WITHDRAWN
WRIGHT STATE UNIVERSITY LIBRARIES

PUBLIC RELATIONS

In Educational Organizations

Practice in an Age of Information and Reform

Theodore J. Kowalski
Teachers College, Ball State University

Merrill,
an imprint of Prentice Hall
Englewood Cliffs, New Jersey ◆ *Columbus, Ohio*

Library of Congress Cataloging-in-Publication Data
Kowalski, Theodore, J.
    Public relations in educational organizations: practice in an age of information and reform / Theodore J. Kowalski.
      p. cm.
    Includes bibliographic references and index.
    ISBN 0-02-366235-2
    1. Public relations—Schools. 2. Public relations—Schools—Case Studies. 3. School management and organization.
    4. School management and organization—Case studies. 5. Community and school. 6. Community and school—Case Studies.
    I. Title
    LB2847.K69   1996
    659.2'9371—dc20

Editor: Debra A. Stollenwerk
Developmental Editor: Linda Ashe Montgomery
Production Editor: Christine M. Harrington
Design Coordinator: Jill E. Bonar
Text Designer: Rebecca Bobb
Production Manager: Deidra M. Schwartz
Illustrations: Kurt Wendling

This book was set in Goudy Old Style by Graphic World and was printed and bound by R. R. Donnelley & Sons Company. The cover was printed by Phoenix Color Corp.

© 1996 by Prentice-Hall, Inc.
A Simon & Schuster Company
Englewood Cliffs, New Jersey 07632

All rights reserved. No part of this book may be reproduced, in any form or by any means, without permission in writing from the publisher.

Printed in the United States of America

10 9 8 7 6 5 4 3 2 1

ISBN: 0-02-366235-2

Prentice-Hall International (UK) Limited, *London*
Prentice-Hall of Australia Pty. Limited, *Sydney*
Prentice-Hall of Canada, Inc., *Toronto*
Prentice-Hall Hispanoamericana, S. A., *Mexico*
Prentice-Hall of India Private Limited, *New Delhi*
Prentice-Hall of Japan, Inc., *Tokyo*
Simon & Schuster Asia Pte. Ltd., *Singapore*
Editora Prentice-Hall do Brasil, Ltda., *Rio de Janeiro*

Foreword

by Albert E. Holliday

The scope of educational public relations is in the midst of a major reevaluation. In the 1950s and 1960s, public relations became a recognized part of the academic preparation of school administrators. But application of this discipline today is usually restricted to last-minute campaigns to pass referenda or to gain public support for a particular project. Many, if not most, superintendents and principals approach communication passively. These behaviors are no longer tolerable. Today, administrators need to become aggressive; they must counter criticism and demonstrate excellence in their own practice.

Public education has received more than its share of criticism over the past two decades. Much of it can be attributed to passiveness on the part of educators, school board members, and national associations. That is, reports about "failures" in public schools have not been adequately countered, although the evidence is overwhelming that public education has not worsened in recent years and has even improved in many respects.

Research indicates that, even today, the majority of school systems do not have a board policy or comprehensive program of communication. A study by Theodore Kowalski and Terry Wiedmer of school districts in midwestern states* revealed that little attention is commonly given to the public relations function.

At the same time that school officials continue to put forth little effort into public relations, the opinion of citizens about public schools has been on a steady downward path. In 1984, in the Phi Delta Kappa/Gallup poll on the public's attitudes toward public schools, 15 percent of those polled gave their local schools grades of D or F; by 1994 that figure had reached 21 percent. In 1988, 19 percent of those polled said schools had "gotten worse," by 1994 that figure was all the way up to 37 percent.

A main reason for the decline in public confidence, I contend, is a steady stream of negative reports about the condition of public education. Many writers in national media have largely ignored ongoing achievements made at the state and local levels.

---

*Published in the *Journal of Educational Public Relations*, 16 (1), January 1994.

The days when superintendents and principals could afford to have a passive approach to their communication responsibilities—apart from last-minute campaigns at tax referenda time—are over. But until school leaders become aggressive, critics and reformers—many with selfish interests—will continue to undermine confidence.

Educational communication has two components. The first is the political aspect. This deals with laying the groundwork for staffing, facility, and programming needs so that the public will adequately fund its schools. The second is the relational aspect. This deals with interrelationships of educators, students, parents, and others in the community. In *this area*, partnerships and parent-volunteer contributions exemplify enhancements that can make a school outstanding.

Both components—the political and the relational—though different in purpose, call for similar attitudes and skills on the part of administrators. School leaders must be able to work cooperatively with publics holding differing perspectives of schools. They must be able to build consensus among staff and the citizenry with regard to relevant goals and approaches to achieving them. They must value sharing, asking, and discussing more than telling.

This book contains practical, research-based information to help prepare administrators to work in the area of public relations. The text reflects the perspectives held by specialists having a variety of backgrounds related to communication and public relations.

The authors focus on issues of technology, reform, and professional practice in discussing the ways in which administrators should be using information to make their institutions responsive to evolving needs.

Albert E. Holliday of Camp Hill, Pennsylvania, has been a public relations director in several education organizations, including a small Michigan school system, the Fairfax County (Virginia) Public Schools, and the Pennsylvania Department of Education. He has also been editor and publisher of the *Journal of Educational Public Relations* since founding it in 1975.

Preface

Although public relations has been an integral part of the graduate curriculum of educational administration for many years, its application in practice is best described as "restricted." This fact is largely attributable to three conditions. First, many administrators have used only one dimension of public relations; they have focused almost entirely on communication efforts designed to improve employee goodwill and organizational image. Rarely have they extended the process to include two-way communication and the purposeful use of information to address existing needs and problems of their organizations. Second, public relations has usually been treated as a specialized function rather than a pervasive activity. The responsibility is generally assigned to a single person (or department in a larger school system); consequently, program functions are not integrated into planning, administration, and evaluation. Third, administrators and school board members have tended to view public relations as a nonessential activity. This is evidenced by the fact that the process is frequently the first program eradicated in budget reductions.

The effects of using rudimentary approaches to public relations in educational organizations have become more consequential in a society increasingly dependent on communication. Policy development and decision making in organizations functioning in the public sector of the economy, processes that are unavoidably political, are enhanced by the effective use of information. Both internal communication and exchanges between the organization and its wider environment are essential. The goal of effectively managing and using information is more likely to be reached if every administrator in a school district understands and accepts responsibility for integrating the public relations process into his or her daily activities. It is more likely to be achieved if administrators seize the opportunities presented by technology to nurture more complete two-way communication exchanges.

PURPOSE OF THE BOOK

The primary objective of this book is to examine the potentialities of educational public relations in the context of contemporary societal conditions. More precisely, the process of public relations is examined in relation to (1) life in an information age, (2) the use of technology in the practice of school administration, and (3) sustained demands for school improvement. The following features are relevant to this goal:

- ◆ The book presents a broad perspective of public relations—one that integrates theory and craft knowledge in promoting two-way communication procedures and extended uses of information.
- ◆ The book advances the belief that every administrator in an educational organization has a responsibility to engage in public relations on a daily basis; hence, the professional knowledge base of a practitioner is incomplete without an understanding of modern practice in public relations.
- ◆ Public relations is cast as a vital element of school improvement. Meaningful change is most likely to occur incrementally and at the micro level—that is, at the level of the individual school. Hence, both the need to create more effective school-community relations and the need to use information to restructure schools (for example, in decentralizing or in moving toward teacher empowerment) are dependent on the appropriate application of public relations.
- ◆ Finally, the book is designed to encourage the process of reflection. The case studies, questions and suggested activities, and suggested readings at the end of each chapter are designed to promote critical thinking in problem solving.

CONTENT OF THE BOOK

The book is divided into four parts. The first outlines the present conditions of practice, focusing on two aspects: (1) the art and science of public relations—where we define terms, give an overview of theory and practice, identify the body of knowledge required of administrators, and discuss legal and ethical issues governing practice—and (2) the conditions of practice—where we provide an overview of contemporary societal issues affecting education and examine the implications of technology for communication and the use of information.

The second part of the book focuses on the organizational dimensions of practice. School districts and schools are organizations, and as such, they function as unique entities composed of groups and individuals. The proper application of public relations requires an understanding of how the process can be used in the wider organization (school district) and within the units of the organization (individual schools). School administrators also need to examine methods for "institutionalizing" the process, that is, making public relations a pervasive activity. These are the topics covered in Part Two.

The application of public relations in educational settings requires myriad critical tasks. Six of the most pressing are examined in the third part of the text. They include planning (that is, how to set goals and develop strategies), working with the media, responding to crisis, collecting and analyzing information, using public relations in funding campaigns and other referenda, and evaluating the PR program.

The book concludes with two chapters placing the practice of public relations in the context of public and private schools. Enrollments in private schools have been increasing, and continued interest in ideas such as school choice, voucher systems, and charter schools increases the probability that this trend will continue. Both the tensions (growing competition) and possibilities for collaboration suggest that school administrators should understand the practice and the use of public relations in both types of organizations.

Each chapter concludes with a case study. These cases are purposely not taken to conclusion so that you may place yourself in the role of decision maker. Using the content of the chapter, you can address common problems faced by practitioners. Questions and suggested activities related to the case study and to chapter content are also found at the end of each chapter. Finally, a list of suggested readings related to the chapter content is provided.

The intent of the book is to present varied perspectives on the practice of public relations in schools. Accordingly, authors with dissimilar academic credentials and experiences are contributors. Some hold academic degrees in journalism, law, communication, business, higher education, and public relations, while others have degrees in educational administration; some are currently employed as professors, while others are practitioners and consultants. Their collective experiences range from the school administration (principalship, superintendency) to higher education administration (department chair, dean, vice president) to consultants in private practice who work directly with educational organizations daily. All the authors are active in professional organizations, and several currently serve as the presidents of these organizations.

ACKNOWLEDGMENTS

Many individuals contributed to this project. I am grateful for the assistance I received from each of the authors who devoted a great deal of time and effort to making the book possible. Walton Small, an instructor at Bethlehem Teachers College in Jamaica and a doctoral student at Ball State University, assisted with research and correspondence. Additionally, I express appreciation to Debbie Stollenwerk, my editor at Merrill Education, who was always encouraging and helpful, and Terry Wiedmer, my colleague at Ball State University, who in addition to authoring one of the chapters provided counsel and constructive criticism throughout the project. Also, I thank my good friend and colleague, Roy Weaver, dean of the Teachers College at Ball State University, for his direction and suggestions at the beginning of the project. Finally, I thank my family for always being patient and understanding.

I would also like to thank the reviewers of this manuscript for their helpful comments and suggestions: Martha Bruckner, University of Nebraska, Omaha; John C. Daresh, Illinois State University; Francis Fowler, Miami University; Gene Gallegos, California State University, Bakersfield; Larry E. Hughes, Houston; John A. Middleton, The Ohio State University; Stephen R. Parson, Virginia Tech; Nancy H. Vick, Longwood College; and Terry L. Wiedmer, Ball State University.

Brief Contents

About the Authors

E. W. Brody is a professor of journalism at the University of Memphis and a veteran of thirty years in public relations practice. He earlier worked in print journalism for a dozen years. Professor Brody has written and/or edited nine books and numerous journal articles. He is accredited by and is a member of the College of Fellows of the Public Relations Society of America.

Glenn Graham is a professor of educational administration at Wright State University. He and co-author Gordon Wise founded the Center for School Tax Levies and Bond Issues at Wright State. They also authored the Phi Delta Kappa Fastback on tax levies and a book on that topic published by the Ohio School Boards Association.

Ann Hennessey is a reporter for a southern California newspaper. She covered schools as an education writer for four years. A graduate of the University of Montana's School of Journalism, she has published articles on school-media relations in journals such as the *Phi Delta Kappan*.

Jerry A. Jarc is president of Catholic School and Parish Development, a firm specializing in recruitment, capital and endowment campaigns, alumni relations, and public relations. He has taught courses in development at numerous universities, including the University of Rochester and the University of San Francisco. He is certified by the National Society of Fund Raising Executives and has served on the board of that organization.

Theodore J. Kowalski is a professor in the Department of Educational Leadership at Ball State University. A former school superintendent, he served as dean of Ball State's Teachers College from 1983 to 1992. He is the author of 11 books and over 120 professional articles. His most recent book, *Keepers of the Flame* (1995), is a study of 17 urban school superintendents. Professor Kowalski serves on several journal editorial boards, including the *Journal of Educational Public Relations*, the *AASA Professor*, and the *Community Education Journal*.

Joseph R. McKinney is an associate professor in the Department of Educational Leadership at Ball State University. He holds both J.D. and Ed.D. degrees and specializes in legal issues affecting schools and administrators. He is the author of numerous articles and is currently co-authoring the book *School Law for Classroom Teachers*, to be published by Merrill/Prentice-Hall.

James F. McNamara is a professor at Texas A&M University with graduate faculty appointments in the Departments of Educational Administration and Educational Psychology in the College of Education and the Department of Statistics in the College of Science. A noted authority on survey research methodology, his most recent book is *Surveys and Experiments in Education Research* (1994).

Maryanne McNamara is a research associate and a program evaluator in the Danforth Foundation School Leadership Program at Texas A&M University. Prior to her current appointment, she supervised student teachers at Texas A&M and was director of an alternative high school.

Doug Newsom is a professor specializing in public relations at Texas Christian University. She is a fellow in the Public Relations Society of America, co-author of three public relations books and co-editor of a book of women's colloquium papers. She has been a Fulbright lecturer in India and has conducted public relations workshops in a number of foreign countries. She is a public relations practitioner and serves on the boards of several public and private organizations.

Mary John O'Hair is an associate professor of educational administration at the University of Oklahoma. She is the founding editor of *Teacher Education Yearbook*. Her research and writings have appeared in leading journals. Her primary research interests include organizational communication, occupational stress, and teacher leadership.

Ulrich C. Reitzug is an associate professor of educational administration at the University of Wisconsin-Milwaukee. He has authored numerous articles and is co-author (with Theodore Kowalski) of the textbook *Contemporary School Administration* (1993). One of his articles, published in *Educational Administration Quarterly* in 1992, won the Davis Award for the outstanding article published that volume year in the journal. He currently serves as associate editor of the journal.

James D. Ricks served as an associate professor and director of the Division of Professional Practice and Research in the College of Education and Human Services at Wright State University. He is author of the Phi Delta Kappa publication *Strategic Planning for Schools*. He has over twenty years of experience as a planner in both the public and private sectors.

Edward H. Seifert is chair of the Department of Educational Administration and associate dean of the School of Education at Southwest Texas State University. He has published over fifty articles and book chapters and has edited two books on educational administration. He is a former teacher, principal, and school superintendent. His current research focuses on change and school reform.

Melvin L. Sharpe is a professor in the Department of Journalism at Ball State University. He previously served as assistant to the chancellor of the State University System of Florida and as director of academic degree programs in public relations at the University of Texas at Austin. He is an accredited public relations professional (APR) and has been inducted into the Public Relations Society of America's College of Fellows. Currently he is president of the Indiana School Public Relations Association.

Angela McNabb Spaulding is a doctoral student in the Department of Educational Leadership at Texas Tech University. Her research interests include micropolitics in schools and conflict resolution.

Arthur Steller is deputy superintendent of the Boston Public Schools. He formerly served as superintendent of the Oklahoma City Public Schools and currently is president of the Association for Supervision and Curriculum Development. The author of a number of articles on public relations activities for administrators, he is a member of the editorial board of the *Journal of Educational Public Relations*.

James S. Trent is acting director of the Division of Professional Practice and Research in the College of Education and Human Services at Wright State University. He has over thirty years of experience as a public school teacher, principal, and superintendent.

Philip T. West is a professor of educational administration at Texas A&M, where he coordinates a graduate specialization in public relations. He directs the University Council for Educational Administration's Program Center for Educational PR and is author of over 150 publications, including the book *Educational Public Relations* (1985). He is editor-in-chief of *Educational Abstracts*, editor of the *AASA Professor*, research and case studies editor for the *Journal of Educational Public Relations*, and Case Corner editor for the *Community Education Journal*.

Terry L. Wiedmer is director of the Resource Center for Educational Services and assistant professor in the Department of Educational Leadership at Ball State University. She teaches in the area of public relations, and formerly served as public information officer of Phi Delta Kappa International. Her research focuses on public relations practices in schools. She currently serves as executive director of the National State Teachers of the Year.

Gordon Wise is a professor of business administration at Wright State University. He and co-author Glenn Graham founded the Center for School Tax Levies and Bond Issues at Wright State. They also authored the Phi Delta Kappa Fastback on tax levies and a book on that topic published by the Ohio School Boards Association.

Robert H. Woodroof teaches in the area of public relations and serves as associate vice president for public relations at Pepperdine University in California. He is active in a number of national public relations organizations and is recognized as one of the outstanding young scholars in his field.

Contents

CHAPTER 4
What School Administrators Need to Understand   58

CHAPTER 5
Public Relations and Technology   73

PART THREE: Critical Tasks

CONTEMPORARY CONDITIONS

CHAPTER 1

Public Relations in an Age of Information

Theodore J. Kowalski

Since the early 1970s, schools, colleges, and universities have faced two stark realities. The first involves major transformations in American society—changes that have not only influenced values and beliefs but have also served to dismantle a manufacturing-based economy that had shaped the country since the Industrial Revolution. As far back as the early 1970s, the thought-provoking book *Future Shock* (Toffler, 1970) warned that American society would go through significant social and economic adaptations. A decade later, futurist John Naisbitt (1982) outlined ten trends he believed were reshaping American society. Three were especially cogent with regard to education:

- ◆ Movement from an industrial society to an information society
- ◆ Movement from a national economy to a global economy
- ◆ Movement from hierarchies to networking

These transitions have helped to frame reform initiatives targeted at both the structure of educational organizations and the behavior of educators. They also have been responsible for new approaches in the use of information and the development of communication systems.

The second reality involves an increasingly negative perception of educational institutions. In particular, the productivity of elementary and secondary schools has been increasingly scrutinized ever since the 1950s. And although it is true that public education in America has always received a fair amount of criticism, the current demands for restructuring have been atypical in that they are exceptionally potent and enduring. Many believe the present quest to transform schools started with the publication of the acrimonious report, *A Nation at Risk* (National Commission on Excellence in Education, 1983). But efforts to reverse the educational policies of the 1960s, policies focused largely on equal opportunity and social concerns, had actually already begun by the mid-1970s (Finn, 1991). The ineffectiveness and inefficiency of education are often attributed to the relative isolation of schools from society—that is, to the fact that many of these institutions have become indifferent to the real needs of their patrons. Thus hopes that school reform will foster a recapturing of public confidence and a rebuilding of symbiotic relationships between schools and communities are to be expected.

This chapter examines the significance and importance of the school-community relationship in an age of information and reform. First we'll examine various definitions of public relations—both definitions in general and definitions with specific reference to schools. Then we'll identify emerging potentialities and expectations for public relations in educational organizations; and finally we'll explore certain foci in contemporary practice:

◆ The potential of technology to enhance the effectiveness of the school in an information society
◆ The link between leadership and public relations in the context of school reform
◆ The importance of the process of reflection in assuring effective practice in the midst of social instability

These foci provide a framework for implementing and enhancing the practice of public relations by administrators in schools, colleges, and universities.

DEFINING PUBLIC RELATIONS

Generally speaking, public relations is a social science—though some consider it an art as well. As a field of practice, it is not yet controlled as are more established professions such as law, medicine, or dentistry—professions requiring specific education and licensing (Seitel, 1992). However, public relations specialists do have access to a growing body of research and theory that can be used to guide practice.

The term "public relations" has many connotations. This is to be expected since it is used at varying times to describe a concept, a profession, a process, and even a goal. Further, the intended meaning may be affected by the context(s) in which the term is used. For example, a large manufacturing company and a public school district are both organizations, but their missions and objectives are distinctively different. In the former, profit is critical to organizational survival, and this reality touches the structure and decision-making processes of every department in the company. Thus those charged with public relations responsibilities are expected to manage information exchanges in a manner that enhances product sales. Public schools, by contrast, are not judged by profits but rather by the extent to which they successfully provide services that satisfy citizen needs and wants. Hence organizational purpose almost always influences how public relations is defined *and* the importance given the process or program.

Because connotation and context are critical, there are many definitions of public relations. Whereas some are rather general, others focus specifically on select aspects of organizational functions. Definitions are examined here in two broad categories: those not directly pertinent to public relations in education and those that are.

Definitions of Public Relations Not Directly Referenced to Education

Public relations can be perceived, if narrowly, as a process of press agentry or advertising. Press agents are specialists who seek publicity for their clients, and advertising specialists prepare controlled messages for transmission to the public through purchased mechanisms (for example, paid ads on television or in a newspaper). But public relations is a broader field than either press agentry or advertising; it is a function wherein the products are subject to media interpretation (Cohen, 1987).

Historically, public relations has often been defined on the basis of intent. Consider this perception of its intent: "[to promote] goodwill toward a company by printed or other means" (Lovell, 1982, p. 402). Such a definition cites a specific goal to be accomplished. Perhaps the most common intent-focused definitions are those emphasizing the shaping of public sentiment, that is, defining public relations as an instrument of persuasion. This conceptualization is exemplified by the very brief definition given by Dilenschneider and Forrestal (1987): "the use of information to influence public opinion" (p. 5).

Over time, the definitions of public relations have become more expansive, often emphasizing two-way communications between an organization and its ecosystems. *Ecosystems* are described as the networks of social relationships in which an organization is embedded (McElreath, 1993). The growing importance of an organization's disposition toward its wider environment is largely attributable to new conditions brought about by a global economy. More specifically, organizations—even private, profit-seeking organizations—that fail to interact with their ecosystems increase the risk of misjudging consumer needs and wants. This error can be fatal to a company functioning in a highly competitive market.

Even the most stubborn executives are beginning to realize that self-imposed isolation is disadvantageous. Efforts to avoid community intervention do nothing more than fritter away energy and resources and block necessary information from entering the company's decision-making process. Over the past three decades, there have been hundreds of examples of the power of governmental agencies and pressure groups to penetrate corporations, even giant corporations. Regulations regarding automobile emissions controls and safety features (for example, seat belts and air bags) are among the most readily recognized. Most executives now realize that the notion of a conflict-free organization is a myth; accordingly, they have become more interested in aspects of public relations that build two-way communication systems.

As technology made the world smaller, social responsibility and communication became essential "costs" of doing business for virtually all organizations (Newsom, Scott & VanSlyke Turk, 1989). Organizational stability and longevity are often dependent on the maintenance of positive internal and external relationships (Seitel, 1992). This emphasis on the interactive nature of public relations is at the base of the following two definitions: "[P]ublic relations is helping an organization and its publics adapt mutually to each other, (Lesly, 1983, p. 4), and "Public relations is viewed today as a management function that uses communication to facilitate relationships and understanding between an organization and its many publics" (McElreath, 1993, p. 4).

Some definitions of public relations extend the emphasis on interaction to include the goal of enlightening top-level executives. Two-way communication is seen as a process channeling vital information to those responsible for major organizational decisions. As Roger Haywood (1991) wrote, "Effective public relations is much more than communications: it should be more fundamental to the organization. Public relations should begin before the decision-making stage—when attitudes towards the issues are being developed by management and policies are being formulated" (p. 4).

Although definitions of public relations have evolved to reflect the growing complexity of both the concept and its application, some of the earliest definitions still endure. Edward Bernay's definition, one he constructed nearly fifty years ago, remains among the most widely referenced. It has three critical dimensions:

◆ To *inform* the public
◆ To *persuade*, that is, to modify attitudes and opinions
◆ To *integrate* the actions and attitudes of an organization with those of its publics and the actions and attitudes of its publics with those of the organization (Cohen, 1987)

In 1978, when the First World Assembly of Public Relations Associations convened in Mexico City, the participants defined public relations as "the art and social science of analyzing trends, predicting their consequences, counseling organizational leaders, and implementing planned programs of action which will serve both the organization and the public interest" (Newsom, Scott, & VanSlyke Turk, 1989; p. 6). This conceptualization places public relations at the very heart of organizational administration. It establishes the process as an integral element of leadership and decision making.

Observing that the myriad existing definitions caused confusion, Wilcox, Ault, and Agee (1992) suggested that students and practitioners focus on recurring key words to enhance their understanding. They identified six of these phrases: "deliberate," "planned," "performance," "public interest," "two-way communication," and "management function." These key words are explained in detail in Table 1–1.

Because some definitions refer exclusively to a process *or* an objective, they often engender restrictive perceptions. Broader conceptualizations are likely when public relations activities are connected to intended results. The work of Melvin Sharpe exemplifies efforts to communicate the meaning of public relations in this more comprehensive context. The basic elements of his ideas are illustrated in Figure 1–1. Sharpe's concept of public relations is especially meaningful to schools and universities, because the outcomes he

TABLE 1–1
Key Words in Defining Public Relations

Key Word	Meaning
Deliberate	Public relations does not occur by chance; it is an intentional activity.
Planned	Public relations does not occur randomly; it is an organized activity.
Performance	Public relations is shaped and made effective by both policies and practices; process is critically important.
Public interest	Public relations serves not only the organization, it also serves society, the general public.
Two-way communication	Public relations is much more than distributing information; it includes receiving information from the publics served.
Management function	Public relations is not an isolated activity delegated to an individual or department; it is most effective when integrated into the decision-making processes of top-level administrators.

FIGURE 1.1
Sharpe's Five Links in Effective Programs (Adapted from Seitel, 1992, p.10)

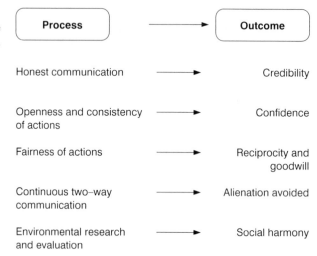

advocates are congruent with the theoretical and actual expectations for these institutions. (We'll look at this again in Chapter 4.) His definition therefore provides a good transition from general definitions to those that attempt to describe public relations in schools.

Definitions of Public Relations in Education

Historically, the term "community relations" has been used synonymously with "public relations" by educators. Why? In part, the use of an alternative term reflected the reluctance of some school administrators to admit they were engaging in public relations—a reluctance associated with fears that taxpayers would see them as using Madison Avenue persuasion techniques (West, 1985). As the term used in this book, public relations is viewed as a broad construct, and community relations is seen as its primary objective. But inner-organizational communication—the internal exchange of information and the building of goodwill among employees—is certainly an essential component of the public relations construct as well.

Not unlike general definitions, those developed with specificity to educational organizations vary in focus and length. For example, Richard Saxe (1984) emphasized the element of persuasion when he wrote that school public relations involves "practices initiated by educators and designed to influence the public" (p. 12). Other authors, however, provide a more inclusive framework. Thirty years ago James Jones focused on information exchanges between schools and their communities: "[P]ublic relations is defined in a broad sense and designates all the functions and relationships that pertain in a two-way exchange of ideas between school and community" (1966, pp. 1–2). More recently, Lutz and Merz (1992) noted that the expanding political dimensions of public relations were best addressed by establishing two-way communication as a vehicle by which school districts could provide and receive information.

Over the years, the influence of public relations specialists on the work of authors in educational administration has been quite evident. For instance, Stephen Knezevich (1969) was apparently influenced by the work of Bernay when he defined school public relations as "information, persuasion, and integration between institution and public" (p. 476). On the other hand, Donovan Walling (1982) constructed a somewhat unique definition, one indicating that public relations was both a philosophy and process. He conceived it as (1) incorporating values and beliefs about communication, and (2) embodying management techniques used by schools to communicate with their constituents. The latter part of this description (the emphasis on techniques) is quite similar to the general definition of public relations authored by Wilcox, Ault, and Agee (1992).

One of the most comprehensive definitions of public relations in education was formulated by Philip West (1985): "Educational public relations," he said, "is a systematically and continuously planned, executed, and evaluated program of interactive communication and human relations that employs paper, electronic, and people mediums to attain internal as well as external support for an educational institution" (p. 23). Of particular note in this definition are its focus on human relations and on the use of multiple media. These elements hold special importance in an " information age" in which technology permits improved communication exchanges.

Public relations also deals with how people feel about issues, services, and individual or organizational personalities. James Norris (1984), for instance, suggested that public relations might be better defined by the term "public relationship." He argued that the process involved building relationships with a great many different publics. This emphasis on the personal dimension of public relations has caught the attention of many practitioners because computers, fax machines, and other devices, which provide quick and easy channels of communication, are often perceived as being impersonal.

Whereas a global economy has been a prime factor in encouraging interactivity in the private sector of the economy, calls for reform have played a pivotal role in renewing an emphasis on school-community relations. Criticisms of elementary and secondary education conveyed two powerful messages to educational administrators:

◆ The public's confidence in schools as social institutions was declining.
◆ The public's perceptions of the purposes, processes, and outcomes in schools were not well informed.

In this respect, the school-reform movement circuitously led administrators to place a greater emphasis on building bridges with their communities, and in the mid-1980s, the National School Public Relations Association (1986) defined educational public relations as "a planned and systematic two-way process of communications between an educational organization and its internal and external publics designed to build morale, goodwill, understanding, and support for that organization" (p. 28).

More recently, Bagin, Gallagher, and Kindred (1994) also emphasized sound and constructive relationships between schools and their ecosystems as a means for coping with an unstable social environment, writing, "[S]ound and constructive relationships between school and community are achieved through a process of exchanging information, ideas, and viewpoints out of which common understandings are developed and decisions made concerning essential improvements in the educational program and adjustments to the climate of social change" (p. 15). As the community environments of educational institutions became more dynamic and less predictable, the value of public relations steadily increased.

In summary, educational public relations is both a social science and an art relating to intentions, process, and outcomes. Both the science and art are influenced by philosophical underpinnings. Because schools and communities are dynamic, public relations is an evolutionary construct focusing most directly on the interrelationships between schools and their ecosystems. The functions most often cited in popular definitions of public relations are summarized in Table 1–2.

TABLE 1–2
Potential Functions of Public Relations in a Public School District

Function	Objective	Example
Goodwill	Creating kindly feelings among the general public	The district makes its facilities available for public use.
External information	Keeping the public informed	The district distributes a newsletter to parents, taxpayers, and students.
Internal information	Keeping employees informed	Periodic meetings, employee newsletters, and open forums are used to share information and answer complaints.
Image promotion	Building and reinforcing a special image of the organization	The district adopts a motto such as "A district where schools are communities of learners."
Service promotion	Letting the public know about available programs and services	Handbooks, catalogs, and other sources of information are distributed.
Interpretation	Defining key issues, programs, and data not readily understood by the general public	The district distributes a letter to students and parents explaining the use of standardized test scores.
Persuasion	Advising and urging the public to take certain positions	The district prepares videos, letters, and other materials designed to gain public support for an impending bond issue.
Interaction	Opening channels of communication to allow school and community to exchange information	School-based councils and advisory committees are used to generate information and encourage participation in decisions.
Reaction	Responding to negative publicity or a crisis situation	The district holds news conferences and prepares informational materials after an arsonist destroys part of the high school.

For our own purposes here, public relations in educational institutions is defined as *an evolving social science and leadership process utilizing multimedia approaches designed to build goodwill, enhance the public's attitude toward the value of education, augment interaction and two-way communication between schools and their ecosystems, provide vital and useful information to the public and employees, and serve as an integral part of the planning and decision-making functions.*

GROWING NEED FOR PUBLIC RELATIONS

Public relations has for many years been a standard component of the professional preparation of school administrators. The primary foci have been the means of communicating news to parents and taxpayers and of building goodwill for the school system. But unlike some other components of administrative practice—components such as finance, law, and facility management—public relations may be, and often was, given a rather low priority status. In large measure this treatment stemmed from the reality that the disregard of public relations historically produced few consequences for administrators and their organization—that is, few consequences in comparison with disregard, say, of fiscal management.

Transitions in society and demands for school reform, however, are changing the relative importance of public relations. Today administrators rely heavily on information exchanges to make timely and relevant decisions. Those who retain outdated notions about keeping information from employees and about preventing community interference are asking for trouble. Yet the implementation of a comprehensive public relations program is no simple matter. There continue to be many impediments on the road to effective practice.

Persistent Barriers

Connor and Lake (1988) viewed barriers to organizational change as belonging to three distinct categories:

- ◆ Obstacles to understanding: The significance of key concepts and/or proposed change is not understood.
- ◆ Obstacles to acceptance: Key concepts and/or proposed changes are rejected by those who have power to influence their implementation.
- ◆ Obstacles to acting: Implementation is blocked by human and material factors.

This typology provides an effective framework for understanding the types of obstacles that lie in the path of public relations programming.

Without a clear perspective of public relations, many patrons and administrators fail to comprehend that the function has a legitimate purpose—even in publicly funded institutions. Their misunderstanding can usually be laid to a restricted view of public relations as nothing more than self-serving acts of persuasion. This misperception was exemplified recently in a small midwestern community where a number of citizens became outraged when the annual school district budget included a $10,000 allocation for public relations.

"Why," the irate citizens asked, "should schools be spending money on something like public relations? Isn't this something that businesses do to promote their products?"

Even more prevalent is the proclivity of taxpayers to view public relations as a frill activity. Here there is some understanding of what is being attempted, but the effort is rejected on philosophical grounds. Consider an incident in a suburban school district where a superintendent spent hours explaining to the school board why additional efforts were needed to build bridges to the community. Yet at budget time, proposed allocations for public relations became the first casualty. Faced with the need to trim $200,000, school board members drew a red line through the program. The board president explained the action to the superintendent: "It's not that we don't support public relations, we just believe we can get along without it."

Barriers to actual implementation may include both human and material resources. For example, administrative staff members fail to achieve comprehensive programming because they lack expertise in public relations or in the use of technology. Or the school district may be in such financial difficulty that program funding is truly impossible.

Factors Elevating the Importance of Public Relations

The need to have a comprehensive program of public relations in schools is tied to several societal conditions. These conditions are caused by the onset of the information age, the creation of global economy, the changing demographic conditions, and the growing dissatisfaction with public institutions. Consider the implications when nonparents—those having no children in the public schools—represent 85 percent of the taxpayers in a public school system. Or consider the difficulty of obtaining additional resources for school restructuring in a climate in which schools are perceived as ineffective. The need for educational public relations becomes even clearer when it is considered in the context of two lingering problems.

Education's Image.   Among the most salient reasons for the new stature of public relations is the issue of *image*. This factor is best understood by comparing past and present circumstances in America. Prior to World War II, schools and universities were usually held in high esteem. Few taxpayers ever challenged the necessity of public education, and teachers and administrators had stature because they were among the select few in their communities who had graduated from college. But since the 1950s, there has been growing skepticism about the effectiveness of elementary and secondary education—and more recently of higher education as well. Today, even those who are themselves poorly educated and ill-informed on educational problems are apt to voice displeasure.

The erosion of public confidence became most visible during the 1960s—a decade of instability. Among the myriad challenges that faced educators were the policy consequences of Sputnik, the social unrest following the passage of the civil rights law, the political divisiveness produced by the war in Vietnam, and controversies created by legally mandated rules for protected groups like special needs students. And in addition to these social and legal interventions, teacher unionism grew to become a widespread and powerful force, often pitting administrators and school boards against teachers (Campbell, Corbally, & Nystrand, 1983).

The turmoil of the 1960s gave way to demands for accountability in the 1970s. The term "back to the basics" became the rallying cry of those who believed that a curriculum preoccupied with social issues had indirectly deemphasized instruction in the core skills. Teachers were seen as spending too much time trying to get students to get along with each other and not enough time helping students to master reading, writing, and arithmetic. By the early 1980s, this disenchantment had grown into a full-blown reform movement. And all during this period, the media were becoming more sophisticated and more pervasive in community life—a condition that simply made it easier for disgruntled citizens to voice their displeasure.

Rather than being held in high esteem, public education now is viewed by many as unproductive and fiscally excessive. Whereas schools were once seen as the great equalizers in American society—institutions providing opportunities for every citizen to become productive and prosperous—they are now blamed for illiteracy, crime, and other ills. Some within the education profession have taken exception to these harsh judgments. David Berliner (1993), for instance, declared that schools in this country have been unfairly damaged by certain unsubstantiated claims—that education is expensive and wasteful; that students are lazy and unproductive; that America's productivity has fallen as a result of inadequate education. But arguments by noted scholars are not likely to be sufficient to change public opinion. In an era when perception automatically becomes reality, each school administrator must be increasingly conscious of the issue of image.

Growing Tensions Generated by School Reform.   Contemporary practice of public relations is made even more complex by the realization that forces attempting to direct the goals of education are frequently incongruent. Consider tensions generated by quests to achieve both excellence and equity. Historically, textbooks treated such differences as management problems and suggested they could be solved by rational applications of knowledge (Kowalski & Reitzug, 1993). Or consider stresses associated with simultaneously seeking teacher empowerment *and* greater community involvement in decision making. Teacher professionalization, especially if it includes giving teachers the power to regulate their own behavior (that is, to decide how and with whom they will make decisions) could indirectly make schools less responsive to parents (Crowson, 1992).

There are also mounting tensions involving liberty, adequacy, and equity. These are especially visible in concepts such as charter schools, school choice (that is, the option to use public funds to enroll in either public or private schools), and vouchers. On one side of the argument are those who believe parents and students should be able to choose any school, including a private school; they believe the resulting competition would serve to force improvement of public schools (Chubb & Moe, 1990; Quade, 1993). On the other side are those who oppose choice plans because (1) such plans do not address the real problems of schooling (Shanker, 1993), (2) they have the potential to create even greater inequities (Henig, 1994), and (3) they undermine citizen responsibility for acting collectively (Moffett, 1994). Standing against private school choice policies, Colin Greer (1992) has argued: "Private and public schools represent two quite opposite sets for goals for public education: a desire for schools to serve the competitive demands of stratified society versus the desire for schools to play a socially integrative and democratic role, serving the right of all parents to participate in the education of their children regardless of

TABLE 1–3

Selected Contemporary Conditions Intensifying the Need for Public Relations

Condition	Ramifications
Public criticism	Resources and support for education will suffer unless negative images are changed.
Information age	Information has become increasingly important with regard to identifying and solving problems. Organizations that cannot productively access and use information will be unable to compete.
Pluralistic culture	Student and community needs, interest, and values are diverse; groups place conflicting demands on schools. As a result, communication becomes a critical process, both within the organization and between the organization and its ecosystems.
Decentralization of governance	School reform is leading to more-democratic schools in which faculty are empowered to function more as true professionals. In such settings, administrators, teachers, parents, and students require accurate and sufficient information.
Concept of lifelong learning	In an information age, learning is no longer viewed as a youth activity. Demands are placed on all schools to be responsive to a wider range of learner needs.
Eroded political and economic support	Fewer taxpayers have family members enrolled in schools. As a result, it is more difficult to gain and maintain goodwill and support.
Expanding demands and shrinking resources	While demands for educational services are increasing, available resources are remaining constant or declining. As a consequence, political activity is becoming more intense because of expanded competition for scarce resources.
Expanded options and competition	Many believe that educational improvement will not occur unless competition among schools is intensified. Ideas such as school choice and charter schools are already being implemented in elementary and secondary education. Many small private colleges are engaged in intense competition for students.
Acceleration of change	Change not only continues, it occurs at an ever-accelerating pace. Citizens seek to gain information about their social institutions.
Rise of global economy	The private sector of the economy relies on educational institutions to satisfy their demands for adequately prepared workers. Two-way communication between business and education becomes critical to satisfying these needs.
Individual student problems	Greater numbers of students enter schools with social, physical, emotional, and learning problems. Schools are expected to provide a wider range of services (for example, expanded health care and social services). In part, the ability to meet this need is dependent on two-way communication between school and community.
Inadequate funding	To secure added funding to meet higher costs and expanded services, educational administrators must do a better job of casting education as an economic good.
Philosophical ambiguity	There continue to be multiple beliefs about the purposes of education. Partially for this reason, decentralization is seen as having the best chance of enhancing school improvement. Building consensus for philosophical goals, even at the community or neighborhood level, requires improved communication systems.

income and other forms of private privilege" (p. 286). Such contentions have not dissuaded proponents of choice; it remains one of those fundamental issues dividing most communities.

Tensions arising from conflicting goals of education are certainly not new, but they are becoming more pronounced in a society where ideas and positions can be exchanged and debated with relative ease. Informed theorists and practitioners approach the tensions of conflicting values not as solvable problems but as recurring outgrowths of diversity and democracy requiring attention. Deeply rooted policy conflicts elevate the importance of sound school and community relationships, making goodwill, mediation, and information exchanges all the more important.

The range of contemporary conditions associated with the need for educational public relations is presented in Table 1–3.

CONTEMPORARY FOCI

Three dominant foci ought to guide both the structure of public relations programs and administrative practices within them. The first relates to the role of technology in an information age; the second emphasizes the links between school reform, leadership, and the public relations process; and the third promotes the use of reflection as a process for leadership effectiveness. These foci are detailed in Table 1–4.

The Importance of Technology in an Information Age

Many current secondary school principals and their assistants remember spending an unbelievable amount of time manually compiling master schedules for their schools. Likewise, there are business managers and personnel administrators who just a decade ago were

TABLE 1–4
Basic Foci and Underlying Beliefs

Focus	Underlying Belief
Importance of technology in an information age	Access to information raises expectations that social institutions will be interactive, responsive, and effective through the process of identifying and solving problems. Technology should provide the tools for increasing both programming and efficiency.
Public relations as an integral part of leadership	Reform efforts have raised expectations that administrators be both managers and leaders, which requires that administrators create effective communication systems. Rather than being an ancillary service, public relations should be infused in all elements of the organization.
Reflection as a critical component of effective practice	Long-term effectiveness is dependent on the ability to integrate experience with professional knowledge and skills in public relations. In handling public relations, reflection should be a valued activity.

using typewriters and posting machines to do most of their work. Before the widespread use of microcomputers, decisions requiring multiple inputs—planning, scheduling, inventorying—were either avoided or were made on the basis of data easiest to obtain. This inability to collect, maintain, and utilize large banks of information clearly placed the organization in a disadvantageous position.

As far back as the late 1970s, several scholars were predicting that technology would not only improve access to information, it would also increase the value of information, a prediction that was not lost on organizational leaders (Lipinski, 1978). West (1981) was one of the first to articulate the public relations potential of technology, especially in school settings. Noting how traditional efforts had failed to produce desired levels of interaction between school and community, he anticipated that technology would become the vehicle for creating a new model for practice. The paradigm shift he envisioned centered on a combination of communication and technorelations, the latter being a process utilizing electronic options devoid of physical contact. He prophesied that technorelations, if properly used, would replace traditional human relations, allowing higher levels of interaction between school and community. The challenge presented by this transition entailed using technology in a way that would not totally sacrifice human interaction for the sake of efficiency.

Several years later, West (1985, pp. 47–48) refined his observations and suggested a new set of communication principles that included

- Immediacy, or instant communication
- Ubiquity, or pervasive communication
- Selectivity, or user control of communication
- Interactiveness, or two-way communication
- Imagery, or the overall character of a communication
- Change, or pervasive communication

The last of these is especially noteworthy because it pertains to a significant transformation in the purpose of educational public relations. West predicted educators would move beyond the traditional goal of merely reinforcing positive views to establish communication links that focused on actually changing public perceptions. Unfortunately, not all administrators have moved in this direction.

To properly weigh the influence of technology on education over the past several decades, one needs to consider its deployment in the context of social, economic, and political conditions. Consider how both school reform and the transition to an information age increased the perceived value of equipment such as microcomputers. For example, many state legislators and governors during the 1980s viewed technology as a means to increase educational productivity without appreciably increasing educational spending. And as Americans gained an understanding of life in an information age, many expected school administrators to employ technology as a means of improving communications with their patrons.

Most schools eventually acquired microcomputers and some even extended the infusion of technology to integrated voice-video-data systems. The mere presence of these technologies constituted new opportunities and challenges for administrators and teachers. They called for new ways of conceptualizing and operationalizing the process of organizational communication (Toth & Trujillo, 1987). In addition to improving internal operations, technology also eradicated, or at least substantially attenuated, obstacles previously deterring information exchanges between schools and their wider environments; richer school-community relations has become a more reachable goal because of technology (Blake, 1991).

There is, however, a potential dark side to practice in an information age. While new technologies are an asset, they can also "lull practitioners into a false sense of security" (Brody, 1988, p. 279). That is, they can lead administrators to take things for granted—to underestimate the value of well-planned, well-executed programming. There is no software package or technology manual guaranteeing a successful public relations program. The scientific products of the information age are really nothing more than the overhead projectors and typewriters of the 1950s and the 1960s—they are tools requiring informed human direction. Without such direction they do not contribute to organizational improvement. Informed leaders realize the goal of technology is to reach what had been unreachable.

Links between Public Relations and the Leadership Process

Although the terms "management," "administration," and "leadership" are often used synonymously, they are generally recognized as distinct concepts. This will be made clearer if we stop to define the three terms:

+ Management: A process of implementing strategies and controlling resources (human and material) in order to achieve organizational objectives
+ Administration: A broad process that encompasses both management and leadership responsibilities and functions
+ Leadership: A process that results in the determination of organizational objectives and strategies, entails building consensus for meeting those objectives, and involves influencing others to work toward those objectives (Kowalski & Reitzug, 1993)

The primary differences between managing and leading entail functions such as planning, consensus building, and influencing. Managers allocate resources and tell people what to do; they observe work performance to see that directions are followed. Leaders, by contrast, are concerned with organizational direction. They continually attempt to redefine vision and mission, and they see conflict as a gateway to change.

Differing perspectives of leaders and managers extend to communication. As Abraham Zaleznik (1989) observed, "Communication is important to both managers and leaders, but the modes differ. Managers communicate in signals, whereas leaders prefer clearly stated messages" (p. 24). Managers are less apt to use information directly; they rely more on sending symbolic messages to others. This approach is less personal and reflects a belief that information is controlled by those with legitimate authority. Leaders concentrate on what to do as well as how things should be done. They are more likely to strive for harmony between the impersonal nature of management and the moral dimensions of dealing with people (Sergiovanni, 1991). Information is seen as a source of empowerment, and when it is exchanged freely in all directions, positive change (organizational development) is more possible.

E. Mark Hanson (1992) referred to such symbolic dimensions of communication when he described how open organizations function internally and externally. "Communication," he said, "can be defined as the exchange of messages and meaning between an organization and its environment as well as between its network of interdependent subsystems" (p. 253). Effective leaders realize that symbols and words define behavior. Both employees and patrons develop perceptions of administrators on the basis of their communications with them.

Unfortunately, at a time when restructuring is so essential, many educational organizations retain long-standing cultures and climates that restrict the flow of information. In the worst situations, information moves in only one direction—from managers to workers. And frequently the message gets filtered—that is, managers restrict or reshape the message. Externally, interactions with the wider environment are discouraged because of the potential of conflict. Parental input, for example, may include criticism of current practices or recommendations contradictory to positions held by administrators.

If leaders are to make decisions about direction, they absolutely have to be well informed. Society is becoming increasingly intolerant of bureaucrats who act on personal conviction rather than on empirical data. In essence, public relations and school leadership are inextricably tied to each other.

Reflective Practice

The third factor that should imbue administrative behavior in public relations is reflective practice. In his enlightening book, *The Reflective Practitioner,* Donald Schön (1983) observed that technical knowledge was insufficient to resolve the problems encountered by practitioners in most professions. School superintendents and principals, for example, occasionally confront situations where standard approaches prove to be ineffective, challenges where tried-and-true methods fail to produce the intended results. This potential for failure exists largely because problems, needs, and other challenges are dynamic and context-specific.

Contextual variations are multifaceted and may be related to the organization's ecosystems (the community), the organization (the school or university), or the individuals specifically involved (students, parents, and/or faculty). Even slight contextual variations may diminish the effectiveness of a proven technique. For example, a principal who recently moved from a rural elementary school to an affluent suburban elementary school was dismayed when she discovered that her trusted techniques for gaining parental involvement were ineffective. Unless properly analyzed, contextual variations can be both enigmatic and stressful. Reflection is an acquired skill permitting administrators to think about intended actions and the outcomes they produce. It is a process dependent on both professional knowledge and previous experiences as a framework for analysis.

Technical rationality is the foundation for most professions where practice evolves from a positivist philosophy (Schön, 1987). Practitioners are viewed as instrumental problem-solvers who apply theory and techniques derived from systematic knowledge. The world of the school administrator, however, is neither rational nor highly predictable. This does not mean that theoretical constructs are unimportant; rather it indicates that they are fallible. Work in public relations activities becomes more meaningful when the practitioner learns to benefit from experience. Experience alone, however, does not guarantee positive growth. It also can have a negative influence—for example, reinforcing poor judgment. Reflection requires analysis and integration in a manner allowing the practitioner to continuously reshape his or her professional knowledge base.

Reflection is especially valuable when the administrator encounters situations where people do not act rationally, where groups do the unexpected. Results do not always conform to intentions; regarding such situations, Kowalski and Reitzug (1993) have written:

> [O]ccasionally surprises occur. Expected results do not materialize and outcomes are incongruent with what has previously occurred in seemingly similar situations. These unexpected results trigger both reflection-in-action and reflection-on-action, causing the individual to reflect on what is causing the unanticipated consequences both as they are occurring and later, after the heat of the moment has dissipated. The individual contemplates questions of how the situation compares with past similar experiences, ways in which it was the same and different, and what may have affected altered outcomes in this situation from previous, seemingly similar situations. (p. 236)

Reflection can occur during the period when an administrator is planning an action, during the period in which the action is taken, and during the period following the action (Reitzug & Cornett, 1991).

Imagine a superintendent who must inform the media that a teacher is being dismissed for incompetence. Before he releases the information, he may reflect on (1) his previous experiences with reporters, (2) the content of his intended message, (3) potential outlets for the message, (4) potential legal ramifications, and (5) implications for relations with the teachers' union. When he actually communicates the message, questions by reporters may also entail reflection. How do I answer the questions? Should I give more information than I originally intended? And after the message has been delivered, he contemplates the results and assesses the relationship between his actions and observed outcomes. Did things turn out as expected? If not, why not? This last stage of reflection is especially meaningful in augmenting one's professional knowledge base—that is, in determining how experience will alter one's professional convictions.

We'll focus on—and we hope enhance—reflective practice in the open-ended case studies that conclude each chapter in this book. By assuming the role of the decision maker, you can use information from the chapter to plan and test alternative responses to the problem presented.

SUMMARY

Two general conditions have increased the need for public relations in educational organizations: (1) society's transition to an information age, and (2) society's demands for school improvement. Collectively, these influences have placed new demands on administrators to maintain effective two-way communication systems in which technology becomes a vehicle for accessing and using information in ways that are timely and accurate.

"Public relations" is a term with many meanings. This is to be expected, since it is used at varying times to describe a concept, a profession, a process, and even a goal. Additionally, it is viewed by many to be both an art and a social science. In this book, public relations is defined broadly to include goodwill, public opinion, community interaction, two-way communication, employee relations, and even planning and decision making.

The need for public relations has never been greater; but unfortunately, program development must occur in the context of several persistent and significant barriers. These obstacles are broadly classified here as being related to lack of understanding, lack of acceptance, and lack of implementation.

The current importance of public relations programs within schools is related primarily to changing images of schools and mounting tensions between conflicting goals brought to the surface by school reform. Changes in the social, political, legal, and economic framework of American society over the last thirty years have made public relations a more essential element of administrative practice. As practitioners move to incorporate the concept into their daily work and the program into their organizational structure, their success will depend largely on their ability to define public relations in the context of an information society, to engage in leadership behavior, to capitalize on the potentialities of technology, and to utilize reflection to enhance personal knowledge and skills.

CASE STUDY

The New Superintendent's Plan

When Janet Ferriter became superintendent of the Boswell School District, it marked the first time this farming community had employed a female in any administrative position. The school board members reacted positively to her confidence and energy, traits she displayed during her interview. But they were even more impressed by her philosophy regarding school and community relations. Dr. Ferriter advocated a broad range of community services, shared decision making, and opportunities for parents and taxpayers to have input into the schools.

During the first six months in Boswell, Dr. Ferriter was shocked to learn how little communication had occurred in previous years between the schools and community. With the exception of occasional notes sent home with students, the only other information about the schools was found in occasional newspaper articles—and these often focused narrowly on school board activities. She was also surprised to learn how little the school district had invested in technology. The business office, for example, was still using antiquated office machinery like posting machines to process work. Even student records were kept manually.

After a few months in Boswell, Dr. Ferriter developed a comprehensive public relations plan to improve communications and information management. Seeking input from administrative staff, she spent nearly three months completing the task. The plan called for (1) the formation of a public relations advisory committee, (2) the establishment of school councils (composed of three parents, three teachers, and the principal) in each school, (3) the publication of a monthly school district newsletter, and (4) the computerization of all information systems in the central office. The plan also included a budget that had a bottom line of $53,000 for the first year.

At the June meeting, Dr. Ferriter presented her plan to the school board, labeling it, "A Plan for Creating a Public Relations and Information Management Program." Reactions from the members were mixed. While most supported specific ideas in the document, all were concerned about the $53,000 price tag.

Dan Jackson, president of the board, questioned how the plan would affect other operations in the school system. "I'm not only troubled by the money," he told those present at the board meeting, "I'm bothered by what the report does not specify. We have all kinds of needs in this district, and I'm not sure how the public is going to react if we approve over $53,000 for a public relations program. We're not General Motors. We can't go spending money promoting ourselves to our taxpayers."

Ella Chambers, another board member, agreed. "I think the plan has some good ideas, but I have to go along with what Mr. Jackson just said. We are going to get a lot of criticism if people think we're spending all this money just to try to create a good image of ourselves."

Dr. Ferriter had anticipated the financial concerns, but she did not expect the questions about the appropriateness of public relations programs in schools. Her first reaction was to remind the board members they had emphasized school and community relations when they employed her. Each of the plan's components, she pointed out, was directed toward achieving that objective.

But the board members remained apprehensive. After a twenty-minute discussion, Chambers finally made a motion to table action on the plan so the board could have more time to study it. Her motion passed unanimously. Dr. Ferriter was directed to provide the board with additional information before the next meeting, to be held in two weeks.

Long after everyone else had left, Janet Ferriter sat in her office thinking about what had just occurred. Mentally, she started questioning her approach to recommending the plan. After sitting in silence for a long time, she reached for a pad and pencil and wrote the following questions:

- ◆ Should I make an even more aggressive push for the plan at the next board meeting?
- ◆ Should I modify the plan?
- ◆ Should I just forget about the issue and move on to something else?

QUESTIONS AND SUGGESTED ACTIVITIES

Case Study

1. Considering the barriers to change discussed in this chapter, identify the nature of the board's reluctance to approve Ferriter's plan.
2. Is it possible for the board members to be *for* better school-community relations and *against* public relations? Why or why not?
3. The public relations plan was developed by the superintendent and her administrative staff. Do you think the board would have reacted differently if one or two of board members had been involved in the planning?
4. What other approaches could the superintendent had used to gain board approval of the plan?

5. Assess the options the superintendent identified for herself after the meeting.
6. Is the superintendent trying to accomplish too much at one time? Why or why not?
7. Discuss Ferriter's contention that the public relations plan will improve school-and-community relations.

Chapter

8. Historically, some writers have preferred to use the term "school-and-community relations" rather than "public relations." Discuss the possible reasons for this preference. Which of the two terms is more encompassing?
9. Discuss how growing demands for school improvement augmented the move to infuse technology into schools.
10. Identify the reasons that timely and complete information is so essential to public institutions.
11. Do you think most school administrators engage in reflection? Defend your opinion.
12. Contemporary definitions of public relations have it going well beyond the act of disseminating information. Do you think that the general public understands this? Do you think that teachers, administrators, and school board members understand this?
13. Discuss the links between school reform, leadership, and public relations.

SUGGESTED READINGS

Berliner, D. C. (1993). Education myths: Eleven current ones that serve to undermine confidence in public education. *Journal of Educational Public Relations, 15*(2), 4–11.

Cannon, C. L., & Barham, F. E. (1993). Are you and your public polls apart? *Executive Educator, 15*(10), 41–42.

Coughlan, S. (1991, Nov. 15). Agent of change. *Times Educational Supplement,* p. 38.

Cutlip, S. M.(1994). *The unseen power: Public relations, a history.* Hillsdale, NJ: L. Erlbaum Associates.

Eisentadt, D. (1994). After the ball: High-tech PR in the no-nonsense '90s. *Public Relations Quarterly, 39*(2), 23–25.

Goble, N. (1993). School-community relations: New for the '90s. *Education Digest, 59*(4), 45–48.

Holiday, A. E. (1994). The ultimate guide to school community relations. *Journal of Educational Public Relations, 15*(4), 3–16.

Howlett, P. (1993). Taming the trends. *American School Board Journal, 180*(6), 35–36.

Kowalski, T. J., & Wiedmer, T. (1994). A study of public relations practices in school districts. *Journal of Educational Public Relations, 60*(1), 21–29.

Lashley, J. E. (1989). Attitude and communication build public relations. *NASSP Bulletin, 73*(513), 34–35.

Ramsey, S. A. (1993). Issues management and the use of technologies in public relations. *Public Relations Review, 19*(3), 261–275.

Schreiber, W. (1993). The proof is in the PR: Five case studies offer conclusive evidence of the value of strategic communications. *Currents, 19*(9), 30–34.

Sparks, S. D. (1993). Public relations: Is it dangerous to use the term? *Public Relations Quarterly, 38*(3), 27–28.

Van Meter, E. J. (1993). Setting new priorities: Enhancing the school-community relations program. *NASSP Bulletin, 77*(554), 22–27.

REFERENCES

Bagin, D., Gallagher, D., & Kindred, L. (1994). *The school and community relations* (5th ed.). Boston: Allyn and Bacon.

Berliner, D. C. (1993). Education's present misleading myths undermine confidence in one of America's most cherished institutions. *Journal of Educational Public Relations, 15*(2), 4–11.

Blake, C. (1991). *Application of new information and communication technologies in public relations.* ERIC Document Reproduction Service No. ED 336 063.

Brody, E. W. (1988). *Public relations programming and production.* New York: Praeger.

Campbell, R. F., Corbally, J. E., & Nystrand, R. O. (1983). *Introduction to educational administration* (6th ed.). Boston: Allyn and Bacon.

Chubb, J. E., & Moe, T. M. (1990). *Politics, markets, and America's schools.* Washington, DC: Brookings Institute.

Cohen, P. M. (1987). *A public relations primer: Thinking and writing in context.* Englewood Cliffs, NJ: Prentice-Hall.

Connor, P., & Lake, L. (1988). *Managing organizational change.* New York: Praeger.

Crowson, R. L. (1992). *School-community relations, under reform.* Berkeley, CA: McCutchan.

Dilenschneider, R. L., & Forrestal, D. J. (1987). *The Dartnell public relations handbook* (3rd ed.). Chicago: Dartnell Corporation.

Finn, C. E. (1991). *We must take charge.* New York: Free Press.

Greer, C. (1992). Why private school choice is not the answer. In A. Must (Ed.), *Why we still need public schools: Church/state relations and visions of democracy* (pp. 278–287). Buffalo, NY: Prometheus Books.

Hanson, E. M. (1992). *Educational administration and organizational behavior* (3rd.). Boston: Allyn and Bacon.

Haywood, R. (1991). *All about public relations* (2nd ed.). New York: McGraw-Hill.

Henig, J. R. (1994). *Rethinking school choice: Limits of the market metaphor.* Princeton, NJ: Princeton University Press.

Jones, J. J. (1966). *School public relations.* New York: Center for Applied Research in Education.

Knezevich, S. J. (1969). *Administration of public education* (2nd ed.). New York: Harper & Row.

Kowalski, T. J., & Reitzug, U. C. (1993). *Contemporary school administration.* New York Longman.

Lesly, P. (1983). The nature and role of public relations. In P. Lesly (Ed.), *Lesly's public relations handbook* (3rd ed.) (pp. 3–13). Englewood Cliffs, NJ: Prentice Hall.

Lipinski, A. J. (1978). Communicating the future. *Futures, 10*(2), *126-127.*

Lovell, R. P. (1982). *Inside public relations.* Boston: Allyn and Bacon.

Lutz, F. W., & Merz, C. (1992). *The politics of school/community relations.* New York: Teachers College Press.

McElreath, M. P. (1993). *Managing systematic and ethical public relations.* Madison.

Moffett, J. (1994). On to the past: Wrong-headed school reform *Phi Delta Kappan, 75*(8), 584–590.

Naisbitt, J. (1982). *Megatrends: Ten new directions transforming our lives.* New York: Warner Books.

National Commission on Excellence in Education. (1983) *A nation at risk: The imperative for educational reform.* Washington, DC: U. S. Department of Education.

National School Public Relations Association (1986). *School public relations: The complete book.* Arlington, VA: Author.

Newsom, D., Scott, A., & VanSlyke Turk, J. (1989). *This is PR: The realities of public relations* (4th ed.). Belmont, CA: Wadsworth.

Norris, J. S. (1984). *Public relations.* Englewood Cliffs, NJ: Prentice Hall.

Quade, Q. L. (1993). Educational choice: Getting there from here. *Momentum, 24*(4), 19–20.

Reitzug, U. C., & Cornett, J. W. (1991). Teacher and administrator thought: Implications for administrator training. *Planning and Changing, 21*(3), 181–192.

Saxe, R. W. (1984). *School-community relations in transition.* Berkeley, CA: McCutchan.

Schön, D. A. (1983). *The reflective practitioner.* New York: Basic Books.

Schön, D. A. (1987). *Educating the reflective practitioner.* San Francisco: Jossey-Bass.

Seitel, F. P. (1992). *The practice of public relations* (5th ed.). New York: Macmillan.

Sergiovanni, T. J. (1991). *The principalship: A reflective practice perspective* (2nd ed.). Boston: Allyn and Bacon.

Shanker, A. (1993). Public vs. private schools. *National Forum: Phi Kappa Phi Journal, 73*(4), 14–17.

Toffler, A. (1970). *Future shock.* New York: Random House.

Toth, E. L., & Trujillo, N. (1987). Reinventing corporate communications. *Public Relations Review, 13*(4), 42–53.

Walling, D. R. (1982). *Complete book of school public relations: An administrator's manual and guide.* Englewood Cliffs, NJ: Prentice–Hall.

West, P. T. (1981). Imagery and change in the twenty-first century. *Theory into Practice, 20*(4), 229–236.

West, P. T. (1985). *Educational public relations.* Beverly Hills, CA: Sage Publications.

Wilcox, D., Ault, P., & Agee, W. (1992). *Public relations: Strategies and tactics* (3rd ed.). New York: HarperCollins.

Zaleznik, A. (1989). *The managerial mystique: Restoring leadership in business.* New York: Harper & Row.

CHAPTER 2

Changing Social and Institutional Conditions

Ulrich C. Reitzug

When we got up to 36th Street, some dudes were showing gang signs and yelling out, "Vice Lords, Vice Lords." Tony said, "We ain't in no gang," and I was backing him up. They noticed my hat, a baseball cap, with the initials "A.G." on it. One of them asked me, "What's up with your hat?" I told them this was my rap name. One guy hit me. We started fighting. When I broke loose, I started running. But they started shooting. They hit me in the back of the knee. I slipped, then I got up and started running again. But they got in front of me. A guy cut me off when I was trying to run through a yard. He shot me. He shot me before I fell; he shot me after I fell. All I could think is am I going to die? Am I going to stay alive? I was telling myself, "Just keep on breathing. But don't look at my leg" (Bothwell, 1994; edited for brevity).

Clarence, age 16, the speaker in the passage above, is just one of 320 children who was shot during a two-year period in a city of approximately 600,000 people. All 320 children were enrolled in the city's school systems, most of them in the major urban district of nearly 100,000 students. These children brought with them the physical and psychological damage of senseless violence as they attended to the reading, writing, and arithmetic lessons presented by their teachers.

But it is not only these 320 who were affected. Countless other schoolchildren are exposed to daily doses of violence and experience the psychological trauma of witnessing friends and neighbors die violent deaths. As a result, many do not expect to be alive for their twenty-first birthdays. Others practice survival strategies—remaining indoors after school to reduce their chances of injury or death, diving to the floor at the first sound of gunfire (Kotlowitz, 1991). Like Clarence, many of these schoolchildren are not gang members. Terry Young, a neuropsychologist who works with children who have experienced bullet-inflicted head injuries, observes, "One thing that strikes me about these kids is exactly that. They're kids. They're into basketball, baseball. They enjoy having normal fun" (Bothwell & Lawrence, 1994; p. A15).

Educating children who are growing up in a violence-laden society is just one of the changing sociocultural conditions with which schools in the late twentieth century are confronted. Other major changing sociocultural conditions that have directly or indirectly affected schools in the last two decades include changing family structures, greater poverty and homelessness, an increasingly multicultural and diverse society, more youth-to-youth violence, and eroding public support for education. These changes have significantly altered the public relations environment confronting today's schools—indeed, have directly affected how we think about public relations. This chapter will detail these sociocultural changes and discuss their implications for public relations in educational organizations.

CHANGING FAMILY STRUCTURES

In the early 1950s the typical American family structure consisted of a working father, a stay-at-home mother, and children. Today this family structure has given way to various other arrangements: large numbers of children are being raised by single mothers, single fathers, grandparents, gay couples, and other combinations of adults. In 1990, traditional families composed fewer than one-third of all families (Kirst & McLaughlin, 1990).

The most significant change in family structure has been the tremendous increase in single-parent families. If you were to poll students in a typical American high school classroom, you would find that almost half of them had spent some part of their youth living in a single-parent family (Hodgkinson, 1991). In fact, since 1970 there has been a 257 percent increase in the number of single parents in the United States, with the increase between 1980 and 1990 alone being 41 percent. African-American children are four times as likely, and Hispanic children are twice as likely, as white children to be raised in single-parent households. However, in recent years the birthrate among unmarried white women has increased dramatically (Smolowe, 1990).

Most single-parent families are headed by women. Hodgkinson (1991) reports that 87 percent of single-parent families are headed by women and notes that since 1970 the number of children living with single, never-married mothers has increased 678 percent. Children living in a female-headed, single parent family are likely to grow up in economically depressed conditions. Many single mothers provide the primary (or sole) financial support for their families, and in 1985 their average income was within $1000 of the poverty level (Kirst & McLaughlin, 1990).

It is not only children living in single-parent families who are experiencing a change in family living conditions. Children from both single-parent and two-parent families have been subjected to a risk factor that Sylvia Ann Hewlett (1991) terms the "time deficit." The time deficit refers to the decreased time today's parents spend with their children when compared with time spent by their predecessors. Hewlett notes that since 1960 children have lost ten to twelve hours of contact time per week with their parents, a decrease of 40 percent. She cites several factors as being responsible for this time deficit:

◆ There are more mothers in the workforce. As Hodgkinson (1991) reports, 70 percent of mothers with school-age children work or are seeking employment outside the home.

◆ An escalating divorce rate (it doubled between 1950 and 1989) results in more single-parent families.
◆ More and more divorced fathers abandon their children; 24 percent did so in 1990, double the 1970 percentage.
◆ There has been an increase in the number of hours required of workers on the job—six hours more per week in 1989 than in 1973. The forty-hour workweek now averages fifty-two hours.

The increase in adult household members in the work force as well as the greater number of weekly hours required by full-time positions has relegated an increasing number of schoolchildren to latchkey status. These children return from school to homes where there is no adult supervision until the end of the workday. It has been documented that latchkey children are more likely to take drugs or drink alcohol than are children who return to homes with adult supervision. While many schools have responded by providing extended-day programs, these programs cannot supply the strong emotional bonds that parental care provides.

Because of the increasingly hectic work schedules of both single-parent and two-parent families, child care often becomes "like a game of Russian roulette" (Gibbs, 1990, p. 44), with children being shuffled from one adult care provider to another. Parental time with children frequently comes at the end of a long, exhausting day and thus is likely to be more stress-filled than it was in previous eras (Hewlett, 1991). This may partially explain the tremendous increase in child abuse cases, which went from 600,000 in 1979 to more than 2.4 million reported cases in 1989 (Gibbs, 1990).

As a result of changing family conditions, increasing percentages of students come to schools with significant psychological or emotional problems. This compounds the schools' educative task. When schools fall short of adequately educating such students, they are as likely as parents to be saddled with the blame. As a result, public confidence in schools erodes.

INCREASED POVERTY AND HOMELESSNESS

For over 20 percent of American children, growing up in poverty significantly affects their childhood experience and impacts their ability to learn. Children are poorer than any other age group in America: Forty percent of all poor people are children; one out of every four children under the age of 6, and one out of every five children overall, is living in poverty (Hodgkinson, 1991; Reed & Sauter, 1990). In fact, the United States has the highest child-poverty rate of any industrialized nation (Reed & Sauter, 1990). Almost half of all children born in the United States today will spend a part of their lives in poverty.

Poverty is closely correlated with race, ethnicity, and gender. Witness the following statistics:

◆ Forty-four percent of African-American children live in poverty (Reed & Sauter, 1990). Additionally, most African-American children will spend four of their first ten years of life living in poverty (Mott Foundation, 1989).

- ◆ Thirty-seven percent of Hispanic children, 27 percent of Asian-American children, and 14 percent of Caucasian-American children live in poverty (Reed & Sauter, 1990).
- ◆ Fifty percent of single women with children live in poverty (Kirst & McLaughlin, 1990).

Although we frequently associate poverty with urban areas, it is actually more prevalent in the rural parts of our nation. The poverty rate for rural children is 50 percent higher than that for urban children, with almost one-fourth of rural children living in poverty (O'Hara, 1988; Cohen, 1992).

The impact of poverty on children is significant. Overall, children from economically disadvantaged families experience greater rates of poor physical health, serious illness, developmental disability, teenage pregnancy, and school dropout. Additionally, children from poverty-stricken families show lower academic achievement and lower self-reports of happiness (Kirst & McLaughlin, 1990; Reed & Sauter, 1990). They spend twice as many days in hospitals as do other children but are unlikely to be covered by health insurance. Thus, poor children generally do not receive preventive health care such as physical examinations and dental checkups (Kirst & McLaughlin, 1990). Conditions for the near-poor (those with incomes slightly above the poverty line) are no better. Frequently they are ineligible for services at public expense and thus do without health care and other services (Erickson, 1990).

The bleak picture of childhood poverty is unlikely to brighten in the near future. Although the federal government has made some recent overtures toward implementing improved health and human services, successful efforts may simply recover ground lost during recent decades. For example, the median Aid to Families with Dependent Children (AFDC) grant has fallen 23 percent in constant dollars since 1970, and only slightly more than half the children nationwide living in poverty receive benefits from AFDC (Reed & Sauter, 1990). Additionally, 38 percent of eligible children do not reap the benefits of food stamps. Public housing is available to serve only 21 percent of poor families (Kirst & McLaughlin, 1990). This reduction in services occurred during a period of time when the real income of poor people dropped 3.2 percent, while their federal taxes increased 16 percent (Mott Foundation, 1989). Interestingly, spending for the elderly increased 52 percent during this period, and spending for defense rose 37 percent (Hewlett, 1991).

The past decade has also seen a tremendous increase in the number of homeless individuals in our society. It is estimated that if recent trends continue, there will be more than seven times the number of homeless people in the year 2003 as there were in 1988 (Erickson, 1990).

As might be expected, homelessness is also correlated with race, age, and gender:

- ◆ Fifty-one percent of the homeless population is African-American, 35 percent is Caucasian, and 14 percent is made up of other races (U.S. Conference of Mayors, 1989).
- ◆ Thirty percent of the homeless population is made up of children (Cohen, 1994).
- ◆ Over 10 percent of the homeless population in a number of major cites is composed of adolescents unaccompanied by parents (U.S. Conference of Mayors, 1989).

- ◆ Forty-three percent of homeless individuals are single men, but another 43 percent are families with children (Cohen, 1994).
- ◆ Most homeless families consist of single women with two or three children under the age of 5. Single mothers typically pay over 50 percent of their income toward housing costs, even though mortgage-approval ratios suggest that no more than 28 percent should be spent on housing costs. As a result, one significant unexpected expenditure can quickly throw single mothers and their children into the ranks of the homeless (Hodgkinson, 1991).

Homeless children experience health, psychological, and school-related problems to a much greater extent than do poor children who live in homes with their families (U.S. Conference of Mayors, 1989). Health-related problems include anemia, malnutrition, and asthma; psychological problems include depression, hyperactivity, listlessness, anxiety, aggression, and low self-esteem; and school-related problems include lower attendance and difficulty establishing peer friendships (U.S. Conference of Mayors, 1989).

It is not that parents of poor and homeless children are shirking their economic responsibility to their children—in 87 percent of poverty families and 24 percent of homeless families, at least one member of the household is employed (U.S. Conference of Mayors, 1989). Unfortunately, a full-time job in a minimum-wage position earns $2500 less than is necessary to bring a family of three to the poverty level (Erickson, 1990).

AN INCREASINGLY MULTICULTURAL AND DIVERSE SOCIETY

In addition to changing family conditions and greater poverty and homelessness, the United States is also becoming increasingly diverse. Between 1980 and 1990 almost 50 percent of the nation's population growth was accounted for by nonwhite individuals. It is projected that by the year 2010, the nonwhite segment of the U.S. population will increase to 38 percent (Hodgkinson, 1991). Currently, about one-fourth of the U.S. population qualifies as being minority (Ward, 1994). This includes an African-American population that makes up 12 percent of the total U.S. population; a Hispanic population that accounts for 8.4 percent; and Asians, Pacific Islanders, and other races who account for 3.6 percent (Waldrop & Exeter, 1991).

Public school populations, particularly in urban areas, are also becoming increasingly nonwhite. In 1989, minority-group members made up 38.7 percent of public school enrollment (Education Vital Signs, 1991), with some large urban districts having over 90 percent minority enrollments (Tanner, 1989). Between 1976 and 1986, the fastest-growing minority group in public schools was composed of Asian students whose population increased 40 percent during this period. By comparison, Hispanics, the second-fastest-growing group, increased their population by 13.2 percent.

A large part of the growth of minority populations in the United States is due to fertility rates, which are strongly correlated with race and socioeconomic group—the economically disadvantaged having the highest fertility rate. By race, Hispanics have a fertility rate of 86.1 births per 1000 women, African-Americans a fertility rate of 72.2 births per 1000 women, and Caucasians a fertility rate of 64.6 births per 1000 women. The median age of Hispanics in the U.S. population is also the lowest (25.0), followed by African-Americans (26.3) and Caucasians (32.2) (McKay, 1986).

Immigration has also contributed to the growth of minority-group populations in the United States. Our country now admits more immigrants annually than ever before. Whereas most immigrants once came from Europe (89 percent in 1910 compared with 10 percent today), most now come from Asian and Hispanic countries (America's Changing Face, 1990). The combination of high birth rates, low median age, and high immigration rates makes the continued growth of the nonwhite segment of our population likely.

Minority-group members typically have low achievement in schools. For example, in 1986 almost 40 percent of Hispanic and African-American students were enrolled below the modal grade for their age compared with 25 percent of Caucasian students (Orum, 1986). While language difficulty may contribute to this figure (especially for recent Hispanic and Asian immigrants) and overt discrimination may account for an additional number, the largest percentage is likely attributable to the cultural incongruency between middle-class, white conceptions of appropriate education and the learning styles of minority groups. (See, for example, Irvine, 1990; Kochman, 1981.)

Other aspects of diversity besides race and ethnicity also exist in schools and should be considered when developing educative practices. For example, some sources estimate that up to 10 percent of the U.S. population is gay (Sears, 1993). However, not only are the needs of homosexual students often overlooked in schools, these students are also regularly and overtly discriminated against by students, faculty, and school policy. Data indicate that many of these students are crying out for understanding. For example, there is a high degree of correlation between teenage suicide and homosexuality (Sears, 1993), which might well be attributed to the "well of loneliness" (Sears, 1987, p. 79) that confronts gay adolescents both in and out of school.

YOUTH VIOLENCE

Recent years have seen a tremendous increase in youth-to-youth violence in our society. Gunshots currently account for one out of every four deaths among American teenagers (Hull, 1993), and children under the age of 18 are now 244 percent more likely to be killed by guns than they were in 1986 (Adler, 1994). Overall, one in six youths between the ages of 10 and 17 has seen or knows someone who has been shot (Adler, 1994).

Although schools remain relatively safe when compared with the streets, violence has become a part of daily life in many schools. A recent survey from the National School Boards Association indicated that 82 percent of schools reported an increase in violence in the past five years and that violence is found not just in urban schools but also increasingly in suburban and rural schools. The study reported that 35 percent of males in crime-ridden urban neighborhoods reported having carried a gun to school and 22 percent reported owning a gun (Portner, 1994). Other reports indicate that 15 percent of sixth- through twelfth-graders carry guns to school in any thirty-day period (Hull, 1993), with over 100,000 students nationwide taking a gun to school on any given day (Kids and Guns, 1994). Additionally, 45 percent of male students in inner-city schools reported that they had been shot at or threatened with a gun on the way to or from school in the past few years (Portner, 1994).

Schools are combatting the gun problem in a variety of ways, including the use of metal detectors, which are now being used in 35 percent of the nation's 100 largest school districts (Portner, 1993). However, measures such as metal detectors simply treat the symptom while ignoring the problem.

Teenagers own and carry guns for a variety of reasons. One recent report quoted one youth who explained, "You fire a gun and you can just hear the power. It's like yeah!" (Hull, 1993, p. 22). Another youth noted, "You feel invincible with a weapon" (Hull, 1993, p. 25). Many youths also see guns as a source of protection from gang violence. One youth noted, "When you have a gun, you feel like can't nobody get you. You can't get got" (Hull, 1993, p. 26). In other cases, guns serve as the tool that allows youths to function as full-fledged gang members. As one recent report concluded, "A pistol says much more than long hair or a pierced nose ever could. . . . With a $25 investment, all the teasing from classmates stops cold. Suddenly the shortest, ugliest and weakest kid becomes a player" (Hull, 1993, p. 23).

Some have blamed the rapid spread of gangs as the reason for increased youth violence and gun possession. Gangs seem to indicate a need on the part of adolescents to belong to an organization that values them and gives them purpose. Interestingly, Heath and McLaughlin (1991) came to a similar conclusion regarding successful youth-serving organizations, noting "What [these organizations] have in common is . . . their insistence that members feel that they belong to an intimate group" (p. 625). More specifically, Heath and McLaughlin found that six factors characterized successful youth-serving organizations:

◆ A common conception of young people as resources to be developed rather than as problems to be managed
◆ Development of a recognizable product—for example, a performance, a team record, a newspaper
◆ Investment of a significant amount of responsibility for the development of the product in the young people themselves
◆ Strong participation by members of the immediate local community
◆ Adaptation to specific local needs
◆ Continual shifts in the structure, role, and processes of the organization in order to stay in tune with the ecology of the immediate neighborhood

ERODING PUBLIC SUPPORT

School violence is only one of a variety of reasons behind the erosion in recent years of public support for public education—particularly financial support. Although one recent poll (Elam, Rose, & Gallup, 1993) indicated a slightly more supportive public, many negative indicators persist. The continued strength of the privatization movement, which is built on such concepts as tuition vouchers, school choice, and charter schools, is one indicator; the increasing difficulty public school districts are having in mustering even marginal support for tax referenda is another. Also contributing to eroding public support are the negative impacts of a swelling population of senior citizens, teacher unionization, and taxpayer revolt.

The Growing Population of Elderly

America is embarking on what Dychtwald (1989) terms the "age wave," the escalating number of elderly and aging citizens in our society. One source places the current over-65 population in the United States at 31 million (Kaplan, 1991). This mass of senior citizens is more affluent than their societal juniors and carries considerable political clout because of their proclivity for voting. And two factors make it unlikely that this group will cast their votes in favor of additional financial support for schools.

1. Senior citizens no longer have children of their own in school and thus are not as committed to investing in education as they might once have been.
2. Many senior citizens are on fixed incomes, and although they frequently have other financial resources, they resist tapping into these almost as a matter of principle.

Current public support for education is high, however, when compared with what is likely to happen in several decades when the baby boomers, some 77 million Americans now 27 to 46 years old, arrive at their golden years. Until schools commit themselves to involving senior citizens as partners in education in some fashion, or provide the elders with valued services, it is unlikely that their support for education will be forthcoming.

Teacher Unionization

Teachers' unions served a valuable role in the past few decades in achieving livable wages and working conditions for teachers. While these unions remain a necessary structure for protecting teachers' rights against the whims of capricious administrators and school boards, they must modify their original focus to respond to a new context. While some unions have reconceptualized their roles and now work collaboratively with administrators and school boards, many unions cling to their original role, maintaining the confrontational stance necessary in a previous era. For example, the executive director of the teachers' association in one large urban district recently indicated that he would use every method he knew to protect incompetent teachers in dismissal hearings. A former teacher, he explicitly stated that he did not care that retaining incompetent teachers was not in the best interests of students—that his job was to protect teachers at any cost (Ernst, 1993). Such a perspective results in a union stance that is not in the best interest of children, is opposed by many teachers in the union, and makes no sense to the public. Further, the public's perception is that all educators feel this way, which only compounds the erosion of public support for education.

Taxpayer Revolt

The passage of Proposition 13 in California, and subsequently of Proposition 2.5 in Massachusetts, is indicative of the taxpayer revolt that has gripped this country for over a decade. In response to public pressure, many state legislatures have placed various direct or indirect restrictions on property tax increases while other states have outlawed property taxes as a source of school revenue.

Taxpayer reluctance to pay increased property taxes is the result of rapid escalation of such taxes over a number of years. Several factors were responsible for this, including a period of double-digit national inflation, more-stringent and costlier requirements for the delivery of special education services, and an eroding tax base (especially in urban areas). The eroding tax base was caused by the flight of manufacturing concerns from cities and the provision of tax breaks and other tax incentives to new businesses settling in the community. All these factors have caused the public to perceive tax increases to be unrealistically high, leading to a taxpayer revolt.

IMPLICATIONS FOR PUBLIC RELATIONS

What are the implications of these changing sociocultural conditions for educational public relations? In answering that question I would like to share with you a bit of my personal education history. I share my story because I think it is representative of the stories of many educators who are well intentioned but shortsighted.

Prior to becoming a university professor I worked in K-12 schools for eleven years as a teacher and principal. The schools in which I worked were attended by primarily white students from upper middle class, two-parent families. Nonetheless, there was sufficient diversity in these schools that there were also children in attendance from economically disadvantaged families and single-parent families. There were African-American students, Hispanic students, and Asian students; students with a variety of disabilities; and students with other characteristics that distinguished them from the "typical" student—for example, students who were wrestling with emerging feelings of attraction for members of their own sex. As I reflect back on those days I realize that while overall I was well respected as an educator, I also know that education in the schools in which I worked was like a cheap tube sock—one size fit all.

Granted, I was sensitive to diversity during my days as a teacher and principal—at least as much as I was capable of being, given my prior experiences. I was against discrimination and prejudice; I believed in equity and justice; I cared for my students and their families; I wanted a top-quality education for all students. However, I viewed these concepts through the narrow lens of a white middle-class male living in a period of time when white maleness so dominated education (and especially school administration) that our focus was seldom challenged. Thus I was insensitive to cultural differences in learning style; I was unaware of certain aspects of student diversity; I did not know enough to question the Eurocentric content of the textbooks we used. I thought equality of educational opportunity meant providing the best "white"* education for all children. If nonwhite children or other children who were culturally different from the mainstream "didn't get

---

*I use the term "white" to denote the typical perspective embraced by white, middle-class, heterosexual males—the dominant power group in educational administration at the time. "White" is not used here to contrast with "black" culture but is used in a broader sense to contrast with any perspectives that are different from the dominant cultural perspective.

it," we would teach them in a group with other children who also "didn't get it." There we would help them by providing white education in finer, more discrete increments. I was never sensitive enough to realize that the Eurocentric focus of the education we provided delegitimized the culture of children of color and ensured *inequality* of educational opportunity for most of these children.

From a public relations standpoint we had an easy sell. Our white middle-class patrons were pleased that we were providing their children with the finest in white education. Our culturally diverse patrons were pleased because we cared enough to provide special "white" programs for their children.

Sadly, in too many of today's schools circumstances have not changed that much. White middle- and upper-class students continue to get the best white education available, while an escalating number of minority and poor students get an education that frequently is culturally incongruent with their needs.

The "Tube-Sock" Response

What has changed since my days as a teacher and principal is that our "tube-sock" education has developed more and bigger holes than it previously had. The turmoil in many students' lives inside and outside of school has increased so dramatically that they ignore or actively resist schools as one more societal structure that oppresses them. The resistance of societally oppressed students has become so strong and so pervasive that it is now affecting the education of white middle-class students and thus is finally drawing the attention of those in business and government—our societal seats of power.

In this context a public relations perspective that focuses on a more efficient, effective, and pervasive campaign to sell old educational packages in new wrappers is not only unethical but immoral. Moral practice requires that we rethink and rebuild the educative role of schools in our society in a way that recognizes and honors multiple cultures and ways of being. (See, for example, Asante, 1991; Tate, 1994; Woodson, 1933.) Simply celebrating Black History Month or adding a Multicultural Issues class may serve as a token response that allows the more systemic and cultural incongruencies of overall school practices to be ignored. I am not arguing that we replace the dominant cultural perspective with a minority cultural perspective. I am arguing that we attempt to understand how education might best proceed when it integrates a variety of cultural perspectives.

In our efforts at understanding, we must ensure that the voices of the disenfranchised—racial and ethnic minorities, single parents, students with disabilities; of the invisible—the poor, the homeless, the homosexual students; and of the excluded—the elderly—are fully included. Without such inclusion any responses that are developed are likely be simply new variations on an old theme—that is, solutions that look good through a white middle-class lens but are distorted when viewed through the lenses of other cultures.

Alternative Responses

Currently there are several efforts being made at a number of sites to ensure that schooling is a process that is more inclusive of its publics. These efforts include parent-involvement strategies and programs, interagency collaboration, school-business partnerships, and site-based management.

Parent-Involvement Strategies and Programs.   In order for parent-involvement programs to make a difference, parents must be involved in meaningful and legitimate ways that extend beyond viewing parents as extra bodies to provide clerical assistance or as revenue generators via their work in PTO fund-raising activities. Parents must be given opportunities to share their hopes and dreams for their children with schoolpeople and to inquire with us as to how those hopes and dreams might be realized. Subsequently, we must work with them, as they must work with us, to attain the hopes and dreams. Rioux and Berla (1994) caution that we avoid "putting the parents in a box," assuming that they and their families "have things wrong with them that have to be fixed" (p. 31). Additionally, we must be cognizant of the need to include parents who are traditionally disenfranchised in schools.

Parents, especially the disenfranchised, may not come to school simply because we invite them. They may harbor unpleasant memories of school from their own student days. Visiting the imposing physical structures that were the sites of unhappy days may be unappealing. Thus we must meet parents on their turf— in community centers, in churches, even in their homes. Additionally, sometimes barriers that are negligible for middle-class whites—for example, child care and transportation to meetings—may restrict the participation of the less economically fortunate (Capper & Hammiller, 1993).

Interagency Collaboration.   Based on a recognition that many community agencies provide services to families and children, school-community collaboration in service coordination and delivery is gaining popularity in many areas. Under this concept the fragmentation and inefficiency that exists in service delivery—consider the 160 programs housed in 35 agencies and 7 departments in California (Kirst & McLaughlin, 1990)—would be reduced. Theoretically, interagency collaboration is intended to resolve the isolation and labeling of problems, the patchwork of solutions, the discontinuity of care, and the underutilization of resources that exist in current service-delivery models.

Interagency collaboration has also been suggested as a means of addressing major problems confronting adolescents. For example, Cross and Jones (1994) advocate collaborative school-community efforts in working to decrease violence among children and to enable them to deal with the violence that is a part of their lives. Beverly Cross, an education professor, and Francine Jones, a nursing professor, describe their initially separate efforts and note, "We began to realize our efforts could increase exponentially if we worked collaboratively and combined the expertise we have in health and education. . . . [T]o have any significant effect on violence, schools and communities must come together" (p. 2).

School and community collaborative efforts, however, are not without problems. Recurring difficulties include defining a mutual philosophy of service delivery among involved agencies, overcoming the narrowness and lack of coordination in the professional training of the various service providers, and resolving turf-protection issues that result from individual agency fears of losing stature or funding (Kirst & McLaughlin, 1990). In some instances coordination of service delivery has resulted in increased centralization, bureaucracy, and depersonalization, moving the point of service further from patrons. Programs that work embrace a treatment perspective that focuses on continuous and evolutionary client development (as opposed to narrow clinical notions that simply treat individual pathologies), involve patrons in self-identification of problem and solution, adapt to local contexts, exhibit cooperation and support from mid- and top-level bureaucrats, and earmark resources for coordination between agencies (Kirst & McLaughlin, 1990).

School-Business Partnerships.   The purpose of school-business partnerships is for schools to profit from the financial and knowledge resources business has to offer. These partnerships are grounded in the debatable assumption that business has succeeded where schools have failed and, thus, that schools can learn effective practices from business. For business the interest is in maintaining an educated and productive workforce.

While many schools have business partners, unfortunately the school-business partnership in many instances can be characterized as transactional rather than transformational. In the transactional partnerships, schools receive funding from their business partners; business has an opportunity to promote their agenda in schools. In the transformational relationship, the vested interests of schools and business recede into the background. Educators and businesspeople engage in discussions that critically examine schooling and its purposes. Troublesome, however, in school-business partnerships is the fact that business, like educational administration, is still white-male-dominated and thus represents the voice that has traditionally been the most influential in schooling. While an inclusive approach to involving the public in education requires business representation, educators must be watchful that the assertive voices of business are not allowed to overpower the emerging voices of the disenfranchised.

Site-Based Management.   Site-based management is one way in which education has attempted to include parents and others in the school governance process. Theoretically, site-based management decentralizes decision-making authority to the school site where teachers, staff, parents, community members, principals, and sometimes students jointly make school decisions. The objective is to give voice to the previously voiceless and, as a result, to make more responsive and effective decisions. While site-based management may still reach this potential, most empirical data to date indicate that although, formally, authority may be decentralized and involvement may be inclusive, informally, principals and district-level bureaucrats use various means to restrict legitimate authority, influence, and involvement (Malen & Ogawa, 1988; Malen, Ogawa, & Kranz, 1991; Reitzug & Capper, 1993).

SUMMARY

Although parent-involvement strategies, interagency collaboration, school-business partnerships, and site-based management each have potential for expanding the circle of school inclusiveness, they remain fairly mainstream approaches and do not guarantee that the deep structure of schooling and its underlying assumptions will be challenged. From my singular perspective I would be arrogant, and naive if I said I had the ideal solution. Nonetheless, of one thing I am certain. A public relations policy that expresses the views of one segment of the population, and then relies on classy brochures and slick videos to impose these views upon patrons, is both ineffective and wrong. Rather, an effective public relations agenda must actively and legitimately involve all patrons—young, old, rich, poor, black, white; from traditional, single-parent, and nontraditional families; homosexual and straight; with and without disabilities—in a continual process of inquiry into the educative process and the rebuilding of schooling.

CASE STUDY

The $366 Million Referendum

This case study is based on actual reports from the *Milwaukee Journal*. Text, however, has been edited.

Milwaukee, Wisconsin, is a city with a population of approximately 700,000 located in a metropolitan area of close to 2 million inhabitants. The Milwaukee Public Schools are attended by nearly 100,000 students, of which more than half are African-American.

From the Milwaukee Journal, *January 25, 1993*

If Milwaukee residents vote February 16 to approve $366 million in long-term borrowing to help pay for a $474.3 million ten-year school building program, what will they get for their money? Some say strictly bricks and mortar. To be sure, there will be a wide range of building projects. They include fifteen new schools—twelve elementary, two middle, and a vocational/technical school—that add up to $276 million, or 58 percent of the plan's total price tag. Another $198.3 million will go for repair, maintenance, and improvement projects that include everything from roof and boiler replacements to major additions at fourteen existing schools.

Many of the new buildings and additions are necessary to support program goals that include:

◆ Reducing class size in kindergarten through second grade from about twenty-six to nineteen students per class.

◆ Providing 4-year-old kindergarten and all-day 5-year-old kindergarten for more than 6000 eligible pupils for whom there now is no space.

◆ Expanding the number of computer, art, and music classrooms. Officials say that 54 percent of the district's 111 elementary schools lack space for computer training, 55 percent have no art rooms, and 70 percent lack music rooms. A total of 63 percent do not have libraries.

◆ Building a $68.8 million vocational school to replace the outdated Milwaukee Trade and Technical School. Another $32.4 million would be spent to upgrade vocational facilities in other schools.

A major portion of the plan—$148.7 million, or 31.4 percent—is earmarked for preserving the district's existing facilities. Without such an effort, officials say, existing buildings will deteriorate to the point where they will need to be replaced.

Officials say the projects would accomplish other goals as well. New schools in the central city would reduce mandatory busing by allowing central-city youngsters to attend neighborhood schools. In addition, students and teachers would be moved out of substandard classroom space. There are now pupils in one of every four elementary schools who are taught in cloakrooms. In more than half the schools, storage areas double as classrooms. In 41 percent of the schools some instruction takes place in hallways.

From the Milwaukee Journal, January 26, 1993

If the proposed school plan passes, it will require average annual property tax increases of 8.1 percent over the twenty-four years it will take to pay off the last of the bonds issued to underwrite the plan. For the owner of a median-priced Milwaukee home, valued at $50,700 today, that translates into average tax increases of $159 per year.

From the Milwaukee Journal, February 7, 1993

Milwaukeeans, overall, are about evenly divided on the $366 million question that goes before city voters next week, but the proposal appears likely to be defeated anyway. Overwhelmingly, the people most likely to vote are opposed.
A survey found several obstacles confronting the building plan:

- ◆ Homeowners feel overwhelmed by property taxes as it is.
- ◆ Milwaukeeans are angry they're being asked to decide on an issue even their leaders can't agree on. Mayor Norquist has proposed spending $184 million instead of the $366 million included in Superintendent Fuller's plan. The mayor said his plan—unveiled just days before the school board voted to take its plan to voters—meets some of the needs while not hitting residents as hard in the pocketbook.
- ◆ Many of those polled feel the higher property taxes that would accompany the plan would drive people out of the city.
- ◆ People aren't convinced the building plan will improve the quality of education, improve the city's economy, or make the city safer.
- ◆ Milwaukee schools seem to have a negative momentum. Only 33 percent of the people polled think the city schools are good. Even so, the poll found strong support for education.

Most Milwaukeeans favor many of the goals in Superintendent Fuller's plan: upgraded job training facilities, more computer classrooms, reduced class size, reduced busing, a new technical/vocational high school, a 4-year-old kindergarten. The problem is the majority isn't convinced the city needs fifteen new schools, fourteen school additions, and more art and music classrooms.

From the Milwaukee Journal, February 17, 1993

Voters turned out in unexpected numbers for a February primary, and 75 percent voted against the school measure while 25 percent voted in favor. According to unofficial returns, the proposal was defeated 93,948 to 30,894. Black voters supported the bond issue as expected. Black turnout was high when compared with past February elections. But in many neighborhoods the turnout among whites, older, and more-conservative voters wasn't simply high; it was unprecedented for a winter election.

The vote broke down sharply along racial lines. In predominantly white neighborhoods the vote averaged 85 percent against and 15 percent for the referendum. In predominantly black neighborhoods the vote averaged 70 percent for the referendum and 30 percent against it.

From the Milwaukee Journal, February 18, 1993

Anxiety about the school plan's impact on property taxes undoubtedly fueled the high turnout. Superintendent Fuller said, in reflecting on the defeat, "While some people may be celebrating a victory, we all need to understand the needs of our children remain."

From the Milwaukee Journal, January 20, 1994

Milwaukee Public Schools released a report card on its performance for the 1992–1993 school year Thursday. Its grades were the kind most children would be afraid to take home to mom and dad. The fourth annual report shows that while MPS continues to work at reform, it still has not shown results in improving test scores, dropout rates, and grade point averages, among other categories.

QUESTIONS AND SUGGESTED ACTIVITIES

Case Study

1. If you were Superintendent Fuller, what action would you have taken *prior* to the vote to help ensure the success of the referendum?
2. If you were Superintendent Fuller, what action would you have taken *subsequent* to the defeated referendum?
3. Why do you think the referendum was defeated?
4. What factor do you think race played in the referendum? If the Milwaukee public schools were attended primarily by white students, do you think the referendum results would have been different?
5. What do you think is the relationship between the 1992–1993 Milwaukee Public Schools report card and the referendum?
6. How do you think the public's overwhelmingly negative perception of education—as suggested by the sound defeat of the referendum—could be changed?
7. How do you think implementing the recommendations from this chapter for greater voice for typically disenfranchised groups would impact future referendum results?
8. List specific ways in which inclusiveness might occur.
9. Do you think the Milwaukee case is unique, or do you think it is representative of the perception of public education in this country?

Chapter

10. In your opinion, have schools contributed to the escalation of violence among America's youth? Do schools have a responsibility for attempting to reduce youth violence? If so, what types of strategies might they use? Which strategies treat symptoms? Problems?

11. Do a demographic analysis of your community that mirrors the demographic analysis presented in this chapter. How is your community similar? Different? What factors explain differences?

12. What implications do changing family structures and conditions have for schools? What implications do they have for public relations as we have traditionally thought of it?

13. What is the responsibility of schools to provide special programs for poor and/or homeless children and their families? What types of programs might be provided? Should they be educationally focused or social-service focused? Which programs for the poor and/or homeless currently exist in your school? School district? In other schools and school districts?

14. The chapter states, "A public relations perspective that focuses on a more efficient, effective, and pervasive campaign to sell old educational packages in new wrappers is not only unethical but immoral." Do you agree or disagree? Do you think that "a new campaign to sell an old package" does, in fact, characterize most current school public relations efforts?

15. Select several policies and practices that are in effect in your school or school district and analyze them from a cultural perspective. Whose culture do they reflect? Learn about the cultural perspectives of various minority and other disenfranchised groups and discuss implications these perspectives have for different ways of constructing the selected policies and practices.

16. Identify any indicators that provide evidence of the degree of public support for your local schools. Analyze and identify the factors that appear to be contributing to positive and/or negative public perceptions.

17. What programs or practices exist to include the elderly in your local schools? What programs and practices might be developed?

18. How are parents involved in your local schools? Whose perspective do these strategies represent? That is, are these the ways *schools* want parents to be involved, or are these the ways *parents* want to be involved?

19. Analyze parent involvement in schools from a demographic perspective. For example, what is the extent of white middle-class involvement? Minority-group involvement? Single-parent involvement? How might parent involvement be made more inclusive of underrepresented groups?

20. What is the extent of collaboration between your local schools and community agencies? What have been the results of any collaborative efforts? What barriers exist to further collaboration?

21. Analyze decision making in your local schools. If your school(s) use some form of shared decision making, which groups are represented? Do teachers, staff members, parents, and other represented groups have legitimate authority and influence, or is their involvement physical only?

SUGGESTED READINGS

Capper, C. (1993). *Educational administration in a pluralistic society.* Albany, NY: SUNY Press.

Capper, C., & Hammiller, R. (1993, October). Multiple perspectives on community-based interagency collaboration. Paper presented at the University Council for Educational Administration conference, Houston, TX.

Hacker, A. (1992). *Two nations: Black and white, separate, hostile, unequal.* New York: Ballantine Books.

Hewlett, S. A. (1991). *When the bough breaks: The cost of neglecting our children.* New York: Basic Books.

Hodgkinson, H. (1989). *The same client: The demographics of education and service delivery systems.* Washington, DC: Institute for Educational Leadership/Center for Demographic Policy.

Irvine, J. J. (1990). *Black students and school failure.* New York: Praeger.

Kochman, T. (1981). *Black and white styles in conflict.* Chicago: University of Chicago Press.

Kotlowitz, A. (1991). *There are no children here.* New York: Doubleday.

Kozol, J. (1991). *Savage inequalities.* New York: Crown Publishers.

Nunn, G. D., & Parish, T. S. (1992). The psychological characteristics of at-risk high school students. *Adolescence, 27,* 435–440.

Reitzug, U. C. (1994). Diversity, power and influence: Multiple perspectives on the ethics of school leadership. *Journal of School Leadership, 4*(2), 197–222.

Reitzug, U. C., & Capper, C. A. (in press). Deconstructing site-based management: Emancipation and alternative means of control. *International Journal of Education Reform.*

Walker, E. M., & Sutherland, M. E. (1993). Urban black youths' educational and occupational goals: The impact of America's opportunity structure. *Urban Education, 28,* 200–220.

Willis, P. (1977). *Learning to labor.* Lexington, MA: D. C. Heath.

REFERENCES

Adler, J. (1994, January 10). Kids growing up scared. *Newsweek,* pp. 43–49.

America's changing face (1990, September 10). *Newsweek,* pp. 46–50.

Asante, M. K. (1991). The Afrocentric idea in education. *Journal of Negro Education, 60,* 170–180.

Bothwell, A. (1994, January 2). Bullets blew holes in young man's basketball dreams. *Milwaukee Journal,* p. A14.

Bothwell, A., & Lawrence, C. (1994, January 2). Gunfire takes huge toll on kids—320 injured in past two years here. *Milwaukee Journal,* pp. A1, A14, A15.

Capper, C., & Hammiller, R. (1993, October). Multiple perspectives on community-based interagency collaboration. Paper presented at the University Council for Educational Administration conference, Houston, TX.

Cohen, D. L. (1992, January 8). Conditions "bleak" for rural children, C.D.F. finds. *Education Week,* p. 7.

Cohen, D. L. (1994, January 19). Children and families. *Education Week,* p. 8.

Cross, B. E., & Jones, F. C. (1994, March). Violence: Bringing schools and communities together. *Wisconsin School News* (Wisconsin Association of School Boards), pp.13–15.

Dychtwald, K. (1989). *The age wave: The challenges and opportunities of an aging America.* Los Angeles: Jeremy P. Tarcher.

Education vital signs (1991). *Executive Educator, 13*(12), A1–A27.

Elam, S. M., Rose, L. C., & Gallup, A. M. (1993). The 25th annual Phi Delta Kappa/Gallup poll of the public's attitudes toward the public schools. *Phi Delta Kappan, 75,* 137–152.

Erickson, J. B. (1990). Poverty in Indiana. *F.Y.I., 2*(3), 1–2, 5.

Ernst, D. (1993, July). Class presentation. University of Wisconsin-Milwaukee.

Gibbs, N. (1990, October 8). Shameful bequests to the next generation. *Time,* pp. 42–46.

Heath, S. B., & McLaughlin, M. W. (1991). Community organizations as family: Endeavors that engage and support adolescents. *Phi Delta Kappan, 72,* 623–627.

Hewlett, S. A. (1991). *When the bough breaks: The cost of neglecting our children.* New York: Basic Books.

Hodgkinson, H. (1991). Reform versus reality. *Phi Delta Kappan, 73,* 8–16.

Hull, J. D. (1993, August 2). A kid and his gun. *Time,* pp. 21–27.

Irvine, J. J. (1990). Black students and school failure. New York: Praeger.

Kaplan, G. (1991). Suppose they gave an intergenerational conflict and nobody came. *Phi Delta Kappan, 72*(9), K1–K12.

Kids and guns (1993, December 1). *Education Week*, p. 4.

Kirst, M. W., & McLaughlin, M. (1990). *Rethinking children's policy: Implications for educational administration*. Bloomington, IN: Consortium on Educational Policy Studies (Indiana University).

Kochman, T. (1981). *Black and white styles in conflict*. Chicago: University of Chicago Press.

Kotlowitz, A. (1991). *There are no children here*. New York: Doubleday.

Malen, B., & Ogawa, R. T. (1988). Professional-patron influence on site-based governance councils: A confounding case study. *Educational Evaluation and Policy Analysis, 10,* 251–270.

Malen, B., Ogawa, R. T., & Kranz, S. (1991). What do we know about school-based management? A case study of the literature—A call for research. In W. H. Clune & J. F. Witte (Eds.), *Choice and control in American education, Volume 2* (pp. 289–342). New York: Falmer Press.

McKay, E. (1986). *Hispanic demographics: Looking ahead*. ERIC Document Reproduction Service No. ED 274 754.

Mott Foundation (1989). *The fraying fabric: A portrait of America's poverty*. Flint, MI: Author.

O'Hara, W. P. (1988). *The rise of poverty in rural America*. ERIC Document Reproduction Service No. ED 302 350.

Orum, L. S. (1986). *The education of Hispanics: Status and implications*. ERIC Document Reproduction Service No. ED 274 753.

Portner, J. (1993, December 8). Fighting a war on weapons. *Education Week*, pp. 24–25.

Portner, J. (1994, January 12). School violence up over past 5 years, 82% in survey say. *Education Week*, p. 9.

Reed, S., & Sauter, R. C. (1990). Children of poverty: The status of twelve million Americans. *Phi Delta Kappan, 71*(10), K1–K12.

Reitzug, U. C., & Capper, C. A. (in press). Deconstructing site-based management: Emancipation and alternative means of control. *International Journal of Educational Reform*.

Rioux, W., & Berla, N. (1994, January 19). The necessary partners: Tips from research on parent involvement programs that work. *Education Week*, p. 31.

Sears, J. T. (1987). Peering into the well of loneliness: The responsibility of educators to gay and lesbian youth. In A. Molnar (Ed.), *Social issues and education: Challenge and responsibility*. Alexandria, VA: Association for Supervision and Curriculum Development.

Sears, J. T. (1993). Responding to the sexual diversity of faculty and students: Sexual praxis and the critically reflective administrator. In C. Capper (Ed.), *Educational administration in a pluralistic society*. Albany, NY: SUNY Press.

Smolowe, J. (1990, Fall, Special Issue). Last call for motherhood. *Time*, p. 76.

Tanner, C. K. (1989). Positive educational policy with negative impacts on students. *The High School Journal, 72*(2), 65–72.

Tate, W. F. (1994). Race, retrenchment, and the reform of school mathematics. *Phi Delta Kappan, 75,* 477-484.

U.S. Conference of Mayors (1989). *A status report on hunger and homelessness in America's cities, 1989*. ERIC Document Reproduction Service No. ED 317 641.

Waldrop, J., & Exeter, T. (1991). The legacy of the 1980's. *American Demographics, 13*(3), 33–38.

Ward, J. G. (1994). Demographic politics and America's schools: Struggles for power and justice. In C. Marshall (Ed.), *The new politics of race and gender*. Washington, DC: Falmer Press.

Woodson, C. G. (1933). *The mis-education of the Negro*. Trenton, NJ: Africa World Press.

CHAPTER 3

Public Relations Theory and Practice

E. William Brody

Education and public relations are two fields whose practitioners are struggling to maintain stability in the face of accelerating social, political, and technological change. Educators are confronted with growing public dissatisfaction over the quality of their "products." Discontent among parents and employers is eroding political and economic support, which compounds the problem and produces ever-louder cries for reform. Circumstances in public relations differ little from those in education. Employers and clients demand durable, measurable behavioral results while many practitioners prefer to measure media exposure.

Both disciplines have lost sight of the reasons they exist and of the needs of the constituencies they serve. Pragmatically, the two are one and the same. Consumer satisfaction in both cases is essential to long-term success. Those who support educational institutions measure performance in the talents and abilities of their graduates. Those who purchase public relations services measure accomplishments in the behaviors of the audiences practitioners address.

Yardsticks applied by traditionalists in education and public relations are meaningless in the eyes of those who pay the bills and control the appropriations. Neither hours of instruction nor volume of media coverage, neither curriculum design nor message content, neither textbooks and audiovisuals nor news releases and brochures ultimately are significant.

Education and public relations are services offered for sale in competitive marketplaces where demand is governed by consumers rather than vendors. While less than uniformly apparent, buyers in both markets weigh costs and benefits—real or perceived—in making purchase decisions. That's why public relations professionals are slowly but surely supplanting publicists in all but entertainment and sports. And that's why private and for-profit schools are displacing the public variety.

The changes buffeting education and public relations are—or should be—bringing professionals in both disciplines to reexamine contemporary communication systems and concepts of human behavior. Both function in a world in which mass communication is becoming progressively less efficient and effective in influencing behavior. Mass media are proliferating. Audiences are fragmenting. Mediated messages thus reach declining percentages of target audiences.

Deterioration in the efficacy of mass communication has been compounded by audience changes. Consumers are becoming better educated, more suspicious of organizational motives, and more skeptical of claims made for products and services. Their behaviors are shaped more by experience than by expectation.

Satisfaction is a function of the interplay of experience and expectation. Favorable responses develop where experience exceeds expectation. Unfavorable behaviors occur where the reverse is true. Experience is demonstrably by far the stronger of the elements. Schools' reputations, for example, are shaped ultimately by the experiences of parents, students, and employers. Implied and implicit promises delivered via mass media, by controlled media such as brochures and other publications, or through the statements of elected or appointed officials are of no more than transient value. Promises, no matter how delivered, create nothing more than expectations. Experience governs behavior.

This principle is best illustrated in education in student disciplinary policies. The object of discipline is compliance rather than punishment, but compliance is a product of enforcement rather than policy. Policies create expectations. Discipline shapes experience—and subsequent behavior.

WHAT THEORY TELLS US

As social scientists, educators and public relations practitioners should be among the first to recognize and act on theory. Available evidence, albeit largely anecdotal, nevertheless suggests that this rarely has been the case. From primary schools to the postgraduate level, educational institutions are plagued by a counterproductive discontinuity between public relations practice and pertinent theory. Less obvious but more important is a general failure on the part of educational institutions to apply behavioral science theory to public relations practice.

These circumstances contribute to less-than-optimal conditions in education. A 1991 study by the Commission on Institutional Relations of the Council for the Advancement and Support of Education, for example, found college and university presidents relatively satisfied with their institutions' public relations functions. The study also found, however, that presidents were more satisfied with the publicity and promotional efforts of their public relations departments than with their environmental scanning and professional counsel.

The lower levels of satisfaction reported for the latter functions can be interpreted in several ways. Practitioners may be providing less-than-adequate support to their presidents, or presidents may merely perceive the support they receive to be less than satisfactory. Practitioners, it appears, may be caught up in the changing focus in public relations. Their success in making the transition from publicity and promotion to relationship-building will be governed by their ability to comprehend and respond to changing environments.

PUBLIC RELATIONS PROBLEMS

Success will not come easily. Developing and maintaining public relationships to induce behavioral change among organizational constituencies requires abandoning all but one of the paradigms of traditional public relations practice. Public relations historically has been treated as a process, albeit with little agreement over process formulae. At least six such formulae have been espoused by as many authors over time (Hallahan, 1992).

The process model or paradigm suffers from a failure to address the origins of public relations problems, a weakness which in part led to the development of the six other practice models cited above. Instead of process, these models focus on (1) public relations plans or programs, (2) alternative practice models, (3) the role of public relations in organizations, (4) behaviors of target audiences, (5) the political and sociological origins of public relations problems, or (6) public relations from a systems perspective.

Kirk Hallahan (1992, p. 6) demonstrated the differences among these perspectives by posing questions that practitioners might ask concerning the success of a public relations effort under each of the models or paradigms:

Process: Were all the steps followed: research, planning, communication, evaluation?

Plan/Program: Was the campaign on the mark and executed well in terms of the situation analysis, objectives, strategies, and tactics?

Communication Practice/Style: Did the effort incorporate accepted principles of effective communication?

Organizational/managerial: Was the effort well received within the organization?

Behavioral: Did the desired change take place in attitudes, beliefs, or behaviors?

Special problems: Was the conflict or political problem averted or resolved satisfactorily?

Systems: Was an equilibrium maintained?

The behavioral model might serve as a basis for relationship-building, but only where adequate research mechanisms are in place to measure anticipated change in constituent attitudes, beliefs, or behaviors. Optimal results even then would require a greater mastery of behavioral theory than prevails among most practitioners.

THREE BODIES OF LITERATURE

Guidance for educators and public relations practitioners seeking to cope with contemporary problems in a fast-changing environment presumably should be found in the literature of public relations and communication. Those who search the literature nevertheless find little theory applicable to contemporary practice. The bulk of what the Public Relations Society of America calls the "public relations body of knowledge" originates in other disciplines. A small but growing number of public relations educators are building a theoretical foundation for the discipline, but progress is slow.

The literature of communication is more valuable, but much of that value originates in decades-old concepts that examine mass communication in the context of other forms of information transfer. Contemporary communication research is an amalgam of several lines of inquiry. Mass communication is among the less-well-explored sectors.

Public relations practitioners can obtain considerable guidance from the behavioral sciences, however, especially psychology and social psychology. Here are to be found the origins of learning theory and the principles of consumer behavior. Psychology and social psychology presumably are major components of most curricula in education. Both also bear directly on the needs of public relations practitioners as they now exist and inevitably will evolve under the conditions described above. Neither discipline, however, appears ready to apply these bodies of knowledge to enhance relationships between educational institutions and their several constituencies.

Behavioral Science Literature

Human behavior has been subjected to intense study in many disciplines. Psychology, educational psychology, sociology, and social psychology are most prominent among them. Collectively, researchers in these disciplines have established a set of complex theoretical constructs that provide considerable insight into human behavior. By inference, the same constructs suggest ways in which organizations can influence those behaviors.

Much of behavioral theory revolves around learning. Exposure to mass media necessarily contributes to learning, but learning involves several mechanisms that have been addressed at length by theoreticians.

Social learning, cultivation, socialization, agenda setting, uses and gratifications, and schema theories have all been used to elaborate the ways in which individuals learn. The literature of human learning and behavior collectively suggest that the influence of the mass media is relatively small and probably declining.

Learning is a universal, lifelong process through which individuals modify behavior in adapting to their environments.

Psychologists generally agree that learning occurs where experience produces change in knowledge or behavior. While focusing on different components of the process, behavioral and cognitive psychologists view experience as created by interaction between organisms and their environments. Cognitive psychologists focus on internal mental activity arising out of the interaction. Behavioral psychologists emphasize the influence of external events. Both assume that learning produces behavioral change.

Behavioralists suggest that learning occurs through four processes: contiguity, classical conditioning, operant conditioning, and observational learning. *Contiguity* is learning through simple association. The principle asserts that two sensations become associated when they repeatedly occur together to a point at which the second (response) is remembered when the first (stimulus) occurs. In *classical conditioning,* as first demonstrated by Russian physiologist Ivan Pavlov, humans and animals learn to respond automatically to stimuli that earlier produced no response or a different response. Where classical conditioning deals with involuntary responses, *operant conditioning* arises out of individuals' goal-directed actions. The actions are called "operants" in that individuals "operate" on their environments to reach specific objectives, and the learning process involved therefore is called operant conditioning. The basis for operant conditioning was established by Edward Thorndike, whose experiments with animals led to what he called the law of effect: Actions that produce satisfying results in specific circumstances will tend to be repeated in those circumstances. From Thorndike's perspective, then, behavior can be viewed as a function of two sets of environmental conditions: those that precede and those that follow, antecedents and consequences. *Observational learning*, occurring in similar fashion, consists of four elements: attention, information retention, behavior, and reinforcement.

While behavioralists believe that behaviors are learned, those subscribing to the cognitive view of learning believe that knowledge is learned and that changes in knowledge lead to behavioral change. Cognitive psychologists view individuals as active processors of information who initiate learning experiences, seek information to solve problems, and reorganize knowledge to achieve new learning. This perspective has led them to focus on individual and developmental differences in cognition rather than to establish general learning principles that might lead to a cognitive learning model or theory.

The void has been filled in large part by social cognitive theorists led by Albert Bandura (1986), who concluded that "social cognitive theory embraces an interfactional model of causation in which environmental events, personal factors, and behavior all operate as interacting determinants of each other" (p. xi). Based on a learning paradigm, social cognitive theory argues that humans seek to gain rewards and avoid punishment. "Learning," Bandura said, "is largely an information-processing activity in which information about the structure of behavior and about environmental events is transformed into symbolic representations that serve as guides for action" (p. 5). Tan (1985, p. 244) took a similar position, arguing (1) that humans learn from direct experience as well as by observing individuals and events in the mass media and (2) that behavior results from a combination of environmental and cognitive factors. Heath and Bryant (1992) summarized this school of thought succinctly:

> Social learning theory argues that people are neither driven by inner forces nor helplessly shaped by external ones. People can set goals and reward themselves; they are insightful as well as foresightful and do not rely exclusively on external forces for rewards. Social learning theory views people as capable of self-regulation, through self-reward and self-punishment. Individuals receive information from their environment [sic] that is used to create motivations. From this information, they learn the consequences of certain opinions and behaviors, and select those that seem most likely to produce reward and avoid punishment. (p. 137)

Peter and Olson (1994) reached similar conclusions in discussing consumer behavior. Affect, cognition, and environment together, they said, shape human behavior. Affect and cognition are psychological responses—"affect" referring to feelings, "cognition" to mental responses. "Environment" refers to the physical and social characteristics of an individual's external world, which in turn influences affective and cognitive responses and behaviors.

"Environment" can be defined in broad or narrow terms. Broadly defined, an environment consists of two dimensions—physical and social. (See Peter and Olson, 1994, pp. 306–308.) The physical environment encompasses all the physical characteristics of organizational facilities, indoors and out. The social environment includes all interactions between and among people. Alternatively, "environment" may be used to indicate only physical facilities (Brody, 1992), while "behaviors" refers to the actions of organizations and their personnel.

Affective responses share several characteristics (Peter & Olson, 1994, pp. 60–62). They are largely reactive and uncontrolled, as in the case of anger or frustration. They are felt physically, as in the "sinking feelings" that may accompany the sudden onset of problems. They can be produced in response to virtually any stimulus, from physical objects to music or odor. Finally, affective responses for the most part are learned. Tastes for specific types of food and reactions to noises may be innate but responses such as evaluations or feelings are acquired.

Cognition, in contrast, involves higher mental processes such as thinking, evaluating, planning, and deciding. The cognitive system interprets personal experiences and environments. It identifies goals and objectives, sorts out alternative courses of action, selects actions, and carries out behaviors.

Individuals process information gained through their affective and cognitive systems to comprehend or make sense of their environments. Comprehension produces knowledge, meanings, and beliefs about concepts, objects, behaviors, and events (Peter & Olson, 1994, p. 118).

How does all of this apply to education? The sum and substance of the theorists' messages to educators and public relations practitioners alike seems inescapable: Reality shapes behavior. Experience is reality. The behaviors of parents, students, legislators, funding agencies, alumni, benefactors, and other constituencies are more susceptible to control by changing reality than through other forms of communication. Educators and educational institutions can best gain and maintain support by (1) understanding the expectations of their constituencies, (2) modifying those expectations where necessary and appropriate, and (3) using the resources at their disposal to meet those expectations, to create what will be perceived as a favorable reality.

Communications Literature

Expectations are shaped by communication, by the transfer of information. The literature of communication deals in responses to transmitted information as opposed to responses to information absorbed through experience. Theory originating in communication can help or hinder public relations practitioners. Communication processes are more easily understood when viewed through theoretical lenses. This perspective can be misleading, however, in that associated discussion commonly neglects or ignores the relatively stronger influence of experiential learning as a governor of human behavior.

Considerable theory and research deal with media-audience interactions and with the role of communication in influencing behavior. The sum and substance of the literature nevertheless suggest that mass communication is a weak tool in influencing audience behavior.

Theory advanced to explain interactions between media and their audiences suggests that mass communication involves interpersonal networks as well as mass media. Paul Lazarsfeld's two-step flow theory, for example, emphasizes the role of opinion leaders in the behaviors of media audiences. (See Katz & Lazarsfeld, 1955.) Everett Rogers suggested a more complex and time-consuming process in his theory of diffusion of innovations (Rogers, 1962). He defines an innovation as a new idea in a social system and declares interpersonal networks far more significant than mass communication in the diffusion process.

The larger body of communications science literature is also helpful to public relations practitioners. It embodies rhetoric and public address, propaganda and media effects, transmission and reception of information, and group dynamics and interpersonal interaction (Heath & Bryant, 1992, p. 34).

Theories of media effects are much akin to public relations theory in that they focus on the efficacy of mass communication and the variables that influence the efficiency and effectiveness of that process. The theories dealing with the transmission and reception of information afford a more helpful perspective for public relations practitioners.

Research and theory building in media effects have focused on the mass communication process and deal primarily with message content, exposure, and effects. Effects, which are our primary concern here, may be behavioral, attitudinal, cognitive, or physiological.

Theorizing about the effects of mass media exposure began with a more-or-less normative theory of uniform effects. Harold Lasswell (1927, 1935) used a hypodermic-needle analogy, for example, to suggest that audiences could be "injected" with messages and thereby manipulated by the mass media. By midcentury, however, theoreticians were developing a more complex model based on human communication.

Joseph Klapper (1960) demonstrated that individual behaviors are governed more by community norms, beliefs, and values than by mass media messages. David Berlo (1960) suggested that humans use all of their senses—seeing, hearing, tasting, touching, and smelling—in communication. He considered all the ways that individuals interact with one another and experience reality to be communication channels.

Contemporary research (see Sprafkin, Gadow, & Abelman, 1992) suggests instead that mass media may produce selective effects—behavioral, attitudinal, cognitive, or physiological—in small segments of audiences based on differences among message recipients.

Behavioral effects, such as buying a product or voting in an election, are emphasized in social learning theory (Bandura, 1977; Bandura, Ross, & Ross, 1961, 1963; Bandura & Walters, 1963; Tan, 1986). Social learning theory suggests that individuals learn behaviors by observing and imitating others as seen or heard in the mass media.

Attitudinal effects are manifested in attitudes toward or preferences for individuals, organizations, concepts, or products. Moviegoers who saw the film *Roger and Me,* for example, exhibited more negative attitudes toward General Motors and business in general. The intellectual and emotional components of attitudes can be inconsistent, however, as seen in the reelection of candidates whose behaviors have been unpopular with their constituencies.

Cognitive effects consist of changes in knowledge or thinking of media audiences. These range from simple learning to more complex effects that can occur through media agenda setting. The latter term refers to the ability of mass media to set agendas for public discussion through editors' or news directors' decisions to emphasize or deemphasize certain topics.

Physiological effects occur often in a variety of forms as the result of media exposure but are seldom sought by public relations practitioners. Television commercials have been found to change heart rates and reflexes. Frightening motion pictures and exciting sports events can produce changes in breathing and pulse rates.

The need in public relations for a new paradigm is perhaps best expressed, however, in concepts advanced by communication scholars several decades ago. Posing the rhetorical question, "What is communication?" Stephen Littlejohn (1978, pp. 375–376) responded "If we are to understand the full richness of communication, we must avoid viewing it as a single event. . . . [C]ommunication . . . is a complex process of psychological and social events involving symbolic interaction. These events occur within and between people in interpersonal, group, organizational and mass contexts."

Almost three decades ago Lee O. Thayer (1968, p. 113) described the process in this way: "The phenomenon basic to all human communication," he wrote, "is the infra-personal process of 'relevanting' or 'messaging' the raw, unstructured event-data of our inner and outer worlds, of organizing and translating event-data into comprehendible, consumable functional units or 'messages.' The one process basic to all human communication," he continued,

> whenever and wherever it occurs, is the *intrapersonal* process of organizing, and converting sensory data into meaningful units ("messages") having some relevance or utility for that individual's past, present or future behavior. Because the psychological system is constantly engaged in making sense of its environment in the service of that organism's adaptive and goal-seeking needs the question is not whether communication is going to occur but *what* communication and with what *consequences*. Communication is a continuous, on-going process, determined by an individual's take-into-account-abilities and his take-into-account susceptibilities. The process is rarely limited to another's communicative intentions vis-a-vis a given individual. . . .
>
> Communication . . . is a co-function of the individual and what is going on in his world(s) that has immediate relevance for him. The world and our conceptions of it co-determine each other. All that we perceive, all that we comprehend, must be perceived and comprehended in and through ourselves. (pp. 111–112)

The breadth of "event-data" was underscored by Michael J. Nolan (1975), who conceived of four "channel categories" or media in human communication: voice, body, object, and environment. Collectively, the writings of Littlejohn, Thayer, Nolan, and others present a significant problem—existing or contingent—for public relations practitioners in educational institutions. The problem: how to ensure that messages transmitted to constituent groups by the behaviors, environments, and quality of services rendered by their institutions are consonant with the messages delivered through emerging or traditional media. If experience produces change in knowledge or behavior, can practitioners afford to deal only with the informational component of the learning process? More important, can professionals who rely on information transfer to stimulate behavioral change succeed in the fast-changing world of mass communication? Logic suggests otherwise.

Public Relations Literature

The literature of public relations offers little theory pertinent to the development of a relationship-oriented, behavioral-based practice model. Three circumstances contribute to these conditions. First, the discipline is relatively young. While press agentry and publicity have existed since the days of Barnum, public relations as relationship-building only recently has become necessary in response to social and technological change. (See Grunig and Hunt, 1984, p. 22.) Second, public relations as an academic discipline is a product of the late twentieth century. Many contemporary practitioners are well educated in college and university departments of journalism and communication, but only a handful of institutions offer degrees in public relations. Third, and most significant, most basic research in any discipline is undertaken by college and university faculty members. Public relations faculties only now are growing to a point at which they generate substantial amounts of research.

Public relations research to date, while unquestionably of value to the field, with few exceptions offers little guidance in relationship-building. Most of the exceptions are the work of University of Maryland Prof. James E. Grunig, who has developed four models of public relations practice and a situational theory to identify publics.

Grunig's four models of public relations practice (see Grunig & Hunt, p. 1984, p. 22) essentially describe the evolution of the discipline from press agentry and publicity to public information and thence to two-way *asymmetric* and two-way *symmetric* communication. The latter model alone is conducive to relationship-building. Organizations that adopt the two-way symmetrical model use balanced, two-way communication to establish mutual understanding and achieve accommodation with their constituencies. Such organizations presumably would go beyond mere communication to achieve these objectives, although Grunig's model is limited to communication techniques.

Grunig's situational theory to identify publics suggests that individuals' communication behaviors vary with their perceptions of organization-related situations in which they find themselves (Grunig & Hunt, 1984, p.148). The extent to which individuals recognize problems and constraints, and the extent of their involvement with the problems, governs their responses, Grunig said.

While the situational theory dealt with communication behaviors, an individual's perceptions of these variables presumably influence other constituent behaviors as well. Customers of organizations perceived as consumer-friendly, for example, are more prone to seek redress of problems they experience than to "vote with their feet" and take their business elsewhere. The growth of single-issue advocacy groups and their use of progressively more radical tactics also can be logically attributed to their perceptions of a target organization's behavior.

The state of the art in public relations research was summarized by Grunig and others in an initial report on an International Association of Business Communicators study entitled *Excellence in Public Relations and Communication Management* (Grunig, 1992). The report dealt with public relations as a mass-communication discipline and offered few insights into how practitioners or their employers might build stronger public relationships by better managing organizational behaviors, environments, and quality of products or services.

The relative weakness of mass communication in inducing behavioral change was underscored, however, in a chapter dealing with the evaluation of public relations programs. If there's a 40 percent chance that a message will reach a specified constituency, a 50 percent chance that recipients will learn key message points, a 20 percent chance that attitude and opinion will change in those who learn the points, and a 10 percent chance that those who hold the desired opinion will behave in keeping with their opinions, the probability that the desired behavior will occur is 0.04 percent—four chances in 10,000. As Dozier and Ehling (1992) put it, "[A] practitioner might find better odds for success in Las Vegas or Atlantic City" (p.166). (See Grunig, 1992, pp. 159–184).

Message to educators and to public relations practitioners in educational institutions and elsewhere: Traditional mass-communication techniques offer little potential to change attitudes, opinions, and behaviors among organizational constituencies. Reality and performance should be the communicator's tools of choice.

RELATIONSHIP-BUILDING

How can public relations efforts be organized to produce enhanced potential for success? A relationship-building model constructed around learning and behavior theory inevitably would change the odds posited by Dozier and Ehling. No substantive barriers exist to a public relations program based on realities as well as messages, on constituent experiences as well as expectations.

Perhaps the best exemplary model at hand is embodied in sophisticated consumer relations programs. Consumer behavior has been studied extensively over time because customer satisfaction is prerequisite to business success. In practical terms, the primary constituencies of all organizations are consumer groups. Organizations whose customers turn to other vendors fail. So do those whose workers decamp consistently for greener pastures. And results are no less troublesome where investors decide that a company's securities are no longer worth keeping.

Pragmatically, all constituencies behave as consumers in one way or another. Workers shop for good jobs as diligently as housewives search for bargains. Investors select securities in similar fashion. Vendors work with precise profiles of "the ideal customer." Organizations that fail to recognize this pattern and view all their constituencies as consumer groups do so at their peril.

The American Marketing Association's definition of consumer behavior is concise, functional, and highly pertinent to public relations practice: AMA calls consumer behavior "the dynamic interaction of affect and cognition, behavior, and environmental events by which human beings conduct the exchange aspects of their lives." The definition, as Peter and Olson (1994) point out, embraces three important ideas concerning consumer behavior. It is dynamic. It involves interaction among cognitions, behaviors, and environmental events. And it involves exchanges.

Exchange requires special attention. Applied narrowly by marketers and often neglected by public relations practitioners, the exchange principle offers considerable insight into relationships between organizations and their constituencies. As embodied in what has been alternatively called "exchange theory" or "social exchange theory"—see Blau (1964, 1977) and Homans (1974)—this principle suggests that humans are essentially transactional creatures, that human behavior can best be viewed as series of transactions, commercial or otherwise. The coinage of human behavior, in other words, involves more than money. Transactions may involve psychological or emotional as well as physical and economic exchanges. Marketing's role is to facilitate economic exchanges. Public relations is—or should be—dedicated to enhancing all exchanges between organizations and their constituencies. Peter and Olson (1994, p. 8) emphasize the point: "To understand consumers . . . we must understand what they think (cognition) and feel (affect), what they do (behavior), and the things and places (environmental events) that influence and are influenced by what consumers think, feel, and do."

Behavior is dynamic—constantly changing and evolving—among all organizational constituencies. The broader view is essential to public relations practice because constituent interests necessarily are in conflict. Constituencies compete directly or indirectly for organizational resources. Organizations succeed to the extent that managers successfully balance resulting demands, implied or implicit. Managers must ensure that resources are distributed equitably whether in the form of quality products, wages and benefits, dividends, or otherwise.

Organizational constituencies also are universally influenced by affect and cognition, behavior, and environmental events. Public relations historically has sought to influence behavior through cognition or cognitive learning processes while neglecting at least equally important affective and environmental factors. Information received through feelings and experiences, in other words, has taken second place in public relations to that which is transmitted through cognition or thinking.

Human behavior, then, is a product of environments and of affect and cognition. Behavior alternatively can be viewed as a product of environmental, affective, and cognitive learning. Cognitive learning, which in part involves assimilating information transmitted through the mass media, long has been the primary domain of public relations. Available evidence suggests, however, that the influence of the mass media is in decline. Public relations practitioners, as a result, must deal more and more with affective and environmental learning as well.

Educators arguably are better equipped than most by education and training to apply theory to public relations practice in behalf of their institutions. Available evidence, largely anecdotal, suggests, however, that few have been able to accomplish this objective despite environmental pressures.

MERGING THEORY AND PRACTICE

Two factors today are driving public relations theory and practice together. The first factor is a continuing decline in the efficiency and effectiveness of mass media—of mediated communication. Recent research conducted by the Harwood Group for the Kettering Foundation (1993) demonstrates that traditional approaches don't work, that people learn through their interactions with other people, that they learn by testing their concepts and ideas in the real world.

Harwood researchers identified nine factors that influence the ways in which individuals deal with public issues:

1. They want to make connections between public concerns rather than treat each in a vacuum.

2. They are concerned about personal context, "the lens through which they view public concerns."
3. They want coherence—the "whys" and "hows," the history, and all sides of the debate.
4. They need "room for ambivalence" to permit "fact-finding, listening, testing of ideas, and figuring out what they believe and how they feel about a concern."
5. Their emotions influence their responses.
6. They demand "authenticity," information that rings true.
7. They want a "sense of possibility," a feeling that progress can be made and that they can play meaningful roles.
8. They are influenced by catalysts—people in their daily lives who spur them to discuss and act on public concerns.
9. They are involved in "mediating institutions" such as churches, schools, and neighborhood councils, where ideas are tested in discussion.

The Harwood Group used the term "meaningful chaos" to describe random interplay among these factors, interplay "that creates for people the sense of meaning, which enables them to form relationships with public concerns" (p. 4). Information sources other than mass media that influence attitudes, opinions, and behaviors are thus necessarily rendered more important.

The second factor driving theory and practice together is change among organizational constituencies. "There are no publics," practitioner Larry Newman told the 1991 conference of the Public Relations Society of America (Newman, 1991). "There are only individual human beings. You've got to know who they are, establish contact with them and engage their interests."

Enduring relationships, loyalty, and third-party endorsements should be public relations' primary objectives, Newman added, and these factors require demonstrating caring, understanding, responsiveness, attention, and respect, as well as delivering value. They require demonstration rather than communication, and demonstration demands enhanced behaviors on the part of organizations and their employees, more comfortable environments for consumers and workers, and better quality in products and services.

The dominant process for gaining influence and thereby winning acceptance in this human climate, according to public relations pioneer Philip Lesly, follows a five-step progression: (1) a basis in fact, (2) credibility, (3) audience self-interest, (4) visibility, and (5) influence. (See Lesly, 1993.)

Lesly's progression, like relationship-building, begins with fact, with reality. Facts and realities shape experience, learning, and behavior. No amount of mass communication can overcome the impact of contrary reality-based messages.

Once positioned to ensure that performance meets or exceed promises, organizations are turning to one-to-one information-delivery systems for all constituents. Public relations and marketing practitioners of late have started applying old and new technologies to establish dialogues with constituent groups. Corporate communicators have adapted satellite-based television systems to communicate with employees, dealers, and others. Increasing numbers of companies are contracting with CompuServe to use that computer utility's networks to maintain communication with personnel around the globe. In response to the fast-changing dynamics of the mass-media marketplace they are concentrating their efforts on what Peppers and Rogers (1993) call "share of customer" rather than "share of market." The objective? To obtain as great a share as possible of the consumer's or investor's lifetime purchases.

The relationship-building concept that Peppers and Rogers call the "one to one solution" is equally applicable, however, in dealing with other organizational constituencies. Enlightened institutions of higher education, for example, no longer think of themselves merely as degree-granting institutions. Instead, they seek to provide a lifetime of continuing education for graduates, and they prosper accordingly. Some have even come to accept the fact that age is no barrier to education and to solicit the parents of undergraduate and graduate students.

Institutional computers, databases, and voice-mail systems are the communication tools of choice in reaching such audiences. If traditional students can be enrolled and their fees collected by telephone, why not extend the same convenience to parents and other nontraditional students? If the institution's course offerings and class schedules are unattractive to older and/or nontraditional students, why not change them? If constituents are concerned over security, parking, and food service, those aspects of campus life can and should be changed as well. If institutional personnel or the services they provide are inadequate—or even merely perceived as inadequate—administrative action is equally necessary.

The same principles are applicable in primary and secondary educational institutions. Other than as mandated by statute, no systemic component should be held sacred and unchangeable. If working parents are more readily attracted to meetings at 6:30 A.M. than at 7 P.M., the times should be changed. If contemporary class schedules can be made more convenient for parents or students, they should be changed as well. Changes such as these are essential components of any relationship-building effort. Relationship-building demands far greater responsiveness to constituent needs than ever conceived of in traditional, mass-media-oriented public relations practice.

Implied and implicit changes in emphasis from mass media and mass communication to the "one-to-one" concept signal a major change in public relations practice. The change requires of practitioners knowledge of a far broader set of theoretical constructs drawn from the social sciences.

The broadened knowledge base is necessary in order to understand the functions of information sources or "message transmitters" other than those embodied in the mass media. While largely ignored by the public relations community, the strong and pervasive influence of nonmediated information sources has long been known and, of late, well understood by researchers in mass communication and the behavioral sciences.

In education, then, the behaviors of institutions, and of their faculties and staffs, will always constitute more convincing messages than those contained in recruiting materials, no matter how artfully packaged. The comfort and convenience of facilities ranging from dormitory rooms and classrooms to administrative offices and parking lots transmit equally convincing messages.

Brochures, videotapes, and persuasive recruiting officers may serve well in enrolling freshmen. Realities will determine whether they remain or depart after their first semesters or academic years. The net effectiveness and efficiency of the best recruiting programs will ultimately be no greater than the sponsoring institution's ability to retain students.

SUMMARY

Traditional public relations techniques have been deteriorating in efficiency and effectiveness over time. Two primary factors are involved. One is the continuing decline in the ability of the media to deliver mass audiences. As late as 1995, the circulations of major metropolitan daily newspapers were dropping at a rate of 1 to 2 percent annually. Network television audiences were also declining in size as cable channels multiplied and direct-broadcast satellite systems came into operation. The impact of these trends is compounded by growing public access to alternative sources of information, ranging from information utilities such as CompuServe and America Online to the Internet.

Deterioration in the ability of mass media to influence behavior requires that public relations practitioners better understand and apply the tools of the behavioral sciences in order to achieve their objectives. Only by controlling the several factors that contribute to human experience can organizations influence learning and behavior.

CASE STUDY

THE PROBLEMS OF A STATE UNIVERSITY

The president of a midwestern state university summoned his public relations officer one morning in the early 1990s and asked for his advice concerning the institution's enrollment problem. The problem had two parts. First, the university's traditional student population was declining in numbers. Undergraduate enrollment was dropping at a rate of about 2 percent annually, although graduate enrollment was increasing and net enrollment was relatively stable. The president perceived that the university was also losing disproportionate numbers of freshmen who were not enrolling for their sophomore years. He asked the public relations officer to analyze the problem and report his findings and recommendations.

The university was situated in a metropolitan area of more than a million residents. The community was primarily a distribution center. There was little manufacturing and few headquarters offices. The population was about 55 percent white, 40 percent black, 5 percent Asian-American.

Competition for students in the area included two private universities and a private college catering to minority students. The city also housed a college of art and a medical/dental school that was part of another state university. Many of the community's more affluent families sent their children out of the city to schools in other states. Others sent their children to the private institutions in the community.

The local university had been founded as a teachers' college and had progressed over time to achieve university status. Research demonstrated that the institution was still perceived as less prestigious, if not of lesser academic stature, than its peers. In reality, the university and all of its programs were fully accredited, and the institution had become known as a center of excellence in a number of disciplines.

The university was less well funded than the state's preeminent land grant institution, however—in part because that older institution and its law school had disproportionate representation in both houses of the state's bicameral legislature. In part to offset the resulting funding problem, the president was contemplating launching a multimillion dollar capital development program within the ensuing twelve months.

The public relations director was asked to consider all of these factors and submit complete strategic and operational public relations plans for the institution.

QUESTIONS AND SUGGESTED ACTIVITIES

Case Study

1. As the public relations officer, what information would you want before responding to the president's request? Describe how you would obtain that information.
2. What constituencies would you anticipate addressing in your strategic and long-range plans? How would you describe the constituencies in demographic and sociographic terms?
3. How would you respond to any negatives that your information-gathering process produced?
4. What behaviors would you seek among each constituency?
5. How would you want the university to be perceived by members of each constituency to predispose them to behave as desired?
6. What recommendations would you make to the president concerning actions that the university should take in order to merit the support of each constituency?
7. How would you ensure that the university addressed all of the factors that shape attitude, opinion, and behavior?
8. Design pertinent research instruments.
9. Design strategic and operational public relations plans, including timetables and budgets.
10. Describe how you would implement those plans.

Chapter

11. How would you adjust the behaviors of organizations to better induce durable, mutually beneficial relationships with specific constituent groups such as employees, consumers, and investors?
12. How can traditional communication techniques best be applied in concert with organizational behaviors, environments, and product-service quality to produce behavioral change?

SUGGESTED READINGS

Albrecht, K. (1988). *At America's service*. Homewood, IL: Dow Jones-Irwin.

Albrecht, K., and Zemke, R. (1985). *Service America: Doing business in the new economy*. Homewood, IL: Dow-Jones Irwin.

Assael, H. (1981). *Consumer behavior and marketing action*. Boston: Kent.

Brief, A. P., & Tomlinson, G. (1987) *Managing smart: A no-gimmick approach to management techniques that work*. Lexington, MA: D. C. Heath.

Carlzon, J. (1987). *Moments of truth*. Cambridge, MA: Ballinger Publishing.

Crosby, P. B. (1984). *Quality without tears: The art of hassle-free management*. New York: McGraw-Hill.

Crosby, P. B. (1986). *Running things: The art of making things happen*. New York: McGraw-Hill.

Desatnick, R. L. (1987). *Managing to keep the customer: How to achieve and maintain superior customer service throughout the organization.* San Francisco: Jossey-Bass.

Fisher, R., & Brown, S. (1988). *Getting together: Building relationships as we negotiate.* New York: Penguin.

Fisher, R., & Ury, W. (1981). *Getting to yes: Negotiating agreement without giving in.* New York: Penguin.

Gray, J. G., Jr. (1986). *Managing the corporate image: The key to public trust.* Westport, CT: Quorum.

Hanan, M., & Karp, P. (1989). *Customer satisfaction: How to maximize, measure and market your company's "ultimate product."* New York: Amacom.

Harrison, M. L. (1987). Diagnosing organizations: Methods, models and processes. Newbury Park, CA: Sage.

Hayes, G. E. (1985). *Quality & productivity: The new challenge.* Wheaton, IL: Hitchcock.

Manning, G. M., & Reece, B. L. (1990). *Selling today: A personal approach* (4th ed.). Boston: Allyn and Bacon.

McGill, M. E. (1988). *American business and the quick fix.* New York: Henry Holt.

McKenna, R. (1992). *The Regis touch: New marketing strategies for uncertain times.* Reading, MA: Addison-Wesley.

Miner, J. B. (1980). Theories of organizational behavior. Hinsdale, IL: Dryden Press.

Naisbitt, J., & Aburdene, P. (1990). *Megatrends 2000: Ten new directions for the 1990's.* New York: Morrow.

Owen, D. B. (1989). *Beating your competition through quality.* New York: Marcel Dekker.

Pascale, R. T. (1990). *Managing on the edge: How the smartest companies use conflict to stay ahead.* New York: Simon & Schuster.

Pascarella, P., and Frohman, M. A. (1989). *The purpose-driven organization: Unleashing the power of direction and commitment.* San Francisco: Jossey-Bass.

Poppe, F. C. (1987). 50 rules to keep a client happy. New York: Harper & Row.

Prus, R. C. (1989). *Pursuing customers: An ethnography of marketing activities.* Newbury Park, CA: Sage.

Thomson, A. A., Jr., & Strickland, A. J., III (1987) *Strategic management: Concepts and cases* (4th ed.). Plano, TX: Business Publications.

Wilson, L. (1987). *Changing the game: The new way to sell.* New York: Simon & Schuster.

REFERENCES

Bandura, A. (1977). *Social learning theory.* Englewood Cliffs, NJ: Prentice Hall.

Bandura, A. (1986). *Social foundation of thought and action: A social cognitive theory.* Englewood Cliffs, NJ: Prentice Hall.

Bandura, A., Ross, D., & Ross, S. A. (1961). Transmission of aggression through imitation of aggressive models. *Journal of Abnormal and Social Psychology, 63,* 575–582.

Bandura, A., Ross, D., & Ross, S. A. (1963). Imitation of film-mediated aggressive models. *Journal of Abnormal and Social Psychology, 66,* 3–11.

Bandura, A., & Walters, R.H. (1963). *Social learning and personality development.* New York: Holt, Rinehart and Winston.

Bennett, P. D. (1968). *Dictionary of marketing terms.* Chicago: American Marketing Association.

Berlo, D. K. (1960). *Communication: An introduction to theory and practice.* New York: Holt, Rinehart and Winston.

Blau, P. M. (1964). *Exchange and power in social life.* New York: Wiley.

Blau, P.M. (1977). *Inequality and heterogeneity: A primitive theory of social structure*. New York: Free Press.

Brody, E. W. (1992, Winter). The domain of public relations. *Public Relations Review, 18*(4), 349–364.

Dozier, D. M., & Ehling, W. P. (1992). Evaluation of public relations programs: What the literature tells us about their effects. In J. E. Grunig (Ed.), *Excellence in public relations and communication management.* (pp. 159–184). Hillsdale, NJ: L. Erlbaum Associates.

Grunig, J. E. (Ed.). (1992). *Excellence in public relations and communication management*. Hillsdale, NJ: L. Erlbaum Associates.

Grunig, J. E., & Hunt, T. (1984). *Managing public relations*. New York: Holt, Rinehart and Winston.

Hallahan, K. (1992, August). The paradigms of public relations: Treading beyond the four-step process. Presented to the Public Relations Division, Association for Education in Journalism and Mass Communication, Montreal.

Harwood Group. (1993). *Meaningful chaos: How people form relationships with public concerns*. Dayton, OH: Kettering Foundation.

Heath, R. L., & Bryant, J. (1992). *Human communication theory and research: Concepts, contexts, & challenges*. Hillsdale, NJ: L. Erlbaum Associates.

Homans, G. C. (1974). *Social behavior: Its elementary form*. New York: Harcourt, Brace, Jovanovich.

Katz, E., & Lazarsfeld, P. F. (1955). *Personal influence: The part played by people in the flow of communication*. New York: Free Press.

Klapper, J. T. (1960). *The effects of mass communication*. Glencoe, IL: Free Press.

Lasswell, H. D. (1927). *Propaganda technique in the world war*. New York: Knopf.

Lasswell, H. D. (1935). *World politics and personal insecurity: A contribution to political psychiatry*. New York: McGraw-Hill.

Lesly, P. (1993). Managing the human climate: The process flow for attaining influence today. In *pr reporter, 36,* (26), 1–2.

Littlejohn, S. W. (1978). *Theories of human communication*. Columbus, OH: Charles E. Merrill.

Newman, L. N. (1991, November). Narrowcasting to reach the right audience. Paper presented to the annual conference of the Public Relations Society of America, Phoenix, AZ.

Nolan, M. J. (1975). The relationships between verbal and nonverbal communication. In G. J. Hanneman & W. J. McEwen (Eds.). *Communication and behavior*. Reading, MA: Addison-Wesley.

Peppers, D., & Rogers, M. (1993). *The one to one future: Building relationships one customer at a time*. New York: Currency.

Peter, J. P., & Olson, J. C. (1994). *Understanding consumer behavior*. Burr Ridge, IL: Irwin.

Rogers, E. M. (1962). Diffusion of innovations. New York: Free Press.

Sprafkin, J. N., Gadow, K. D., & Abelman, R. (1992). *Television and the exceptional child: A forgotten audience*. Hillsdale, NJ: L. Erlbaum Associates.

Tan, A. S. (1985). *Mass communication theories and research (2nd ed.)*. New York: Wiley.

Tan, A. S. (1986). Social learning of aggression from television. In J. Bryant & D. Zillman (Eds.). *Perspectives on media effects*. Hillsdale, NJ: L. Erlbaum Associates.

Thayer, L. O. (1968). *Communication and communication systems: In organization, management and interpersonal relations*. Homewood, IL: Irwin.

Thorndike, E. L. (1913). Educational psychology. In *The psychology of learning* [Vol. 2], New York: Teachers College, Columbia University.

CHAPTER 4

What School Administrators Need to Understand

Melvin Sharpe

Organizational performance in the area of public relations requires the understanding and support of top-level administrators. In part, this advocacy is needed because administrative behavior and organizational image are interdependent. That is, the effectiveness of an organization's public relations performance is directly related to the commitment and behavior of the chief executive officer. Thus if the superintendent of schools or the university president places little emphasis on communication, other administrators are likely to do the same.

The intent of this chapter is to explain (1) what effective communication and public relations programming require of an administrator and (2) what an administrator has the right to expect from the public relations professionals employed to assist with the administrative task. Both issues are explored with regard to current conditions in society and schools and practice within the public relations profession.

WHAT PUBLIC RELATIONS REQUIRES OF ADMINISTRATORS

Effective communication will not be achieved with the indiscriminate use of relatively inexpensive communication tools such as newsletters or carry-home letters to parents. The process is far more complex, and success begins with a recognition that two-way communication is essential to organizational leadership. Success is also predicated on the realization that the management of communication is as vital as any other single area of responsibility within educational administration.

School administrators are the executive officers of public corporations with responsibilities comparable to the management responsibilities in private corporations. Some elements of the jobs are virtually identical. For example, managing resources and evaluating personnel are duties commonly assumed by both business managers and school administrators. But the human management responsibilities can be the greater in schools since school executives have responsibilities extending beyond customer satisfaction, internal employee communication, and profit margins. Administrators usually are expected to achieve a broad base of support both within and outside their organizations; they must repeatedly show other governmental officials and the public at large the achievements of their organizations.

There are other factors adding to the complexity of school system communication and public relation management responsibilities:

◆ School systems mirror society; consequently, school administrators are confronted with societal problems over which they have little control—for example, illegal drugs, violence, and teenage pregnancies.
◆ They work in conditions where a variety of special interest and pressure groups generate conflicting role expectations.

Other types of organizations usually have less complex communication needs because managers exercise more control over internal membership and the extent of external interaction. Public school systems, by contrast, are almost always composed of individuals and groups who bring a wide range of needs, wants, beliefs, and motivations to the organization. This condition is most obvious in the area of student admission; public school administrators typically have little control over this matter because it is shaped in state laws and policy. Equally important is the realization that schools serve a heterogeneous customer base. Unlike a manufacturing company that can target its product to a specific group of consumers, schools must satisfy a broad audience holding different and, at times, conflicting expectations. This fact is critical in understanding the complexity of the communication needs of school systems and, in particular, in understanding why the achievement of public confidence and support is directly related to the stability of the financial base.

Three Foundational Principles

Black and Sharpe (1983) observed that effective public relations performance in schools cannot occur unless the top administrator and the remainder of the administrative team recognize and accept three principles that provide a philosophical framework allowing the organizational commitment needed for achievement. The three philosophical principles are the following:

1. The economic and social stability of the school is dependent on the support of public opinion.
2. All human beings in democratic societies have the right to information about decisions affecting their lives.
3. The management of two-way communication enables an organization to adjust to change.

These principles constitute a belief system enabling good planning and organizational performance. Accordingly, each is examined in detail here.

The Support of Public Opinion.   Thomas Jefferson stated that in a democratic society everything depends on the consent of the public. Edward L. Bernays, a pioneer in the public relations profession, used this Jeffersonian concept to develop his philosophy of public relations, which he called "the engineering of public consent." The concept can be more fully understood when it is recognized that all organizations share various types of interdependence within social systems, which in turn form larger living ecosystems. Forces within both social systems and ecosystems serve to control, regulate, form values and cultures, and continually evaluate the usefulness of organizational roles. And because of the power of the ecosystem to constrain or even eliminate organizations, organizations must stay in reasonable harmony with their ecosystem if they are to survive. Robert Dilenschneider (1987), one of the nation's leading public relations consultants and a Harvard Business School lecturer, has stated that "the latitude with which a business can operate is directly related to its ability to maintain—at minimum—a neutral and—at best—favorable public opinion" (p. 7).

Studies of organizational behavior clearly show that many organizations ignored public opinion in the past. For example, nineteenth-century industrialists basically believed they could do what they wanted without public consultation or approval (Cutlip, Center, & Broom, 1985). The "public be damned" attitude of bureaucratic management gradually changed as (1) communication technology increased the potential for media exposure, (2) managers confronted a growing number of laws designed to protect consumers, and (3) American industry faced the realities of a global economy.

Does this cavalier attitude exist among school administrators? At a recent conference sponsored by a state public relations association, a school superintendent stated that he did not want parental involvement because he simply had enough problems without parents sticking their noses in his business. This misguided administrator obviously failed to recognize that his business is public business; without parental support, he is probably going to be unable to carry out the mission and reach the goals of the school district he heads. Without parental support, a school system is likely to meander in a state of instability, and the consequences of this condition may not be recognized by administrators until the support is needed and it isn't there.

When administrative support is lacking for the public relations function, the organization may be unable to respond adequately to changing societal needs and demands. This prevents or discourages organizational adaptability. As a consequence, the organization is in a disadvantageous position, and internal instability may reach a level that (1) threatens the job security of the top administrator, (2) destroys valuable programs, and/or (3) further erodes public support.

The Right to Information.   Because of the nature of schools as social institutions, and because of the current importance placed on information, administrators and board members should recognize and accept the principle that internal and external publics have the right to information about decisions affecting them. Consider the following negative behaviors that often result when this principle is rejected:

- Information is concealed as long as possible in an effort to prevent and control opposition.
- The organization engages in carefully controlled one-way (usually marketing) communication techniques.

◆ The news media are viewed as the enemy; reporters are cast as adversaries rather than communication facilitators who serve the public interest in democratic social systems.
◆ Information is used largely for the benefit of management and special interest groups.

These behaviors have increasingly serious consequences in today's world. Administrators may find themselves constantly involved in legal disputes over access to information; they may cause alienation and mistrust; they may force their organizations to become reliant on third-party interventions to resolve conflict. These outcomes not only serve to reduce the credibility of administrators, they needlessly consume the organization's resources. Attorney fees, the costs associated with protracted collective bargaining, and arbitrator fees are common examples of the negative by-products.

Communication and Organizational Change.   Dilenschneider (1987) has stated that "The management of a firm's image and identity is as fundamental a chief executive officer responsibility as managing the financial performance, strategy, or organization of the company" (p. 8). He also emphasized that "a facility for employing public relations and an understanding of the PR mindset will increasingly become a make-or-break criterion for top executive advancement" (p. 9). Yet far too many school administrators continue to manage organizational communications as if their own eyes and ears were sufficient to determine the need for change.

Individuals hear what they *want* to hear, not always what they *need* to hear. Thus, executives opposed to change will often exert much of their energy to argue their position rather than to collect and analyze accurate information. The relationship among communication, information, and change has become more critical in a rapidly changing society. Business leaders, for example, have continuously criticized schools for not adequately preparing students for the workplace. These criticisms are often fueled by the reality that schools and local businesses may have little or no contact with each other; business managers lack accurate information about what students are learning, and administrators lack accurate information about job qualifications in their local markets (Kowalski, Weaver, Greene, & Pfaller, 1993).

The solution is the management of communication in such a way that administrators are able to listen fully and accurately to all the voices, both negative and positive, in their social environments. Research, feedback, and evaluation are half of the communication process; the other half is message projection. When communication is inadequately managed so that the projection function has not been balanced by the organization's ability to hear and listen, administrators have blocked their own managerial ability to facilitate gradual harmonious change. The alternative is all too often confrontation and major disruption.

Recognizing the Importance of Behavior

Rodney Davis (1986), in a National School Public Relations Association publication, made the point: "Too many school districts looking to develop a public relations program fail to realize that they already have one, and it may be a disaster" (p. 27). Employees in a school communicate with the public and community every single day both through verbal statements and through their actions. Thus the question is not *whether* a school district will have a public relations program; rather it is this: Will the public relations program be properly organized, planned, executed, and supported?

The time-honored adage—"Actions speak louder than words"—remains highly accurate. It provides administrators with a behavioral recognition of what their public relations performance requires. More so, it reminds administrators that effective public relations performance cannot be achieved through limited marketing or one-way communication techniques that whitewash reality or attempt to brainwash targeted publics.

Despite an increasing emphasis on subjects such as organizational theory, leadership behavior, and public relations in the preparation of school administrators, many practitioners appear to ignore the symbolic importance of their behavior. In part, this may be explained by socialization—the shaping of behavior within the social context of the organization (school). It may also be explained by continuing ambiguities surrounding the link between administrative behavior and public relations performance. That is, the application of public relations to education is still improperly conceptualized by some administrators.

A study conducted by a task force of the Public Relations Society of America described public relations as the "lubricant that makes the segments of an order work together with minimum friction and misunderstanding" (Black & Sharpe, 1983, p. vii). A clear picture of public relations performance for administrators emerges when one examines those behaviors *lubricating* and *harmonizing* social interactions (Sharpe, 1989). But specifically, what are these behaviors and what are their consequences?

The behavioral principles for achieving harmonious public relationships and their consequences are

- ◆ *Honesty* for *Credibility*
- ◆ *Openness* and *Consistency of Actions* for *Confidence*
- ◆ *Fairness* for *Reciprocity*
- ◆ *Continuous Communication* to build *Relationships* and prevent *Alienation*
- ◆ *Continuous Image Analysis* for *Corrective Adjustments* in *Behavior* or *Communication*

Each of the behavior-consequences merits closer examination.

Honesty for Credibility.   Friends and acquaintances who are dishonest are often ostracized in personal relationships. In fact, once trust is lost, individuals find they must struggle to regain it. Honesty may be, therefore, the most vital behavior related to the achievement of effective, continuous, stable personal relationships.

For organizations, the cost of losing trust is ineffective communication. Without credibility, messages will not be accepted. Hanging in the balance are

- ◆ Employee loyalty and support (those upon whom an organization is dependent for production of services or products)
- ◆ Customer/consumer confidence (those upon whose support the survival of the organization is directly dependent, for example, students and parents)
- ◆ Stockholder/taxpayer/legislator support (those with a direct economic interest or responsibility in the success or failure of the organization)

◆ Stakeholder support (those with a self-interest in the success or performance of the organization, for example, dependent businesses, community leaders, and employers)

Put simply, organizations cannot afford to lose credibility within their social environments. Organizations, however, often find it easier to regain credibility than do individuals. This is true because organizations can change leaders, policies, and procedures in an effort to build a new image. People are generally more skeptical about an individual's ability to change behavior totally.

The maintenance of organizational honesty in today's changing world environment is a complex process. It is made so by an ever-expanding knowledge base and the presence of technology. These conditions serve to modify public expectations of social institutions; that is, schools are expected to be increasingly responsive and relevant. Honesty of communication, therefore, requires continual analysis of existing organizational behavior and beliefs in relation to the new knowledge available to assure that what is being communicated remains accurate and that existing behavior supports the communication.

Organizational honesty requires a supporting corporate culture—one in which leadership behavior and regular evaluation promote the acceptance of appropriate values and beliefs. Honesty also requires a continual objective search for truth. This quest is often made more difficult by virtue of the differing values, beliefs, and expectations held by the various publics served by schools. Honest communication is dependent on the continual self-analysis of societal needs and wants and organizational programs. This process is commonly called "environmental monitoring," and it has been identified as "the fastest growing category of public relations research" (Baskin & Arnoff, 1988, p. 122).

Openness and Consistency of Actions for Confidence.   No one has confidence in an individual who appears to hide information. Likewise, the general public distrusts organizations that withhold or otherwise protect information. The complexity of achieving organizational openness and consistency of actions increases with organizational size and age. Both factors tend to cause an increasing number of rules and controls, and highly bureaucratic organizations maintain closed climates shielding them from their wider environments (Owens, 1995).

Openness can, and often does, increase conflict, because more views enter the organization. But conflict can be productive as well as cause inefficiencies. For example, open communication can minimize rumors or other forms of misinformation; the process can alert administrators to the need for change.

All states now have open-record laws defining (1) what information is classified as public, (2) what types of meetings must be open to the public, and (3) what types of information and meetings may remain confidential. These laws are not, however, uniform from state to state. The mere compliance with open-record laws does not assure public confidence. The behavioral principle, "openness for confidence," teaches that circumstances dictate the degree of openness needed—and sound public relations research helps to determine the degree of need.

As a general guide, public relations experts advise that administrators should release information to those who will be affected by the information. Barbara Posner (1993), vice president of human resources and corporate relations for Tenneco Automotive, has said,

"If we use the old rule of need to know, then we wouldn't share much of anything. But far more problems arise from knowing too little than from too much" (p. 3). Posner further emphasized that "in an environment of teamwork, cooperation and trust, we should share as much as is appropriate to inform, explain and possibly elicit action" (p. 3). Simply put, if affected audiences don't know what the problem is, they can't be part of the solution.

How does an administrator determine an appropriate level of openness? The answer depends on information obtained through environmental research of targeted audiences made possible by an established program of two-way communication. For schools, focus groups and advisory committees are two common sources of this information.

Fairness for Reciprocity.   At first glance, being fair in relationships appears to be an easy management goal. In reality, it is one of the most difficult aspects of administration. Adherence to this principle is an organization's biggest public relations challenge—and usually its greatest communication problem. The difficulty relates to differences in the ways that administrators and others define fairness. What a teacher, parent, or student may deem to be fair may be substantially different from the principal's conception. Every self-interest group may have a slightly different view of "fairness"; as a consequence, they will evaluate the fairness of administrative decisions from their personal perspective. Accordingly, the public relations behavioral principle of fairness teaches administrators to communicate and defend the basis of "fairness" used to make organizational decisions.

The computer-access that public relations professionals have today to news stories and legal decisions before they have been communicated in the local or national media enables the preparation of administrators for media inquiry. Advance information via Internet allows administrators to take proactive action in creating or adjusting policies based on the information learned or to be fully prepared to explain and defend school-system positions. In most cases, the media questions will probe the fairness of the school system's plans for handling a similar situation if it should occur in the local community. The media, of course, are looking for a localized story based on what is about to be a nationally communicated incident. Repeated preparedness rather than reactive clumsiness in response communicates a school administration prepared to treat students, teachers, and members of the community fairly in all situations. The reciprocal response is parent, taxpayer, and legislative support.

Continuous Communication to Build Relationships and Prevent Alienation.   Can communication be so successful that it can be discontinued for a period of time without effect? The answer is no! The simple truth is that family, friends, employees, customers, and business associates will feel alienated over time when communications cease or decrease.

Administrators often learn the problems related to inconsistent communications when they enter new, demanding jobs that change their communication priorities. In these situations, principals may have to spend more time directing their attention to new audiences, and consequently they give less attention to their family members; their time restrictions may cause them to use short notes instead of letters; personal contact may be replaced with telephone conversations. Whatever the case, they risk alienation by decreasing or changing communication.

Organizations can have the same communication problems. This is especially true as the demand for information increases. Often unknowingly, administrators create alienation by reducing the attention they give to an audience or by altering the way in which they communicate with that audience. As individuals advance to increasingly more complex positions in educational administration, this aspect of communication becomes a more critical issue. For example, a principal who becomes a superintendent may not alter her communication technique, despite the fact that she is now exchanging information with more and different audiences. In today's context, top-level administrators often discover that effectiveness requires them to have communication assistance.

Continuous Image Analysis for Corrective Adjustments in Behavior or Communication. Image analysis facilitates individual and organizational change. The most successful members of society have developed the ability to engage in self-analysis and to improve themselves. But the reality is that for all individuals, even those who are successful in their personal communication, accurate image assessment is difficult.

Because organizations are composed of many individuals and groups, the task of self-analysis is even more complex. Yet it is an essential process for the achievement of long-range stability in a dynamic society. Without an objective analysis of the perceptions of management effectiveness, school administrations will find change to be essentially impossible without a change in the administration. Equally serious are situations where the wrong image exists or is being unknowingly projected. Corrective communication programs will not be implemented unless the problem is known.

This principle teaches that images must be continuously analyzed, protected, and corrected. This is a function apart from creating an image. Analysis can produce safeguards assuring effective public relations and communication.

A model of the behaviors required for the performance of public relations and the reasons for the behavior is provided in Table 4–1, which also details the difficulty of behavioral achievement, the means of achievement, the cost to an organization's public relations performance if the behavior is not achieved, and the ultimate cost to the organization itself for lack of performance. In summary, the model explains how the lack of achievement of public relations performance affects the bottom line of all organizations.

Recognizing the Importance of Administrator Commitment

Administrator commitment to the success of public relations programs must be reinforced and demonstrated if the program is to be effective. Such commitment is demonstrated by

- ◆ Appointment of a qualified public relations management administrator and qualified supporting staff
- ◆ Creation of a job description establishing direct access to the top administrator and full participation in the formulation of management policies and decisions for the public relations executive officer
- ◆ Establishment of communication policy and a communication strategic plan designed to maintain organizational harmony with both internal and external publics

TABLE 4–1

Behavioral Requirements for Achievement and Maintenance of Effective Public Relations: A Behavioral Theory Model for Public Relations

Behavior	Reason	Difficulty	Means of Achievement	Cost to PR Performance if Not Achieved	Cost to Organization if Not Achieved
Honesty	Credibility	New knowledge and changes in social values	Environmental research and continual self-analysis	Message rejection and ineffective communication	Loss of internal and external support
Openness and consistency	Confidence	Situational aspect of the need	Public opinion analysis and management commitment and control	Message rejection and mistrust	High cost of ineffective communication and loss of internal and external support
Fairness	Reciprocity	Concepts differ	Communication of basis; public opinion analysis; continuous self-evaluation of basis; willingness to adjust	Damaged relationships and message rejection	Loss of repeat sales; punitive govt. regulation; loss of support; increased taxation; loss of employee loyalty
Continuous communication	Preventing alienation and building relationships	Overcoming communication roadblocks; maintenance of two-way communication	Continuous evaluation of communication effectiveness; strategic public relations planning	Message rejection; misinformation; uneducated audiences; lack of adjustment	Increased cost of repairing relationships; time required in rebuilding relationships; loss of support for management goals; target audience self-interpretation of organizational messages
Accurate image analysis	Corrective adjustments	Achievement of accurate self-analysis; reluctance of management to change existing behavior	Continuous analysis of target public opinion; corrective communications strategies; behavioral change	Ineffective programs; dependence on one-way communication strategies; misinformation without awareness; image damage without knowledge	Expense of using ineffective communication and public relations strategies; inadequate information upon which to base sound management decisions; lack of achievement of full productivity potential; unionization

Source: Developed in 1994 by Dr. Melvin L. Sharpe, APR, Fellow PRSA, Ball State University, from a concept conceived in 1987.

Commitment must also be reflected through support for the continued professional development and education of public relations staff advisors.

The most desirable situation is one in which the superintendent or college president (1) appoints a director for communications who is accredited by the National School Public Relations Association (NSPRA), the Public Relations Society of America (PRSA), or the International Association of Business Communicators (IABC); (2) provides support for a staff with educational backgrounds in public relations; (3) appoints staff qualified to conduct strategic communications planning; and (4) requires the public relations officer to hold membership in the NSPRA and its state chapters or in the PRSA or IABC. Commitment is also demonstrated by the presence of a planning process assuring two-way communication and the use of timely, accurate information. Finally, it is demonstrated by policies and administrative regulations promoting the effective use of communication and information.

Some of the historical problems associated with an inadequate commitment to educational public relations are

◆ Identification of the public relations function as largely promotional and frequently deceptive
◆ Collective bargaining conflicts affecting the quantity and quality of communication
◆ Organizational culture that supports the concept that communication should be carefully controlled by administrators
◆ Lack of understanding on the part of administrators regarding the broad applications of public relations

Two areas of opportunity for improved understanding of the value of communication and of effective public relations performance relate to (1) the role communication can play in improving the quality of education through increased support and involvement and (2) the additional educational contributions school systems can provide communities through improved educational communications programs. Administrator commitment is often most genuine when it is associated with these broader and widely endorsed goals.

WHAT ADMINISTRATORS SHOULD EXPECT FROM THE PUBLIC RELATIONS OFFICER

An administrator who is employed to direct a public relations office in a school district or institution of higher education may have any one of a dozen titles. The more common director of public relations, director of public information, director of communication, and director of community relations. In some districts, the titles of "coordinator" or "assistant superintendent" may be used instead of "director".

Public relations and communications administrators, regardless of title, have a special responsibility to provide the organization with an accurate assessment of the status of image and communication effectiveness. Many leading public relations professionals see these two facets of their work as the most important. But the job responsibilities extend well beyond these duties. Actual expectations, however, will vary somewhat from one school district to another because of unique needs in school districts (as organizations) and unique needs in the wider environments (as communities). In general, however, several associated responsibilities are nearly universal. They include

- ◆ Providing the organization and its administrative staff with communication and public relations goals and objectives supportive of the organization's mission and general goals
- ◆ Producing measurable results for communication activities
- ◆ Recommending policies and procedures designed to improve organizational communication
- ◆ Conducting reliable research and public opinion evaluation that provide information for sound decisions
- ◆ Providing dependable counsel to administrators with regard to their personal performance in the areas of communication and public relations
- ◆ Remaining current in the professional knowledge base of communication and public relations
- ◆ Adhering to the professional and ethical standards of public relations specialists
- ◆ Serving as a spokesperson for the media in the absence of the top school administrator
- ◆ Conducting employee public relations training designed to improve the total organizational performance in communication and public relations

A superintendent or college president ought to set appropriate but high expectations of the public relations officer. These expectations should be included in the job description and understood by employees throughout the organization. Job requirements for the public relations administrator should include strategic planning, environmental monitoring, and communication effectiveness evaluation.

The person selected to be the public relations officer ought to have an appropriate academic background; he or she should hold a degree in public relations, journalism, or communication—preferably from a program having national accreditation in journalism or mass communication or PRSA certification. The person should be a member of the National School Public Relations Association, the Public Relations Society of America, or the International Association of Business Communicators. To remain current on matters most directly affecting school districts, the person also should be active in the state association for educational public relations.

SUMMARY

This chapter examined two essential elements of a successful public relations program, both of which pertain to the educational administrator's role. The first is what administrators need to know about their own responsibilities in the areas of organizational and personal communication. The top executive ought to (1) recognize the need for a public relations program, (2) create programs built on sound principles, (3) focus on action as well as intent, and (4) demonstrate a commitment to the process. These responsibilities were defined in the context of behavior and expected outcomes.

Secondly, administrators should understand what can be accomplished with a qualified public relations officer on the administrative staff and demand acceptable performance from those who are designated to operate the program. This issue was discussed in terms of expectations and qualifications.

CASE STUDY	The Difficulties Encountered in Applying PR Principles

Janet Karson was named superintendent of the Maswell School District after having worked in the system for over two decades. She was a classroom teacher for fourteen years and then an elementary school principal for ten years. She was flattered when several members of the school board encouraged her to apply for the superintendency of this predominately rural, 1200-student district. Although reluctant at first, she pursued the job and was selected with unanimous support from the seven school board members.

In recent years, relationships between the teachers' union and the administration had deteriorated, and this issue had become the primary concern of the school board. A bitter strike, the first in the district's history, had closed schools for eleven days the previous year and divided the community. The strike was ended largely through the efforts of a mediator, and neither the board nor the union was pleased with the outcome. The intense conflict before, during, and after the strike had prompted the former superintendent, John Ashland, to retire.

In seeking a new superintendent, the board members had wanted to employ someone who could reduce the continuing strife between the school board and the teachers' union. Up until he announced his resignation, Ashland had been the lightning rod for union attacks, but once he announced he was resigning, that dubious honor shifted to school board president, Burt Arnold, owner of a farm implement business. Arnold had been anxious to find a superintendent who would take him out of the spotlight. He and the other board members wanted to name a superintendent who could reason with the union leaders; they were tired of the conflict. This goal was largely responsible for their interest in Janet Karson. During the strike, she had managed to keep her school open (the only one that did remain open), and yet she was not attacked by the union leaders. Her rapport with teachers was the critical factor. Teachers trusted her, and union officials feared they would alienate their members if they said derogatory things about her. Thus she managed to persuade her teachers to work during the strike, and union officials carefully avoided attacking her.

When Karson became superintendent she made a commitment to continue the open-door policy that had been her trademark as principal. Additionally, she announced that she would devote much of her time to instructional leadership and would spend two days every week in the schools. Her policy toward the union would be to treat them fairly, she had told the board. "I'll talk to their officials just like I talk to everyone else," she'd said. "They have the same access to me as any teacher, parent, or student."

After just three months in the job, however, Karson was struggling to keep up. Telephone calls, many of which were from school board members, were not returned for two or three days. Purchase orders and other documents requiring her signature often went unsigned for longer periods. But the work piling up on her desk did not dissuade her from spending about 40 percent of her workweek visiting classrooms and talking to principals and teachers.

At the start of the second semester, several board members complained to board president Arnold about Karson's not responding immediately to their telephone calls. He too was becoming impatient with her apparent lack of responsiveness. Arnold called his cousin John, principal at the high school, and asked him if administrators were having the same problem. John Arnold indicated that the reverse was true. "She's in my building quite a bit. But overall, I think she has trouble managing her time. She has this thing about not wanting to be seen as a manager."

The day after the discussion with the high school principal, Burt Arnold called Karson's office and told her secretary he would be there at 4 that afternoon to see the superintendent. "It's important. So, whatever she's doing, tell her to cancel and be there," he told the secretary.

A person who believes in direct communication, Burt Arnold told Karson exactly what was on his mind. "I and the other board members think you are spending too much time away from your office. You're not a principal anymore. And besides, you have got to understand that board members expect you to return their calls immediately. They're not just anybody. They're your bosses, he said, then added, "Mr. Ashland had problems as superintendent, but he always knew enough to answer board members' questions before anything else. These people are used to having a superintendent who gives priority to their questions."

Karson was a bit surprised by the comments. She felt that many of the board members' questions concerned trivial matters. "I return the calls as soon as I can," she told the board president. "I think every call, every request for an appointment, and every visit to a classroom is important. And besides, have there been any serious problems because I don't return a call immediately? Most of these calls are not that important. For example, one board member called last week because her neighbor complained about the quality of food service in the schools. Is this something that needs immediate attention?"

Arnold was not used to a superintendent who did not immediately agree with him. Looking Karson straight in the eyes, he said, "We appreciate the good job you're doing, especially in keeping the union quiet. But you have to learn that this job has a lot of management responsibilities. Like it or not, you work for the school board; when school board members call you, you call them back as soon as possible. I think you're flirting with trouble if you keep this up."

QUESTIONS AND SUGGESTED ACTIVITIES

Case Study

1. Is there any evidence suggesting the presence of a public relations plan in this school district?
2. Should a school district of this size have a full-time public relations administrator? Why or why not?
3. Assess the superintendent's experience in the school system. With regard to public relations, is her experience an asset or liability?

4. Is the school board really interested in a good communications program? Why or why not?
5. Is it common for school board members to call the superintendent frequently? If they do, should this be a source of concern?
6. If you were Karson, would you give preferential treatment to school board members?
7. Are the frequent school visits evidence that Karson is a good communicator? Why or why not?
8. How can the superintendent provide evidence that she is committed to open, honest communication?
9. Evaluate Karson's behavior with regard to being fair and open in her communications.
10. Relating this case study to the issue of communication, what elements of this chapter are relevant to the concern being expressed by the board president?
11. What is the purpose of a teachers' union? Does their presence have any relevance to organizational communication?
12. Develop a job description for a director of public information in a school district of 5000 students and a job description for a direction of public information in a liberal arts college with 1500 students. Compare the two job descriptions.

SUGGESTED READINGS

Dickey, B. B. Internal communications. *Communication: Journalism Education Today, 27*(4), 2–6.

Dilenschneider, R. L. (1987). Platform. *International Public Relations Review, 11*(3), 6–9.

Geddes, D. S. (1993). Empowerment through communication: Key people-to-people and organizational success. *People and Education, 1*(1), 76–104.

Henderson, E. H.(1990). Cast a wide net. *American School Board Journal, 177*(3), 38–39.

Hines, R. W. (1993). Principal starts with PR. *Principal, 72*(3), 45–46.

Howlett, P. (1993). Politics comes to school. *Executive Educator, 15*(1), 14–20.

Johnson, V. R. (1994). Connecting families and schools through mediating structures. *School Community Journal, 4*(1), 45–51.

Sharpe, M. L. (1987). Recognition comes from consistently high standards. *Public Relations Review, 12*(4), 17–25.

Sharpe, M. L. (1994). Can any type of promotional or communication activity be classified as public relations? *International Public Relations Review, 17*(4), 19–25.

Vann, A. S. (1992). Ten ways to improve principal-parent communication. *Principal, 71*(3), 30–31.

Wakefield, G., & Cottone, L. P. (1987). Knowledge and skills required by public relations employers. *Public Relations Review, 13*(3), 24–31.

West, P. T. (1987). Out of sight—out of work: A case study about a PR director who returns after a year's sabbatical to discover his function has been supplanted. *Journal of Educational Public Relations, 10*(1), 26–30.

REFERENCES

Baskin, O., & Aronoff, C. (1988). *Public relations: The profession and the practice.* Dubuque, IA: Wm. C. Brown Publishers.

Black, S., & Sharpe, M. L. (1983). *Practical public relations.* Englewood Cliffs, NJ: Prentice Hall.

Cutlip, S. M., Center, A. H., & Broom, G. M. (1985). *Effective public relations.* Englewood Cliffs, NJ: Prentice Hall.

Davis, B. R. (1986). *School public relations*. Arlington, VA: National School Public Relations Association.

Dilenschneider, R. L. (1987). Platform. *International Public Relations Review, 11*(3), 6–9.

Kowalski, T. J., Weaver, R. A., Greene, J. E., & Pfaller, J. E. (1993). Developing a world-class work force: Business and industry, government, and schools respond to school reform. *Contemporary Education, 64*(2), 94–98.

Owens, R. G. (1995). *Organizational behavior in education* (5th ed.). Boston: Allyn and Bacon.

Posner, B. (1993). Q&A on corporate communications. *The Ragan Report, 24*(16), 3.

Seitel, F. P. (1992). *The practice of public relations*. New York: Macmillan.

Sharpe, M. L. (1989). Cases and commentaries, Commentary 4: Avoiding ethical problems. *Journal of Mass Media Ethics, 4*(1), 113–117.

Sharpe, M. L. (1994). Can any type of promotional or communication activity be classified as public relations? *International Public Relations Review, 17*(4), 19–25.

CHAPTER 5

Public Relations and Technology

Robert H. Woodroof

Edward Bernays's *Crystallizing Public Opinion* (1923) launched the intellectual era for public relations and the first rumblings of a movement to gain respectability as a recognized profession. Views are mixed as to whether or not the movement, now sixty years old, has reached its objective. Proponents would argue that today public relations has the five major characteristics of a profession:

1. A set of professional values
2. Strong professional organizations
3. Adherence to professional norms
4. An intellectual tradition and an established body of knowledge
5. Technical skills acquired through professional training (Grunig & Hunt, 1984, p. 66)

Even our industry's most vocal critics admit that PR engages professionals to accomplish its purposes. They argue, however, that dubious motivations often guide our actions, calling into question the values on which our profession is based. The most vocal in this category are print and electronic media journalists and other watchdogs of the PR industry, who subscribe to the theory that public relations is a conspiracy cleverly designed to manipulate public opinion through deception for corporate or political gain.

Whether or not we deserve the criticism, the reality is that we are all under greater scrutiny today by a more savvy public. Our work is more visible and thus more susceptible to criticism. (Newson, Scott, & Turk, 1993). The leading force in opening our industry to greater visibility and public scrutiny is the technology of the information age. In fact, public relations has been on a collision course with the information age ever since Bell Laboratories invented the transistor in 1947 . . . and impact is imminent.

For nearly fifty years public relations practitioners have embraced each new technological advancement in succession, retooling each step of the way: integrated circuits, microprocessors, mainframe computers, desktop computers, modular emulators (modems), electronic mail, electronic database information research, portable computers, facsimile machines, image scanners, laser printers, color laser printers, real-time electronic news monitoring, cellular phones, desktop publishing, laptops, notebooks, subnotebooks, palmtops, satellite communications, even video telephones.

Our defense for continually retooling our work is that we truly believe we are improving our effectiveness. Technology, we say, allows us to plan campaigns more strategically, target our messages better, improve the content and style of those messages, continuously monitor results, and achieve objectives quicker and with greater efficiency. This is true for the best of us.

However, the rapid pace of continual transition has its downside because technology is only as effective as the professionalism of those who use it. In this sense, the information age is testing our professionalism, creating a shakedown period for us. While we are learning to adapt the potential of technology to increase our effectiveness, we will also be tested in ways we are only beginning to understand.

Instead of asking the question "How do we unlock the potential of technology?" we should ask, "How do we control its potential?" Or perhaps more to the point: "How do we keep technology from controlling us as we work to advance our schools and educational systems?"

Emerging technology will help, even force, public relations to move from a *practice* to a recognized *profession*, providing the resources to calculate effectiveness in measurable terms, to reduce ambiguity, and to increase accountability. The result will be a significant practitioner cleansing, a major shakedown reducing the flack factor and transforming public relations into a respected, indispensable, strategic planning tool of senior management.

No organization type will experience these eventualities more acutely than schools, school systems, colleges, and universities, where public relations will play an integral role in regaining public confidence and building a strong case for dramatically increased public and private funding.

FORECASTING TRENDS OF DRAMATIC CHANGE

In his much-touted and much-referenced *Future Shock* (1970), Alvin Toffler offered an eye-opening snapshot of future society. Toffler masterfully painted visions of the America of the future, pushed without restraint down a twisting luge of unprecedented transformation, overwhelmed by "the roaring current of change, a current so powerful that it overturns institutions, shifts our values and shrivels our roots" (p. 3).

His picture was a powerful wake-up call for America because he focused on the "soft or human side of the future," damping the "harsh metallic note" that accompanied most attempts at prediction in the '60s.

However, Toffler failed in one critical area. He looked at the future while walking down a thirty-year through-way, built logically on historical perspectives and present-day trends, observing change that was visible in a cognitive sense from his carefully laid path. His vision was limited because he built his through-way at a time when dramatic social change was occurring from decade to decade.

By the mid-1980s, however, half-way through his time frame, dramatic change was occurring in real-time perspective, creating shifts of social direction he could not have anticipated. Thus many of his predictions for society at the turn of the century have a curious 1980s feel to them.

While acknowledging that "future shock is a time phenomenon, a product of a greatly accelerated rate of change in society" (p. 13), Toffler, even with his uncanny insight, could not envision how fast the rate of acceleration would be and thus could not plan for some of the significant changes in direction his through-way would need to predict.

A magnified version of Toffler's dilemma exists today. We have entered a time when our farthest-reaching dreams are merely portents of the very near future. In fact, it is becoming increasingly difficult to outdream the future, an exciting but sobering reality.

For our purposes there is limited practical value in trying to predict the marvels of technological change that will occur over the next decade. A more important exercise is to consider how we can adapt to the demands these changes will bring to our professional behavior.

TECHNOLOGY AND NEW DEMANDS ON PROFESSIONAL BEHAVIOR

As technology improves, demands on the professional increase at a rate equal to expectations of improved effectiveness. Advancements in technology force practitioners to exercise more professional behavior in at least seven critical areas. The public relations practitioner must

- ◆ Seek the highest levels of communication skills
- ◆ Learn to be a communicator-on-the-run
- ◆ Develop the habit of lifelong learning
- ◆ Become expert in adapting communication science
- ◆ Use critical thinking for strategic purposes
- ◆ Accept accountability for actions and counsel
- ◆ Integrate PR with other disciplines

Seeking the Highest Levels of Communication Skills

The product of public relations work is communication. Every activity leads ultimately to communicating one or more messages to a target audience. Theorists have debated for decades about what constitutes the most important ingredient in the communication mix for reaching a target audience at the cognitive level: the *source* of the message, the *medium* through which the message is sent, or the *content* of the message.

For example, according to Canadian professor Marshall McLuhan, advances in technology, specifically television, elevated the *medium* of the message as the important element in the communication mix. He argued that regardless of the content of the message, communication occurs more easily through television because less work is required of the receiver, who can put himself or herself into the interaction more easily than with other types of media.

Others argue that the *source* of the message is more important, that regardless of the content of the message or the channel through which the message is delivered, communication occurs only when the source is believable, authoritative, and/or charismatic. Thus the source drives the machinery of effective communication.

The most popular view, according to Fraser Seitel (1992), is that without appropriate and well-conceived *content*, communication does not occur, regardless of the source or the medium. There are two factors in modern communication efforts that justify the popular view that the message is the message: improved targeting and increased competition, both resulting from recent advances in technology.

Thanks to improved methods of tracking individuals in our publics, understanding their opinions and lifestyles, and reaching them with personalized messages, the public relations professional has a greater opportunity for effective communication than ever before. However, as more organizations have utilized these advances to reach their publics, competition for an individual's attention has increased dramatically, elevating the importance of the content of the message that is delivered.

Consider, for example, a school district seeking public approval during the next election for a new bond issue to fund improvements. A new bond issue often calls for increased tax assessments, not a particularly appealing proposition to the average homeowner. Furthermore, a tremendous quantity of political campaign messages bombards the public during an election period, adding to the torrent of messages that are a part of every individual's day. Therefore the public relations task of a school district to sell the need for a tax increase has two obstacles to overcome: getting the attention of the right audience in the midst of communication overload and communicating a persuasive message that results in action.

While neither the scenario nor the obstacles are new, they are more critical today because advancing technology has created such tremendous competition for the attention of the general public. But, even if the public's attention is gained, the message must be persuasive or the objective of the campaign to seek voter approval is not achieved. Thus, the message becomes the critical element in the communication mix.

Technology has the power to increase our effectiveness in reaching our target audience, but at the same time it forces us, because of increased competition, to develop the highest levels of communication skills to craft a message that will stand out in the crowd. If there is no message, or if the message is not compelling, technology loses its power to aid the communication process.

Learning to Be a Communicator-on-the-Run

An editorial in the *Public Relations Journal* highlights the impact of technology on communication: "We're in the era of instant information, with faxes buzzing around the globe at dizzying speeds. While the positives of this technological revolution far outweigh the negatives, rapid change is disruptive and creates new stresses, even as it improves communication. It's literally possible to work a 24-hour day if you're in a global business! Because instant communication is possible, clients and customers might now expect instant service, in effect, instant gratification" (Bovet, 1992, p. 2).

Improved technology and increased competition have created the potential of a twenty-four-hour workday because *timing* has become as crucial to success as both the *message* and the *messenger*. Consider this example.

The president of a major private university is approached by a small sister institution—3000 miles distant and on the verge of closure—with a merger proposal. On the surface, the location of this small college near Washington, D.C., provides a compelling opportunity to establish a year-round internship program for the university in public policy and political science.

A professor of public relations at the university has recently consulted with the struggling institution to help identify strategies for a turnaround. The university president now calls him to a meeting to gain his advice on the potential merger. The college has opened its files for full disclosure to the university, but, because of potential problems of conflict of interest, the professor calls the president of the small college for his approval to share information obtained during the consulting process. Approval received, the professor agrees to meet with the university president.

Armed with an electronic trove of research notes and critical analyses of the strengths and weaknesses of the institution, the professor sits down before the meeting to draft a three-page brief, isolating the critical points and concluding that the merger is not in the best interest of either institution. The university would inherit millions of dollars of financial distress, severe deferred maintenance, and lack of qualified staff. The struggling college would, in effect, be dissolved and lose its identity, which it is reluctant to sacrifice. It would be more strategic and less costly, the professor advises in his report, for the university to simply establish a new campus for a Washington-based program.

The professor is able to present this strategic report because he is familiar with the use of technology—and its adaptation to his work. During the time he consulted with the small college, his research and analysis of the institution's historical marketing and fundraising performance, its competitiveness, fiscal condition, positioning within the region, and personnel were aided by technology: on-line information databases, computerized content analysis, and sophisticated word processing.

While the data collected—and the resulting list of pros, cons, and recommendations—were based on his experience and sweat equity, much of the data gathering, sorting, and reporting was done with the aid of technology. And the speed with which he could produce a targeted, concise, meaningful report was also the result of technology. The professor is a communicator-on-the-run because he was able, with the aid of technology, to insert into his busy schedule a demand that would otherwise have been impossible.

The caveat to this scenario is that the process raised the expectations of the university president in terms of what he could expect in the future from the public relations office of the institution. This is the direction technology is pushing public relations, to be ready to respond with quick results, particularly in those areas of our expertise. Those unable or unwilling to adapt to heightened expectations created by technology will find the profession leaving them behind, victims of the practitioner cleansing of the '90s that has already begun.

Developing the Habit of Lifelong Learning

Access to important and relevant information to aid our work is virtually instantaneous today, transforming trend analysis to a real-time function. Professionals must maintain a constant vigil of local, regional, national, and international trends that impact short- and long-range strategic planning for their institutions.

The "information highway"—now a catchphrase for a national movement that is changing forever the way Americans live, work, and play—will become the primary communication resource for our work, linking our institutions with our audiences in exciting new ways.

The information highway is a good example of how increasingly difficult it is to outdream reality. Far sooner than we might expect, virtually every byte of knowledge or sensory experience in all genres of human composition will be available in our homes and offices on command. The leaders in this movement, telecommunication and entertainment companies who control the electronic linkages across the continent and the civilized world, are engaged in an entrepreneurial one-upmanship to be the first to take advantage of each dramatic, and profitable, advancement. This competitive spirit will be dampened only by our ability as a nation to pay for the progress.

The information highway presents promises and problems for the public relations professional. Generally speaking, it promises opportunities to streamline the dissemination of news and other messages to more narrowly targeted audiences. It promises the ultimate in clipping services through the satellite transmission and retrieval of full-text WYSIWYG ("wizziwig," or what you see is what you get) articles and electronic broadcasts on the unlimited topics of our choosing. It promises multisite, interactive news conferences and educational programs from any vantage point in the world. It promises research capabilities for issues monitoring and trend analysis that would otherwise be impossible. And the list goes on, limited only by the creativity and needs of the user.

The problems are more singular, but ultimately more dramatic. The first problem is slow adaptation to the resource. Many in our profession have only recently and reluctantly begun to use a simple computer word processor. They would suggest that they are too busy to adapt. This problem will likely dissolve in the next generation or two when all professionals will have used advanced technology from a very early age.

Marvin Cetron and Owen Davies (1989) describe the second, more damaging problem in simple terms: "The information you need may be accessible electronically, but now the problem is shifting to knowing where to look—and then distilling what you really want from the data deluge that can be triggered by the most mundane request" (p. 146).

In short, the problem presented by the information highway is not learning how to use it, but how to control it. The solution is twofold. First, the professional must develop the habit of continuous learning, staying up-to-date on the effective use of evolving technological resources. The process builds a modern expert, a prerequisite for professional recognition, and for gaining greater respect. Second, a plan of action for using evolving technology to enhance our learning should be based on strategic planning, as in any other major PR endeavor. For the educational public relations professional, the plan can be divided into two broad categories: (1) daily monitoring and retrieval and (2) project-based access.

Two subcategories fall under the rubric of daily monitoring and retrieval: *issues monitoring and trend analysis* and *electronic clipping services* (media scanning). Both subcategories require key-word references and knowledge of which database resources to use in maintaining a daily vigil. A growing number of professional services—Nexis/Lexis, CompuServe, Dialog—offer access to thousands of on-line information databases. They will, for a fee, research existing files and monitor databases daily for new data, saving each "hit"—often in full text—into a user's own personal electronic file. Downloading the information to disk for editing, content analysis, sorting, viewing on screen, or sending directly to a printer for hard copy can be done at the user's leisure.

Resources for personal electronic clipping services—DataTimes, MediaLink, PR Newswire, CompuServe, America Online, and Prodigy—are growing rapidly. For example, on CompuServe's Executive News Service, a series of electronic requests can be launched, using key terms such as the name of your institution, where scans of selected wire services occur at least every hour. Retrieved articles, typically in full text, are then saved into the user's personal electronic folder for retrieval later. Specific major newspapers can also be monitored, and electronic versions of daily newspapers provide increasing access in full-page graphic format.

A new trend that will likely become the norm is a satellite service that monitors print and electronic news coverage in real time, playing a ticker tape of the titles of articles within the search parameters across the top of a user's computer screen, saving the full text of retrieved articles in a special file for later retrieval. These services offer retrievals from major media and wire services. Future plans include a service that downlinks televised news—as broadcast—for playback on screen. (Burrelle's Broadcast Database offers this service in full-text form now.)

Project-based access to the information highway is unlimited and can, with careful planning, be an invaluable resource in improving effectiveness. For example, when assisting in planning a major fund-raising effort—a growing demand on secondary and higher-education PR professionals—the information highway can assist in identifying target regions and target audiences based on demographic and psychographic analysis, monitoring economic trends that might impact the effectiveness and timing of the campaign, transmitting campaign news and features simultaneously to hundreds of targeted media, and locating lost alumni. The list of project-based uses is limited only by knowledge of the resources available and the funds to pay for the services. Though costly today, the expenses of these services will undoubtedly go down as the information highway expands.

The PR professional cannot afford to ignore the resources at his or her disposal. Becoming educated in what is available and how to use it prudently will, to use license with a quote from Patricia Walker (1992), "distinguish those [professionals who will] thrive" (p. 19).

Becoming Expert in Adapting Communication Science

Multidirectional communication between a school, college, or university and its mix of publics becomes more complex as technology improves, creating smaller and more narrowly defined target groups. The *masses* become the *individuals,* and theories of persuasion, group dynamics, social learning, and cognitive dissonance take on rich new meaning and practicality.

Students in all disciplines, not just public relations, question the value of studying theory in college, wondering how theory will be applicable to anything they might do. In one sense, their concern is valid, because the real value of a theory in principle is in how it plays out in reality.

For example, theories of persuasion and the cognitive dissonance theory are popular with public relations professions who know how to use them to tailor messages. Persuasion theory (Yale model) teaches that messages have a greater chance of reaching the audience if the source is credible and authoritative (Newsom, Scott, & Turk, 1993). The theory of cognitive dissonance, authored by Leon Festinger (1963), states that when others try to persuade us to do something our conscience, beliefs, attitudes, or opinions tell us we should not do, cognitive dissonance occurs. "The existence of dissonance, being psychologically uncomfortable, will motivate [us] to try to reduce the dissonance and achieve consonance [by justifying our action, rationalizing our behavior, and modifying our opinion]. When dissonance is present, in addition to trying to reduce it, the person will actively avoid situations and information which would likely increase the dissonance" (p. 3).

A direct-mail campaign planner seeking funds from private academy alumni who have traditionally not given to the school's annual fund might use these two theories to craft persuasive messages. After the database of alumni is confirmed as being as accurate as possible and—after testing—the appropriate (that is, credible and authoritative) signatory of the communiqué is chosen, research is conducted to determine the points of cognitive dissonance that might be supporting the alumni tendency to ignore requests for funds.

For example, if there are specific graduation classes or a range of classes over several consecutive years who have a very low giving rate, there may be issues in the history of the academy that impacted the experience of those students, resulting in their reluctance to give. If so, research may help identify the key issues, information that would be valuable in developing new approaches to communicating with and involving alumni from those classes. Given enough time, significant changes in attitude and giving patterns can be made.

A university used this approach to develop a three-year campaign that helped increase giving by 200 percent over previous efforts. The theory of cognitive dissonance was used in this instance to help explain why alumni were not giving and was then used to rewrite targeted messages designed to reduce dissonance and increase the percent of positive response.

Today the concept of using communication science to aid in drafting effective messages has been taken to new heights, thanks to the benefits of technology. PhaseOne, a California-based research firm, spent more than a decade developing a sophisticated computer program to analyze the effectiveness of messages in all forms: advertising, marketing, promotion, and more recently, student recruitment and fund raising for education.

The basis for their analysis is a combination of the leading theories and assumptions of persuasion, with content analysis as the primary research technique. Their objective is to analyze the persuasive effectiveness of a message in reaching planned objectives. Their client list is long and impressive, suggesting a high rate of success. While they are the only firm to use this technology, their approach launches new possibilities in linking technology with effective communication and affirms the thesis of this section that theories of communication science are valuable resources for the professional in public relations.

Using Critical Thinking for Strategic Purposes

No organization type is in greater need of effective strategic planning than are educational institutions. However, strategic planning is only as effective as the accuracy of the forecasting that accompanies the process.

Forecasting occurs at many levels, and effective strategic planning should draw from the full range of forecasting techniques. The lowest level of forecasting is trend analysis, the highest is impact analysis, and both are aided significantly by technology—trends are identified through electronic database research.

Trend analysis uses observed consequences of past actions to predict future tendencies. *Impact analysis* predicts the range of consequences that may result from future actions taken to exploit observed trends. Impact analysis requires critical thinking to identify the full range of potential consequences. While critical thinking is largely a cognitive skill, and thus a learned discipline, improved technology is reducing the learning curve significantly by placing the tools necessary at the fingertips of professionals.

While the details of these processes do not fall within the limits of this chapter, it is important for educational PR professionals to understand their significance in our work today.

Education is one of the revered safeguards of our society. But today our institutions are in trouble. Numerous published reports, TV and print editorials, and educational activists suggest that education is failing. Educators across the country have designated the '90s as a time for critically needed change. Of particular note are two reports: *Educational Renaissance: Our Schools at the Turn of the Twenty-First Century* (1991) and *An American Imperative: Higher Expectations for Higher Education* (1993).

There is a movement in America calling for a renewal of education, calling for a reassessment of where we are going and for the development of strategies for dramatic improvement. The call goes out to all levels of the educational system.

Public relations professionals in education are ideally suited to assist in this renewal with strategies based on critical thinking and decisions based on impact analysis. At the core of the process is the tenacity and dedication of the professional to take an active role in communicating success in recovery and future plans of action to broad target audiences. Technology used strategically is a primary resource in the process.

Accepting Accountability for Actions and Counsel

Quantifiable proof of effectiveness is demanded of professionals today. The movement toward quantification of our work makes many in our profession uneasy, primarily because research is a high-skill function. Fortunately, it is not a requirement of the professional to be a qualified research analyst. What is required, however, is that the professional know the kind of research needed, how to obtain it, and how to use it to advantage.

Newsom, Scott, and Turk (1993) suggest that accountability through quantification is long overdue in public relations practice. Rather than carefully pretesting message effectiveness and monitoring message impact, practitioners tend to commit significant campaign resources solely on the basis of gut instinct or past experience. Emerging technology can assist in correcting this problem, but there is one caveat. Technology, as powerful and wonderful as it is, is only an adjunct resource in gaining quantifiable evidence of our effectiveness. It cannot relieve the human effort necessary for true accountability.

Technology can aid in developing effective and persuasive communication, but it cannot create it. Technology can help identify trends and monitor issues of significance as they unfold, but it cannot translate that knowledge into strategic planning. Technology can perform complicated statistical functions based on hundreds of variables, but it cannot translate the significance of the results into relevant, usable conclusions about attitudes and opinions.

Ultimately, without human involvement, technology used in research is no more valuable to our efforts than the emergency action plan that never leaves the shelf. In this sense, it will take the will of the profession and the determination of the professional to make research, with the support of technology, a standard part of planning and evaluation.

Integrating PR with Other Disciplines

The ability of technology to more narrowly define and target audiences is blurring the lines of authority separating public relations, marketing, market research, advertising, and fund-raising disciplines. Two emerging concepts gaining increasing acceptance are "marketing public relations" and "integrated marketing." The first relates to all types of organizations; the second is associated primarily with corporations, but the principles are applicable to nonprofits as well.

A third concept, which enjoys less consensus than the first two, suggests that fund-raising and public relations efforts in nonprofit organizations are hierarchically more similar than the traditional organizational structure that places PR under fund-raising management (Kelly, 1991).

These concepts represent a philosophical shift to link communication outreaches in all functional areas of an organization as a symphony of message dissemination. To continue with this analogy, we are moving rapidly to an organizational design where an independent communication office (marketing, public relations, or advertising) may or may not be first chair, according to the objectives of a particular outreach or program. First chair is assumed by the office most responsible for ensuring that the objectives are met, and the other disciplines work in concert to achieve maximum effectiveness.

In this sense, technology can help change the functional design of how we communicate with our audiences, so that the multiple messages being sent by different offices to the same publics are unified. Public relations must assume a leadership role in the transition by ensuring that organizational messages, regardless of the source, are unified and credible (Newsom, Scott, & Turk, 1993).

ACT: GAINING POWER THROUGH TECHNOLOGY

As an acronym, "ACT" refers to the process of gaining power through technology: True power in our society is granted to those who have *access* to knowledge, who have *control* over the transmission and dissemination of knowledge, and who make strategic use of *timing* in communicating knowledge. Power is granted to these individuals because they are an indispensable resource for decision makers in our society.

Technology used effectively in the ACT process is the vessel through which power is delivered. Following is a description of each major ACT category and a list of processes dramatically streamlined by emerging technology.

Access to Knowledge

Technology enables the educational public relations professional to collect an enormous amount of knowledge relevant to the success of the institution, with instantaneous access and relative low cost. Following is a list of specialized public relations activities that demand access to targeted information.

Media scanning: Using electronic media "clipping" services.

Issues monitoring: Similar to media scanning in process, but expanding the search parameters to include such sources as journals, government documents, and research studies and dissertations.

Trend analysis and forecasting: Using historical and current data on interrelated topics to aid in planning. For example, information related to use of technology in education, budgetary constraints on schools, and costs (savings) related to use of technology can identify current trends that may assist in lobbying efforts for state and federal funding for upgrading technology in the classroom.

Action impact analysis: Using a combination of issues monitoring, trend analysis, and forecasting to assist in predicting the impact of future strategically planned actions on a particular issue.

Key players/programs monitoring: Tracking media coverage, for example, of a school's new program that links students with community service projects to help assess the impact of the program on the school's image.

Target audience identification: Using electronic databases to target groups for communication, typically based on demographic and psychographic information.

Economic analysis: Determining a local community's economic condition, identifying social services that are underrepresented, and determining recreational preferences of citizens to assist in community relations efforts between an institution and the surrounding community.

Economic impact studies: Determining the ultimate economic impact of an institution on the surrounding community.

Control over the Transmission and Dissemination of Knowledge

Technology enables the public relations professional to deliver targeted messages to appropriate audiences with greater efficiency, less waste, and lower effective cost than ever before. Consider the following list of services and resources for controlling the transmission and dissemination of information and targeted messages.

Video news releases: Many network, local, and cable news outlets eagerly seek video footage of newsworthy events or programs. VNRs are also valuable in targeted constituent communication.

Multisite, interactive satellite video-conferencing: This resource is valuable for making major announcements or telecasting programs, and particularly valuable during times of crisis.

Electronic mail for internal communication: Communication via electronic mail on a computer-networked campus is generally more efficient and effective than mass memoranda distributed through the mail—assuming that a majority of potential users check their electronic mail daily. New systems now provide notices on screen when new mail is received.

Broadcast fax: Simultaneous transmission of news and photos to target media worldwide, while currently available, will be one of the most significant growth industries in public relations as technology expands capabilities.

Information-on-demand: A resource providing target audiences with instant access to an institution's stored documents at any time, this is currently referred to as "fax-on-demand." Technology will expand this service to include all types of information products, from videos to collateral pieces. (See On-line publishing and Interactive video recruiting items below.)

Personalized messages to individuals within target audiences: With the advent of micro-marketing techniques, public relations outreach will address recipients electronically, by name, with specially tailored messages similar to the personalized direct mail processes used today.

Cable access, the new frontier: With hundreds of cable channels available through the information highway, the ability to target messages to narrowly defined audiences is increased dramatically.

On-line publishing: This resource involves periodicals and collateral material produced electronically from concept through finished "product" and broadcast direct or on-demand to constituent home computers. College guidebooks will be sold as CD-ROM packages, featuring color materials from thousands of academies, proprietary schools, colleges, and universities. This service is already available from a limited number of colleges.

Interactive video recruiting: Similar to on-line publishing, traditional recruiting videos will be available on CD-ROM and cable-access channels or will be transmitted electronically at the viewer's request. The viewer may interact with the video to select specific information via touch-screen technology. If the video is transmitted electronically, the prospective student will have the option of submitting a formal application—also electronically—immediately after viewing the video. A narrator will "walk" the prospect through the application, answering concerns and questions in interactive style.

The electronic meeting: Meetings come alive with computer presentation technology. Imagination and creativity are essential to gain the most of this resource.

Distance learning: The school or college campus is extended through on-site, live, interactive, worldwide satellite transmissions featuring unique educational programs, such as museum tours in Florence, Italy, or archaeological digs in Israel.

Timing in Communicating Knowledge

Technology enables the public relations professional to transmit messages of any complexity to anyone, anywhere, in seconds. Being able to operate within a microwindow of opportunity creates significant flexibility, increases the potential for effectiveness, and is especially beneficial in times of crisis. Consider the following two activities, impacted by technology, where timing is critical:

Project management: Sophisticated computer software simplifies the management of complex projects—particularly those where one activity must be completed before another begins (sequential) and is critical to its success (typical of most complex projects).

Technology in times of crisis: Resources identified in the access and control categories of the ACT process will greatly improve effectiveness in times of crisis. The challenge is to integrate access and control technology into emergency action plans so that implementation (timing) is seamless. Project management software is particularly helpful in merging technology with the details of emergency action plans.

Using Technology to Integrate ACT Processes

Using technology effectively often means integrating multiple technologies for the greatest impact. From a simple weekly office meeting to a multisite, national video news conference to crisis management, most public relations efforts will be more effective when multiple technologies are integrated strategically. In this sense, each aspect of the ACT process is incorporated into PR planning and implementation, dramatically improving the chances for success, regardless of the situation or project.

The following examples will show how integrating future technology will streamline the PR process and aid in situation analysis, planning, and action. Each activity identified in these two examples has been traditionally very labor-intensive. For example, media scanning (press clipping services) and issues monitoring are labor-intensive because people are required to sit at a work desk, scanning, identifying, and clipping relevant articles, which are then mailed to the client in a formal report.

New technology, however, shifts much of the workload from human power to electronic power, providing instant results at significantly lower cost (when personnel costs are considered). Consider the following examples.

Example 1

A school system in a large metropolitan area is experiencing a wave of violence among students on three campuses. In the past three weeks, one student and one principal have been killed; eight other people have been injured. All incidents involved handguns.

Every morning the public relations director for the school system reviews media coverage on the crisis by viewing an electronic newspaper—compiled, formatted, and designed by computer—on her newspaper-sized screen. The WYSIWYG document displays editorials and news reports in full text, complete with headings, photographs, and other graphics. Quotes are italicized and names of school personnel and students that appear in the articles are highlighted in red. Touch-screen technology allows the director to see file data, including photographs, on personnel and students cited in the articles.

A second file holds full-length versions of local and national televised news reports on the crisis, in chronological order, ready for viewing. Sophisticated voice-recognition software reduces the televised broadcasts to written text for distribution in the morning crisis-control meeting with school system administrators, with accompanying hard-copy print-outs of the newspaper reports. Presentation software is used to prepare a graphic report, which is sent to a large viewing screen in the crisis-control meetingroom, updated instantly as coverage on the crisis is released.

Media outlets receive alerts and updates at least daily via broadcast fax. Morning briefings for media are scheduled every day as officials begin implementing plans to deal with the violence. Simultaneous, interactive teletraining sessions for school personnel, using experts from across the country, are held at all campuses of the district.

A local university offering on-location psychology clinics for crisis situations—using graduate students in training for clinical certification—offers pro bono services to area schools impacted by the violence. Electronic media kits on the project are transmitted to key media outlets across the country, with photos and biographies of key participants. Psychology professors of the university are used as expert resources for televised interviews.

A special electronic circuit carries releases and editorials submitted by gun-control activists and lobbyists in the press galleries of both the state capitol and Washington's House and Senate press galleries.

Example 2

A major midwestern university is planning to build a science laboratory and work farm on a part of their campus considered "environmentally sensitive." Identifying the history of the issues involved and the potential impact of the situation on university image is a key concern of the president and her vice president for university advancement.

Databases covering media, journals, books, and government documents worldwide are scanned for relevant historical information and reports on related environmental issues. Previous university-related coverage is also scanned. The electronic vigil also monitors the situation daily as it unfolds.

Similar retrieval and reporting techniques used in Example 1 above are applicable here. In addition, sophisticated statistical software eases the process of content analysis so that human energy can be devoted to weighing implications, strategic planning, and reporting.

The university has a standard policy of cooperation and openness with media, a policy that is threatened as the issues become more sensitive. Since the university is committed to doing whatever is necessary to avoid damaging the environment with this project, public relations strategy links environmental control agencies, activist groups, university science faculty, construction engineers, and media together as a national "think tank" to aid in planning and to maintain the university's policy of open communication.

After a three-day conference is held near the site of the proposed construction, participants are linked via satellite in biweekly interactive teleconferences. Media alerts and articles, complete with color photos, are sent via satellite technology to hundreds of media outlets.

As the plan of action unfolds, all aspects of the project are controlled via project management software. Every morning, administrators involved with the project can view progress on screen, with the day's activities and plans—including meetings, correspondence, and other responsibilities—"announced" at the top of the screen. The previous day's media coverage, correspondence from constituents, and other communications are available by verbal command, retrieved from the on-campus computer network. Confidential information is controlled by the system's "need-to-know" password or voice-recognition system. Within a few minutes, administrators are updated on the project without encroaching on other responsibilities of running a major university.

THE PROMISES AND PROBLEMS OF EMERGING TECHNOLOGY FOR PR

Consider the following promises and problems of emerging technology for public relations.

Promise.   Globalization and transient lifestyles allow for a high level of mobility among our publics, making it difficult to stay in touch. Improved technology provides the resources to maintain contact and to use this trend—seen as a hindrance to consistent communication with constituents—to advantage.

Promise and Problem.   The concepts of time and speed have been transformed with emerging technology. Maintaining contact with constituencies, particularly for colleges and universities with international programs and/or international clientele, demands a twenty-four-hour vigil. Improved technology turns this dilemma into a manageable, albeit threatening essential.

Problem.   Because technology and competition have increased the demands of constituents, instant communication becomes the expectation rather than the exception, increasing the potential for burnout for the professional.

Problem.   The demand for instantaneous communication creates the opportunity for instantaneous *miscommunication*. Public relations professionals must take care to live by the rule that just because it *can* be broadcast in two minutes does not mean that it *should* be or that it is *ready* to be broadcast.

Promise and Problem.   Technology is creating the ultimate in specialization, redefining the target audience as the target individual. While this trend promises greater opportunity for targeting the right message to the right audience, it forces the public relations professional to fight against ultracomplexity in campaign planning, which can be costly and time-consuming and further increases the chances of burnout. On the bright side, the very nature of technology is to manage complexity with more efficiency, providing a window of escape for the thoughtful, strategic planner.

Promise.   Computers. Even though computer technology is incredibly sophisticated today, its ultimate potential is impossible to predict. It is clear, however, that as a resource for public relations, the computer will remain at the top of the list far into the twenty-first century.

Problem.   The potential of computers as a priceless tool in public relations lies solely in the ability and tenacity of the public relations professional to understand, command, and strategically use its potential. Those who refuse to adapt will suffer the consequences of any species unwilling or unable to adapt to its environment: extinction.

Promise.   The need for public relations professionals to be good communicators, both in written and oral communication, will not diminish with the transformation of technology. Computers will not make better communicators out of poor communicators, unless there is a willingness to learn. With the dramatic increase in the quantity of messages generated through upgraded technology channels, the need for well-conceived messages will increase, not decrease, in value. In this sense, the call in the twenty-first century will be "The message is the message," a call that should be welcomed with great enthusiasm.

Promise.   Forecasting will become more than a luxury in the most effective offices. No field will feel this trend more critically than will secondary and higher education, which is undergoing significant transformation even today. Technology improvements will create immediate feedback and provide opportunity for instantaneous analysis—highly valuable resources in proactive, strategic public relations planning. The result will be healthier institutions and a stronger system of education.

Promise.   Improved research techniques will be at the disposal of every professional. The ability to determine audience opinions and attitudes using many clearly defined variables will be available in new versions of user-friendly research software. Additionally, professionals will be able to conduct *nuance* evaluations by incorporating quantitative and qualitative research techniques. The effective professionals will use research as a standard aid in planning.

SUMMARY

The power of technology is humbling, especially when its potential is limited only by our ability to dream and to adapt to change. As the drama of emerging technology for public relations continues to unfold, the debate on its benefits and downsides will be ongoing. Current evidence suggests that the promises far outweigh the problems.

The caution is that we learn how to control its power to meet targeted objectives. If the means by which we do our business ever becomes more important than the ends we seek, our organizations, like the proverbial dog at the mercy of his tail, will suffer from what our constituents will view as serious misdirection and lack of focus.

CASE STUDY   **Pepperdine University and the Global Technology Initiative**

Pepperdine University is an independent, medium-sized university enrolling approximately 7000 students in four colleges and schools. The university's undergraduate Seaver College and the School of Law are located on 830 acres overlooking the Pacific Ocean at Malibu, California. The Graduate School of Education and Psychology and the School of Business and Management are based in West Los Angeles, with three additional branch locations. Full-time international campuses are located in Heidelberg, London, Florence, and Tokyo. Additional short-term programs are offered at strategic locations throughout the world.

Pepperdine University is engaged in a $300 million capital campaign that will conclude in 1999. A priority goal of the campaign is to fund a $3 million global technology initiative. The objective of the initiative is to restructure the university's communication network at all of its campuses worldwide to take advantage of emerging technology provided by the information highway.

Major areas impacted by this initiative include:

1. University Relations, that is, alumni affairs, community relations, fund raising and donor relations, public information, publications
2. Undergraduate/Graduate Domestic and International Academic Programs, that is, admissions, faculty, instruction, internship programs, libraries
3. Management and Financial Accounting, that is, administration, financial aid, university finance and student accounts
4. Interoffice networks

Beginning in 1985, Pepperdine initiated energetic plans to phase in computerization in its academic, administrative, and operations areas. Electronic mail services and other networking capabilities were added in later years. Additionally, student housing was retrofitted so that students could electronically access university library databases.

Today every faculty and staff office on domestic campuses is computerized. Faculty and administrative offices are linked via the network and electronic mail systems, and selected users have access to finance, admissions, and development records databases. International campuses are computerized in their main administrative offices. Most offices universitywide have direct access to fax machines, including the administration offices of all international campuses.

With the basic structure in place, the university is prepared to launch the next phase of the program, the Global Technology Initiative. This plan proposes opportunities for real-time distance learning via satellite from locations throughout the world and direct linkages via the information highway to electronic databases relevant to the many areas of academic and administrative interest.

An area considered a priority by the university for significant technological upgrading is the public information office. Presently, the university has a three-person full-time staff and several student interns in public information. The operation is supported by writers who work primarily in periodicals offices at each of the four university schools. Additionally, a public relations firm is under contract to assist with national media, community relations, and general university public relations.

The public information office is computerized and linked to the university network, has access to a multidepartment fax machine, and has limited access to electronic resources outside the university. The office, which is responsible for all university media coverage worldwide, employs a clipping service and occasionally uses a firm specializing in broadcast fax services for limited releases.

Upgrading the public information office will be one of the first goals of the new Global Technology Initiative.

QUESTIONS AND SUGGESTED ACTIVITIES

Case Study

1. How would you rate the public information office's ability, as it is presently designed, to take full advantage of the information highway for the benefit of the university?
2. If you were responsible for upgrading the public information office as a part of the university's Global Technology Initiative, how would you establish need and what would be the elements of your proposal?
3. Would you recommend a complete upgrade of the office to current state-of-the-art standards, or would you recommend a phased upgrade, taking advantage of new technology as it is released? Why?
4. In terms of personnel, would you recommend additions to the staff? If so, how so? If not, why not?
5. Prepare a written proposal defending a detailed plan to upgrade the university's public information office. Be specific and support your proposal with research from other similar institutions.
6. Identify the pros and cons of both a centralized management approach, where all public information efforts flow from one central office, and a decentralized approach, where the university maintains a small main office with branch public information departments at each of its graduate schools. In the decentralized approach, the undergraduate school would be the responsibility of the main office.

Chapter

7. Review Example 1 in this chapter. Then interview the director of public relations of a large school district in your region to determine how well prepared they are to respond to a similar crisis. Present the results of your analysis in a formal report.

SUGGESTED READINGS

Bollentin, W. R. (Ed.). (1993). All articles referenced. *Educom Review, 28*(3).

Bovet, S. F. (Ed.). (1992). Discovering databases: On-line services put research at practitioner's fingertips. *Public Relations Journal, 48*(11), 2.

Brzezinski, Z. (1993). *Out of control: Global turmoil on the eve of the 21st century.* New York: Macmillan.

Cetron, M., & Davies, O. (1989). *American renaissance: Our life at the turn of the 21st century.* New York: St. Martin's Press.

Cetron, M., & Gayle, M. (1991). *Educational renaissance: Our schools at the turn of the 21st century.* New York: St. Martin's Press.

Educom. (1993). Expanding the information highway debated at national NET'93. *Educom Update, 2*(3), 2.

Hauss, D. (1993). Measuring the impact of public relations: Electronic research techniques improve campaign evaluation. *Public Relations Journal, 49*(2), 14–21.

Kelly, K. S. (1991). *Fund raising and public relations: A critical analysis.* Hillsdale, N J: L. Earlbaum & Associates.

Paul, R., & Binker, A. J. A. (Eds.). (1992). *Critical thinking: What every person needs to survive in a rapidly changing world.* Santa Rosa, CA: Foundation for Critical Thinking.

Shell, A. (1994). A map of the information highway. *Public Relations Journal, 50*(1), 27.

Toffler, A. (1970). *Future shock.* New York: Random House.

Wiesendanger, B. (1994). Plug into a world of information: Use technology to deliver messages and monitor impact. *Public Relations Journal, 50*(2), 20–23.

Wingspread Group on Higher Education. (1993). *An American imperative: higher expectations for higher education.* Washington, DC: Johnson Foundation.

REFERENCES

Bernays, E. L. (1923, 1961). *Crystallizing public opinion.* New York: Liveright Publishing.

Bovet, S. F. (Ed.). (1992). Discovering databases: On-line services put research at practitioner's fingertips. *Public Relations Journal, 48*(11), 2.

Cetron, M., & Davies, O. (1989). *American renaissance: Our life at the turn of the 21st century.* New York: St. Martin's Press.

Cetron, M., & Gayle, M. (1991). *Educational renaissance: Our schools at the turn of the 21st century.* New York: St. Martin's Press.

Festinger, L., & Schramm, W. (Ed.). (1963). The theory of cognitive dissonance (pp. 17–27). *The science of human communication.* New York: Basic Books.

Grunig, J. E., & Hunt, T. (1984). *Managing public relations.* New York: Holt, Rinehart and Winston.

Kelly, K. S. (1991). *Fund raising and public relations: A critical analysis.* Hillsdale, N J: L. Earlbaum & Associates.

Newsom, D., Scott, A., & Turk, J. V. (1993). This is PR: *The realities of public relations.* Florence, KY: Wadsworth.

Seitel, F. P. (1995). *The practice of public relations.* Englewood Cliffs, N J: Prentice Hall.

Toffler, A. (1970). *Future shock.* New York: Random House.

Walker, P. A. (1992). Forecast 1992. *Public Relations Journal, 47*(1), 19.

Wingspread Group on Higher Education. (1993). *An American imperative: higher expectations for higher education.* Washington, DC: Johnson Foundation.

CHAPTER 6

Legal and Ethical Aspects
of Public Relations

Joseph R. McKinney

Court decisions over the past four decades have set in motion social changes that have fundamentally altered the relationship between public schools and the communities they serve. Supreme Court decisions concerning school desegregation, the role of religion in the schools, the rights and freedoms of teachers and students, race discrimination, sex discrimination, the rights of individuals with disabilities, and the teaching of values have had important and lasting ramifications for the larger society. The increased role of the courts in education has drawn much comment from legal and education scholars. In *School Days, Rule Days*, Kirp and Jensen (1986) refer to the substantial involvement of the judiciary in shaping school affairs as the "legalization" of education. In *Law and the Shaping of Public Education*, Tyack, James, and Benevot (1987) document the dramatic increase in litigation and the heavy reliance on the courts in shaping American educational policy since World War II.

The field of school-community relations, which dates to the 1920s, is guided and informed today by the law both in policy making and practice. To understand the relationship between both case and statutory law and school-community relations we must first identify the contemporary view and practice of school-community relations. Albert E. Holliday (1988) defines school-community relations (and school public relations) as "a systematic function on all levels of a school system, established as a program to improve and maintain optimal levels of student achievement, and to build public support" (p. 12). Kindred, Bagin, and Gallagher (1990) define educational-community relations this way: "Educational public relations is management's systematic, continuous, two-way, honest communication between an educational organization and its publics" (p. 15). Philip West (1985) explains that the province of educational public relations consists of "essentially a blending of two elements: communications and human relations" (p. 45).

Who is involved in blending communication and human relations in the context of school-community relations? The literature of school-community relations is replete with references to communication between educational organizations and internal and external constituencies or publics. (See, for example, Bagin, Gallagher, & Kindred, 1994; and West, 1985.) The *internal* public generally consists of school board members, school administrators, teachers, all other school employees, and students. *External* publics variously include parents, nonparents, volunteers, parent-teacher groups, the media, the business community, community groups, special interest groups, politicians, and, to a certain extent, collective bargaining units. Schools interact with these publics in different forms and activities, and the law accordingly touches on individual school-community relations programs in ways that reflect the differences in school-community relations activities. Schools overlooking the significance of the legal aspects of school-community relations not only face the risk of financial liability for running afoul of the law but also stumble in failing to educate and lead their many publics in understanding the importance of safeguarding America's democratic values and individual constitutional rights.

THE VARIETY AND VOLUME OF LITIGATION AFFECTING SCHOOL-COMMUNITY RELATIONS

Studies available to date on litigation rates in education indicate the extent and pervasiveness of the impact of the law on school-community relations. Most studies are based on analyzing reported (published) judicial decisions. The general conclusion that emerges from these studies is that the total amount of education-related litigation greatly increased from the 1960s to the middle 1970s, then decreased modestly from 1977 to 1987—mainly because of a decrease in new school desegregation filings. But litigation rates remain today at historically high levels. Imber and Thompson (1991) estimated, on the basis of their study, that in any one year one lawsuit is filed against a school in the United States for every 3500 students attending public school.

And the litigation rates in many categories of school law, including those particularly affecting school-community relations, have significantly increased in recent years. These include such suits as those related to the rights of individuals with disabilities, negligence, and equity in funding (Imber & Gaylor, 1991). Other areas of school law with rising litigation rates affecting school-community relations are search and seizure suits, church-state cases filed in federal courts, challenges to the curriculum, and suits by outsiders.

The empirical studies of education-related litigation do not begin to fully capture the legal ramifications associated with school-community relations (or any other educational practices). Most studies are based on actual lawsuits filed against school districts and do not consider threatened or potential lawsuits. Another complicating factor is that many legal challenges are brought pursuant to extrajudicial or alternative dispute procedures. These alternative forums to court proceedings include local and state grievance procedures (often personnel-related), administrative procedures, and challenges brought directly to a local school board. And of course, schools must comply with a complex body of federal and state statutes and regulations. The picture of the volume and variety of litigation related to school-community relations is not complete without taking these factors into account.

DESEGREGATION AND THE SCHOOLS

The Supreme Court decision in *Brown v Board of Education* (1954) stands as the most important case ever in terms of judicial impact on school-community relations. In *Brown* (1954), the court ruled the separate-but-equal doctrine unconstitutional but established no remedy for desegregating the public schools. In *Brown II* (1955), the Supreme Court fashioned an ambiguous remedy when it declared that school desegregation would proceed with all deliberate speed. The Court left to the local schools and communities the responsibility of desegregation. Almost every facet of school operations touching on school-community relations was covered by the *Brown II* (1955) decision: "problems related to administration, arising from the physical condition of the school plant, the school transportation system, personnel, revision of school districts and attendance areas" (p. 295). The resistance to school desegregation is well documented elsewhere, and a recitation of its long history is not necessary or possible here. As Alexander and Alexander (1992) explain, "[O]ver a generation after *Brown*, judicial decisions are still required to settle social and legal issues emanating from the circumstances surrounding desegregation" (p. 417). Desegregation cases exemplify the interplay of communities, schools, and the law. Where progress in school desegregation has been made since *Brown*, it has been achieved only as a result of open two-way communication between schools, their many publics, and the courts.

LIABILITY TORTS

A school district's greatest exposure to lawsuits in the context of school-community relations lies in the category of tort law. In attempting to build and maintain effective relationships with its many publics, a school must find ways to generate community participation. Increasing the flow of information among internal and external publics and involving the community in the education enterprise through increased participation in school and school-related community functions carries many benefits, but it also carries increased legal risks.

In an action based in tort against a school district, the injured party seeks a judgment holding the school district and/or a school employee responsible for the consequence of a wrongdoing. By allowing compensation for injuries sustained by individuals in school, tort law requires schools to take appropriate steps to provide for a safe and orderly environment. Tort law imposes liability on schools for injury or harm to individuals using the school, including students, parents, and outsiders injured at school. There are three major categories of tort law: (1) negligence; (2) intentional torts, including defamation; and (3) strict liability. The categories of negligence and intentional torts are relevant to school-community relations.

Negligence

The most prevalent tort action involving schools and school personnel is negligence. Negligence may be defined as conduct falling below an established standard fixed and imposed upon the parties by the law, common or statutory, that results in injury (Keeton, Dobbs, Keeton, & Owen, 1984, p. 288). Negligence encompasses all human behavior. The commonly employed test used by the courts to determine negligence is grounded in the nature of a formula created by the courts, which have created a hypothetical person who "has never existed on land or sea: the reasonable man of ordinary prudence" (Keeton, Dobbs, Keeton, & Owen, 1984, p. 174). The "reasonable" person conducts himself or herself in an ideal manner; he or she is a community standard. Although the reasonable person operates as a community model, his or her conduct varies appropriately with the circumstances under which he or she acts. In a negligence lawsuit the question becomes Would the reasonable person have been expected to foresee, and as a result, to have been able to take action to prevent the injury that occurred? An affirmative answer to the question suggests that the defendant in a negligence action was negligent.

There are four elements in a cause of action for negligence:

1. There must be duty of care between the plaintiff and the defendant.
2. There must be breach of the duty of care by the defendant.
3. The defendant's breach of duty must have been the proximate cause of the resultant injury to the plaintiff.
4. The plaintiff must have suffered actual loss or damage as a result of the injury. For liability to be proven, all four elements must be shown by the plaintiff.

Adequate Supervision in the Use of School Facilities.   An effective school-community relations program will encourage the use of school facilities and school visits by citizens of the community. Making the school available for community use builds confidence in school personnel and programs and assists the school in gaining financial support. In a more global sense, "[A]llowing people to use the buildings is consistent with the function of the school as a social institution and is clearly a service in the public interest" (Bagin, Gallagher, & Kindred, 1994, p. 177).

School personnel have a duty to maintain school buildings and grounds and equipment in proper condition. A school corporation will be held liable to an injured person if it knew or should have known of an unreasonably dangerous or hazardous condition at the school and failed to take steps to eliminate the danger. Courts impose a high standard for the proper maintenance of school facilities and equipment, and concomitantly the judiciary has looked favorably on schools that have developed preventive maintenance programs that provide for regular facility and equipment inspection.

Within the general framework of negligence tort liability as discussed above, most states have developed special liability rules concerning owners and possessors of property and buildings and their duty toward occupiers of the property (premises liability). Individuals who enter upon the property of another are legally classified according to the level of duty owed them as either trespassers, licensees, or invitees. A "trespasser" is an individual who enters upon the property of another without a privilege to do so or without consent from the possessor. A "licensee" is a person who enters upon the property of another with permission (express or implied). An "invitee" is defined as an individual who is invited (express or implied) to enter and remain on the premises of another for a particular reason. Invitees include individuals on premises as members of the public for purposes for which the property is held open to the public. (See American Law Institute, 1986.)

Traditionally, most individuals entering a school who are not students, parents, or employees are considered to be licensees. Licensees include community groups and organizations using the school facility for meeting purposes. A school district only owes a licensee a duty to be warned of concealed dangerous conditions of which the school district has actual knowledge. A school district owes a greater degree of care to an invitee than it does to a licensee. School districts that open the doors to their facilities to external groups and individuals run the risk of creating invitees out of groups traditionally characterized as licensees. A school district owes an invitee a duty to exercise reasonable care for his or her safety and to take reasonable steps, including regular inspection of the premises, to make sure the premises are safe for the invitee. This heightened duty to invitees means in practical terms that school districts must, among other things, be vigilant in mopping and drying slippery floors, in removing dangerous snow and ice from entrances and sidewalks, in adequately lighting halls and parking lots, and in providing or increasing security measures when attacks on school invitees are foreseeable. These precautions are generally met when school is in session, but they become problematic when a school not in session allows community groups to use its facilities as part of a school-community relations program.

What constitutes due care and adequate supervision depends largely upon the circumstances surrounding an injury. The traditional standard of care and supervision applicable in most situations is the level of care and supervision an ordinary prudent person would exercise under the circumstances. However, when on the job supervising students, school personnel are held to a higher standard of care and supervision than is the ordinary, reasonably prudent person. In general, school district liability for injuries sustained to individuals other than students will be decided within the framework of the general and special (premises liability) tort liability framework.

Adequate Supervision and Violence in the Schools.   Violence in American schools is a significant problem. In a 1993 survey conducted by the National School Boards Association (NSBA) titled "Violence in the Schools," 82 percent of the 720 school officials responding said that school violence had increased in the past five years and 35 percent of the respondents reported that violence had risen significantly. NSBA officials called for parent and community involvement in curbing school violence. School authorities have a legal obligation to maintain safe and violence-free environments. The duty to provide adequate supervision and security extends to parents and citizens invited to school. School officials should go on the offensive and take proper precautionary action if assaults on school personnel, students, and members of the community using the school are reasonably foreseeable. These safety measures might include warning the public, beefing up on-campus security, increasing crowd control at sporting events, keeping all but the front door to the school locked, installing metal detectors (in the worst situations), and establishing mentoring programs. The legal reasoning applied in school violence cases appears to be grounded in whether or not a school could reasonably have foreseen the violence and prevented the injury under all the circumstances of the case.

Many school districts attempt to get nonparents involved in the schools through volunteer programs. Schools often invite senior citizens and others to read to students, eat lunch with students, and volunteer in the library. A school district that utilizes volunteer activities exposes itself to liability for the tortious acts of volunteers. Schools may want to consider personal background checks on volunteers engaged in long-term programs.

Defenses against Negligence.   Several defenses against liability are available to educators. The most common defenses are contributory negligence, assumption of the risk, and governmental immunity. In order to prove contributory negligence, a school district must demonstrate that the plaintiff (the party filing the suit) failed to exercise reasonable care for his or her own safety and that that failure contributed to the plaintiff's own injury. Contributory negligence is a potent defense for educators because, if shown, the defense totally excuses a school district from liability. Because of the harshness of the "complete bar to recovery" rule of contributory negligence, the majority of states have adopted the defense of comparative negligence, which permits damages to be apportioned according to the assessed degrees of fault of all parties. However, in some states where comparative negligence has replaced contributory negligence, the comparative fault provisions do not apply to tort claims brought against government entities, including school districts.

Another defense available to schools is the defense of *assumption of the risk.* It involves a plaintiff's consent or voluntary acceptance (express or implied) of a specific risk or danger of which the plaintiff has actual knowledge. Assumption of the risk operates to relieve a school district of liability even if the risk or danger has been created by the school district. The doctrine of assumption of the risk has been frequently and successfully raised in the sports-injury arena. In a number of cases against school districts where damages were requested for injuries that were allegedly sustained by spectators and other members of the community as a result of actions by players or other spectators at sporting events sponsored by schools, recovery has been denied on the basis of assumption of the risk. School districts have successfully used the defense of assumption of the risk in circumstances where spectators were struck by batted or thrown baseballs, struck by football players executing plays, knocked down by children (also spectators) engaged in horseplay, and struck by a tennis ball while watching a match. (See Korpela, 1971.)

Prior to the 1970s, litigation against public schools and most government entities was limited or entirely prohibited by the doctrine of immunity. *Governmental immunity* in America is based largely on English common law, exemplified by the ancient maxim that "the king can do no wrong." The prevailing doctrine in the United States has been that both the state and federal government are immune for torts committed by their officers and employees unless the government consents to such liability. The doctrine of sovereign immunity was traditionally extended to school districts in most states for injuries to individuals that were caused by the negligent acts of governmental employees. However, today in more than half of the states, the doctrine of governmental immunity for torts has been eliminated or substantially diminished by legislation or judicial actions (McCarthy & Cambron-McCabe, 1992).

In many states where governmental immunity does not protect school districts from tort liability, state legislatures have passed legislation that limits the amount of damages an injured party may recover as compensation for losses as a result of governmental negligence. Many states also allow school districts to purchase liability insurance that covers the school district and its employees from being held personally liable for damage awards. Moreover, several states have passed statutes (tort claim acts) that must be complied with as a prerequisite to recovery by anyone claiming an injury as a result of governmental negligence.

Protection of educators against personal liability varies among the states. Traditionally, states have made a distinction, for tort liability purposes, between whether the educator was performing a ministerial function or a discretionary function. States permit immunity for torts committed while performing discretionary acts but hold school personnel responsible for the ministerial actions. "Discretionary actions" involve the exercise of professional judgment, formulation of school policy, setting of goals and planning. "Ministerial activities" involve compliance with mandates of legal authority not requiring the exercise of judgment.

As a last resort, to protect against financial ruin, schools can purchase adequate insurance coverage. Drake and Roe (1994) suggest that school districts purchase all-risk property insurance, comprehensive liability insurance, and errors and omissions liability insurance for teachers, administrators, and school board members.

Defamation

The tort that most directly touches on all aspects of school-community relations is defamation. The law of defamation, like school-community relations, is centered on communication. *Defamation* consists of the twin torts of libel and slander. *Slander* is spoken defamation, and *libel* is written defamation. Defamation is an injury or invasion of a person's interest in his or her good reputation, name, and character by a false and defamatory communication concerning the person (*Restatement of Torts, Second,* 558, American Law Institute).

In seeking to keep the community informed about their programs, needs, and problems, schools use various communication tools. Since school-community relations is properly viewed as a two-way communication process, citizens are encouraged to discuss school issues and even criticize school policy where appropriate. All of these interactions between the school and the community open the door to misinformation, propaganda, and false statements.

Cases involving alleged defamatory communication among parents, students, citizens, and school authorities concerning school matters have been the subject of defamation suits. But proving a defamation action is quite difficult. Effective defenses are available to school personnel who become defendants in defamation actions. Of course, a defamatory statement that is true is not actionable in a defamation suit.

Defenses against Defamation.   An absolute privilege completely excuses a defamatory statement. It is usually accorded speech made in legislative, judicial, or executive proceedings. Such statements are protected if made in the performance of legitimate public duties (Restatement of Torts, Second, 590, American Law Institute). Statements made by school board members and superintendents in the course of evaluating school personnel or investigations into wrongdoing are often protected by an absolute privilege. (They are certainly protected by a qualified privilege.)

A *conditional* or *qualified privilege* excuses defamatory speech made in good faith and without malice. It has been used extensively as a defense by school personnel. The qualified privilege arises from common law and is pertinent to communications between parties sharing an interest or duty, including school personnel. The judiciary has noted the public's interest in education and has extended the qualified privilege to teachers engaged in evaluating students and to school administrators communicating information about teacher performance. Parents also have available the defense of qualified privilege when communicating about teacher performance and other matters directly bearing on the welfare of their children at school.

The Supreme Court in *New York Times, Inc. v Sullivan* (1964) ruled that the First Amendment requires that a "public official" who files a defamation suit against critics (for example, individuals or the press) of his or her "official conduct" must show that the defamatory statements were made with "actual malice" and that the defendant(s) made the statements with knowledge of their falsity or with reckless disregard of whether they were true or false. The courts have been divided on the issue of whether school administrators and teachers who have been defamed are public officials within the meaning of *Sullivan*. The judicial trend has been toward not considering administrators and teachers public officials. However, school board members and superintendents have been considered public figures (Alexander & Alexander, 1992). When viewed as private citizens, teachers need only to prove that defamatory statements made against them are untruthful.

In disseminating information about the school to the community through the mass media the *Sullivan* (1964) rules concerning defamatory communication are applicable. After *Sullivan*, defamation liability is extremely difficult to prove against the media when the defamatory communication concerns a public figure or official. This in no way obviates a school from practicing honest, well-researched journalism.

CONSTITUTIONAL TORTS

Many of the school-community relations issues facing contemporary educators touch on some aspect of constitutional law. Issues related to the freedoms of speech, religion, assembly and the press; voting rights; and invasion of privacy, due process, and equal protection rights are some of the more frequent and important constitutionally protected rights that come into play in school-community relations. School districts that interfere with the federal constitutional rights of individuals may be liable to the party injured in an action known as a "constitutional tort." Constitutional torts protect and secure individual rights under the U.S. Constitution from being interfered with by the state. Schools have witnessed dramatic increases in the number of constitutional tort actions brought against them. The legal authority for maintaining a constitutional tort against a school district is found in the Civil Rights Act of 1871, which was codified in the federal laws as Title 42 of the United States Code shortly after the Civil War. Congress intended that awards under the Civil Rights Act of 1871 would deter the deprivation of the constitutional rights of newly freed black citizens.

The most prevalent statute under Title 42 used by plaintiffs to bring constitutional tort actions against school districts is 42 U.S.C.S. 1983. Section 1983 provides in part: "Every person who, under color of any statute, ordinance, regulation, custom or usage, of any state or Territory . . . subjects or causes to be subjected any citizen of the United States or other person within the jurisdiction thereof to the deprivation of any rights, privileges, or immunities secured by the Constitution and laws shall be liable to the party injured in an action at law" (42 U.S.C. 1983, 1988).

In *Monell v Department of Social Services of New York* (1978), the Supreme Court held that Section 1983 suits could be brought against government units like school boards. However, the Court held that governmental bodies cannot be held liable under Section 1983 on a respondeat superior theory whereby employers are liable for the acts of their employees. Therefore school districts are liable under Section 1983 for a constitutional wrong committed by an employee only when the actions represent well-established custom or official policy of the school district.

In *Wood v Strickland* (1975), a case involving student discipline, the Supreme Court held that individuals, including school board members, could be held liable for committing constitutional torts. Before *Wood v Strickland* school employees had been completely immune from Section 1983 actions. However, in *Wood*, the Supreme Court granted school employees a "good faith immunity." The Court said that a school board member or school employee loses the immunity and may be liable for damages under Section 1983 if "he knew or reasonably should have known that the action he took within his sphere of official responsibility would violate the constitution rights of the student affected" (*Wood*, p. 322). In *Harlow v Fitzgerald* (1982), the Court explained that as long as a school employee's action does not "violate clearly established statutory or constitutional rights of which a reasonable person would have known" (p. 818) he or she will not be held liable under Section 1983.

Political Speech

Teachers and other school employees play a central role in a school-community relations program. Bagin, Gallagher, and Kindred (1994) maintain that a strong external communication program is impossible without the support and participation of school employees. Positive employee relations depend on a school's recognizing human needs in order to build a community spirit among school employees. High morale among employees is associated with a strong school-community relations plan. Teachers should feel free to express themselves on matters related to the welfare of the school. However, school employees cannot be expected to always agree with school leaders or school policy. Sometimes what a teacher believes to be constructive criticism is viewed by school administrators as insubordinate behavior.

Prior to the 1960s, public employment, including the employment of teachers, was considered a privilege rather than a right. Accordingly, teachers were expected to limit and give away their First Amendment rights to their employers. However, during the 1960s, with the public's attention focused on individual rights, the courts determined that the "privilege doctrine" was inappropriate, and the relationship between teachers and school boards began to change (Alexander & Alexander, 1992). The U.S. Supreme Court in *Pickering v Board of Education of Township High School District 205* (1968) established the legal principle that public school teachers have the First Amendment right of freedom of expression. In *Pickering*, a school board terminated the employment of a teacher for writing a letter to a local newspaper that was published, criticizing the school superintendent and school board for spending school funds on athletic programs and neglecting to inform the district taxpayers of their decisions. The Supreme Court applied a "balance of interests" test in determining that the teacher's letter did not disrupt the orderly educational process. The Court struck the balance in favor of the teacher, recognizing the right of teachers as citizens to express their views on matters of public concern. However, a teacher's right of speech and expression is not of unlimited scope. If a teacher's comments seriously damage the relationship between employer and employee—or are deliberately or recklessly false or seriously impede the educational mission of the school—then the exercise of such speech may be grounds for dismissal. However, the burden of proving any of these matters rests with the school district.

Where an educator's First Amendment right is at issue, the judiciary uses a three-step analysis. The court must first determine if the teacher's speech is constitutionally protected. Here the court determines whether the statements made by the teacher, taken as a whole, are on a matter of public concern. Second, a court must ascertain whether the school board's dismissal was motivated by the teacher's exercise of his or her First Amendment rights. Third, the school district must be given an opportunity to demonstrate that it would have taken the same action in the absence of the teacher's constitutionally protected conduct.

Right of Privacy: The Teacher

Increased community participation and public interest in education results in a better understanding of community concerns and values. While this is most often positive in building the future of public schools, it can also cause legal problems for school districts. Certainly, schools belong to the community, but the concept of community ownership does not imply that the community can unilaterally impose its values and morality on the schools and their employees at the expense of individual constitutional rights. However, the courts recognize the role of community values and attitudes in the context of teacher employment.

Although the U.S. Constitution does not expressly mention privacy, the Supreme Court has interpreted the Constitution to include a fundamental right of privacy. A teacher's conduct outside of the classroom may be the basis for cancellation of a contract or disciplinary action. The problem in cases involving protection of personal privacy is to arrive at a balance among the privacy interests of the teacher, community morals, and the school's interest in maintaining an appropriate educational environment. Teachers have been discharged from public school employment for matters arising in their private lives that conflict with community sentiment.

Most states have tenure laws that variously set forth grounds for terminating a teacher's employment. One ground for dismissal that often leads to conflict between privacy rights and community values is commonly referred to as "immorality." In an often-cited case involving allegations of teacher immorality, the Pennsylvania Supreme Court defined immorality as "not essentially confined to a deviation from sex morality; it may be such a course of conduct as offends the morals of the community and is a bad example to the youth whose ideals a teacher is supposed to foster and to evaluate." (*Horosko v Mount Pleasant Township School District*, 1939, p. 868).

Immorality often involves matters related to teachers' sexual conduct. Courts have been almost unanimous in upholding teacher dismissals based on sexual involvement with students. Teachers are considered to be role models, and courts will not approve sexual activity with students. Teachers have been discharged for sexual conduct with nonstudents where there is a nexus between the teacher's behavior and an adverse impact on the school. Courts may consider community attitudes with respect to a teacher's sexual activities and the ability to satisfactorily carry out his or her teaching duties. In a small rural community in South Dakota a teacher was discharged for immorality for openly living with her boyfriend (*Sullivan v Meade Independent School District No. 101*, 1976). The court upheld the dismissal because the teacher violated local mores. In addition, she was popular with her students, making it likely they would imitate her behavior. However, a Florida court held that sexual relationships involving consenting adults may not constitute immorality where the activity takes place away from school and a teacher's ability to satisfactorily carry out his or her professional responsibilities is not impaired (*Sherburne v School Board of Suwannee Co.*, 1984).

Teachers have been dismissed for homosexual conduct with nonstudents. Generally, courts have required proof of a negative impact on a teacher's effectiveness in teaching stemming from the teacher's homosexual conduct. If the homosexual conduct does not adversely affect students, other teachers, or the learning environment, then the teacher may not be dismissed.

School boards have dismissed teachers who are unwed and pregnant. Generally, the courts have held that dismissal of unwed, pregnant teachers is impermissible because it violates a teacher's privacy rights and the Fourteenth Amendment.

Right of Privacy: The Student

The news media often seeks information from school employees, especially in crisis situations involving students. Controversial news stories about students involved in criminal activities or students with AIDS attending school have recently attracted the attention of the news media. In these situations the student's right of privacy must prevail over the public's right to know. Information contained in student records pertaining to health, family background, and serious disciplinary problems cannot be released to the public (20 U.S.C. 1232g, 1988).

In 1974, on the basis of widespread allegations of abuse and misuse of student records, Congress enacted the Family Educational Rights and Privacy Act (FERPA), which is commonly referred to as the Buckley Amendment. The handling of student records by school officials was criticized on several grounds, including the release of information to third parties—such as police, news media, social service agencies, and vendors—without the consent of parents, failure to provide parents with access to records, and maintenance of inaccurate records. In response, Congress passed legislation that provided substantive and procedural safeguards for the privacy rights of students and their parents. FERPA grants parents, and students upon attaining 18 years of age, a legal right of access to student records. Within a reasonable period of time from their request, parents must be allowed to inspect and review (and make copies of at their own expense) all records directly related to their child. In no event may the school stall for more than forty-five days from the parent's initial request for records. With respect to inaccurate records, FERPA provides parents with an avenue to amend records, and if not satisfied, parents may request an impartial hearing on the issue. Parents may also file complaints concerning violations of FERPA with the Department of Education. Schools found not in compliance with FERPA face the ultimate sanction of losing federal aid.

FERPA mandates that most information contained in student records be kept confidential. Personally identifiable information contained in school records may be released only with written consent from the student's parents. The most common exception to the rules regarding confidentiality is that student records may be made available to school officials, including teachers within the school district where the child attends school, who have legitimate educational interests in the student. Schools must keep a record of individuals and agencies who are given access to the records of a student. Under FERPA, public schools may release general information to the public, including a student's name, address, telephone listing, date and place of birth, major field of study, participation in activities and sports, dates of attendance, and degrees and awards received.

In addition to the privacy rights protected by FERPA, the Individuals with Disabilities Education Act (IDEA) contains specific confidentiality requirements covering the records of students with disabilities. Moreover, most states have enacted legislation according confidentiality rights in records containing personal information kept by state agencies, including public schools. In some instances state privacy statutes grant more privacy rights to students than does FERPA.

Religion, Community, and Public Schools

The relationship between religion and the public schools is an extremely important, delicate, and controversial issue in the context of school-community relations. Wide-ranging issues of community concern such as prayer, Bible reading, distribution of religious materials, student-initiated devotional meetings on school property, and the use of school facilities by religious groups are among the thorniest church-state separation issues confronting a school-community relations program. Many school systems have seen their school-community relations undermined and/or dominated by issues related to the role of religion in the public schools.

The First Amendment of the U.S. Constitution provides that "Congress shall make no law respecting an establishment of religion or prohibiting the free exercise thereof." The majority of church-state cases in the public education setting arise under this establishment clause.[11]

In most church-state cases since 1970 the Supreme Court has applied a three-part test derived from the Court's ruling in *Lemon v Kurtzman* (1971). Although the so-called *Lemon* test has been severely criticized by many of the current Supreme Court justices, the Court has not eliminated the test from establishment-clause adjudication. The tripartite test developed in *Lemon* is as follows: First, the governmental action or statute must have a secular purpose; second, its primary effect must neither advance nor inhibit religion; finally, the governmental action must avoid excessive governmental entanglement with religion.

In two landmark Supreme Court decisions in the early 1960s the Court struck down school-sponsored Bible reading and daily prayers. These decisions were controversial and unpopular with the general public. Supported by popular opinion, almost half the states enacted legislation permitting some form of prayer (silent meditation or voluntary prayer, for example) in the public schools. In *Wallace v Jaffree* (1985) the Court found an Alabama statute calling for a daily one-minute period of silence for meditation or prayer to violate the First Amendment. However, the Court suggested that a statute authorizing a moment of silence for meditation or prayer during the schoolday might pass constitutional muster if the state legislature's intent in passing the law was not motivated by a religious purpose.

One school-sponsored activity involving the entire community—graduation exercises—has turned into a hotbed of legal activity. In fact, a national debate over prayers at graduation ceremonies erupted after the Supreme Court, in *Lee v Weisman* (1992), struck down school arranged–clergy led benedictions and invocations at graduation ceremonies. The prayers contested in *Lee* were designated nondenominational and given by a local rabbi who was invited by the school principal. The Court found the active participation of school authorities in organizing the prayer, students' susceptibility to peer pressure, and the importance of graduation ceremonies to students ("coercive pressure" to attend) coalesced to create a violation of the "establishment clause." However, the Court left unresolved the constitutionality of student-organized and student-led prayers at graduation. Indeed, in 1993 the Supreme Court let stand a Texas high school policy that permitted student-initiated invocations and benedictions at graduation ceremonies (*Jones v Clear Creek Independent School District*, 1993).

Students and community groups and organizations often request the use of school facilities for religious purposes. Requests by students and community groups for the use of school facilities for meetings and other activities have been distinguished and treated differently by the judiciary. In 1990 the Supreme Court upheld the constitutionality of the Equal Access Act (passed by Congress in 1984), which permits student-initiated religious groups to meet on school premises during noninstructional time. If a public high school has at least one noncurriculum-related student group, then *Board of Education of Westside Community Schools v Mergens* (1990) holds that a school must recognize a wide array of groups, regardless of the philosophical, political, or religious content of their members' speech.

In *Lamb's Chapel v Center Moriches School District* (1993) the Supreme Court held that a school board's refusal to permit a church access to school facilities, after hours, to show a film series on family and child-rearing issues was unconstitutional. A close analysis of the case reveals that the Court ruled narrowly on the issue of public access to school facilities for religious purposes. David Schimmel (1993) summarized the implications of *Lamb's Chapel* for educators:

> (1) The First Amendment does not generally require public schools to allow outside groups to use their facilities. (2) If public schools allow some community groups to use their facilities after school hours to present films, speakers, or forums on one or more subjects, they cannot prohibit religious groups from presenting their views on the same subjects. Such viewpoint discrimination against a religious perspective (or any other legitimate perspective) is a violation of the Free Speech Clause of the First Amendment. (3) Nevertheless, public schools may restrict or prohibit religious speech or religious activities on their property, if necessary, to avoid violating the Establishment Clause. (p. 395)

One other volatile church-state separation issue involves the distribution of religious literature by students on school property. Beginning in the late 1980s, most courts have held that students have a free-speech right to distribute religious materials on school property. Schools maintain the right to set reasonable rules regarding the time, place, and manner of distribution of religious literature on school premises.

COMMUNITY VALUES AND THE CURRICULUM

One paradox of an effective school-community relations program is that increased community involvement in school affairs does not always result in agreement on school programs or school purposes. The tension between community values and attitudes and the goals and mission of the public schools is particularly felt in curricular decisions. Ralph Tyler (1949), known as the father of curriculum making, identified three major sources of the curriculum: society, learners, and knowledge. Curriculum makers must consider information, beliefs, and values from each source. Parents and interest groups aligned with myriad causes attempt to influence the curriculum, experiences, and information provided in public schools. The influence and efforts of special interest groups and organizations cannot be underestimated.

Reports of censorship in America's public schools has steadily increased for several years. Acccording to one study conducted during the 1992-1993 school year, 395 attempts to ban books, other curriculum materials, and educational approaches from classrooms occurred in forty-four states. This number represents an increase over the previous year's record high of 376. The censors were succcessful in 4l percent of the reported cases during 1992-1993. The states with the most censorship challenges during that year were California, Pennsylvania, Oregon, Texas, and Washington. Among the most frequently targeted areas: sex education, religious content, self-esteem curricula, books describing immoral activity, and outcomes-based education (People for the American Way, 1993).

One particular educational approach known as "outcomes-based education" (OBE) has been at the center of censorship controversy during the 1990s. Bill Zlatos (1993) reported that "All across America, the battle lines are drawn over OBE. From Pennsylvania to Washington, from Iowa to Oregon, hundreds of angry parents have jammed public hearings, and thousands of opponents have taken to the streets" (p. 12). What is OBE? While no single definition exists, at its core, OBE stands for the proposition that all students can learn. Zlatos summarized the many variations of OBE: "Its approach, in short, is to define clearly what students are to learn (the desired outcomes), measure their progress based on actual achievement, meet their needs through various teaching strategies, and give them enough time and help to meet their potential" (p. 13).

Twenty-four states have enacted some form of OBE as part of broader assessment and accountability reform programs. The most common approach to OBE is to develop sets of core outcome goals for specific academic areas, for such areas as self-esteem, ethical judgment, and tolerance, for skills in collaborating and in working alone—and to measure student progress locally. Critics of OBE claim that its costs are unknown and that the outcomes cannot be measured; religious groups claim that OBE promotes values and morals inconsistent with their religious beliefs.

Courts have granted local school leaders broad discretion to determine matters related to the school curriculum. However, the discretion granted to school authorities is not absolute; the courts also consider the constitutional rights of students, teachers, and parents. Most state legislatures have granted primary responsibility for public school education to local school boards, which generally have considerable power in regulating the instructional program. Local school authorities have broad powers concerning curriculum, textbooks, and other educational matters. But the Supreme Court made it clear in *Board of Education, Island Trees Union Free School District No. 26 v Pico* (1982) that books may not be removed from a school library by school officials if they are motivated by an intent to suppress or deny access to ideas with which they disagree. In *Pico* the Court maintained that school boards could remove books from a school library if motivated by the "pervasive vulgarity of the book," its "educational unsuitability," its "bad taste" or "irrelevance" or because of age and grade inappropriateness. Alexander and Alexander (1992) warn that the direction of the courts in the 1990s on issues related to the curriculum "appears to place less emphasis on a broadly conceived standard that secures the expansion of knowledge preventing the 'casting of a pall of orthodoxy' and allows more flexibility in allowing curriculum decisions to be made on the basis of local school board judgment and, possibly, local political pressure" (p. 245).

COPYRIGHT ISSUES

Every school-community relations program disseminates information about the school to the community through print and audio and visual media activities as well as through performances and school displays. Every school district uses and produces copyrighted work and must be aware of copyright law. The purpose of copyright law is to protect the ownership and use of original works of authorship. Copyright provides the creator of an original work control over many activities, including the right to reproduce, distribute, display, perform, adapt, and translate the work (17 U.S.C. 101, et. seq.).

Congress passed the Copyright Act of 1976, substantially amending the Copyright Act of 1909 that made copyright law a matter of federal law. Federal copyright protection attaches upon any original work of ownership, fixed in any tangible form of expression. Registration of the copyright with the U.S. Copyright Office is not a condition of a valid copyright. However, registration is a prerequisite to filing a copyright infringement action. The copyright law extends to such items as literary works, computer programs, musical works and lyrics, dramatic works, graphic and sculptural works, sound recordings, and audiovisual works. Significantly, copyright does not cover ideas, procedures, and concepts (17 U.S.C. 101, 102).

The 1976 copyright law places some limitations on the exclusive rights enjoyed by copyright owners. Section 107 of the act sets forth the "fair use" doctrine, which is particularly relevant to educators. This doctrine states in pertinent part that "the fair use of a copyrighted work, including such use . . . by reproduction . . . for purposes such as criticism, comment, new reporting, teaching (including multiple copies for classroom use), scholarship or research is not an infringement of copyright" (17 U.S.C. 107). Further guidelines for educators regarding reproducing multiple copies of copyrighted work for educational purposes (and cited by courts) are found in the Classroom Guidelines of the Fair Use Doctrine (H.R. 94-1476, 94th Congress, second session 66, 1976). These guidelines represent part of the legislative history of the 1976 act but are not considered part of the law. They permit educators to make multiple copies (not to exceed in any event more than one copy per pupil in a course) for classroom use or discussion—provided that the copying meets the tests of brevity and spontaneity and the cumulative effect test and that all copies contain a notice of copyright. It is clear that the copying of anthologies containing substantial portions of copyrighted books or articles without the permission of the copyright owner—even for educational purposes—violates the fair use doctrine (*Basic Books Inc. v Kinko's Graphics Corp.*, 1991).

Computer software is given protection under the copyright laws. The owner of a copy of a computer program may make copies of the program only when the new copy is created as an essential step in using the program in conjunction with a machine or when the new copy is for archival purposes only. All archival copies of the program must be destroyed when the program is no longer used (17 U.S.C. 117). It is clearly illegal for a school to load a copy of a program on one machine and "boot" that copy into the fixed memory of its microcomputers. The state of the law in the area of computer software is complex and rapidly evolving. School districts are well advised to inform teachers and students of the changing law regarding the use of copyrighted software.

ETHICS AND SCHOOL-COMMUNITY RELATIONS

The set of nonlegal rules—those outside the legal system that guide human relationships—is known as "ethics." What is generally called the ethics of a profession is actually the consensus of expert opinion as to the human responsibilities and obligations involved in a profession. References to ethics suggest that the term relates to moral action, human character, and a sense of duty; that it pertains to what is fair, equitable, good and professionally right, conforming to professional standards of conduct.

During the past ten years American educators have shown a growing interest in, and a genuine concern for, ethical and moral issues related to educational theory and practice. Textbooks on ethical leadership in school administration, the inclusion of ethics courses in educational administration preparation programs, and a proliferation of scholarly articles devoted to exploring the ethics of school leadership are evidence of a heightened awareness of the importance of ethical issues in education. (See, for example, Kimbrough, 1985; and Strike, Haller, & Soltis, 1988.) Indeed, Robert Crowson (1989) suggested that educators face ethical issues on a daily basis. As he explained, "To a large degree all [educational] administrative decisions are rooted in moral codes and cultural values, thus all decisions have an ethical component" (p. 418).

Many of the legal issues discussed above raise recurring ethical issues in the context of school-community relations. Incident-specific issues related to teacher dismissal, values inculcation, freedom of the press, parental rights, copyright infringement, student and teacher privacy rights, teacher and student free-speech rights, compliance with federal and state laws and regulations, and teacher evaluation pose ethical choices in individual cases. Beyond these incident-specific legal issues, policy and governance matters concerning school choice, allocation of resources, school-based management, teacher preparation, class size, school consolidation, and student assessment practices present ethical dilemmas in the context of school-community relations.

Many education scholars argue that incident-specific issues must be examined as taking place in a much broader ethical context. Robert Starratt (1991) contends that the educational program "is supposed to serve moral purposes (the nurturing of the human, social and intellectual growth of the youngsters)" (p. 187). As a consequence, "[T]he administrator who assumes that the educational environment, the organization, the system, the institutional arrangements (the curriculum, the daily and weekly schedule, the assessment and discipline and placement and promotion policies) enjoy a value neutrality, or worse, already embody the desirable ethical standards, is ethically naive, if not culpable" (p. 187). Ulrich Reitzug (1994) summarizes the importance of recognizing and understanding the ethical issues faced by educators: "Surfacing and addressing ethical issues of daily practice is perhaps the most crucial task in which administrators engage. The specific ethical issues that are analyzed and the way in which they are resolved will mold the culture and character of the school; define the school's purpose and the measures of effectiveness it considers crucial; and determine whether the school is a static entity or a transformational and empowering community" (p. 37). If the engine driving a school's purpose and defining its empowering capabilities is fueled by that school's ability to address ethical issues on a daily basis, then it is incumbent upon educators operating within the school-community relations mileu to be familiar with the ethical precepts, theory, and the practice relevant to education.

Codes of Ethics

The search for the meaning and the practice of ethics in any profession generally begins with an examination of the profession's code of ethics. An ethics code is a set of standards and guidelines aimed at promoting the ideals of social responsibility within the context of a profession. From the standpoint of school-community relations it is important to note that most of the professional mass-communications organizations have established ethics codes. Compliance with these codes is generally voluntary. The Public Relations Society of America (PRSA), the Society of Professional Journalists (SPJ), the American Society of Newspaper Editors (ASNE), and the International Association of Business Communications (IABC) have laid down ethical principles for communication professionals to follow. In fact, a recent issue of the widely read journal *Public Relations Review* was devoted to public relations ethics, and several articles called for creating a universal ethics code to cover the entire public relations professional community (Hiebert, 1993).

The National Education Association (NEA) adopted a code in 1929, and since then there have been many amendments to that code. The basic standards of the NEA code are meant to apply to all educators. The National Association of Secondary Principals (NASSP) adopted a statement of ethics in 1973 for all educational administrators. The NAASP Code of Ethics specifically addresses the relationship between school administration and school-community relations. The code states that "The administrator acknowledges that the schools belong to the public they serve for the purpose of providing educational opportunities to all. However, the administrator assumes responsibility for providing professional leadership in the school and community" (*NASSP Bulletin*, 1988).

The NASSP ethics code sets forth ten principles that make it incumbent upon the educational administrator to

1. Make the well-being of students the fundamental value in all decision making and actions
2. Fulfill professional responsibilities with honesty and integrity
3. Support the principle of due process and protect the civil and human rights of all individuals
4. Obey local, state, and national laws and not knowingly join or support organizations that advocate, directly or indirectly, the overthrow of the government
5. Implement the governing board of education's policies and administrative rules and regulations
6. Pursue appropriate measures to correct those laws, policies, and regulations that are not consistent with sound educational goals
7. Avoid using positions for personal gain through political, social, religious, economic, or other influence
8. Accept academic degrees or professional certification only from duly accredited institutions
9. Maintain the standards and seek to improve the effectiveness of the profession through research and continuing professional development
10. Honor all contracts until fulfillment or release (*NASSP Bulletin*, 1988, p. 95)

The NASSP Code of Ethics is useful, as a beginning point, in reflecting on ethical issues in education because it represents the profession's shared values. However, codes of ethics are of little help in actual decision making because educational judgment involves more than simply following preestablished rules. Ethical decisions are contextually bound and are made only after independent and reflective thought. Stories by and about individuals making ethical decisions document the multiplicity of experience in a way that shows the inadequacy of applying a static code of ethics. Questions like "What do our relationships ask of us?" "Who controls and how shall we govern ourselves?" and "Who benefits by these arrangements?" (Starratt, pp. 189, 199) cannot be answered by codes of ethics.

Administrative Ethics

Kowalski and Reitzug (1993) suggest that administrative ethics can be divided into three categories:

1. *Nonroutine issues of morality and personal practice.* This category includes ethical choices administrators confront on an irregular basis, where one choice may result in personal pleasure or personal (as opposed to professional) gain. Examples falling into this category include misuse of funds, sexual indiscretion, and certain conflicts of interest.
2. *Nonroutine issues of professional practice.* This category includes ethical choices administrators confront on an irregular basis that deal with professional matters. Examples falling into this category include nepotism, yielding to influential constituents in order to avoid trouble, and terminating teachers (for example,

those who need the salary provided by teaching and try hard but are ineffective teachers).

3. *Daily issues of administrative practice.* This category includes the application of power (for example, the imposition of one person's will upon another), the shaping of people and organizations, the determination of "correct" values, the justification of power usage, and the justification of choices exercised (p. 368).

William Greenfield (1993) identifies four main sources of values relevant to guiding educators involved in school-community relations: (1) society's standards of good conduct; (2) the education profession's rules of conduct; (3) the school's or school district's standards (found in school board policy and state and federal laws); and (4) the community attitudes and standards. The question immediately arises: Which set or source of values should guide school personnel involved in resolving ethical issues related to school-community relations?

Starratt (1991) proposes a model or framework within which one may ground ethical judgments in the school environment. This framework recognizes the intersection between school-community relations, social responsibility, and ethics. Starratt incorporates three perspectives into this framework for identifying, evaluating, and making ethical decisions. The three perspectives are the ethic of critique, the ethic of justice, and the ethic of caring. The *ethic of critique* is focused on confronting "the moral issues involved when schools disproportionately benefit some groups in society and fail others" (p. 190). Central to this ethic is an examination of the structural (managerial) issues involved in educational leadership, such as bias in the workplace. School personnel viewing the world through the lens of the ethic of critique reflect upon and explore such constructs as bureaucratic leadership, power, and domination. Questions raised by the ethic of critique seem especially useful when considering the school administrator's relationship with internal publics.

The *ethic of justice* is concerned with values such as individual rights, the common good, and democratic participation in school governance. Starrett points out that, in educational institutions where consideration of the ethic of justice takes place, "[S]pecific ethical learning activities are structured within curricular and extracurricular programs to encourage discussion of individual choices as well as discussions of school community choices" (p. 193). The ethic of justice requires an examination of the tension between the claims of the individual and community needs. Starratt observes that "[T]he claims of the institution serve both the common good and the rights of individuals in the school. . . . [D]iscussions about the curriculum, about appropriate textbooks, about a visiting speakers program and the like will need to be carried on . . . for the moral questions they raise about public life in the community" (p. 194). An understanding of the underpinnings of the ethic of justice is helpful in the search for a balance between individual rights and the larger good of the community. The ethic of justice offers the possibility of alternatives to practices that often benefit the majority but encumber others.

The *ethic of caring* emphasizes human connection and relationships. The ethic of caring provides a perspective for dealing with both a school's internal and external constituencies. Most centrally, the ethic of caring is "grounded in the belief that the integrity of human relationships should be held sacred and that the school as an organization should hold the good of human beings within it as sacred. This ethic reaches beyond concerns with efficiency" (Starratt, p. 195). The ethic of caring examines the motives and reasons attendant on the administration of a school. The ethic of caring draws attention to stereotyping and language that interferes with honest two-way communication. The elements of a positive school culture are found in the ethic of caring, which is reflected in a school-community relations program where school officials stress empathy and concern and caring for others, value cooperation over competition, and emphasize participative forms of decision making.

Attention to diversity has moved Reitzug (1994) to challenge educators to become more sensitive to the ethical issues of diversity. As he asserts, "[S]ensitivity to diversity recognizes *cultural differences* due to race, ethnicity, gender, and class, as well as *opinion differences* due to varying beliefs concerning educational practice. Evidence of sensitivity to diversity is found in practices such as multicultural curricula, and shared decision-making interventions such as site-based management" (p. 1). Today, school-community relations are played out in an increasingly pluralistic society, and educators should be acutely aware of ethical issues arising out of cultural diversity.

Ethics and the Educative Role of School-Community Relations

The interplay between ethics and school-community relations is most directly located in the educative function of the public school. Education for life must be the ultimate mission of any school-community relations program. Bellah, Madsen, Sullivan, Swindler, and Tipton (1992) deliver a clarion call for schools to transform their districts, towns, and cities into learning communities. They explain that Americans must begin to view schools less as part of the "infrastructure for competition and more as an invaluable resource in the search for the common good" (p. 175).

This is the kind of school-community relations plan that John Dewey sought when he urged schools to assume the role of educating the public not only to the needs of the school but to the needs of the community as well (McKinney & Place, 1992). Dewey said: "The schools are not doing, and cannot do, what the people want until there is more unity, more definiteness, in the community's consciousness of its own needs; but it is the business of the school to forward this conception, to help the people to a clearer and more systematic idea of what the underlying needs of modern life are, and of how they are really to be supplied." (1901/1940, p. 37).

In sum, the ethical challenge to school-community relations today is to create and use the culture of the school in ways that will involve the schools' pluralistic constituencies in a common effort to build a just and caring school and community.

CASE STUDY	The Superintendent Learns about Community Values

Mary Wright was excited as she drove to the first school board meeting of her second year as superintendent of the Gallup Community Schools (G.C.S.). Gallup, with a population of 100,00, is an aging industrial community in the Midwest, and Wright had enjoyed a first-year "honeymoon" with the school board and surrounding community as she attempted to learn about the schools and the community and concentrated on not rocking the boat. But now she was determined to address a litany of educational concerns that she felt had been previously ignored by the school district.

In hiring her, the school board had conducted what they considered to be a complete background search. Wright had been pleased that the school board had not discovered that she had recently filed for bankruptcy and as a result had been virtually penniless when she first came to Gallup. She was also glad that the board had not discovered that she had been seeing a psychiatrist for the past three years after suffering from psychological fatigue. Although members of the G.S.C. school board had asked her previous employer (members of the Blueline school board) if Wright had any medical or other "in-the-closet" problems that might interfere with her performance as superintendent, the Blueline board had not informed G.C.S. about Wright's financial or psychological problems—although the Blueline school board was familiar with these problems.

On the basis of information that she and her school-community relations director, Tom Sample, had gathered, Wright was now prepared to make the annual "state-of-the-G.C.S. address." In that address at this first school board meeting of the year, Wright announced the following initiatives:

1. Because of the growing AIDS epidemic and an increase in local teenage pregnancies, G.C.S. would explore offering a sex education program (beginning in kindergarten).
2. Because of school disturbances motivated by racial and ethnic animosities, G.C.S. would immediately introduce courses on promoting understanding and tolerance among students from different racial and ethnic backgrounds (a multicultural program beginning in ninth grade).
3. In an effort to curb gang activity and prevent school dropout G.C.S. would immediately implement a community-oriented program to be cosponsored by the schools, law enforcement agencies, and the Gallup prosecuting attorney's office. G.C.S. counselors, principals and deans would target students with extensive disciplinary problems for mandatory conferences involving parents, school personnel, the police, and a representative from the prosecuting attorney's office. The team of educators, police officers, and attorneys would advise students and parents of the ramifications of getting in trouble and dropping out of school.
4. Having obtained a waiver for three G.C.S. elementary schools (as a pilot program) from state-mandated testing, G.C.S. would now implement an alternative assessment (AA) program at those schools covered by the waiver, with a view toward developing a districtwide AA program in the elementary schools.

The day after the meeting, Wright encountered a wave of criticism of her proposals for new programs. Rev. Robert Wunder, minister at King's Garden Church, appeared on local television and called Mary Wright an "antifamily nut." He demanded that the school board not approve the sex education program. Wunder claimed that sex education interferes with parental rights and violates his congregates' (and their school-aged children) freedom of religion. Next, Wright received a phone call from the president of the local chamber of commerce, Buck Speakes, who said that any attempt to introduce multicultural education into the school curriculum would be challenged by his group and other community groups already concerned about declining test scores because of a "watered-down" curriculum. Speakes also stated that he feared multicultural education would lead to a further "disuniting" of the community.

Three days later, Wright received a letter from the local chapter of the American Civil Liberties Union (ACLU), which claimed that her plan to work cooperatively with the police and the prosecuting attorney's office would lead to serious violations of students' privacy rights. The ACLU was prepared to challenge the program in court.

By the end of the week, Wright was feeling the political heat from her school board presentation. She picked up the morning newspaper, only to find a letter to the editor from a G.C.S. elementary principal, Bea Line, criticizing Wright's position on sex education as radical and unnecessary. Line also wrote that she had located and sent local community leaders copies of an article written by Wright and published in a scholarly research journal. The article advocated condom distribution in public high schools.

After a short weekend, Wright returned to her office to be confronted by two school board members and several influential members of the community. They were particularly upset about the sex education program, claiming it was offensive to local values; and they were incensed over the AA program. One citizen remarked that the AA program "sounded a lot like outcomes-based education, and Gallup won't stand for that."

Wright contacted Tom Sample, who seemed to be the only person she could trust in Gallup. In fact, one evening over drinks she had told Sample about the bankruptcy proceedings. Now she asked him to prepare and distribute a quick—but slick-looking—response to the criticism of the AA program. She told him to deny that AA had any parallels with outcomes-based education. Sample was perplexed because just a month earlier Wright had sent him a summary report of AA objectives, a report replete with positive references to outcomes-based education.

QUESTIONS AND SUGGESTED ACTIVITIES

Case Study

1. What ethical and legal issues are raised in the case study? What ethical perspectives would you employ in the case study to make decisions? In your opinion, which legal challenges to Wright's proposals for new programs are most likely to succeed? to fail?

2. The case study lends itself to role playing. Form a group and assign (or choose) characters. Try to empathize with the character you are playing. What points of view are not compatible? What are the alternatives to filing a lawsuit for the characters opposed to Wright's view? What should Tom Sample do about writing a response regarding outcomes-based education for the press?

3. Are there legal or ethical limits concerning a school board's authority to remove books and other materials from the curriculum? Is there any legal or ethical difference between removing books from the regular school curriculum and removing books and other materials from the school library? Would the removal of religiously oriented books from the school library violate the First Amendment? If a book is offensive to a minority student should it be removed from the curriculum or the school library?

Chapter

4. What interests do the courts balance in cases involving a teacher dismissal?
5. Define defamation and explain the difference between absolute and conditional or qualified immunity as it relates to school-community relations. Discuss the theory of governmental immunity and how it relates to school-community relations.
6. Should all outsiders to a school be considered trespassers? Licensees? Explain your answers from a legal and a school-community relations point of view.
7. Is there any place for religion in the school curriculum? If parents object to textbooks or course offerings on religious grounds, should schools exempt their children from using the textbooks or taking the courses? What legal and ethical considerations are relevant to your decision making?

SUGGESTED READINGS

Association for Supervision and Curriculum Development. *Religion in the curriculum*. Alexandria, VA: Author.

Champion, W. T. (1993). *Sports law in a nutshell*. St. Paul, MN: West Publishing.

Cubb, J. E., & Moe, T. M. (1990). *Politics, markets, and America's schools*. Washington, DC: Brookings Institution.

Dewey, J. (1966). *Democracy and education*. New York: Macmillan.

Foster, W. (1986). *Paradigms and promises: New approaches to educational administration*. Buffalo, NY: Prometheus.

Giroux, H. A. (1988). *Schooling and the struggle for public life*. Minneapolis: University of Minnesota Press.

Goodlad, J. I. (1984). *A place called school*. New York: McGraw-Hill.

Hogan, J. C. (1985). *The schools, the courts, and the public interest* (2nd ed.). Lexington, MA: Lexington Books.

MacIntyre, A. (1984). *After virtue*. Notre Dame, IN: University of Notre Dame Press.

McCarthy, C. (1990). *Race and the curriculum*. London: Falmer Press.

Noddings, N. (1984). *Caring: A feminine approach to ethics and moral education*. Berkeley, CA: University of California Press.

Orfield, G., & Monfort, F. (1988). *Racial change and desegregation in large school districts*. Alexandria, VA: National School Boards Association.

Smolla, R. A. (1991). *Law of defamation*. New York: Clark Boardman.

REFERENCES

Alexander, K., & Alexander, D. (1992). *American public school law* (3rd ed.). St. Paul, MN: West Publishing.

American Law Institute. (1986). *Restatement of torts, second*. St. Paul, MN: American Law Institute Publishers.

Bagin, D., Gallagher, D. R., & Kindred, L. W. (1994). *The school and community relations* (5th ed.). Boston: Allyn and Bacon.

Basic Books Inc. v Kinko's Graphics Corp., 754 F.Supp. 1522 (S.D.N.Y. 1991).

Bellah, R. N., Madsen, R., Sullivan, W. M., Swindler, A., & Tipton, S. M. (1992). *The good society*. New York: Vintage Books.

Board of Education, Island Trees Union Free School District No. 26 v Pico, 457 U.S. 853 (1982).

Board of Education of Westside Community Schools v Mergens, 496 U.S. 226 (1990).

Brown v Board of Education, 447 U.S. 483 (1954).

Brown v Board of Education (Brown II), 349 U.S. 294 (1955).

Crowson, R. (1989). Managerial ethics in educational administration: The rational choice approach. *Urban education, 23*(4), 412–435.

Dewey, J. (1940). "The people and the schools. In J. Ratner (Ed.), *Education today.* New York: G.P. Putnam's Sons. (Reprinted from *The elementary school teacher,* 1901.).

Drake, T. L., & Roe, W. (1994) *School business management.* Boston: Allyn and Bacon.

Greenfield, W. O. (1993). Articulating values and ethics in administrator preparation. In C. A. Capper (Ed.), *Educational administration in a pluralistic society* (pp. 267–287). Albany, NY: State University of New York Press.

Harlow v Fitzgerald, 457 U.S. 800 (1982).

Hiebert, R. (1993). Public relations review (Vol. 19, 1). Greenwich, CT: JAI Press.

Holliday, A. E. (1988). In search of an answer: What is school public relations? *Journal of educational public relations. 11*(2), 12–16.

Horosko v Mount Pleasant Township School District, 6 A. 2d 866 (1939).

Imber, M., & Thompson, G. (1991). Developing a typology of litigation in education and determining the frequency of each category. *Educational administration quarterly, 27*(2), 225–244.

Jones v Clear Creek Independent School District, 930 F. 2d 416, cerf.deny 113 S.Ct.2750 (1993).

Keeton, P., Dobbs, D., Keeton, R., & Owen, D. (1984). *Prosser and Keeton on the law of torts* (5th ed.). St. Paul, MN: West Publishing.

Kimbrough, R. B. (1985). *Ethics: A current study for educational leaders.* Arlington, VA: American Association of School Administrators.

Kindred, L. W., Bagin, D., & Gallagher, D. R. (1990). *The school and community relations* (4th ed.). Englewood Cliffs, NJ: Prentice Hall.

Kirp, D. L., & Jensen, D. N. (1986). *School days, rule days: The legislation and regulation of education.* Philadelphia: Falmer Press.

Korpela, A. E. (1971). *American law review* (Vol. 35). San Francisco: Lawyers Co-operative Publishing Co.

Kowalski, T. J., & Reitzug, U. C. (1993). *Contemporary school administration.* New York: Longman.

Lamb's Chapel v Center Moriches School District, 113 S.Ct. 2141 (1993).

Lee v Weisman, 112 S.Ct. 2649 (1992).

Lemon v Kurtzman, 403 U.S. 602 (1971).

McCarthy, M., & Cambron-McCabe, N. (1992). *Public school law* (3rd ed.). Boston: Allyn and Bacon.

McKinney, J. R., & Place, A. W. (1992). John Dewey and school-community relations. *Journal of research for school executives, 2,* 30–36.

Monell v Department of Social Services of New York, 436 U.S. 658 (1978).

NASSP Bulletin 1988. Statement of ethics. *NASSP Bulletin, 72*(512): 95.

National School Boards Association (1993). Violence in the schools. Alexandria, VA: Author.

New York Times, Inc. v Sullivan, 476 U.S. 254 (1964).

People for the American Way. (1993). *Attacks on the freedom to learn.* Washington, DC: Author.

Pickering v Board of Education of Township High School District 205, 391 U.S. 563 (1968).

Reitzug, U. C. (1994). Diversity, power and influence: Multiple perspectives on the ethics of school leadership. *Journal of school leadership,* 197–222.

Schimmel, D. (1993). Discrimination against religious viewpoints prohibited in public schools: An analysis of the Lamb's Chapel decision. *Education law reporter, 85,* 387–396.

Sherburne v School Board of Suwannee Co., 455 So. 2d 1057 (Fla. App. 1984).

Soma, J., & Pringle, D. (1986). Computer software in the public schools. *Education law reporter, 28*, 315–324.

Starratt, R. J. (1991). Building an ethical school: A theory for practice in educational leadership. *Educational administration quarterly, 27*(2), 185–202.

Strike, K., Haller, M., & Soltis, J. (1988). *Ethics of school administration*. New York: Teachers College Press.

Sullivan v Meade Independent School District No. 101, 530 F. 2d 799 (D.S.D., 1976).

Tyack, D., James, T., & Benevot, A. (1987). *Law and the shaping of public education*. Madison: University of Wisconsin Press.

Tyler, R. (1949). *Basic principles of curriculum and instruction*. Chicago: University of Chicago Press.

Wallace v Jaffree, 472 U.S. 38 (1985).

West, P. (1985). *Educational public relations*. Beverly Hills, CA: Sage.

Wood v Strickland, 420 U.S. 308 (1975).

Zlatos, B. (1993). Outcome-based outrage. *Executive educator, 15*(9), 12–20.

ORGANIZATIONAL DIMENSIONS

CHAPTER 7

Effective Programming at the Institutional Level

Arthur Steller

School safety was a hot topic for the Oklahoma City Public Schools district; it even became the focus of a bond-issue campaign. The administrative staff planned and executed a public relations strategy. All the right things were brought into play—citizen input, speakers' bureaus, media publicity, and opinion-leader (individuals who shape public opinion in the local community) support. After twenty years without winning a bond issue, the school community was confident of victory this time.

However, a critical piece of the public relations strategy was missing. Effective public relations involves more than just giving information to the public. It also entails anticipating problems. The first rule a public relations officer should honor is "What *can* happen, often *does* happen." In the case of Oklahoma City, the planners knew teacher negotiations were underway, but they never considered the possibility that this process could derail the bond referendum. Weeks before the citywide vote, negotiations with the teachers' union hit a snag. Unexpectedly, union officials declared public opposition to the bond initiative. Suddenly the issue of teacher salaries and the referendum became inextricably linked. The board members, however, were unwilling to approve salary increases (for which they believed funds were not available) to gain the union's endorsement. Over 10,000 votes were cast in the referendum, the highest number in the history of the school district; the bond issue failed by less than 200 votes.

This true case exemplifies the fact that school officials must be prepared to do more than just implement the standard aspects of a public relations program. In the real world of practice, the ability to handle *unplanned* events often determines success. Public relations literature focuses largely on researched, rational plans, programs, and events, frequently ignoring the controversies, vendettas, nastiness, crises, and other totally unexpected situations that can attenuate even the most effective plans. Public relations guru Edward Bernays compared planning with drama, "a drama that hasn't happened yet, in which every step of the drama, every appearance of every actor, every scene is outlined . . . yet, all are subject to change"(Davis, 1986, p. 29). This does not mean that programs should not be planned, rather it points out the need for administrators to integrate flexibility so they are able to overcome unexpected barriers.

This chapter offers suggestions about orchestrating one's drama with researched detail, planning, and foresight. Just as important, this chapter presents ideas on how to plan for the unexpected. Both ingredients are essential to producing a public relations program capable of developing the attitudes, perceptions, actions, information, and results important to an educational institution.

CHANGING TIMES

Twenty years ago, a school public relations program that included a good newsletter, six positive stories in the local newspaper, a strong PTA, and consistent bond levy promotions was likely to be judged effective. But communities have changed, and so have the standards for good practice. Families a century ago obtained information from sources close to home—church, school, neighbors. Today, information is readily available from multiple sources, not the least of which are the print media, television, and radio. Equally momentous has been the increasing tendency of the general public to question and criticize public institutions and those who operate them. This has been especially apparent in public education over the last two decades.

Contrary to popular thought, however, intense criticism of public education is not a recent phenomena. Approximately a decade before the well-known report, *A Nation at Risk*, was published in 1983, Unruh and Willier (1974) wrote that public criticism "has placed educational institutions on the defensive, perhaps because it has come from so many sources and in so many unexpected ways" (p. 150). They suggested that educators get off the defensive and begin to accentuate the positive: "It's entirely possible that what's right with the schools is far greater than what's wrong" (p. 150).

Both technology and the drive for school reform create unprecedented opportunities for educational institutions. Technology facilitates communication, and school reform has kept education in the public eye. Hence, administrators can accentuate the positive by working effectively with employees, community, and media. But success is not a product of kismet; it requires well-planned, well-executed effort. It requires both a top-level administrator (superintendent or college president) who understands and accepts a broad definition of public relations and a public relations specialist who has knowledge and skills in areas such as issues management, needs assessment, marketing, and planning.

The Public Relations Plan

Planning must come first. Robert Topor (1992) noted that public relations plans should strongly resemble a mosaic communicating a dynamic and powerful message to viewers. It should focus on the big picture, ensure a balance between individual elements, and include smaller pieces, each with its own marketing value. Whether it is the district's mission statement, an employee newsletter, an awards ceremony, a superintendent's speech, or a conversation—each contains intrinsic power. As Topor wrote, "As with tesserae within a mosaic, the power of each piece is not fully revealed unless it is arranged (marketing strategy) as part of a grander, more comprehensive plan (a marketing plan)!" (p. 46).

There are a number of basic elements to an effective plan. These range from data analysis to goal setting to establishing a public relations office and employing a public relations administrator. The more cogent and common features of the plan are discussed here.

Defining the Organization

The organizational mosaic, the public relations plan, should be composed only after history, goals, accomplishments, trends, and internal (within the organization) and external (in the wider environment) perceptions have been properly identified and analyzed. Often this is referred to as "defining research." In some instances, much of this information may already be available. For example, local chambers of commerce and businesses may have conducted studies of community life that include education components. Or individual principals may have completed surveys of parents and students. By compiling an inventory of available data, school officials can learn rather quickly what additional tasks may be necessary to complete a sufficient research data bank for planning.

Among the more critical elements of defining research are the following:

- A *demographic review* of the community, including income, age, race, sex, location, occupation, hobbies, interests, lifestyle and connection to the organization
- *Results from opinion polls and bond or finance elections and public reactions to critical issues* over the last several years
- *Surveys of staff and community* that reveal opinions, perceptions, and attitudes about schools
- *Data from needs assessments* conducted with students, parents, potential employers, and higher education officials
- *A list of opinion leaders*
- *Follow-up studies of graduates*
- *Information distribution lists* detailing who wants information and the nature of their priorities

Benchmarking

In addition to gaining a full understanding of their own organization, administrators should consider studying other educational institutions that have been highly successful. The purpose is to focus on the processes most associated with goal attainment. This concept is called "benchmarking," the art of discovering how others do something better so that one can imitate and possibly improve the techniques. Fortune 500 corporations such as AT&T, Du Pont, Ford Motor, Motorola, and Xerox use benchmarking as a standard management tool.

Benchmarking also offers much promise for schools. Most educational administrators are willing to share their knowledge and skills, including detailed plans and strategies they have developed. Consider telephone interviews and field trips to other educational organizations by small teams as part of the defining-research process. Additionally, a wealth of information about exemplary public relations programs can be attained by attending national conferences, such as those sponsored by the National School Public Relations Association and the American Association of School Administrators.

Although information about successful programs can enhance the planning process, administrators ought not believe that programs will have equal success in all settings. That is to say, information from other organizations is valuable so long as administrators weigh the material in the context of their work environments, their problems and needs, and their communities.

Setting the Organizational Mission and Goals

When the research component is completed, the planners can move to reshaping mission and goals. Today the terms "vision" and "mission" are frequently used synonymously. The mission statement provides a brief indication of the organization's intent. Some statements are only a few sentences. For example, one school district adopted a mission statement that read, "Creating a model urban school district." The specifics on how "model" was defined came from the staff and the public. These interpretations were integrated into goals that were prepared for a five-year time frame.

A mission should clearly and concisely communicate the general intent of the organization. Topor (1992) observed that a good public relations program had to have its roots in fertile soil. He wrote: "[As] with many things in life, [public relations] needs to have its roots in fertile soil to succeed. The 'nutrients' that feed marketing should grow out of the institution itself" (p. 18). A good public relations program is grounded in a general mission and its corresponding goals.

Goals should be written from both short-term and long-term perspectives. Bond issues and levy campaigns, for example, should be planned long before they are announced to the public. Most importantly, goals should be written in a fashion allowing periodic modifications. In keeping with the theme of dealing with the unexpected, the continuous gathering of information allows administrators to adjust specific goals when conditions warrant. For instance, a goal to improve school facilities by a specified date may have to be altered if state laws governing the financing of capital outlay are changed. Placing long-term goals in concrete—that is, essentially making them immutable for five or more years—is a mistake.

The mission and goals of an organization are the grout holding the mosaic together; they are the bridge connecting internal and external themes. Mission and goals become central to all communication efforts; they accommodate cohesion and balance. From placing district and school logos side by side at an awards program to working with the news media in a fashion that balances school district and individual school interests, the mission and goals provide the administrator with a framework for practice.

Setting Messages and Themes

Once mission and goals are written, administrators are in a position to craft the organization's *messages* and *themes*. These elements of the public relations plan serve two critical purposes: (1) They help garner support for the organization, and (2) they help people understand the directions in which the organization is moving. Good themes are usually concise, rhythmic, memorable, and easy to understand. Themes used by schools include such ringing phrases as "Quest for Quality," "Getting Better for Kids," "Public Education: A Sound Investment in America," and "Champions of Learning" (Bagin, Ferguson, & Marx, 1985, p. 112). More so than the mission statement, messages and themes express the values and beliefs of the organization; they communicate symbolically both the philosophy and culture of the organization.

Themes and messages can be very powerful, as evidenced by successful corporations in the private sector (Deal & Kennedy, 1982). To be effective, though, they should be predicated on reality. Consider, for example, administrators who decided on the theme "Established Excellence" when in fact test scores in their district had been declining for fifteen years. False claims are likely to be challenged, and if they are proven false, the organization suffers. Themes and messages should be positive and honest. They should have a clear association with the mission and goals of the organization.

Including the Public Relations Specialist

One of the most critical decisions made by the chief executive officer of an educational organization relates to employing a public relations administrator. What type of person is needed? Do the responsibilities justify a full-time position? Additionally, the superintendent or principal must consider responsibilities and working conditions for this person. Life in an information age dictates that, compared with conditions just a decade ago, (1) qualifications for this position should be more stringent, and (2) the position should have higher stature in the organization.

Qualifications. When public relations is defined and applied as a broad construct, the job requirements of a chief public relations officer become more extensive. This person must be a planner, an analyst, a communication expert, a manager, and even an evaluator. And because the public relations administrator is involved in so many fundamental activities, he or she is an integral part of the administrative team. Alluding to this fact, Unruh and Willier (1974) wrote that this person should have certain capabilities: "To see the beginning of an educational movement, be it a problem or an innovation, and to identify it early for what it is and what it can do is the foundation of administrative and public relations judgment. Identifying the problem early and formulating and evaluating potential solutions are essential in arriving at a practical way to deal with it" (p. 147). Public relations professionals need to create dialogue internally and externally; they must be able to use various communications techniques ranging from internal publications to mass media; they must understand communications opportunities in print, on air, in speeches, and in conversations and know how to use any communications possibility and what challenges to expect.

Only ten years ago it was common for educational institutions to relegate public relations responsibilities to a full-time English teacher or an administrator who appeared to have a knack for communicating. Both the present context of schools and communities and the refinement of the public relations profession (that is, the infusion of sociological, psychological, and economic theory) emphasize the thoughtlessness of extending past practice to contemporary administration. Ideally, the chief public relations officer has knowledge and skills in both public relations and administration, and even more importantly, he or she is able to apply this expertise within an organizational setting.

Stature.   The public relations administrator should have easy and open access to the chief executive officer of the organization. In public school districts, this means paralleling the position with associate or assistant superintendents, even if that particular title is not used. (In some states, the individual might have to have a superintendent's license to hold the title of assistant or associate superintendent.) Having to go through an intermediary may cause delays and related communication problems for the public relations official. For example, when a school district is contemplating closing a school, announcing test scores, or changing a school board policy, the public relations specialist should be involved in formulating the strategy, timing, nature of communications, and evaluation procedures. Today communication is at the center of virtually all administrative activities.

Creating the Public Relations Office

Related to decisions about the position of public relations administrator are decisions about the public relations office. Where will it be located? How many staff are required? What resource allocations have to be made? And even, what title should be given to the office?

Many school leaders grapple with what to call their communications offices. Various program titles have been used: school community relations, public affairs, public relations, employee relations, even customer service. Quoting Bernays, B. Rodney Davis (1986) wrote, "[W]ords are as fragile as lace or a soap bubble. The words and their meanings get kicked around . . . so today the words 'public relations' are so muddy in meaning that to some they do mean press agentry or flackery" (p. 14). "Public Relations" is increasingly seen as the appropriate title, because it provides the broad construct encompassing communication activities. For some superintendents, this term may be objectionable because of the way it is interpreted by the general public. If another title is used, it should be sufficiently broad so as not to suggest a narrow range of activities. An "Office of Employee Relations," for instance, indicates no responsibility for communication with the community.

No public relations office can function effectively without an adequate budget. When budgets are slim and teachers' salaries are frozen, the public relations staff is often an easy target, criticized as "fluff" and described as something the district can live without. The budget of any division of a school district has both direct and symbolic importance. The amount of money dictates program scope, but it also conveys a message to employees and the community about the importance of communication within the organization. Thus, when a public relations program is planned, consideration must be given to creating a budget for it. This should include a specific amount of money and notations as to the source of revenues.

Establishing Time Lines

All plans require time parameters. An effective approach is to develop five-year goals that are reviewed annually. This time frame has several primary benefits:

- ◆ Department and unit heads (for example, principals) can develop one-year goals tied to the organization's goals. Annual reviews encourage broad input that helps to determine if the long-range goals should be adjusted.
- ◆ Annual reviews inform central administrators of the progress being made throughout the organization.
- ◆ No goal is frozen in time. There is the benefit of having a long-range target while at the same time having the flexibility of altering those targets on an annual basis.
- ◆ The longer time dimension makes it more difficult to abandon initiatives easily. In today's world, leaders are frequently tempted to make abrupt shifts in direction.

A superintendent can develop a "tickler" file identifying all departmental and unit goals, progress data regarding those goals, and anticipated attainment dates. This information can prove to be extremely valuable to the chief administrator in making day-to-day decisions.

APPLYING THE PLAN

Application becomes easier when a comprehensive plan is in place, but the plan itself does not assure good practice. There are myriad considerations to take into account now, considerations involving employees, students, parents, other patrons, school board members, and the media. Although several of these topics are the themes of other chapters in this book, they are briefly reviewed here.

Internal and External Communication

Targeted public relations plans focus on both internal and external audiences. Traditionally, public relations was seen largely as an external function involving transmitting information to the community. Although this aspect remains important, such communication is likely to fail if it is contradicted by students, employees, or school board members. Individuals within the organization are expected to know, firsthand, what is really occurring. And in the case of education, individuals and groups tend to offer their opinions frequently and freely. Consider that every person coming in contact with an organization will tell an average of twenty-two people about it, and a little over 10 percent of them will tell even more people. These messages are both good and bad (Levinson, 1989).

Rather than attending to internal communications, educators are at times their own worst enemies. As Davis (1986) wrote:

School boards argue among themselves, and with the community, and many times with the superintendent they hired. Teachers argue with administrators and the school board. Administrators unionize and talk tough and lob verbal hand grenades back at teacher union invectives. We argue about back-to-basics versus relevant education, about class size and working conditions and fringe benefits, about who is to blame for declining test scores, about accountability and pro-ductivity, and about vandalism and violence. We castigate each other over declining enroll-ments, closing schools, desegregation, politics, bureaucracies, finances, community advisory committees and plenty of other things. (p. 16)

Communications can work only when sucessful from the inside out. Bagin, Ferguson, and Marx (1985, p. 39) offered four reasons why internal communication is an important element of a public relations program:

- ◆ An organization can meet its mission only if internal staff know what the mission, goals, and objectives are.
- ◆ All members have information that can make organizations more effective.
- ◆ A sense of ownership depends on having opportunities to be involved in decisions.
- ◆ All institutions work better if the right hand knows what the left hand is doing.

Effective internal communication requires honesty, openness, and accessibility. That is to say, top-ranking administrators need to have contact with people and groups within the organization; and when those contacts occur, there should be an open and honest ex-change of information. In larger organizations, this requires time management, especially if nonprofessional staff and students are to be included. (Issues related to internal com-munication are discussed in detail in the next chapter.)

Topor (1992) warned that educational organizations were prone to "*not* thinking, plan-ning, executing, and evaluating services from an *external* point of view" (p. 21). External communication entails far more than just sending newsletters and pamphlets to targeted publics. Collecting information about needs and wants, for instance, requires external communication. Advisory committees, shared governance councils, and ad hoc groups of-fer channels for gaining community input.

When we compare past and present conceptualizations of educational public relations, we find that the two most glaring differences with regard to communicating are (1) the dedication of energy and resources to the open exchange of information within the orga-nization and (2) the creation of two-way communication with the wider communities served by the schools. Both have become essential elements of administrative behavior in an information age.

The Media

Although public relations is a broad construct, media relations remains a central feature. Advising administrators of this fact, Ordovensky and Marx (1993) wrote: "When you de-cided to get involved in education you also committed yourself to working with the news media. The media are a part of each educator's professional life for several reasons. Here are just two: People want to know how well schools are teaching students. People want to know how their tax dollars are being invested. In short, our schools deal with two things very clear to people, their children and their tax dollars" (p. 1).

A community's perceptions about its schools are greatly influenced by the media. Most people obtain most of their information about schools from local newspapers. Increas-ingly, cable television and radio talk shows are extending the options for obtaining infor-mation.

Educational organizations ought to have a prescribed plan for working with media. This can be incorporated into the public relations plan or it can be published in a separate handbook. Further, administrative staff should receive guidance in this area. Workshops involving reporters, for example, provide a good way to prepare individuals for this task. Specific suggestions about media relations are detailed in Chapter 11.

Board Meetings and Other Public Meetings

School board meetings or board of trustees meetings are the easiest and most effective communications tool available to educational organizations. But the outcomes may be either negative or positive. For example, meetings seemingly out of control and lasting five or six hours may give the public the impression that operations are chaotic. Or if the entire meeting delves on the negative, popular criticisms may be reinforced. In any public meeting, the organization is on stage. Both the substance and procedures of the meeting convey messages contributing to public image.

Because of their impact on image, meetings of the governing board should be planned with input from the public relations administrator. Some elements of the agenda should address positive features of the schools; some should detail cogent accomplishments. Likewise, procedures should reflect the prevailing culture. If open and honest communication is valued, then procedures ought to be in place to allow these behaviors to be exhibited at the meetings. If research, planning, and evaluation are valued activities, then this fact should be exhibited in actions that are taken. If communication is deemed essential, then reports, both verbal and written, should be planned and free from grammatical errors and inaccuracies. These meetings are also an opportunity to showcase an outstanding program, group of students, or faculty member.

Citizen Participation

Over the past three or four decades, there has been a growing recognition that schools do not function well when they are isolated from their communities (Kowalski & Reitzug, 1993). Accordingly, one of the goals of public relations programming should be to involve as many parents as possible in the process. This task is made both more necessary and more difficult by virtue of the fact that many taxpayers do not have direct contact with their schools through children, grandchildren, or employment. Their opinions about schools are usually based on second- and thirdhand sources of information. Many experienced superintendents and principals have discovered that in the case of education, familiarity often breeds support.

Among the ideas that can be used to enhance citizen participation are the following:

◆ *Parent-teacher associations* are one of the most common avenues to citizen participation, and these groups continue to make valuable contributions.
◆ *Open houses* allow parents and other taxpayers to actually see the school facilities and to talk to teachers. Effort should be made to entice nonparents to attend.
◆ *Parent-teacher conferences* can serve multiple purposes. If properly conducted, they can be a source of information for the school system.

◆ *Special events* such as plays, musicals, and award ceremonies offer an opportunity for patrons to visit schools. At times, principals have used such events to convey messages about the school.

◆ Other contacts with parents can include *telephone calls* or *home visits*. Both encourage information exchanges.

◆ Creating *community dialogue* is another way to broaden citizen participation. Focus groups can be formed to periodically discuss relevant issues affecting the schools and the community. School officials may hold open forums, especially related to major decisions such as building a new school.

◆ *Community partnership programs* are rapidly becoming one of the most common links between schools and community. The most successful are forged around mutual needs and benefits. Such joint efforts broaden the scope of communication.

◆ A *principal-for-a-day program* is an idea designed to bring business leaders to the school. Shadowing the principal for a day, they learn firsthand what is occurring. These experiences are usually then shared with a wider audience.

◆ *Advisory groups* can be formed on an ad hoc or permanent basis to provide input about problems, ideas, or programming. Administrators should always define the group's purpose, specify time lines for action, and strive for broad representation.

◆ *Local school councils* are emerging as one of the most powerful means of broadening citizen participation. Used largely in conjunction with decentralization concepts, these groups tend to have more authority than do advisory groups. As such, participation is likely to be more regular and input more candid.

Wider participation, in and of itself, does not guarantee improved education (at least in terms of student learning). For example, the structure of local school councils and the way they fit into the governance system are key factors in determining if these groups will be positive or negative (American Association of School Administrators, 1994). Gaining participation is a first step, but management and leadership must follow. In this respect, a comprehensive public relations plan increases the likelihood that community participation will have a positive influence on the primary functions of the school.

DEALING WITH CONTROVERSY

Dealing with unexpected crisis or controversy further tests the quality of the public relations program. Controversy, like crisis, can result in unpleasant situations requiring administrative action. Consider teacher pickets, lawsuits, vendettas, or parental displeasure with a science curriculum.

The impact of controversy was easily seen in a situation that involved budget cuts and the closing of a high school in an urban district. Parents and other community members who opposed these decisions tended to create their own facts. They speculated as to why this particular high school was targeted, and their stories ranged from creative to absurd. Soon their anger was directed toward top administrators in the school district. Rumors spread about the superintendent and led to a grand jury investigation; his telephone and travel records were subpoenaed. And although the grand jury found no merit to the accusations, the superintendent and other officials had to expend a great deal of energy to deal with the controversy. This situation shows how controversy can take unpredictable turns, how it can serve as a catalyst for new problems.

The importance of including contingencies for public controversy in public relations has been illuminated by the school-reform movement. Any time educators propose change, they can be virtually assured of some opposition. The relationship between change and communication was noted by Ledell and Arnsparger (1993) when they wrote, "Educators who propose substantive change in public schools have an obligation to engage and inform the public. They also have an obligation to protect schools from being manipulated by special interest groups who seek to misinform the general public or advance a narrow agenda" (p. 35). Because school leaders make tough, public decisions, their integrity, professionalism, and decision-making skills are apt to be challenged.

In preparing for controversy, the following steps may prove useful:

◆ Recognize that controversy will exist. There are people who are likely to pursue their purpose(s) with almost any means.
◆ Recognize that when controversy erupts, the media will cover it—even if it entails personal attacks.
◆ Collect the facts. An appropriate response requires accurate information.
◆ Share the facts. Create fact sheets; make information available through media outlets.
◆ No matter how emotional the situation, act fairly, honestly, and legally. There is nothing to be gained by unprofessional, unethical, or illegal acts.

SUMMARY

Public relations programs are developed and put into effect at both the institutional and the unit levels of an organization. Both school districts and schools, for example, benefit from leadership that accommodates the use of accurate information for planning, programming, and evaluation. Here we explored those issues most cogent to institutional planning and application.

The chief executive officer of any organization sets the tone for public relations. If he or she sees the process as a self-serving effort, then this perception is apt to become reality. This fact is becoming increasingly apparent in a world where information plays such a dominant role. The top administrator must not only possess the professional knowledge and associated skills to pursue public relations, he or she must be committed to open and honest two-way communication. If the proper values and beliefs are in place, decisions about a public relations director, a public relations program, and the use of information can be put in place.

This book is about the convergence of technology, school reform, and use of information to improve schools. These factors have changed what society expects from schools and they have redefined effective administration. Today's outstanding practitioner is more likely to be a leader than a manager and more likely to seek information than attempt to control it. If every segment of the organization is to contribute to the public relations effort, the top administrators must demonstrate their commitment to the process.

High Hopes Gone Sour

Three years ago Tom Clancy arrived in Lawrence, hailed as the superintendent who was going to radically improve the Lawrence Public Schools. In the eyes of the public, that expectation has not yet been fulfilled. Although patrons readily agree that the school system has not deteriorated under his leadership, most are quick to point out that he has failed to produce any meaningful improvement. The survival clock is ticking, for Dr. Clancy's contract is up for renewal in another year.

A small, working-class midwestern city, Lawrence has escaped many of the problems plaguing urban areas. Yet, the public schools have been in the doldrums for nearly two decades. The city fathers (the leadership is still all-male) have frequently made the schools their scapegoats, suggesting that most community problems are linked to education. When the economy turned sour, the schools were blamed for not properly preparing graduates. When juvenile crime increased, the problem was attributed to poor discipline practices in the schools. While the schools are often seen as the problem, they were also, with Clancy's arrival, projected as the solution.

The belief that schools were at the center of the community's problem had led to the dismissal of the former superintendent, the first female superintendent in the district. She had been hired by a five-member school board composed of three women and two men. When the next school board election had wiped out what the local newspaper called "the overrepresentation of females," the superintendent knew she was in trouble. She was increasingly portrayed in editorials and letters to the editor as "an academic who is too soft on discipline." Initially, many parents liked her motto, "All Children Can Learn," and many had believed her when she talked about the possibilities of long-term reform. Teachers and administrators, however, were more skeptical. When the expected changes had not occurred within a year or two, the criticisms from the staff had become louder, and even those parents who had once supported her became disgruntled.

Clancy had applied for the job in Lawrence knowing the last two superintendents had had a combined tenure of only four years. An experienced superintendent, he knew there were risks in all jobs, but his apprehensions about Lawrence had been particularly strong, and they had not diminished when he interviewed for the job. But once it became apparent that the mayor and school board were behind him, he had convinced himself he could succeed, and he negotiated a five-year contract.

Clancy had barely placed the family pictures on his new desk when he realized that Lawrence was far more complex than his last superintendency. He was inundated with paperwork, a situation to which he was not accustomed. Purchase requisitions for any item over $500 required nine signatures, including his. He had also made several other discoveries rather quickly:

◆ He was the only "outsider" on the administrative team. All the others had grown up in Lawrence and had graduated from local high schools.
◆ There were dozens and dozens of committees functioning in the district. No decision of any consequence was made without a roomful of people being present.
◆ No administrative staff member had been fired or even disciplined for years. When they got into trouble or encountered problems they could not solve, they were simply moved to another assignment.

- ◆ The school board was engaged in micromanaging, involved in the day-to-day operations of the school system.
- ◆ The employee unions were unusually powerful. Not only did they have lucrative contracts, they had exerted influence in recent school board elections.
- ◆ There was no organized method for communicating with staff or the public. For example, telephone calls and letters from patrons were often ignored.
- ◆ The culture and climate of the organization was highly bureaucratic. There was little effort to involve the community in school matters.

After two months on the job, Dr. Clancy had shared his concerns with several trusted colleagues. They'd advised him to become his own public relations agent. They told him to get out into the schools and community and meet directly with teachers and patrons. He decided to follow their advice.

Much of routine work of the superintendency was relegated to an assistant, Bill Evans—a long-time employee with thirty-eight years of experience in the district—and Clancy started spending a good bit of time away from the office. He joined local organizations to broaden his contact with the public, and he accepted every invitation to speak before community groups. The results were not exactly what he had expected. Discussions with teachers often focused on complaints about other employees. Parents seemed to complain about everything except their childrens' current teachers, and this was partially explained by parental fears that teachers would retaliate if they found out they were being criticized. Those who were more candid complained about antiquated teaching methods, a lack of structure, and low expectations.

Through his first year in Lawrence, Clancy had remained committed to his course of action. But Bill Evans, his key assistant, had retired that first summer, and the board president had exerted tremendous pressure on Clancy to promote a principal, Gene Glenn, to the vacated central office position. At first, the superintendent had objected, but eventually a compromise was reached. In return for promoting Glenn, the superintendent was given authority to create a position for a public information officer. He was also given assurances that he could pursue a reorganization of his administrative staff.

The local media had applauded the superintendent's initiatives, declaring that improved media relations and an administrative shakeup were both long overdue. Clancy was portrayed positively in the stories.

The newly created position of public relations director was filled quickly by Betty Simmons, an award-winning high school journalism teacher. The fact that she was a "local" was seen as an asset by most board members. The reorganization of staff was a far more difficult matter. The effort, which took six months to complete, turned out to be a disappointment for the superintendent. Clancy was able to oust only one administrator; all the others had political ties directly to the school board members or indirectly to them through the unions. As a result, the reorganization had been sarcastically described by one reporter as "a senseless game of musical chairs."

Now at the start of his fourth year in Lawrence, the media has set their sights on Dr. Clancy. They have criticized his failure to bring new administrators into the district. They have pointed out that test scores have not improved. Anonymous comments from employees and parents frequently make their way into the newspaper, virtually all criticizing

Dr. Clancy. Quotes from school board members and off-the-record comments about school board executive sessions and administrative cabinet meetings are made available to reporters. Clancy has had to reduce his time away from the office because he is increasingly distrustful of Gene Glenn, who has become a publicity hound. Making himself available to the media, the assistant superintendent typically exaggerates accomplishments and raises false hopes about program changes.

One bright spot for Clancy has been the success of Betty Simmons. Since assuming her post, she has won several awards for the newsletters and brochures she's prepared. She is also the only administrator not immersed in local politics.

QUESTIONS AND SUGGESTED ACTIVITIES

Case Study

1. Do you think Tom Clancy was "set up" for failure? Why or why not?
2. What could Clancy have done differently when contemplating taking the position in Lawrence?
3. This school district has both a closed climate (that is, there is little effort to involve the community) and a high amount of political activity. Do you think these characteristics are common in public school systems?
4. To what extent do public expectations play a role in this case?
5. Assess the status of the administrative staff. Do connections between the administrators and school board members contribute to the climate in the school system?
6. Assess the superintendent's decision to devote a good bit of his time to visiting schools and the community. Was this a good idea?
7. Was Clancy prepared to employ a public information officer? What factors in the case influence your answer?
8. Assess the compromise Clancy reached with the board president. Was this an effective approach to establishing public relations? Why or why not?
9. Outline the steps that could be taken to create a public relations plan for this school district. What roles would the superintendent and public information officer play in the planning?
10. To what extent could good public relations solve Clancy's problems?
11. What are the limits to what quality communications can accomplish in Lawrence?

Chapter

12. Early in this chapter the point was made that criticism of education is not a new phenomenon. Do you agree? How can criticism be lessened in the future?
13. Develop a job description and title for a school public relations official.
14. Prepare a public relations budget for a school district of 6000 students with a per pupil expenditure of $4900.
15. Plan a school board meeting with the intent of addressing the image portrayed by the school district to the public.
16. What are four ways to enhance citizen participation that you believe would be particularly effective? Why did you select these particular activities?
17. How can administrators protect themselves and their school districts from controversy, while meeting the demands of educational leadership?

SUGGESTED READINGS

Berry, L. L., & Parasuraman, A. (1991). *Marketing services competing through quality*. New York: Free Press.

Hanson, E. M., & Henry, W. (1993). Strategic marketing for educational systems: A guide for implementation. *NASSP Bulletin, 77*(556), 79–88.

Howlett, P. (1993). Taming the trends. *American School Board Journal, 180*(6), 35–36.

Kaplan, G. R. (1992). *Images of education—The mass media's version of America's schools*. Arlington, VA: National School Public Relations Association.

Kotler, P., & Fox, K. F. (1985). *Strategic marketing for educational institutions*. Englewood Cliffs, NJ: Prentice Hall.

National Commission on Excellence in Education (1983). *A nation at risk: The imperative for educational reform*. Washington, DC: U.S. Department of Education.

Nebgen, M. (1991). The key to success in strategic planing is communication. *Educational Leadership, 48*(7), 26–28.

Sharpe, F. (1994). Devolution—Towards a research framework. *Educational Management and Administration, 22*(2), 85–95.

Townsend, R. (1993). Coping with controversy. *School Administrator, 50*(9), 24–27.

Van Meter, E. J. (1993). Setting new priorities: Enhancing the school-community relations program. *NASSP Bulletin, 77*(554), 22–27.

Wanat, C. L., & Bowles, B. D. (1993). School-community relations: A process paradigm. *Community Education Journal, 20*(2), 3–7.

REFERENCES

American Association of School Administrators. (1994). *Local school councils . . . Where we stand*. Arlington, VA: Author.

Bagin, D., Ferguson, D., & Marx, G. (1985). *Public relations for administrators*. Arlington, VA: American Association of School Administrators.

Davis, B. R. (1986). *School public relations: The complete book*. Arlington, VA: National School Public Relations Association.

Deal, T. E., & Kennedy, A. A. (1982). *Corporate cultures: The rites and rituals of corporate life*. Reading, MA: Addison-Wesley.

Kowalski, T. J., & Reitzug, U. C. (1993). *Contemporary school administration*. New York: Longman.

Ledell, M., & Arnsparger, A. (1993). *How to deal with community criticism*. Denver, CO: Education Commission of the States.

Levinson, J. (1989). *Guerrilla marketing*. Boston: Houghton Mifflin.

Ordovensky, P., & Marx, G. (1993). *Working with the news media*. Arlington, VA: American Association of School Administrators.

Topor, R. (Ed.). (1992). *No more navel gazing*. (Articles from *Marketing Higher Education Newsletter*.) Mountain View, CA: Topor & Associates.

Unruh, A., & Willier, R.A. (1974). *Public relations for schools*. Belmont, CA: Lear Siegler/Fearon Publishers.

CHAPTER 8

Effective Programming at the Unit Level

Philip T. West

Few people would deny the importance of good human relations, nor would they wittingly shun any practice that helped to achieve such goodwill. As a movement in industry and education, human relations was, to many, a kind of salvation for the worker who had heretofore toiled under rigid scientific-management principles. As a way of relating to one another in the home, at work, and in the marketplace, human relations is not only sensible but also a step toward inviting harmony into one's existence. Good human relationships engender respect, cooperation, and collaboration and are essential to organizational efforts such as site-based management and total quality management. But good human relationships do not happen in and of themselves; they must be planned and implemented with careful deliberation. This kind of planning in any organizational context requires an effective public relations (PR) program, which, if viewed analytically, incorporates the best in human relations and communication practices (West, 1985a).

ESTABLISHING THE NEED FOR A PR PROGRAM AT THE UNIT LEVEL

All boards of education do not naturally opt for PR programs in their districts. Looking upon them as a form of gimmickry best left to big corporations who want to attract potential product users, many boards are prone to consider PR programs more as luxuries than as necessities. And their stance is quite understandable, for the benefits derived from a PR program often go unnoticed until a crisis occurs within a school system, while the additional and continuous expense they represent to already-overburdened taxpayers is immediately apparent.

When boards do approve such programs, the programs are frequently centralized. The PR director operates from the school system's central office, from which all communiqués and responses to inquiries emanate and through which all matters pertaining to PR are channeled. In this approach to PR, individual schools or units follow, rather than lead, in any orchestrated PR efforts.

Creating Awareness

Unfortunately, in the process of orchestrating efforts at the central-office level, even the most well-intentioned superintendent and PR director, working hand in hand, sometimes overlook or underestimate the potential contributions building-level units can make to the system's PR program. Being a member of an administrative team, council, or cabinet, along with the system's PR director, unit-level administrators become increasingly aware of the importance of PR in conducting system affairs. But awareness cannot stop here. Unit-level administrators must initiate their own PR programs.

Such programs are severely limited, however, if the system's superintendent is indifferent to the need for a systemwide PR program. Isolated efforts at the unit or system level too often run counter to each other. On the other hand, if a PR program is backed by policy, it is not only financially accommodated within the system budget to assure it some measure of continuity within that system, it also becomes an inherent part of the system's culture and an accepted way of organizational life. As a consequence, individual units have access to the expertise of the system's PR director to help them with their own programs, plus the necessary encouragement from their superintendent to use their limited resources as creatively as possible to make their programs work.

Garnering Support

The unit administrator, or principal, cannot hope to create staff support for a PR program instantly. An effective program develops over time. Although system PR policy may specify certain parameters in which any unit PR program can operate, it is the PR practices of the unit itself, when coupled with the PR practices of other units, that determine to what extent a system's PR program is going to be effective. Without a shared vision predicated on egalitarianism, extensive opportunities for participation, trust, and open channels of communications, units differ drastically in their approach to PR, both internally and externally.

Support is a two-way street. The superintendent must serve as an exemplar to principals, the principals as a protocol for staff. Modeling appropriate PR behavior is a first step toward getting others to reciprocate. A second is to recognize and reward such behavior. When the organizational climate is conducive to good human relations, it is also ready to launch a concerted PR effort. A third step in getting support is through wholesale involvement, at which time potential PR contributions of all staff members are addressed. This third step, however, does not occur without a plan and the people to make sure it is carried out.

DEVELOPING A PR PROGRAM AT THE UNIT LEVEL

While system policy makes it legitimate, a PR program can be initiated by a principal without such a policy. What policy does is lend organization, unity, and direction to disparate efforts at the unit level. Some principals pride themselves on the good PR program they have, boasting that staff, students, and community members enjoy a strong sense of togetherness and camaraderie. Staff and student attendance is high, open-house events are filled to capacity, and media relations are excellent—all of this occurring in the absence of system policy. Other principals, not as aware of the ingredients of an effective PR program, experience haphazard results in their PR efforts. Unfortunately, the efforts of both types of administrators too often become disjointed and misdirected in the absence of formalized policy when the rare crisis occurs.

Creating a Building-Level Committee

A PR program functioning at its optimal level in any school district has a systemwide PR committee ideally composed of about fifteen members: administrators, staff, students, parents and nonparents, senior citizens, and business and industry leaders (West, 1985a). It also has a similar committee at the unit level. While the systemwide PR committee is presided over by the school district's PR director, the unit committee may be chaired by the principal or assistant principal or a designee, who may be a teacher with abbreviated duties, charged with carrying out the unit's PR program.

These committees meet separately about once a month throughout the school year. Then in fall and spring, representatives of unit committees meet with the total membership of the systemwide committee to pool and address community concerns. In this way the unit and system become very much aware of each other's problems and are able to make recommendations to the system's chief executive officer to either alleviate or eliminate these problems.

Fall and spring meetings are also instrumental in assessing unit progress toward systemwide goals for the PR program. At the same time, the system's support mechanisms are evaluated. The input and feedback from these committees keep lines of communication open throughout the district.

The terms of committee members should be staggered so that two-thirds of the membership is always retained. For example, if a committee numbers fifteen and terms of appointment are for three years, each year has a turnover of five. This staggered approach gives new members the benefit of always having experienced members on hand to assist them in learning committee fundamentals.

Relating the Unit Program to System Policy

A unit's program should not exist in a vacuum, operating independently as seen fit by principal and staff. It must be related to the school district's systemwide PR policy, which may be developed by the systemwide PR committee under the auspices of the superintendent and/or the system's PR director. Or it may be developed by the PR director alone, subject to the approval of the superintendent; or by the superintendent alone, if neither a committee nor a director yet exists. On some occasions, a standing committee of the board, working with the superintendent, may be engaged in PR policy formulation. In any event, whatever is developed must ultimately be submitted to the board for its approval.

Actual PR policy formulation takes into consideration six aspects (West, 1981; West, 1985a):

1. *Participants:* Who will develop the policy? Preferably, it is a systemwide PR advisory committee, operating in tandem with unit-level committees
2. *Values:* What do school officials believe in with regard to information flow and exchanges? The public's right to know? Citizen participation? Gaining/retaining public confidence? Open school climates? The public's attitudes and expectations for its schools? Administrator/staff/student relationships?
3. *Goals:* To create a two-way communication system between central office and building-level units and between school district and community? To develop a good working relationship between school district and the various media? To implement a systemwide PR in-service program?
4. *Structure:* To whom does the systemwide PR director report and why? Who designs and carries out PR activities? What is the role of the unit in the systemwide program? How flexible is this role?
5. *Strategies:* Who develops what PR strategies?
6. *Assessment:* How often and in what manner does PR program assessment occur?

The outcome of this process is, of course, a PR policy that is implemented at both system and unit levels. And what applies to the system has the same relevance for the unit. Indeed, if policy is ideally implemented, it retains sufficient flexibility for unit interpretation in designing activities that enhance goal accomplishment. The converse would be a straitjacket that denies the relative uniqueness of individual units as they attempt to meet consumer needs, interests, and aspirations.

Addressing the Unique Needs, Interests, and Aspirations of Unit Clients

The needs of unit clients may vary from school to school. While latchkey programs may be vital in one school, a program to prevent student dropout may be crucial in another. While the former may entail enlisting volunteers or hiring paraprofessionals to operate these programs, the latter may suggest a whole array of activities to involve parents in the education of their children.

The interests of clients in various units may also differ. Some clients are enamored with a unit's athletic opportunities for their youngsters while others favor a unit's academic offerings. On the other hand, if a community education program is in place for community members, some of the unit's clients may deem computer training as a desirable course for the unit to make available; others may reveal a strong interest in aerobics, ceramics, or stained glass courses.

The aspirations of a unit's clients may be largely contingent upon their success or their children's success in the unit. If an adult successfully completes a high school equivalency program, he or she may give much consideration to entering college or some specialized technical school. If a youngster repeatedly experiences success in a writing program, he or she may aspire to become a professional writer or to go on to college to major in English.

Coordinating Unit and System PR Activities

While unit PR programs may enjoy some degree of uniqueness, they must never be so unique that they undermine the commonality of purpose they share with each other in the attainment of system goals. Some systems have a standard reporting form that each unit uses to keep the system's PR director informed about unit activities. It is then up to the PR director to make the appropriate media contacts. Other systems, having only a single PR director and several units to coordinate, give units much more latitude in reporting information to the media about ongoing activities. In these systems, a directory is generally made available to the media, listing unit administrators as well as key central-office personnel.

The success of either approach is largely contingent upon the degree of openness that exists throughout the system. If communication is at an optimum level among units and between units and the central office, coordination can be relatively simple. By the same token, if channels of communication are always kept open, it is also easy to target a unit when it is not in compliance with system PR policy goals.

One channel of communication is the administrative team, cabinet, or council, which brings administrators together to plan, coordinate, and assess ongoing programs and activities. Another, extending participation and channeling information from school to community and back again, is best reflected in the recent trend toward site-based management, which is sometimes coupled with a total quality management approach. Still another, mentioned earlier, is the use of unit-level and systemwide PR advisory committees.

There is, as well, the communication channel provided by computer technology, which allows unit principals and the central office to network and to consolidate PR efforts. PR issues management at the system level and PR issue-oriented in-service (identification and problem resolution) at the unit level present other opportunities to computerize information flowing in both directions. The least creative, but a bureaucratic necessity, is the use of the computer for transmitting and storing records and memoranda.

Identifying the Elements of An Effective PR Program

There are seven dimensions in any educational PR program, regardless of whether it is carried out within a unit or throughout a system. Each of these dimensions operates at high and low levels of public relations. The first, *selling,* is at its lowest level no more than hype. Unconcerned with any ethical obligations, it tends to sell whatever is as right. At its highest level, however, this dimension uses marketing strategies to target and meet the needs, interests, and aspirations of the system's constituency. These strategies may also create needs and stimulate greater interests and aspirations when constituency awareness of available products is somewhat lacking. At this level, selling becomes a client-oriented, decision-making approach that employs extensive research, citizen involvement, and opinionnaires to gauge not only client satisfaction with existing products but also client receptivity to new products (West, 1985a).

The second dimension is *persuading,* which is, at its lowest level, little more than propaganda. Here the school story is told to clients in a way that is ambiguous and misleading, but not necessarily untrue. The message that constituents receive is that all is well in unit or system, even when flaws are becoming noticeable. In contrast, the highest level of persuading is educating the organization's various publics to become more discriminating in making their choices about schooling for their children (West, 1985a).

The third dimension, *informing*, has, at its lowest level, a narrow dissemination of the facts. Here the client receives only a partial representation of the facts, which, because of their narrowness, are insufficient for making an appropriate decision. By telling only part of the story, and the best part at that, the unit or system limits and controls potential client responses. At its best, this dimension promotes comprehensive news reporting and reveals both sides of an issue, while assuming that an informed clientele will be more likely to provide needed participation and support than one that has to act on limited knowledge (West, 1985a).

The fourth dimension, *defining*, is, at its lowest level, the telling of the school story in educational jargon. The assumption here is that professionalism is best served when terminology is arcane. Unfortunately, jargon is not the way to communicate to a unit or system's various publics, if any degree of understanding is to be assured or if goals are to be shared. Thus, at its highest level, defining means administrators and teachers communicating in the simplest terms possible with their clientele (West, 1985a).

The next two dimensions—*exchanging* and *responding*—if carried out at their highest levels, result in large-scale interaction and involvement. Finally, there is the dimension of *synergy*, which, in linking one dimension to another, as well as unit to system, forms a web of public relations that assures an effective PR program (West, 1985a).

SITE-BASED PR MANAGEMENT

In systems where site-based management has been mandated, decisions formerly made by superintendents alone are increasingly being made at the unit level by advisory councils composed of teachers, parents, and other community members (National School Public Relations Association, 1993). Within this new decision-making context, the role of the pricipal is to facilitate rather than to dictate (Aronstein, Marlow, & Desilets, 1991), while the role of those further up the hierarchy is not only to allow but to encourage principals to share decision making with their teams (Maeroff, 1993). Sharing "their leadership role with individuals long considered to be their subordinates" (p. 12) may be difficult for some administrators, but if ample developmental opportunities are made available to them and a whole-hearted commitment can be elicited, site-based management will continue to enjoy its current prominence (West, 1994).

Meanwhile, the emerging role of the PR director is to coach and advise unit-level personnel in matters that deal with public relations (NSPRA, 1992). In one school district, for example, some of this preparation has been directed not only at dealing with the media and developing coalitions but also at managing conflict and crisis (NSPRA, 1992). PR directors have also been engaged to work with teachers and advisory groups to help them understand precisely what site-based management is all about (NSPRA, 1992, p. 1). Too, the PR director has been instrumental in assisting councils to develop both communication strategies and a mission statement that will guide them in their relationships with each other and with other groups (NSPRA, 1993).

With the advent of site-based management and the ever-increasing need for community support to attain educational goals, there is no longer anything faddish about effective public relations at the unit level (Armistead, 1992). Goal accomplishment is an outcome of an effective unit and system public relations program, which uses two-way communication strategies to transmit information to and receive information from their various publics, preferably through activities that involve them, so as to gain support for mutually rewarding educational goals (Ascough, 1993).

TOTAL QUALITY MANAGEMENT

Just as site-based management is on the rise in school districts across the country, so too is total quality management. Emphasizing shared decision making and collaborative goal setting, both approaches have much in common. The difference is that while site-based management may reflect a legal mandate or a local school board policy, total quality management represents a highly structured option to accomplish mandates and policies. Evolving over the past four decades in this country and in Japan, it is a methodological approach that is derived from the best of a variety of organization models and systems, theories to control quality, and instrumentation (Coate, 1990). Based on the fourteen points advocated by the movement's originator, W. Edwards Deming, total quality management requires educators to view unit and system as an amalgam of both people and process that constantly interact (American Association of School Administrators, 1992).

It is a concept that virtually makes customers and suppliers out of everyone within a school system, with anyone receiving a service viewed as a customer and anyone providing a service viewed as a supplier. In many instances, the same individual is both, with exchanges being reciprocal and supportive (AASA, 1992). Vision-driven, total quality management stresses the highest standards of consumerism; continuous quality control; and overall improvement through extensive information sharing, stakeholder input—particularly from those most closely associated with a process—and process improvement teams. The basic assumption in this approach is that people are motivated to do the best job they can and that system errors are due mostly to faulty processes—90 percent, according to Coate (1190)—and not to people (AASA, 1992). Since improvement and measurement are directly related in total quality management, individuals are expected to make improvements in their work that can be measured (Shonberger, 1992).

In stressing the importance of consumerism and the contributions of people, total quality management reflects a philosophy that invites and depends upon good public relations. In such an environment, the role of the PR director takes on considerable importance, especially in helping to structure and maintain communication processes that harmonize relationships between team members and among teams as they strive to achieve unit and system goals. In turn, these groups, along with the PR director, open and maintain a variety of two-way communication channels between a school district and its community. In total quality management a unit or system's clients, as well as its suppliers, interact to bring about programmatic change and improvement (Wanat & Bowles, 1993).

In systems just beginning to implement total quality management, some team members may be quick to assign blame to individuals rather than to faulty processes and to restrict, rather than expand, information flow—to compete, not cooperate. The same may be true of those further up in the administrative hierarchy, where competition is even keener. The result may be a good deal of scapegoating at unit and system levels. However, if both unit-level principals and teams, as well as their superiors, are accoutered with the appropriate public relations skills and practices to carry them through this trial period, the transition will be much easier to experience. In those school districts where site-based management and total quality management are reinforced by pairing, broadening dramatically the circle of participation, public relations skills become even more important.

STRATEGIC PLANNING

Strategic planning, a collaborative form of management, originated in business and industry in the 1950s and enjoyed growth during the 1960s and 1970s. However, mixed reviews in the 1980s prompted a move from process to technique (Webster, Reif, & Bracker, 1989). In any event, strategic planning has now found its way into the public schools as a result of site-based efforts. In effect, the strategic plan guides an organization through the vagaries of the present toward some sought-after future (Hellebust & Krallinger, 1989). With regard to its relationship to total quality management, Richard Shonberger (1992) points out that while the principles of total quality management do not address some of the complex aspects of competition that are dealt with by strategic planning, they seem to impart to them both simplicity and balance.

In a booklet entitled "Sharing a Vision," which describes the essentials of the strategic plan of the Waco Independent School District in Waco, Texas, the district's school board and administrators showed how strategic planning can become a way for a school and a community to join efforts to achieve desirable and needed change. Developed by a strategic planning committee and eight action teams, the district's strategic plan has a mission statement that sets forth a shared vision and ethical priorities and outlines the best ways to implement and attain them. Efforts are to be directed toward achieving identified student outcomes. Meanwhile, close attention is to be paid to critical issues facing school and community that impede overall goal accomplishment (Sharing a Vision).

In the Cupertino (California) Union School District, the strategic planning process was used by board and administrators to bring together members of the community to decide what the district's educational expectations should be for the future. By addressing a multiplicity of changes occurring within the district, a broad representation of school and community leaders, assembled into fifteen task forces, was able to forecast and plan for identified needs and develop a mission statement to guide the district into the future. Also emerging from the district's strategic planning process was a technology plan to facilitate educational access into the twenty-first century (del Prado & Armstrong, 1990).

In summing up the merits of strategic management, Jauch and Glueck (1988) pointed out that strategic management is predictive rather than reactive. It is founded on a decision-making process that, in looking to the future, achieves an awareness of trends and fosters the capability to plan early and effectively to manage those trends. This planned decision-making process must be kept flexible to deal with change that is unexpected. In a similar vein, Hellebust and Krallinger (1989) indicate that the true effectiveness of strategic planning occurs when strategies and goals become rooted in an organization's culture and impact all its decisions. They also indicate that the future of strategic planning is not with planning staffs but with line management in the organizational hierarchy; in educational environments this translates into both school and community members.

THE MARKETING OF EDUCATION

The importance of the customer emphasis in both total quality management and strategic planning is perhaps best addressed by Peter Drucker who maintains that the only aim of a business is to make customers (Hellebust & Krallinger, 1989)—people who, by preference, repeatedly purchase a product. Today education is really big business, with entrepreneurs on the sidelines waiting to offer alternatives to traditional schooling, should the schools fail to meet the needs of their community constituents, who until recently have seldom been viewed as customers. But marketing—and all it implies—has now found its way in the schools, and its importance is undeniable.

It is said that by necessity a marketing plan determines all other organizational plans (Hellebust & Krallinger, 1989). Because its grasp cannot exceed its reach, a marketing plan is directed both inward and outward, influencing, on the one hand, every phase of production and all personnel decisions and, on the other, extending into the marketplace to meet community needs and desires. Just as complex as the marketing plan are concomitant practices, which should include information collection, storage, and patterned retrieval to determine advantageous distribution outlets, customer preferences, and strengths and weaknesses of competing products. Products should also be differentiated to appeal to customers, and markets should be segmented to target specific customer needs (Hellebust & Krallinger, 1989).

The role of marketing in education is a relatively new one, dating back only about a decade and a half. For example, in 1980, Barry Ostow was claiming that marketing was an important part of a district's PR program, and Bonnie Ellison was promoting advertising in the schools. That same year William Banach and staff conceived and implemented the Macomb County Marketing Plan for Schools, which the Michigan Education Department endorsed for statewide use in 1981 (Banach, 1981). In 1981, Don Bagin recommended that community educators market their programs, emphasizing, among other things, that a successful marketing program would make them aware of unwanted services, which may be costing the district a lot of unnecessary time and money. In 1982, Joanie Flatt identified three roles for the PR director that highlighted marketing, one of which stressed advertising, a technique that schools in the past had considered inappropriate.

Since then much has been written about the application of marketing strategies to schools. In advocating a marketing plan that reflects a strong consumer orientation and in stressing what it must have to be successful, Mary Nebgen (1985) called for top management support, an institutional image that reflects high quality, the hiring of a marketing specialist, a variety of two-way communication channels internally and externally, differentiation of products to increase their attractiveness, and multiple opportunities for immediate feedback. Moreover, she claimed that any attempt to operationalize a customer-oriented philosophy would require that staff receive formal training not only in its value but also in how it can be accomplished.

With regard to the use of marketing strategies in schools, Philip West (1985b) said, "[T]he public . . . needs to be sold on the idea that the public schools are better than ever and that, if faced with a choice, the wise citizen opts for a public school education" (p. 17), adding, "[T]he approach schools eventually adopt will be sophisticated. It will employ artful marketing strategies, many of which will mainly bring people into the schools to become involved in school affairs" (p. 17).

In discussing the merits of using the computer as an educational marketing tool, West and Elkins (1990) noted that "[W]ith a computer to classify and arrange a database for a management information system, a marketing plan can be designed and operationalized with relative ease" (p. 18). For example, the computer can track the short- and long-range goals that grow out of a school district's mission statement; it can track participants, competitors, and issues arising from special interest groups; and it can track product development and consumption. It can also be used to facilitate policy development activities and to relate budget to the demand for services. Finally, it can be used electronically as a promotional strategy and as a tool for evaluation (West & Elkins, 1990).

In explaining what a school or unit would have to market, West (1986–1987) identified four categories: students, administration/staff, curriculum, and community. Included among the items contained in the first category are number of scholarships awarded to students and quality or reputation of colleges students will be attending. In the second category are education and experience, along with honors and awards received and articles published. In the third are special showpiece curricular approaches and available remedial, developmental, and enrichment opportunities available to students. And in the fourth are availability of educational opportunities for adults, number of school-business/industry partnerships, and favorable citizen poll results. Interestingly enough, in a survey that assessed the perceptions of PR directors and superintendents nationwide with regard to the function of marketing in the public schools, both groups were in most agreement on the statement: "The media should be fully used to advertise the strengths of the school district's faculty" (Gardner & West, 1990, p. 30).

It would seem that marketing strategies, admittedly on the rise in schools and compatible with both the tenets of TQM and strategic planning, are likely to continue to flourish. As they do, public relations at the unit level must also grow, and along with it so, too, must the PR role of both principal and staff.

PR ROLES OF UNIT-LEVEL PERSONNEL

When a school district is said to have good PR, it is not because of some magical art performed by a district's superintendent or PR director, or the two working in tandem, nor is it simply due to the combined efforts of central-office personnel. This does not mean that what happens at the system level is unimportant. What it does mean is that while a system may have effective PR as one of its primary goals, it is at the unit level where the accomplishment of this goal must really take place.

Role of Public and Private School Principals

The PR role of a school principal is much like that of a superintendent. Both may be instrumental in getting a board to adopt a PR policy: the superintendent directly, principals indirectly through their superintendent. Both may assign the PR function to someone else: the principal to a teacher, the superintendent to a districtwide PR specialist. The efforts of both are aimed at achieving internal and external harmony within their purviews. The principal focuses on improving relations with and among building-level personnel and between unit and neighborhood. The superintendent targets the improvement of administrative, staff, and community relations throughout the district. Both may also conduct surveys: the principal at the unit level and superintendent at the system level. The principal is spokesperson for the unit; the superintendent, for the district. And both deal with the media: a principal periodically, the superintendent fairly often. As a consequence, both are obliged to develop good relations with the media. Both must also have the necessary personal attributes to relate to people effectively (West, 1985a).

A survey taken in Texas (Schueckler & West, 1991) to assess the perceptions of both principals and PR directors concerning the actual and ideal PR role of senior high school principals found that the principals saw them themselves as doing a better job than did the PR directors. On the other hand, there were five areas in which principals thought they needed to improve their PR role:

* Strives to operate an effective school office.
* Possesses common sense, judgment, discretion, and a sense of proportion.
* Listens carefully when others speak with him/her.
* Is tactful and diplomatic in all relationships.
* Promotes an open-door policy with students, teachers, parents, and others. (p. 25)

It is interesting to note that two of these areas (the second and third listed) were also among the top five areas in which PR directors sought improvement for principals. Three other areas where PR officers saw a need for improvement in principals were the following:

* Continually strives for the best public relations program possible.
* Recognizes the accomplishments of individuals and groups.
* Strives to keep the superintendent informed of any potential problem in the area of public relations. (p. 25)

Assistant principals in high schools also have an important PR role to play, as indicated in a recent Delphi study, which had a panel of experts identify critical tasks for Texas assistant principals in two time periods: 0 to 5 years and 10 to 20 years (Eaton & West, 1988). In the first time period, or the immediate future, there were six critical PR tasks for assistant high school principals:

* Maintain rapport with teachers (agreement among experts on the importance of this task was 83%),
* Motivate students and faculty (78%),
* Communicate with parents/students (78%),
* Present professional demeanor to faculty (72%),
* Maintain rapport with students (72%), and
* Improve teacher morale (66%). (p. 31)

In the second time period, or more-distant future, there were eight critical tasks to be performed by assistant high school principals, six of which appear in the first time period, with about the same degree of group consensus. The remaining two were "Improve school climate (78%)" and "Elicit parental cooperation (66%)" (p. 31).

At the elementary school level principals also have a significant PR role in school-community relations. According to West (1993a),

> [They] communicate with a variety of groups daily, most typically students, teachers, support staff, and parents, but also central office personnel, their peers, and sometimes their superintendents, depending on the size of the system. They also communicate with business/industry representatives engaged in Adopt-a-School Programs. In these relationships they may at one moment assume an instructional leadership posture and at another an entrepreneurial stance. As leaders of instruction they are not only agents of quality but also of change. As entrepreneurs they strive to communicate their school's excellence to the neighborhoods that support them. (p. 10)

Principals in private high schools have much in common with their public school counterparts with regard to the PR role they must play, according to the perceptions of principals in Texas private high schools (Powell & West, 1991). For example, four of the five top PR tasks in which these principals would like to improve are the same as reported by high school principals in public schools. Where they differ is in their perceived need for improvement in recognizing the accomplishments of their staff, the area in which PR directors recommended improvement for Texas public high school principals. Key PR activities performed by these private high school principals include:

- ◆ Informing parents of school activities with newsletters.
- ◆ Involving parents in formal programs.
- ◆ Meeting with parents formally and informally.
- ◆ Meeting with students.
- ◆ Informing and interacting with the community.
- ◆ Involving the school, faculty, and students in the community. (*Powell & West*, 1991, p. 30)

Role of Public and Private Schoolteachers

The PR role of teachers in public and private schools is the same. Only their clientele differ. The public school has a guaranteed clientele, while the private school has to attract students to its program and is, therefore, much more aware of the importance of consumerism than is its counterpart. However, with the rise of marketing in public schools and the appearance of total quality management and strategic planning in these schools, public schools are taking on a similar customer orientation.

One of the most effective PR postures teachers should, therefore, assume is to treat students as customers or clients. However, to have a satisfied customer a teacher must be able to meet his or her needs. This means that teachers must know their subject matter well and be able to package it in a manner that is educational and interesting, if not entertaining. It also means that teachers must have high expectations for students and recognize and reward appropriate behaviors. It means, too, that lines of communication between teacher and parent must kept open and available. And in carrying out their PR role, teachers must be model behavior that they would like their students to emulate. One of several factors that creates satisfying relationships between home and school is a properly qualified and proficient teacher of high moral standing who works hard and cares about children (Swink, 1989).

According to Pope and West (1989) the PR role of teachers is to be instructionally effective and grammatically correct at all times, while modeling behavior in the dress and manner of a professional. The teacher should also behave as a responsible citizen—voting, for instance, in public elections. Too, teachers should refrain from criticizing students and peers; they should be responsive to the needs of their clients, students and parents—the former by making homework meaningful and the latter through pupil progress reports and parent-teacher conferences. By welcoming parents into classrooms that they have made appealing for learning and by getting involved in a school's PR program, teachers further enhance their PR role.

Roles of Other Public and Private School Personnel

Unquestionably, all school personnel have a PR role to play, be they publicly or privately employed. By doing the best job they can to meet the needs of their clientele and by taking pride in their work, they fulfill much of their role. By showing appreciation for the job others do, they further complement this role. Though their contributions to an effective PR program are many, only a few will be addressed here.

Guidance counselors often develop close relationships with students and parents through their aid and advice in academic matters. And they help both child and parent to realize educational aspirations for the student. School nurses may also develop close relationships with students through frequent school contacts and with parents through notes carried home by students, occasional phone calls, and home visitations. Librarians open up a world of books to children and sometimes prepare annotated reading lists for faculty members to make them aware of new library holdings. They are also involved in the sensitive issue of making library acquisitions that might incur community disapproval. Working just outside the principal's office, secretaries and clerks generally come in contact with a large number of people, and their attitude toward and treatment of these people—be they staff, students, or visitors—tend to characterize the kind of morale existing within a school. Because an attractive and well-kept building reflects a school family's pride of ownership—and because this pride typically encourages better care of the school facility by the rest of the community—a custodian surely has an important PR role to play.

What is served daily in the school's cafeteria, and how it is served, is extremely important. Food prepared and served well by cafeteria workers can enhance the morale of virtually the entire school, while making an individual diner's lunch a high point in a busy and demanding day. Like cafeteria workers, bus drivers are also potential PR emissaries, who gain the respect and confidence of parents by showing concern for their children while transporting them safely along busy streets or highways in all kinds of weather. According to Paul Kimmelman (1982), bus drivers are also dependable information sources for parents.

IDENTIFYING THE UNIT-LEVEL PR PERSON

Having a districtwide PR director these days is not a frill, as some educators seem to think. It is, instead, a dire necessity if schools are to communicate effectively with their various internal and external audiences. While some school districts, generally the larger ones, have several full-time PR directors operating on the system level, many school districts still consider themselves fortunate to have a single full-time PR director at this level. But times are changing. And as the need for educational public relations increases, so too will the number of part-time and full-time PR directors employed in school districts.

Part Time / Full Time

A recent national study (Genzer, 1993), which sought to determine actual and ideal workloads of PR directors, found that 90 percent of responding PR directors were employed full time, and 64 percent had a staff of more than one. In contrast, a much-earlier study by West in 1980 revealed that only 67 percent of the PR directors sampled were employed full time.

Over the years it has been quite commonplace for part-time PR directors to work themselves into full-time jobs as a district expands and PR responsibilities multiply. Today, as districts continue to grow and a variety of site-based management approaches are implemented, the importance of having someone function in that position at the unit level, at least part time, is almost as great as having someone do the same at the system level full time. This is especially true if districts adopt a unit PR advisory committee to network with a system's PR advisory committee or, for that matter, with the system PR director.

According to Brian Kendall (1986), site coordinators are the key to an effectively networked communication program. For example, once trained in the fundamentals of communications, fifty site coordinators—60 percent of them secretaries, 35 percent of them teachers, and the rest unit managers—in California's Vallejo City Unified School District helped the district move from a centralized form of reporting information to one that coordinated and networked all its communication efforts and charged each unit with the responsibility of planning and disseminating through a variety of information channels.

Relationship with the System-Level PR Director

The individual given released time to perform unit PR responsibilities is responsible to both the school principal and the site-based management team, if one exists. The unit PR director either provides leadership or acts as a resource person for the unit PR advisory committee. The relationship between unit and system PR director is collegial rather than supervisory with regard to unit PR matters, affording each unit the opportunity to communicate directly with its publics. However, in those PR matters that affect the total system, the district PR director has the final word, the assumption being that the district PR director is an experienced PR professional and the unit PR director is a PR novice.

Periodically, unit PR directors meet with the system PR director to apprise him or her of unit and community concerns, expressed through site-based management teams and local PR advisory committees. In this way, unit site-based management teams and PR advisory committees are directly linked to the larger system and its administrative team, cabinet, or council to produce a broad database upon which decisions affecting students, staff, administration, and community can be made with reasonable accuracy.

Qualifications for the Unit-Level PR Position

In Susan Genzer's 1993 study, slightly more than half of those now occupying the position of PR director, or its equivalent (director of community relations, director of information services, public information officer, and the like), had an undergraduate major in journalism (25 percent), communications (14 percent), English (12 percent), or public relations (5 percent). At the master's level, however, education (10 percent) and, more specifically, educational administration (8 percent) majors and those majors so prevalent at the undergraduate level—communications (12 percent), English (4 percent), and public relations (1 percent)—were virtually equal in number with regard to the preparation of the educational PR director.

In performing their jobs, PR directors stressed the need for both training and experience in journalism (West, 1980), suggesting that a likely candidate for a unit PR person is one having some training in that area. Opportunities do exist, though, for the designated person to increase his or her proficiency without pursuing formal training. For example, the National School Public Relations Association (NSPRA) has an annual seminar that brings together experienced and novice PR directors to exchange ideas and obtain needed skills. NSPRA's state chapters provide similar training opportunities. NSPRA also has an array of publications that are designed to help all educational PR directors do their jobs better. Useful ideas may also be gleaned from the *Journal of Educational Public Relations*, a quarterly publication directed toward meeting the needs of educational PR specialists.

In any event, the individual chosen to assume the public relations responsibilities of the unit should possess excellent writing and speaking skills and evince some ability to lead. Some competence in photography would also be an asset, as would a working knowledge of how the various media operate, but both can be learned in time. The PR person at the unit level must also be a people person, more so perhaps than the system PR director, who is often isolated from the daily activities in schools.

CULTIVATING INFORMATION NETWORKS

Two-way communication, horizontally and vertically, is vital in any organization. If information channels are not kept open, rumors flourish and morale suffers. The flow of information within units and between units and the system is crucial to goal assessment and continuous improvement. Without information, units are compelled to function within a vacuum. Similarly, when communication breakdowns occur between school and community, the system becomes alienated from the community, and its efforts tend to invite indifference and criticism instead of support.

Unit to Unit (Formal and Informal)

Although there are many formal ways by which one unit can communicate to another, perhaps the very best is through the individual who presides over each unit's PR advisory committee. Preferably, this individual is the one charged with the unit PR function. Through periodic meetings with other individuals who have similar unit committee charges, the unit PR person is presented with opportunities to crossfeed information. This information is then carried back to the unit and shared with committee members and the unit's site-based management team, all of whom become information agents within the unit.

A monthly unit newsletter is another way units can keep each other apprised of their activities. This newsletter should be prepared by the unit PR person in consultation with the building principal and endorsed by the site-based management team. Unit-level PR directors can also exchange school activity schedules and publications. They may prepare video programs to be aired on cable TV, which can be viewed by other units as well as community members. Again, an exchange of unit communication plans would be helpful.

Informal opportunities for information exchanges occur many times during a year. Staff members who work in the district may be neighbors, with informal exchanges taking place over backyard fences or in neighborhood socials. If their children attend various unit schools, they, too, serve as information carriers. The local shopping center is a hotbed of information as unit members casually come together and discuss what is happening in their schools. Given the fact that virtually everyone is an information carrier, it would be wise for the unit PR director to keep staff constantly informed. A little information can be a dangerous thing.

Unit to System (Formal and Informal)

The same kind of periodic meetings that bring unit PR persons together to exchange information can be used to bring them together with the system PR director, who is faced with the awesome task of keeping everyone informed, internal as well as external publics. Unit PR persons also draw upon the expertise of the system PR director to design information plans and networks and to establish and cultivate media contacts. They are also kept abreast of system affairs through newsletters and newspapers that cover board, staff, school, and community events. Most important, they are privy to information that affects staff members prior to formal publication or announcement. Too often, staff members say they are the last to know about anything that occurs in their school district.

Informal information exchanges can occur on the system level in many ways: before and after periodic PR meetings with the system PR director; during staff development PR sessions over which the system PR director presides; and on picnics instigated by the local teachers' association where all school personnel have an opportunity to visit with each other. What actually transpires, of course, is something that is largely contingent upon a system's openness.

Determining Other Information Channels

In every neighborhood there are formal leaders to whom residents turn for information and advice. They may have a seat on the city council or on the school board, be a minister in a church or the scoutmaster of a local Boy Scout group. Easy to target and anxious to accept civic responsibilities, these people can serve as information agents for the site PR person. Less obvious, though, are the many informal leaders (the local barber, grocery clerk, deli manager, bank teller, and the like) who serve as information sources for neighborhood members (Bagin, 1981). One needs only to query a random selection of residents to determine who these people are. The greater the number of times their names are mentioned, the more valuable they will be in the creation of a network of potential communicators that receives and disseminates information from both residents and school. In commenting on the importance of such a network and the use of key communicators to make it work, Bagin (1981) said that people are more prone to accept change if they hear about it from acquaintances rather than read about it or hear about it from someone they do not know.

Utilizing Technology

By networking, unit PR persons can transmit information by computer to each other and to the system PR director almost instantly. They can have on-line conferences without ever leaving their stations. They can leave messages for each other as well as keep a record of all electronic exchanges. Because of this instancy, said Sharon L. Yoder (1985), networks can add to or eliminate many traditional forms of communication, among them bulletin boards and newsletters. And with notebook computers encroaching on the territory of desktops, mobility is assuredly enhanced and distance a thing of the past.

Some school systems have used cable television to link their schools with each other and with the community. In these systems the camcorder takes its place alongside the camera for recording information about the schools for media dissemination. And with the everyday use of projection television and 100-inch screens, every member of a site-based management team, not just its PR designee, can be networked for video-conferencing.

ASSESSING THE UNIT-LEVEL PROGRAM

A unit's PR program cannot be deemed effective or in a continuous state of improvement unless there is ongoing assessment. While there are many ways to assess a PR program, the most productive way is to direct all efforts toward achieving predetermined and concrete goals (West, 1985a). Because unit and system are linked irretrievably in PR goal accomplishment, there is considerable overlapping in most assessment procedures. Inventories, for example, that target system PR programs typically include sections that have relevance for unit assessment. Doyle Bortner (n.d.), for example, in offering 168 items that can be used to evaluate a system PR program, includes an array of items that are applicable to unit programs. Albert Holliday (1987), in his PR climate-assessment inventory, offered a specific section for building-level evaluation. An assessment inventory called PROWESS developed by Oberg and West (West, 1985a) also provides items than can be adapted for unit use.

Using Opinionnaires

Easy to construct and just as easy to administer—by telephone, mail, or face to face—the opinionnaire can serve as a method of assessing a unit PR program. Opinionnaires can target any or all aspects of a unit's program, at one time assessing the perceptions of staff as to PR program effectiveness; at another time, students; and at still another, community members.

And the items they contain may be generated from the unit PR advisory committee, key communicator groups, and site-based management focus groups and teams. PR consultants may be called in to develop these opinionnaires, but the best approach is to use those individuals who are most committed to making the unit PR program a success.

Quantifying Levels of Involvement

Levels of involvement, usually an indicator of PR effectiveness, are determined by a quantitative assessment. For example, how many parents attend school functions or are involved in the unit's PTA or PTO? How many accolades or criticisms does a unit receive from its constituents? How many parents, nonparents, and senior citizens are involved in its volunteer program? How many local businesses have pledged support to the unit's adopt-a-school program?

The number of articles a unit has gotten published in the local press, as well as the number of public service announcements it has had aired on radio and television, can serve as quantitative assessment points. In effect, virtually anything associated with PR that can be counted serves as a way of quantitatively assessing a unit PR program.

The Case-Study Technique

The case-study approach is a qualitative method of PR assessment that can be utilized at the unit level to analyze PR program effectiveness. An assessment of this kind depends mostly on gathering unit demographics and making observations and interviews within the unit.

However, paper tracking to determine the effectiveness of dissemination strategies is important, as is a qualitative assessment of unit publications, faculty notices, and media coverage.

Cost-Benefit Analysis

The monetary value of an educational PR program is often considered by board and administrators. While many will readily admit that a PR program is worth having, most have some difficulty in putting a price tag on one. In an effort to translate PR program outcomes into dollars and cents, West (1993b) had several advanced PR classes analyze, over a seven-year period, the potential monetary value of the seven PR evaluation categories of PROWESS (West, 1985a): school image, school financial referenda (that is, bonds and budgets), school media coverage, community feedback and involvement, staff involvement, administrative involvement, and program effectiveness. To perform these analyses, students had to create their own school districts and then apply the categories to them.

In these analyses the contribution a PR program might make to the success of a school district was assigned an arbitrary value of 1 percent out of a possible 100 percent, with the difference attributable to the many other variables (instructional or fiscal leadership, curricular effectiveness, instructional technology, special services, to cite but a few) that have a similar impact on a unit's effectiveness. Thus, if school image results in attracting parents and their children to the district and, concomitantly, real estate values go up, shopping malls are built, factories are relocated or built, and all of these activities are translated into new tax dollars, then the PR program is privy to 1 percent of the bounty. Similarly, if the school's image increases student attendance while reducing teacher absenteeism and turnover, then the additional monies coming from these savings contribute to the worth of a PR program. The 1 percent bounty is also applicable to repeated passages of bond and building referenda, media coverage, school business partnerships, and the like (West, 1993b).

When the dollars generated from the cumulative analyses were totaled, the worth of a systemwide PR program ranged from about $200,000 to about $750,000, with monetary differences largely due to the size of the system students had created. Though no attempt was made in these analyses to gauge the specific worth of unit contributions, system totals, when divided by number of schools, would seem to suggest that having some kind of organized PR program at the unit level is highly beneficial. However, until PROWESS and the assumptions that governed these analyses can be tested in the field in school districts that have well-established PR programs, the monetary value of a PR program can only exist within the realm of good logic.

SUMMARY

The need for PR programs at the unit level has never been greater. Long-term efforts to foster broad and meaningful participation within school districts have given rise to site-based management and the resurgence of a grass-roots philosophy that invites community involvement at the local level. To ensure that the outcomes of shared decision making be carefully planned and implemented and be of the highest quality, school administrators have employed strategic planning and total quality management as management tools. Finally, to convey the message to the school district's various publics that system and unit goals are being accomplished and that district needs are being met, administrators have begun to market their schools.

Because the success of site-based management and the management tools it uses is largely contingent upon how well school personnel and community people can work together and how well they can communicate and market their achievements and innovations, effective public relations becomes critical at the unit level. In every unit someone must be charged with the PR responsibility, and this individual must work closely with unit-level teams as a PR resource person and with the district PR director in coordinating unit PR activities with systemwide PR goals.

CASE STUDY

A Program Disintegrates

When Principal Jack Arnold assigned Mary Crane the responsibility of initiating and carrying out a building-level PR program, he was in step with the district's move toward site-based management and a total quality management approach. Unfortunately, he did so without consulting the site's management team members, who, resenting his unilateral action, began spreading the word that empowerment was a hoax at Hector High School. They also resented having to work with Crane, who was supposed to be in charge of something she knew nothing about.

In the meantime, Crane was trying to perform her job without any released time, all the while attempting to pacify the principal and placate the team. Because she taught four classes of English each day—and supervised a study hall and the school's student newspaper—she could not be present at most of the team meetings. On those rare occasions she did attend, the team seemed to transact little or no business, tabled most motions, and adjourned early. With hardly any knowledge of what went on in team meetings and with practically no time to coordinate any of her efforts with the district's PR director, Crane was generally unprepared to address inquiries from staff, parents, the media, and other community members. Because of her inexperience, she was also not much of a PR resource person for the management team.

One of Crane's responsibilities as a unit-level PR person was to publish a staff newsletter twice a month. Not being privy to most site management team decisions and without adequate time to do any reporting of her own, she was hard-pressed to find content for the newsletter. Sick of Crane's recipes, book and movie reviews, poems, vacuous editorials, and a principal's column that was all puffery, faculty members tended to rate the newsletter as a waste of a paper.

Feeling overburdened, unappreciated, and somewhat alienated, Crane asked to be relieved of her responsibilities. Not wanting to go through the trouble of finding a replacement for her at this time, Arnold coaxed her to stay on the job just a bit longer. It was then that she asked for a period of released time so she could be more effective on the job. She had Arnold promise he would look into the matter and get back to her as quickly as he could. But swamped by problems of his own, the principal delayed taking any action.

Just when a frustrated Crane was ready to throw in the towel a second time, Arnold approached her. "I haven't settled the matter about your released time yet," he said, "but what I'm going to do is give you an entire day off to work on PR. I've arranged for a substitute to take your classes tomorrow." Smiling pleasantly, he added, "I hope that will help you out some." And before she could say anything, he was gone.

With the free time that Arnold had given her, Crane created a unit PR advisory committee, drawing from both staff and neighborhood for its membership. The committee, which had a dozen members, convened the following week. At the meeting, a question about the committee's constitution arose, pitting staff against neighborhood. Crane tried to resolve the issue but was overruled by an assistant principal, also a member of the committee. His unyielding position precipitated an early departure by community people, who wanted to be full-fledged members of the committee, not tokens.

Bad news traveled fast at Hector High, and Principal Arnold had Crane facing him on the other side of his desk by midmorning of the following day. "I heard you created quite a rumpus last night at your first advisory committee meeting," Arnold began.

"I did nothing of the kind," retorted an indignant Crane, her voice quaking. "It was Mr. Mackeworthy who caused all the trouble. I have no authority around here. I am really not a member of the site team. I have no released time, and the only training I have in PR is what I'm getting from reading whatever books I can find on the subject. Yet I am supposed to dream up and run a PR program at the unit level. I can't do it, and I want out." Abruptly, she did an about-face and left the room.

Alone, Arnold shrugged his shoulders and turned to his computer to prepare a memo for the site team, instructing them to select a new unit PR person at their next meeting. He said nothing about why Crane had resigned. Later, whenever the business about finding a suitable replacement for Crane came up at site-team meetings, the item was inevitably tabled. Eventually, the matter was assigned to a subcommittee and ignored entirely. Quite aware of the game the team was playing—snubbing him for assigning Crane the PR function without discussing the matter with them—Arnold washed his hands of the entire effort.

But when Superintendent Haberson mandated that all schools establish building-level PR programs, the principal was caught in a dilemma, not wanting to lock horns with the site team again yet knowing that he would have to do something fast. He knew Haberson was under the impression that he still had a PR person. In fact, the superintendent was planning to use Hector High as an implementation model for the district's other schools. He was most interested in the unit's PR plan—mainly in how it was being related to district PR policy and to what extent it was being coordinated with the district PR person. At the last cabinet meeting he had applauded Arnold's PR efforts and had announced to attending administrators that an effective unit PR program had great value to the district.

QUESTIONS AND SUGGESTED ACTIVITIES

Case Study

1. What arrangements should Arnold have made at the building level to support Mary Crane? What should his role have been with regard to gaining support for her with unit faculty members, other units, and the central office?
2. What actions could Arnold have taken with team members to restore their confidence in him?
3. Assume the role of Principal Arnold and respond to a request made by Superintendent Haberson for a status report on his school's program.

Chapter

4. Why is it important to have a building-level PR program? What should it look like? What is the principal's role in it?

5. What should be the role of the site-based management team in the selection of a building-level PR person?
6. In small groups, develop a list of qualifications for a building-level PR person and write up a job description for the position.
7. Invite about six class members to stage a meeting of a site-based management team to select a building-level PR person. Then have the remaining class members reflect upon the team's decision-making process.
8. In small groups try to put a price tag on a building-level PR program.
9. How is a building-level PR program compatible with total quality and strategic management approaches?

SUGGESTED READINGS

Bagin, D., Ferguson, D., & Marx, G. (1985). *Public relations for administrators*. Arlington, VA: American Association of School Administrators.

Bostingl, J. J. (1992). *Schools of quality: An introduction to total quality management in education*. Alexandria, VA: Association for Supervision and Curriculum Development.

Deming, W. E. (1982). *Out of the crisis*. Boston: Massachusetts Institute of Technology Center for Advanced Engineering Study.

Kindred, L. W., Bagin, D., & Gallagher, D. R. (1990). *The school and community relations* (4th ed.). Englewood Cliffs, NJ: Prentice Hall.

Kohn, A. (1986). *No contest: The case against competition*. Boston: Houghton Mifflin.

Ordovensky, P., & Marx, G. (1993). *Working with the news media*. Arlington, VA: American Association of School Administrators.

Quinn, J. B., Mintzberg, H., & James, R. M. (1988). *The strategy process: Concepts, contexts, & cases*. Englewood Cliffs, NJ: Prentice Hall.

Saylor, J. H. (1992). *TQM field manual*. New York: McGraw-Hill.

Schmoker, M. J., & Wilson, R. B. (1993). *Total quality in education*. Bloomington, IN: Phi Delta Kappan.

Senge, P. M. (1990). *The fifth discipline*. New York: Doubleday Currency.

Walton, M. (1986). *The Deming management method*. New York: Dodd, Mead.

REFERENCES

American Association of School Administrators. (1992). *Creating quality schools*. Arlington, VA: Author.

Armistead, L. (1992, September). PR at school level no frill. *Network*, p 7.

Aronstein, L., Marlow, M., & Desilets, B. (1991). Detours on the road to site-based management. *Journal of Educational Public Relations, 14*(3), 20–22.

Ascough, L. (1993). Different challenges: School public relations strategies change with times to be effective. *Texas Lone Star, 11*(4), 36–38.

Bagin, D. (1981). Marketing your program. *Community Education Journal, 8*(3), 14–15.

Banach, W. J. (1981). The marketing of education—Part one, two, and three. *Journal of Educational Public Relations, 5*(2), 4–18.

Bortner, D. M. (n. d.).1 Benchmarks for school public relations. *Journal of Educational Communication 3*(2), 8–19.

Coate, L. E. (1990, July). Implementing total quality management in a university setting. Paper published by Oregon State University.

del Prado, Y., & Armstrong, B. (1990). Schools of the future: One district's vision. *Journal of Educational Public Relations, 13*(1), 13–16.

Eaton, E. R., & West, P. T. (1988). Assistant high school principals will have an important PR role. *Journal of Educational Public Relations, 11*(1), 31.

Ellison, B. (1980). It pays to advertise. *Journal of Educational Public Relations, 4*(2), 10–15.

Flatt, J. L. (1982). The role of the educational public relations director. *Educational Considerations, 9*(1), 10–12.

Gardner, B. P., & West, P. T. (1990). PR directors and superintendents generally agree on the function of marketing in public schools. *Journal of Educational Public Relations, 12*(4), 30–32.

Genzer, S. M. (1993). Actual and ideal workloads of educational public relations directors in the United States. Unpublished doctoral dissertation, Texas A&M University.

Hellebust, K. G., & Krallinger, J. C. (1989). *Strategic planning workbook.* New York: Wiley.

Holliday, A. E. (1987). What's your public relations/communications/relationships climate? *Journal of Educational Public Relations, 10*(1), 10–15.

Jauch, L. R., & Glueck, W. F. (1988). *Business policy and strategic management* (5th ed.). New York: McGraw-Hill.

Kendall, B. E. (1986). Breaking with tradition. *Journal of Educational Public Relations, 9*(3), 4–9.

Kimmelman, P. (1982). Provide PR training for your transportation staff. *Journal of Educational Public Relations, 5*(3), 12–13.

Maeroff, G. I. (1993). Team building for school reform. *The School Administrator, 50*(3), 44–47.

Nebgen, N. K. (1985). Marketing and the management of public schools: Borrowing from business. *Journal of Educational Public Relations, 8*(2), 20–24.

National School Public Relations Association, (1992, October). Site-based management changing school PR role. *Network,* pp. 1, 3.

National School Public Relations Association. (1993, October). The care and feeding of school-site councils. *It Starts on the Frontline,* p. 1.

Ostrow, B. J. (1980). Marketing—A necessary addition to a school system's communication program. *Journal of Educational Public Relations, 4*(2), 4–9.

Pope, T. L. B., & West, P. T. (1989). How PR directors and superintendents perceive the role of teachers in PR. *Journal of Educational Public Relations, 12*(2), 11–13.

Powell, J. W., & West, P. T. (1991). Principals in private high schools seek an improved PR role. *Journal of Educational Public Relations, 14*(1), 30–31.

Schonberger, R. (1992). Is strategy strategic? Impact of total quality management on strategy. *Academy of Management Executive, 6*(3), 80–87.

Schueckler, L. P., & West, P. T. (1991). Principals and PR directors mostly agree on the ideal PR role for senior high school principals, but substantially disagree on their PR performance. *Journal of Educational Public Relations, 13*(4), 24–26.

Sharing a vision: A strategic plan for Waco ISD. (n.d.). Waco, TX: Waco Independent School District.

Swink, E. (1989). What factors in a school create satisfying home-school-community relations? *Journal of Educational Public Relations, 12*(1), 19–20.

Wanat, C. L., & Bowles, B. D. (1993). School-community relations: A process paradigm. *Community Education Journal, 20*(2), 3–7.

Webster, J. L., Reif, W. E., & Bracker, J. S. (1989). The manager's guide to strategic planning tools and techniques. *Planning Review, 17*(6), 4–13, 48.

West, P. T. (1980). The making of a school PR director. *Journal of Educational Communication, 4*(1), 28–29.

West, P. T. (1981). The basics of a written PR policy. *Journal of Educational Public Relations, 4*(4), 23–24.

West, P. T. (1985a). *Educational public relations*. South Beverly Hills, CA: Sage.

West, P. T. (1985b). To sell or not to sell: Marketing in the public schols. *Catalyst for Change, 15*(1), 15–17.

West, P. T. (1986–1987). Projecting a marketable image. *National Forum of Educational Administration and Supervision Journal, 4*(1), 1–10.

West, P. T. (1993a). The elementary school principal's role in school-community relations. *Georgia's Elementary Principal, 1*(2), 9–10.

West, P. T. (1993b). What is a PR program worth? *The AASA Professor, 15*(4), 8–12.

West, P. T. (1994). Shared decision making in the public schools of America. *The AASA Professor, 17*(1), 9–12.

West, P. T., & Elkins, P. W. (1990). Using the computer as a marketing tool. *Community Education Journal, 17*(4), 18–20.

Yoder, S. L. (1985). Five steps to develop an internal communication plan. *Journal of Educational Public Relations, 7*(4), 24–27.

CHAPTER 9

Institutionalizing Public Relations Through Interpersonal Communication: Listening, Nonverbal, and Conflict-Resolution Skills

Mary John O'Hair
Angela McNabb Spaulding

When any evil arises within a republic, or threatens it from without . . . the more certain remedy by far is to temporize with it, rather than attempt to extirpate it; for almost invariably, he who attempts to crush it will rather increase its force, and will accelerate the harm apprehended from it.

—Niccolo Machiavelli, 1517

As schools face today what Thomas Paine called in the dismal years of the American Revolution "times that try men's souls," educators must reach out to diverse and often unsupportive groups of parents and community members and explain (temporize) the logic behind innovative school practices and reforms. School public relations play an important role in making connections by sharing information, determining actions within school organizations and the community, and facilitating valuable services for American children and their families.

   As we move into a highly technological information age, helping educators to reach diverse groups of students and their parents will become increasingly important. As Alex Molnar said in a recent issue of *Educational Leadership:* "Educators too often do a poor job of reaching out to diverse groups of parents and community members and drawing them into life of their schools. Part of the job of public school educators is explaining the logic behind the school curriculum to community members, soliciting their ideas, and being willing to participate with them in defining and directing the school program. . . . It now seems to me that educators should reach out . . . *before* there is a crisis in their school

157

district" (p. 5). A well-defined school public relations program allows for early analysis and intervention and results in precrisis management.

No substitution exists for personal contact. New information technology such as electronic mail, video-conferencing, cellular phones, and fax machines may be thought to reduce the need for personal contact in schools. In reality, the need for school professionals to personally share information; to persuade and guide actions within a community; and to develop partnerships with business, government, and community service organizations has never been greater.

By institutionalizing a public relations program, educators have the opportunity to guide the actions of others—whether it's the media, community service organizations, businesses, or right-wing extremists—in the best interest of children. In the past, educators adopted a laissez-faire approach to public relations. When negative news was highlighted in the media, educators ignored (unsuccessfully) the reports in hopes that they would soon blow over. When irrational attacks were made on programs such as whole language, outcomes-based education, critical thinking, and cooperative learning by groups who see these innovations as contrary to their religious values, educators were amazed at first and later resentful. Rarely, however, did educators take any action.

In an information age, ignoring negative news is counterproductive and naive. Mark Twain observed that "[T]he person who grabs the cat by the tail learns about 44 percent faster than the one just watching." Rather than ignoring controversial attacks on public education, educators must "grab the cat by the tail" and adopt a proactive, inquiry mode that emphasizes the human touch of caring and personal commitment. The "human touch" is characterized by the educator's ability to understand the diverse needs and interests of others and to personalize the content of the message to address those needs and interests. Adopting the human touch allows educators to find a common ground, adjusting the message according to feedback (often in the form of a challenge) received from parents and community members.

Through an institutional public relations program, educators can provide the public with accurate information rather than allowing, by impassivity, the radical reformists and the media to interpret educational news. Through a proactive public relations plan, educators can confront inaccurate and unfavorable reports and explain or qualify difficult-to-understand or distorted content. In addition, adopting a school public relations plan helps reduce negative educational reports by keeping the public fully informed and actively participating in school governance. As a result of active participation, a school public relations program impacts the school's organizational culture and climate, developing a trust between schools and the media, business, and community members that leads to new working relationships. Only in an atmosphere of cooperation and collegiality will healthy, productive partnerships be developed to address the needs of America's youth and enhance student learning and productivity.

In order to provide the human touch and proactively negate propaganda by public school opponents, educators must examine the key ingredient necessary for successful public relations programs: *communication*. Communication holds the key to unlocking hidden suspicions and fears in our educational system and to encouraging constructive dialogue on important issues. Unless a concerted effort is made through effective communication, the gaps between educators and opponents of public education will continue to grow.

Principals in restructured schools view communication skills as the skills most needed for success as schools move from a traditional, isolated stance to one fostering shared vision and collegiality (Fullan, 1991; O'Hair & Bastian, 1993). Thurston, Clift, and Schacht (1993), in emphasizing the development of an educator's ability to reflect and communicate, state that "Communication will be crucial in establishing a schoolwide commitment to a mission and in sharing the decision-making process" (p. 262). Communication is key to establishing trust, promoting collaboration, and managing conflict.

Unfortunately, communication skills are an often-neglected part of an educator's formal and informal education. Generally when one thinks of communication skills, the first image that comes to mind is that of speaking. Unless accused of poor listening or of being unobservant, educators tend to downplay the importance of listening and nonverbal communication. However, when a crisis exists, skills in listening and observing are more fruitful than are skills in speaking.

While speaking and writing skills can always improve, those communication skills are not what needs the greatest attention in regard to establishing a successful school public relations program. Specific communication skills needing the greatest attention by school principals include skills in sharing information, in seeking feedback, in listening, in nonverbal awareness, and in conflict resolution (O'Hair & Bastian, 1993). In a similar finding, Miles (1993) reports that seventeen New York educators found the following communication skills to be key for effective school change: reducing conflict, enhancing collaboration in interpersonal and group situations, and gathering feedback. Without adequately developed communication skills, the public relations process is simply incomplete. In this chapter, we will examine the foundation of successful school public relations as reflected in three core communication competencies:

Competency 1: Listening effectively

Competency 2: Decoding nonverbal communication

Competency 3: Resolving conflicts

All three competencies are a must for any educator who is to successfully institutionalize public relations and thereby persuade, guide, and impact the school and the children he or she serves.

COMPETENCY 1: LISTENING EFFECTIVELY

The importance of listening skills in successful school public relations cannot be overemphasized. Consider the following scenario.

Example

Ray Curtis, Willow's high school principal, shuddered as he looked again at the purchase receipts spread across his desk. He had requested these receipts after receiving a harsh memo from the central office stating that the school was already over budget for the year. How could this be? His school was only five months into the budgetary calendar. This was a tough year financially for the school district, and Curtis knew that he would have to answer for his school's financial mismanagement. One by one he began to seek information from his staff. "Why did you purchase an additional set of math manipulatives?" "Where did you get permission to buy a new stage curtain?" "Who approved the purchase of six new sewing machines?" The staff seemed to echo the same theme, "Well, I asked you before I made the purchase, and you shrugged your shoulders and said to go ahead." Curtis couldn't believe that he had approved such purchases, but other members of his staff and even his trusted secretary confirmed his purchase approvals. Deep down the principal resented his staff for taking advantage of him and making him look bad with the central office. His staff knew better than to approach him with such requests when he had other things on his mind.

Analysis

Examine Ray Curtis's listening behavior. What advice can you give him?

Individuals from diverse professions document the importance of listening. Physicians cite communication and listening as the single most important skill in medical practice (Weston & Lipkin, 1989). Attorneys believe listening is key to success in the legal profession (Merrill & Borisoff, 1987). From a business perspective, Tom Peters (1988) and Lee Iacocca (1984) devote major sections of their books to describing the value of listening. Iacocca (1984) concludes, "I only wish I could find an institute that teaches people how to listen. After all, a good manager needs to listen at least as much as he needs to talk. Too many people fail to realize that good communication goes in both directions" (p. 54).

Research findings confirm that successful employees are good listeners. In twelve major research studies, good listening skills have been cited as one of the most important skills (often *the* most important skill) for employees to possess at all levels of the organization (Wolvin & Coakley, 1988). In addition to enhancing professional growth, good listening heightens one's personal good health. Studies have shown that when we talk our blood pressure goes up; when we listen it goes down (Lynch, 1985, p. 160). Clearly, when we listen we are more relaxed and less excited than when we speak.

If professionals from law, medicine, and business recognize the need to develop good listening skills, why, then, the lack of emphasis on listening in education? Perhaps, as schools become less traditional and less isolated from the community and begin to reflect shared decision making, educators will recognize the importance of listening skills in institutionalizing public relations. Teachers and principals must actively listen to community members, parents, and the media. Unfortunately, many barriers to effective listening exist in schools.

Barriers to Effective Listening

Once school leaders begin to recognize listening barriers and reduce negative behaviors, they are free to develop successful public relations plans.

Let's look at some indicators of poor listening. We'll begin by analyzing the following scenario.

Example 2

Maria Sanchez, principal at Herring Elementary, left for a school networking conference that included twelve schools committed to school restructuring and change. In addition to teachers and principals in attendance, each school was represented by parents, school board members, business leaders, and the media. Sanchez decided to arrive a few minutes early in order to locate Lori Hutton, a science teacher at Herring, to discuss a story that Hutton had sent to the central office and the news media about Herring's new fire safety plan.

Sanchez had recently received a memo from the superintendent, Bob Walton, congratulating her school on designing an exceptional plan. The memo had really upset her because it outlined a fire safety program designed by Herring teachers and parents but never approved by the principal. In addition, at a recent administrators' council meeting, Sanchez had been embarrassed by Walton's request that she describe the plan and detail several of its components. Sanchez felt betrayed that Hutton had bypassed her and gone directly to the sueprintendent's office. For no apparent reason. Hadn't she always been available for her staff and made it clear that all teachers discuss new proposals with her first before taking them outside the school?

As Sanchez drove through the hotel parking lot now to find a space, she thought it strange that Hutton's car was nowhere in sight. Hutton had been on the planning committee of the conference, and she should have arrived early to prepare for conference registration. Disgruntled, Sanchez parked her car and picked up a large stack of unopened mail to read while she waited. She could not imagine any principal receiving more mail than she did. Actually, the better part of her day was spent reading and responding to mail. No wonder she didn't have time to be in classrooms or in district strategic planning meetings and was often overlooked by Superintendent Walton in developing new district projects.

Glancing up, Sanchez saw Hutton walking across the lot toward the hotel. Perhaps she should confront her now rather than later. Seeing her principal, Hutton looked confused. She spoke first. "Mrs. Sanchez, I'm surprised to see you here today. I thought you would be at the district planning retreat with Mr. Walton at Lake Wannabe. I thought the retreat was mandatory for all principals."

Sanchez was mortified to learn that the retreat had been announced several months prior and had been discussed again at last week's administrative council meeting. She had attended the meeting but had not been listening.

Analysis

Analyze Maria Sanchez's feelings. What indicators of poor listening are present in this example?

The following indicators characterize poor listeners:

1. *Poor listeners are bypassed by others*, especially if the topic is deemed vital. For instance, in the example above, Hutton may have felt that a fire safety plan was critical for the school and that she could not afford to waste time presenting it to Sanchez, given her lack of attention.

2. *A large amount of written communication is an indicator of poor listening*. When face-to-face encounters prove fruitless, others may feel that the only communication channel available is written. If Sanchez had checked her mail, she probably would have found a note from Superintendent Walton's assistant reminding her of the retreat—*and a copy of the fire plan*.

3. *Poor listeners may feel left out of important projects* because they are perceived as inefficient or lazy when actually they are deficient only in their listening skills.

4. *Missing important meetings is characteristic of individuals with poor listening skills*. Poor listeners are perceived as unreliable and are often passed over for promotions and special projects.

5. *Poor listeners react to rather than prevent problems*. Poor listeners rarely assume a proactive stance. They miss verbal and nonverbal cues that indicate future problems and only become aware of problems at the last minute, when such problems are full-blown and perhaps unresolvable.

6. *Poor listeners are manipulated easily by others*. For example, if Sanchez had accused Hutton of bypassing her and going directly to central office, the teacher's response might have been: "Mrs. Sanchez, you're not serious, are you? I can't believe that you don't recall our conversation about the fire safety plan. You told me that you supported the plan and whenever the minor issues were worked out to run the plan by Mr. Walton's office. I thought that I had your total support. You know that I would never go over your head!" Poor listeners are easy marks.

Poor listening is costly to the individual—and to the institution. Poor listeners are often perceived as less intelligent and consequently are passed up for promotions and special advancements. Communicating with a poor listener is tiring and stressful for others. Repetition of information, physical and mental distractions, and misinterpretations are time-consuming and costly for schools. Minor inconveniences such as missing an appointment because of failure to listen or not bringing the requested materials to meetings result in negative expenditures for both the school district and individuals involved. In the business world, Lyman K. Steil (1980), corporate consultant, describes the monetary problems that poor listening creates: "With more than 100 million workers in this country, a simple $10 mistake by each of them, as a result of poor listening, would add up to a cost of a billion dollars. And most people make numerous listening mistakes every week" (p. 65).

In the *Journal of Business Communication*, Steven Golen (1990) listed the most common listening barriers; these are presented in Table 9-1. As you study the table, note the barriers you have experienced within the past week; describe the specific incident. Don't be surprised if you experience difficulty analyzing your listening behavior. It's often difficult to recognize listening barriers without prior listening training.

TABLE 9–1
Top-Ranked Barriers to Effective Listening

Rank	Barrier
1	Listening primarily for details or facts
2	Becoming distracted by peripheral noises like those from room office equipment, telephones, or other conversations
3	Daydreaming or becoming preoccupied with something else
4	Thinking of another topic or following some thought prompted by what the speaker has said
5	Having no interest in the speaker's subject
6	Concentrating on the speaker's mannerisms or delivery rather than on the message
7	Becoming impatient with the speaker
8	Disagreeing or arguing outwardly or inwardly with the speaker
9	Trying to outline everything mentally
10	Faking attention to the speaker
11	Jumping to conclusions before the speaker has finished
12	Becoming emotional or excited when the speaker's views differ from yours
13	Ceasing to listen because the subject is complex or difficult
14	Allowing your biases and prejudices to interfere with your thinking while listening
15	Paying attention only to the speaker's words rather than to speaker's feelings
16	Avoiding eye contact while listening
17	Not putting yourself in the speaker's shoes or empathizing
18	Refusing to relate to and benefit from the speaker's ideas
19	Refusing to give feedback
20	Refusing to paraphrase to clarify a point
21	Overreacting to certain language, such as slang or profanity
22	Not listening because it takes too much time
23	Not reading the speaker's nonverbal cues

Source: Adapted from Golen, 1990, pp. 30–31.

Unfortunately, the greatest barrier to effective listening is ourselves. Our general attitude about listening is often detrimental to our listening success, making us our own silent enemy. It is no secret that most educators prefer to talk rather than listen. Talking is more self-centered, whereas listening is more other-centered. Common cliches such as "Professors are absent-minded," "Doctors have poor bedside manners," or "Used car salesmen talk ninety-miles-an-hour" point to an inability to listen actively, adopt turn-taking strategies, and ultimately establish rapport with others. Effective listening improves rapport, establishes trust, and generally improves professional and personal relationships. Listening skills are essential in developing new working relationships with parents, community members, businesses, and the media.

Educators all possess the capability for effective listening. The challenge involves an individual *desire* or *willingness* to listen. Effective listeners are individuals who know that they must do more than passively allow sounds to enter their ears. Effective listeners participate actively in the communication process by attempting to develop a positive attitude toward the speaker's message and consciously anticipate the importance of the message. Furthermore, effective listeners constantly seek interest areas and remind themselves that something of value can be learned from every message.

Improving Listening Skills

As discussed earlier, for successful school communications it is necessary to understand the importance of effective listening and to recognize the barriers to effective listening. In order to build trust between schools and establish healthy and productive public relations, listening skills must be honed. The *strategic listening process* (O'Hair, O'Rouke, & O'Hair, in press) can be used to assist school leaders in listening development. Key components of this process include the following activities:

- ◆ Understanding and committing to the listening process
- ◆ Listening between the words
- ◆ Improving memory
- ◆ Providing supportive feedback
- ◆ Clarifying messages through second-guessing
- ◆ Using excess thinking time productively
- ◆ Adopting mental guidelines for effective listening

Figure 9-1 provides a visual image of the strategic listening process.

Understanding and Committing to the Listening Process.   "Listening" comprises three elements: what is heard, what is understood, and what is remembered. Listening includes hearing, or receiving aural stimuli from the environment; connecting or processing the stimuli into meaningful messages; and storing messages for immediate or delayed retrieval. Listening occurs at different levels, depending on the message. For example, a simple request, such as to close the door or to turn off the lights, generally requires basic processing and rarely the more complex process of reflective thinking. On the other hand, reflective listening would require that the listener understand the sender's personality, culture, and environment. As schools become increasingly diverse, reflective listening is more difficult—and more necessary. While the teaching force grows predominately white and female, the student population shows more and more diversity in terms of race, class, language, and sex-role socialization patterns (Grant & Secada, 1990, p. 404). Understanding and committing to the listening process will become crucial as students and families become more diverse and teachers and administrators less diverse.

Listening between the Words.   Effective listening requires more than listening to the words alone. In his 1988 campaign, Pres. George Bush seized on the slogan: "Read my lips. No new taxes." The impact of the message was supported by his paralanguage, or the *way* he said those six words. Later, when he broke his promise, this statement caused Bush and

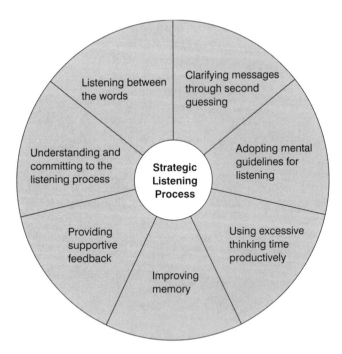

FIGURE 9–1
The Strategic Listening Process (From O'Hair, O'Rouke, & O'Hair, in press)

his advisors much embarrassment. Perhaps his critics and voters in general would not have remembered so vividly the original message if his paralanguage had not been so compelling (O'Hair, O'Rourke, & O'Hair, in press).

Effective listeners must do more than merely read lips—or words. Effective listeners must learn to listen for deeper meanings. Listeners can miss 100 percent of the "feeling content" of spoken messages by not listening *between* and *beyond* the words. To understand deeper meanings in oral communication educators must listen for the paralanguage elements of speech. "Paralanguage" refers to *how* something is said rather than *what* is said. More specifically, paralanguage involves aspects of verbal communication that are unrelated to the words used. For example, after Jack Mehan has worked for weeks on a PTA program, his principal stops by his classroom and congratulates him on a job well done. However, Mehan notes that the principal's voice lacks enthusiasm and excitement, and he begins to question his principal's sincerity; he wonders what his principal *really* thought about the PTA program. Tone and loudness of voice are some of the more obvious types of paralanguage, but there are other, less obvious elements of paralanguage.

Improving Memory.   Memory is crucial to the listening process. Improving memory increases listening comprehension. After examining the purely informational level of listening, researchers claim that 75 percent of oral communication is ignored, misunderstood, or quickly forgotten (O'Hair, O'Rourke, & O'Hair, in press). It makes little sense to hear, attend to, comprehend, and then fail to remember oral communication.

Memory is often thought of as "storage." The memory can store great amounts of information and is often examined through the temporal classifications of short- and long-term memory. Short-term memory (STM) involves pattern recognition by transfer from sensory storage to the form of memory described by memory researchers as "attention" (O'Hair, O'Rouke, & O'Hair, in press). Unfortunately, STM consists of a very brief unit of information, usually about fifteen seconds, unless the unit is rehearsed, which allows for an extension of up to sixty seconds. Generally, the term "memory" refers to long-term memory. However, long-term memory is rarely activated until at least sixty seconds after the presentation of a stimulus. Actual entry into long-term memory may depend on both rehearsal and organizational schemes. In other words, long-term memory requires a linkage between the new stimulus and the old information previously stored in memory. The storing and retrieval of information that is unconnected and meaningless is extremely difficult.

Teaching individuals to develop visual images in listening situations results in a significant increase in comprehension and memory for both children and adults (O'Hair, O'Rourke, & O'Hair, in press). The visual images produced while listening to a conference speaker or while watching a video can provide the framework for organizing and remembering key information.

Providing Supportive Feedback. Conversation with individuals who do not provide feedback—that is, give no nods of the head or utter "uh-huhs"—is extremely uncomfortable. Under normal conversational conditions, it is difficult to carry on a conversation with someone who is unresponsive. Without feedback, the sender does not know if the receiver is in agreement or disagreement with the message, is bored and ready to terminate the conversation, or is daydreaming and not properly hearing the message. Feedback is essential if strategic communication is to occur.

Good listeners provide appropriate supportive feedback by

- Demonstrating interest in what the speaker says
- Maintaining appropriate eye contact
- Smiling and showing animation
- Nodding occasionally in agreement
- Leaning toward the speaker to demonstrate an attitude of interest and confidentiality
- Using verbal reinforcers like "I see" and "yes"
- Phrasing interpretations of the speaker's comments to verify understanding
- Consciously timing their verbal and nonverbal feedback to assist rather than hinder the speaker (O'Hair, O'Rourke, & O'Hair, in press)

If listening is gaining meaning from situations involving the spoken word, then feedback is crucial in gaining meaning. Feedback helps us continue conversations, which in turn provide us with verbal and nonverbal cues that help inform and guide us in understanding others' motivations, fears, and goals. Without feedback, listeners are robbed of fundamental information required in understanding others.

Clarifying Messages through Second-Guessing. It is common, while strategically listening, to be skeptical of the initial interpretation of the message received from a speaker. This skepticism is referred to as "second-guessing," or seeking the "truth" in a message. The theory of second-guessing expands the role of cognition in communication to help clarify the hearer's understanding of the truth behind the message. Second-guessing is a mental process through which listeners attempt to make better sense of what they believe to be a "biased" message. By reviewing and analyzing additional information pertinent to the original biased message, listeners gain a clearer picture of the true state of affairs rather than a slanted and prejudiced view from only the sender of the message (Hewes & Graham, 1989).

Second-guessing is only used when a perceived need for accuracy in information exists. For example, Caitlin Caldwell's superintendent tells her that the shared governance report that she has worked on for the last several weeks is "interesting and informative." Caldwell is not sure what the superintendent means by "interesting and informative." Does she mean literally "interesting and informative" or does she mean "not exactly what I wanted but I know that you worked hard"? Rather than take the comment at face value, Caldwell may have reason to doubt the message. At this point, she may decide that her superintendent's feelings about the project are not important and she really doesn't need complete accuracy of the message; thus she accepts the initial interpretation and stops analyzing the message. However, if message accuracy *is* important to her, Caldwell might begin to second-guess.

Second-guessing as a listening strategy can help redefine and clarify messages and can guide the listener to respond appropriately. The second-guessing process involves exploring alternative interpretations, prioritizing interpretations, and selecting the best interpretation. The reinterpretations are assumed to be closer to the truth than the initial face-value interpretation of the message, though it is still possible that upon reflection in the reinterpretation phase an individual will return to the original interpretation.

Using Excess Thinking Time Productively. Most people do not realize the amount of excess thinking time that is available during listening. Speech speed is much slower than thought speed (approximately 90 to 200 words per minute versus 1000 to 1500 words per minute). The arduous speaker uses only a fraction of the listener's thought capacity. Thus listeners have a great amount of "free time" while listening. The difference between good and poor listeners is that good listeners use excess thinking time to concentrate on the message while poor listeners indulge in negative listening behaviors such as daydreaming. Few individuals can daydream without losing a great part of the speaker's message.

In comparison, effective listeners use excess thinking time to

◆ Outline mentally the speaker's message
◆ Identify the speaker's purpose and determine how the speaker's points support that purpose
◆ Evaluate the soundness of the speaker's logic
◆ Verify and integrate information presented with past knowledge and experience

- ◆ Maintain eye contact in order to observe and interpret the speaker's nonverbal signals
- ◆ Formulate questions to ask at appropriate moments in order to verify the accuracy of their understanding
- ◆ Provide encouraging verbal and nonverbal feedback (O'Hair, O'Rourke, & O'Hair, in press)

Without constantly processing information received, listeners may experience daydreaming.

Adopting Mental Guidelines for Effective Listening. Consider these general mental guidelines for achieving effective listening in educational settings:

1. *Believe that effective listening is crucial to school public relations and school success.* Some listeners tune out during a meeting because of disagreements with the messages being communicated. However, listening, even under protest, is informative and crucial to school success. New ideas and concepts may be sparked at any given time, even under protest. Successful educators are committed to the listening process and rarely tune out conversations.

2. *Learn to tolerate and even enjoy silence.* Consider the following personal suggestions for learning to tolerate and enjoy silence: (*a*) Turn off the car stereo when driving to and from work and listen to the road noises. (*b*) When in conversation, encourage the other person to fully develop his or her idea before you speak. (*c*) Think of someone to whom you have failed to listen, either on purpose or inadvertently, and make special time in your schedule just to "lend them an ear." Learning to tolerate and enjoy silence is essential for meaningful communication.

3. *Relate new information to old information.* The "new-to-old" connection can be made by relating new information to established policies and procedures or by mentally creating new policies and procedures for the new information. For example, if a new smoking policy prohibits smoking in the teachers' work area of the school building, this new policy can be related to the old policy by concluding that smoking is prohibited both inside and outside the building.

4. *Adjust to problems of poor listeners.* Poor listeners have a habit of interrupting speakers. To prevent this, verbally request that all interruptions or comments be held until the speaker has completed his or her communication. Interruptions prevent speakers from thoroughly developing and explaining key points and ideas. If interruptions do occur, the speaker should return to the topic so as to adequately complete the discussion. Repetition is advantageous when communicating with poor listeners.

5. *Organize listening by constantly summarizing previous points and identifying main points with key words or phrases.* At the conclusion of a conversation, identify three major points and describe each. Educators often use small tape recorders to summarize main points after important educational meetings.

6. *Mentally ask questions to evaluate, process, and use incoming information.* Formulate questions such as: What point is the speaker trying to make? How can I apply the information the speaker is giving me? Are the points consistent with what I already know about the topic? Is there an underlying message?

COMPETENCY 2: DECODING NONVERBAL COMMUNICATION

Improving listening behavior is a difficult and time-consuming task. Careful attention to overcoming listening barriers and eliminating the silent enemy, a negative attitude toward listening, helps educators institute effective public relations programs. However, improving listening behavior alone will not provide educators with complete communication competence. Understanding the nonverbal message is equally important in that task.

Example 3

Arturo Gomez, principal of Southpark School, was frustrated and bewildered. Lindsey Kately, a ruthless local newspaper reporter, had just left his office. Kately had just discovered that a large number of students at Southpark School had failed their achievement tests. Storming into the principal's office, she had placed both hands on the front of his desk, leaned toward Gomez, looked him directly in the eye, and asked, "Why haven't you answered my phone messages? I informed your secretary that it was urgent that I talk with you."

Gomez was immediately intimidated. Remaining seated, he looked down at a stack of papers on his desk and began, "Well, I . . . uh . . . well, I . . . uh . . . was really busy and uh . . . I, ah, planned to call you when I found time." The truth of the matter was that Gomez had had plenty of opportunities to return the reporter's calls. In reality, he had hoped to avoid communication with her.

Kately rolled her eyes, took a deep breath, and exhaled loudly and impatiently, "I can't wait forever. I need some information now." Tapping her pencil on Gomez's desk, she came straight to the point: "Is it true that your school's test scores are the lowest in the district?"

The principal hesitated. When he finally spoke, he hardly recognized his own voice. "Well, I, ah, I wouldn't necessarily say it was . . . a, ah, large . . . well, I, ah . . . can't discuss the test results . . . uh, because, uh . . . they are confidential," he said softly, even timidly.

"Confidential!" Kately exploded, slamming her notepad down on the desk. "I'm not asking for *individual* scores but how the *group* scored. The public has a right to know what kind of education they are paying for." The reporter hesitated a moment, then moved toward the door. As she threw open the door, she turned and said, with a smirk on her face, "If you won't give me information, I know where I *can* find it." Then, with the slam of the door, she was gone.

Analysis

Examine Arturo Gomez's nonverbal behavior. What advice can you give him?

In this section we'll explore nonverbal communication, the behaviors that convey meaning to other people without the use of language. Nonverbal communication includes any behavior that does not use words. The manner in which principals use their voices, faces, and bodies—even how they arrange their offices—communicates meaning to their publics. Nonverbal behaviors can even convey information we might not want others to know—for example, feelings of dislike or disapproval.

As the school community becomes increasingly diverse, understanding nonverbal communication becomes vital for educators. Everything—from lifestyles to products to technologies to the media—is growing more heterogeneous. This new diversity brings with it more complexity, which in turn, means that schools need more and more data and know-how to function effectively. Awareness of nonverbal communication can help provide educators with essential information.

The verbal communication process is, by and large, controllable and intentional, but nonverbal behavior is often difficult to manage and control. Communication scholars consider nonverbal communication to be a double-edged sword (O'Hair & Friedrich, 1992). If used effectively, it can enhance one's ability to communicate with others. It can also damage one's ability to act constructively.

This section examines nonverbal communication research over the past thirty years and focuses on those areas that are relevant to institutionalizing public relations through effective school communication. We'll discuss the major functions of nonverbal communication and synthesize these functions into the framework of visual communication skills.

Major Functions of Nonverbal Communication

Nonverbal communication serves a number of functions in a school context. Michael Argyle (1988) defines four functions of nonverbal behavior. The first function is to *express emotions*. Emotional expression is as important in school settings as it is in personal encounters. When school members communicate excitement through their voices and gestures, it is possible to get a sense of their commitment to what they are saying. In addition, educators can have an idea of how school members feel about their duties and responsibilities by how they sit or by their facial expressions. Without nonverbal behavior, the understanding of emotions would be difficult, and schools would have less knowledge of how others feel and respond to educational issues.

The second function of nonverbal communication is to *convey interpersonal attitudes*. Expressing opinions through nonverbal communication reveals interpersonal attitudes. When a parent enters the school office, a perceptive principal can tell how the parent feels about the visit by her nonverbal behavior. If she says "Hello" without much expression in her voice and without looking directly at anyone, she may simply be going through the motions required of all humans. If, on the other hand, she smiles, turns, and looks directly at the principal, she is perceived to be genuine in her greeting.

The third function of nonverbal communication is to *present one's personality to others*; this is sometimes labeled the process of "impression formation and management" (Burgoon, Buller, & Woodall, 1989). Without tone of voice, gestures, facial expressions and so forth, humans would appear and sound mechanical and uncaring. As human communicators, educators can obtain an accurate sense of what others are trying to communicate by knowing their personality. How others use language can give educators an indication of their personality to some extent, but their nonverbal behavior also provides a rich source of information about their character, disposition, and temperament. An awareness of another's personality characteristics allows principals to make and confirm predictions about school members' actions, plans, and behaviors. This makes communicating easier. For example, a parent who talks loudly and positions himself directly in the principal's face could be perceived as aggressive and pushy. On the other hand, parents who avoid eye contact, talk softly, and use few gestures may be perceived as shy and reluctant to confront others on issues. Without understanding culture, race, and gender expectations, it is difficult to accurately interpret nonverbal cues that convey another person's personality.

The fourth function of nonverbal communication is to *accompany verbal communication*. Nonverbal behavior can *reinforce* what is said verbally (smiling while stating satisfaction for a project); it can help *regulate* verbal behavior (breaking eye contact to signal that a conversation is over); it can *complement* oral communication (talking very slowly and deliberately to make an important point); it can *substitute* for verbal behavior (nodding, winking, or gesturing approval); and it can even *contradict* verbal language (stating pleasure at meeting someone without establishing eye contact) (O'Hair & Ropo, 1994). When verbal and nonverbal messages contradict, the receiver of the message relies on the nonverbal message. Principals must carefully monitor nonverbal behaviors that accompany verbal communication to ensure that they reinforce rather than contradict verbal messages.

The Framework of Visual Communication

The *framework of visual communication skills* (O'Hair, O'Rourke, & O'Hair, in press) describes the essential components of nonverbal communication in business and educational settings. The framework has five major components: facial expression, eye and visual behavior, gesture and body movement, space, and dress. (See Figure 9-2). Each component is described below and discussed in relation to nonverbal communication in educational settings.

Facial Expression. One of the most expressive channels of nonverbal communication is the face. Although only a few words are available to describe them (for example, frown, smile, sneer . . .), there are, in fact, more than 1000 different facial expressions (Ekman, Friesen, & Ellsworth, 1972). The challenge becomes interpreting the various facial expressions and decoding their message content. Facial expressions are the most reliable signal for determining the emotional state of an individual. A principal who pays close attention to facial expressions may get a glimpse of an individual's true feelings. Early identification of a school problem can help principals encourage discussion that ultimately aids in conflict resolution.

In addition, facial expressions provide feedback as to how communication is being understood. For example, a teacher may *state* that she understands a particular assignment but *look* confused. A principal who is aware of facial expressions and uses feedback appropriately is alerted immediately to a potential problem.

Furthermore, facial expressions are beneficial in determining the real motivations and intentions of others. Often individuals try to change their facial expressions to

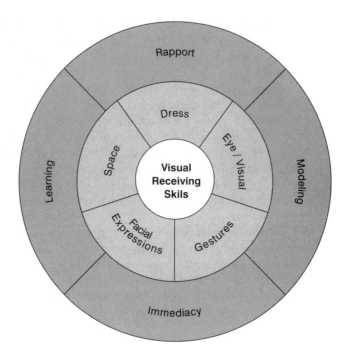

FIGURE 9–2
Framework of Visual Communication Skills (From O'Hair, O'Rourke, & O'Hair, in press)

deliberately mislead others about how they feel. Although facial expressions are important for principals to observe and analyze, this information alone is probably not enough to establish a high degree of accuracy concerning another's emotional state. According to the framework of visual communication skills, other nonverbal clues are needed.

Eye and Visual Behavior.   The eyes provide rich information. Because humans are becoming more and more visually oriented, the movement of the eyes and how they are focused on other people and objects provide a great deal of knowledge and insight.

   Eye gaze indicates that one person is looking directly at another individual's face, particularly the eyes. *Eye contact* refers to mutual and simultaneous eye gaze between two people; that is, both people are looking directly into each other's eyes (Harper, Wiens, & Matarazzo, 1978; O'Hair & Ropo, 1994). With eye gaze, one person is searching for information about another. With eye contact, both individuals are committed to the communication process (O'Hair & Friedrich, 1992). Research on nonverbal communication through the eyes alerts educational leaders to the need to consider cultural, social, and gender differences and provides clues to communication avoidance.

   Cultural, social, and gender differences.   Cultural differences in eye gaze and eye contact are well documented. The eyes are important in regulating the flow of communication among people. For example, when one person greets another, a certain sequence is generally followed: gaze—smile—eyebrow lift—quick head nod (Eibl-Eibesfeldt, 1972).

This behavior may seem to be one of those things known through common sense until educators realize that all parents, staff, and community members do not share the same nonverbal behaviors. The most distinguishing feature in the cross-cultural use of eye contact is the focus of the listener's eyes (Burgoon, Buller, & Woodall, 1989). Anglos are socialized to gaze directly at the speaker's face when they are listening. Native Americans and African-Americans often refuse to look directly into the eyes of any authority figure. In their culture, direct eye gaze with an authority figure is considered rude and inappropriate. Japanese-Americans avoid eye contact when listening by focusing on the speaker's neck. Educators may damage professional relationships by being unaware of and insensitive to cultural differences.

A summary of research findings reveals other factors involving eye behavior and nonverbal communication (O'Hair, O'Rourke, & O'Hair, in press):

- People have a tendency to "match" the gaze duration of their conversational partner.
- Speech rate is higher when the speaker looks at the listener.
- Eye gaze increases when one is communicating positive information and decreases when information is negative.
- Smiling causes a decrease in eye gaze.
- In groups, there is a tendency to look more while speaking and look less while listening. (The opposite is true when only two people are talking.)
- People who gaze longer are better-liked.
- Increased gazing causes favorable impressions when positive information is communicated and unfavorable impressions when negative information is revealed.
- Compared with high-status people, people with lower status (less power) look more when listening than when speaking.
- Females gaze more than males.
- Females are looked at more than males.
- Females are more uncomfortable when they are unable to see their conversational partner.

An awareness of cultural, social, and gender differences may prove helpful in understanding visual behavior and improving communication.

Communication Avoidance. Visual behavior is a good indicator of communication avoidance. It is important for educators to understand that certain meanings are to be found in both intentional and unintentional avoidance. In addition, educators must remember that there are several reasons why an individual may avoid eye contact. First, the individual may be *unwilling to communicate.* An individual may feel unprepared to answer a question, may be busy thinking about something else, or may even be unhappy with someone and, as a result, avoid eye contact. *Emotional arousal* may also reduce eye contact. As mentioned earlier, the face is an excellent source of clues for determining the emotional state of an individual. The eyes can provide that type of information as well. Sometimes adults avoid eye gaze to cover up emotions such as despair, depression, and even stress (O'Hair, O'Rourke, & O'Hair, in press). For example, consider the nonverbal behavior of a parent who feels embarrassed. The parent will probably divert his or her eyes to objects rather than look directly at people. This is an effort to recover lost self-esteem (O'Hair & Ropo, 1994). Once the parent recovers, normal eye behavior will resume. A principal's awareness of nonverbal communication will allow the parent time to regain self-esteem and return willingly to the conversation. Understanding eye and visual behavior is important in understanding people and building the trust needed to develop productive relationships between educators and the public.

Gesture and Body Movement.   Gestures and body movements, sometimes referred to as "kinetics," are another aspect of nonverbal communication. Individuals use gestures to complement what they say verbally. Communication problems occur whenever a person's gestures suggest a meaning different from the verbal message. As mentioned earlier, it is important for educators to remember that whenever a contradiction exists between the verbal and the nonverbal message, listeners believe and accept more readily the nonverbal message (Burgoon, Buller, & Woodall, 1989).

Emblems and *posture* are two types of body gestures. "Emblems" refers to gestures that take the place of words. *All* cultures have emblems. Some are universal in meaning, others are not. "Postures" refers to the positions of the body. For example, postures include the crossing of legs, folding of arms, slouching, and sitting on one's knees. Cultural awareness of nonverbal emblems and posture is a necessity.

Space.   Often school leaders and the public respond differently to space. Space may be examined from two differing viewpoints: personal space and environmental space.

Personal Space.   *Proxemics,* or the distance that exists between communicators, is referred to as "personal space." School leaders must consider two aspects of personal space: first, the distance measured in feet and inches, and second, the perceived distance measured only by how comfortable people feel about the spatial distance between them and their communicating partners (O'Hair & Ropo, 1994). People differ according to their tolerance for personal space; some individuals prefer very close communicating distances, and others require further distances. Edward T. Hall (1973) developed a system of determining personal space preferences that was later updated by other researchers (O'Hair, O'Rourke, & O'Hair, in press). Four zones in which all communication takes place consist of the intimate, the personal, the social, and the public. (See Table 9-2.) If principals violate the rules of personal space as dictated by these zones, others may be offended or repulsed. Entering the intimate zone with a casual acquaintance can be misleading and troublesome. On the other hand, if principals choose to interact at distances that are greater than what the situation requires, they may be perceived as cold and aloof.

The culture, age, and gender of individuals may also affect personal space preferences. For example, many cultures display gender differences in spacing and touching distances. In general, adhering to the norms of the situation, culture, and degree of acquaintance is the best advice for educators in using personal space appropriately.

Environmental Space.   This space refers to how individuals perceive, construct, and manipulate physical space in educational settings. Environmental space is important because people are influenced by what they see. Office arrangement, reception areas, decorations, wall hangings, colors, plants, and furniture are what school visitors see first when enter-

TABLE 9–2
Zones of Personal Space

Type	Definition	Example
Intimate zone	People interact at the closest distance in this zone (skin contact to 18 inches). Not often observed in educational setting, this spacing is usually reserved for those very close to us—spouses, best friends....	A parent whispers a message to a teacher in a meeting to avoid disturbing the speaker.
Personal zone	Interactions that are personal or private in nature take place in this zone (18 inches to 4 feet). Voice level tends to be soft and gestures increase with this distance.	A teacher asks the principal for assistance on a report.
Social zone	This zone ranges from 4 to 12 feet and is used a great deal in educational settings. Educators use normal vocal inflections and volume and tend to feel comfortable both verbally and nonverbally.	Teachers, students, parents, business leaders, and community members gather in a small group problem-solving session.
Public zone	The largest interacting-distance space (12 feet and beyond), this zone reduces the chance for immediate feedback and the ability to read facial expression and visual behavior. Vocal pitch and volume are at higher levels, and gesturing may be exaggerated in order for everyone within the zone to see.	The PR officer presents a public relations plan at a faculty meeting.

Based on Hall, 1969.

ing the building. Not only are first impressions of school personnel important to keep in mind when developing a school's professional image, but first impressions of the building, classrooms, cafeteria, and principals's office are also important to consider.

The effective use of environmental space offers schools the "power of suggestion" in that they can suggest to their school community through space arrangement that they are student-centered, professional, personable, effective, and accessible. Principals can communicate professionalism and accessibility through their office arrangement. The best arrangement is one that puts the least distance and fewest barriers between communicators. The objective is to produce walkways, functional sitting areas, and relaxed meeting space. Making effective use of environmental space is a constant challenge for educators.

Dress. What others wear and their general appearance communicate a great deal about the wearer and the school organization. It has been found that human relationships are established, reconfirmed, or denied within the first four minutes of contact (Zunin & Zunin, 1972). Dress has much to do with the early stereotyping and misconceptions that occur. Acceptable dress may reduce inaccurate perceptions and improve first impressions. What is "acceptable" may vary according to community, climate, geographical location, and fashion trends.

Accurately decoding the nonverbal communication of others and being aware of one's own nonverbal behavior can help educators project a positive, caring image to the public. Providing the human touch in school public relations involves understanding the personalities, emotions, and feelings of others. Awareness of nonverbal communication provides educators with an in-depth analysis of human behavior often otherwise overlooked.

COMPETENCY 3: RESOLVING CONFLICTS

No longer does the old flying-by-the-seat-of-the-pants approach to conflict work, if it every truly did. Now, more than ever, a successful public relations program must proactively plan for conflict, for conflict is an undeniable and inescapable reality in the life of any educational organization. The success of a public relations program—and more importantly, the success of the organization it represents—depends upon how well conflict is understood and handled. In the example below, the principal has some serious considerations to reflect on in solving conflict in her school. Handled ineffectively, the conflict could lead to dysfunctional behavior. Handled effectively, the conflict could be beneficial, moving individuals and groups to adopt new and innovative school practices.

Example 4

Late one evening, Marcia Broast received a call from an influential parent whose child was in the elementary school she headed. The parent was irate that an "immoral and undesirable book" had been made required reading for the fifth-grade language arts class. Broast gathered as much information from the parent as possible.

The phone continued to ring. Before the evening was over, Broast had received two more calls from outspoken parents demanding different assignments for their children. Without exception, each caller was critical of Broast and of the school for permitting the assignment of a book said to contain sexual overtones and profanity. One parent warned Broast that other parents were upset and had been calling each other.

The next morning, the principal was met at her office door by two more angry parents. By now Broast knew that the matter had become an important issue in the community, even among parents whose children were not in the language arts class.

Analysis

Assume that you are Marcia Broast, faced with a conflict that is likely to become a "faculty-community" and "faculty-administration" conflict. How would you handle the situation?

To deal with conflict and to use conflict constructively, educators must develop and institutionalize proactive, public relations plans that seek resolutions emphasizing and communicating a human touch. Nothing substitutes for the human touch, which is characterized by personal contact and commitment and effectively utilizes listening and nonverbal communication skills. This type of communication reduces people's mistrust of one another. And communication that reduces mistrust greatly enables people to cooperate in reaching agreements that lead to the betterment of all.

To institutionalize a proactive public relations program, educators must first understand the context in which conflict occurs and is communicated. Secondly, educators must structure communications so as to promote cooperation through strategies of conflict resolution.

The Communication of Conflict:
Understanding the Contexts of Conflict

Conflict arises when individual actors or groups of actors seek to impose their will upon others in order to further their interests and concerns over and against the interests and concerns of the others (Ball, 1989). *Cooperation*, on the other hand, occurs when individual actors or groups of actors seek to blend their will with others and to work with others for mutual benefit. Relationships inevitably allow for both conflict and cooperation. In most cases, this balance of conflict and cooperation creates a strong bond between individuals and groups. However, intense or disruptive conflict upsets the conflict-cooperation balance and produces pernicious results for all. Thus, it is necessary not only to recognize conflict as a fundamental base of organizational life but to distinguish between beneficial and harmful conflict by understanding the contexts or causal conditions from which conflict evolves. There are five distinct contexts of conflict: resource scarcity, perceived injustice, goal incompatibility, misperception, and unrealistic expectations.

Resource Scarcity.   Resource scarcity stimulates conflict. Scarce resources may include materials, time, territory, personnel, capitation, information, and/or influence (Ball, 1989). Conflict within educational organizations has steadily escalated as resource availability has declined and as the influence of special interest groups competing for scarce resources has increased. The members of special interest groups, equipped with education, access to information, and the backing of larger coalitions, have a considerable amount of power to influence resource allocation decisions.

Perceived Injustice.   When people feel that they have been treated unjustly, conflict results. "That's unfair!" "What a raw deal!" "We don't deserve this!" Such communications are frequently used when injustice is perceived. In this context, people disagree on the equity or equality of outcomes. *Equity* is perceived injustice based on an individual's or a group's deservingness. *Equality* is perceived injustice based on an individual's or a group's needs. Intense protests of injustice based on equity usually come from those who believe themselves worthy of more than they are receiving, while protests of injustice based on equality come from those who feel that rewards and resources should be distributed equally to those within one's group according to each individual's abilities and needs (Leung & Bond, 1984; Murphy-Berman, Berman, Singh, Pachauri, & Kumar, 1984). For instance, in schools, perceived injustice can create conflict over teaching salaries. This conflict can have a basis in either equity (paying teachers according to their merit) or equality (paying all teachers equal amounts).

Goal Incompatibility.   When individuals who must coexist within the same school environment have incompatible goals, conflict is likely to arise. Incompatible goals are often the result of differing social, cultural, economic, or ideological backgrounds. For example, principals have been known to manipulate teachers' school-based decision making when teacher-principal ideologies over important school issues differ (Spaulding, 1994a).

While shared goals can unify diverse groups of teachers, parents, students, and other community members, the lack of such goals can hamper cooperative effort—and conflictive actions between individuals and groups will persist. For example, lacking goals shared with teachers, parents may form coalitions to influence classroom practices and undermine a teacher's authority (Spaulding, in press).

Misperception.   Conflicts frequently contain a small core of truly incompatible goals, surrounded by a thick layer of misperceptions of the adversary's motives and goals. People in conflict frequently form distorted images of one another. These distorted images cause people to jump to conclusions about the motives and goals of others. According to Meyer (1987), conflicting parties often have mirror-image perceptions of one another—each attributes the same virtues to themselves and vices to the other. For example, when both sides believe that "what *we* are doing is beneficial for students, while what *they* are doing is detrimental for students," each may treat the other in ways that incite support of that perception.

Unrealistic Expectations.   Conflicts arise when one or both parties in a relationship have unrealistic expectations. It has been found that students often get caught between the differing expectations of their parents and their teacher (Spaulding, 1994b). For example, if a parent demands that his child be placed in an advanced academic program, and the teacher feels that, given the child's academic ability, the request is unrealistic, conflict is likely to occur.

Analysis

Refer back to the example at the opening of this section on conflict resolution: What do you suppose is the context in which the conflict arose? How will knowing the context of the situation help the principal resolve the conflict?

Strategies for Conflict Resolution: Promoting Cooperation through Communication

The second component in institutionalizing a proactive conflict-resolution program is to structure communication so as to promote cooperation through the use of conflict-resolution strategies, lines of actions that educators use for reducing, dissolving, or modifying conflict. Six diverse strategies for conflict resolution are presented below: uniting behind a common enemy, creating shared goals, appealing to social responsibility, providing grouping opportunities, seeking outside intervention, and initiating conciliatory gestures.

Uniting behind a Common Enemy.   Organizations and their leaders have been known to create or expose a common threat as a strategy for building group cohesiveness and cooperation. Social, economic, and educational barriers are often dropped as people help each other cope with a common enemy. The struggle creates a cohesive and cooperative spirit, enbusing people with the idea that "We are in this together." For example, Pauline B. Gough, editor of *Phi Delta Kappan*, identified a common enemy—the national press—when she editorialized on their coverage of a study on adult literacy in America. Very few educators would have trouble uniting behind Gough's "common enemy": "[A] report that should have reinforced the public's view of the value of education was instead allowed—by the nation's press—to demoralize teachers and administrators and to reaffirm the widely held (but erroneous) view that public education is failing to educate. Shame on the press for its widespread failure to set the study's finding fully in context. American education deserves better" (1994, p. 355).

Creating Shared Goals.   A shared goal is one that is more important, under normal circumstances, than any individual goal. Shared goals create harmony between conflicting groups. It is possible that the most important challenge facing education today is the identification of agreement on shared educational goals among diverse groups of students, parents, and community members.

In many classrooms, teachers and students have created shared goals through cooperative learning, which in turn has improved both classroom relations and student learning outcomes.

Appealing to Social Responsibility.   Social psychologists concur that most people do have feelings of social responsibility (Meyer, 1987). Educators must learn to tap such feelings. In many cases people may be convinced to forgo immediate personal gain for the common good. For example, students have been found to give up occasional recess periods in order to sort lunchroom trash for environmental conservation. In education organizations, appeals to social responsibility can most often be heard during tax-increase campaigns in which the school attempts to garner monetary support for budgetary considerations.

Providing Grouping Opportunities.   Placing conflicting groups together is another strategic option for promoting cooperation and resolving conflict. For example, inner-city gang violence often destroys community property. As compensation, select members of opposing gangs could be carefully placed together on service teams whose projects would include, among other activities, restoring community property. Grouping opportunities of this nature allow conflicting groups to spend time together so as to better know and understand each other. In this way, misperceptions can be clarified, goal compatibility can be identified, and conflicts can be resolved.

To get the most out of grouping opportunities, group size must be small. The smaller the group, the more responsibility each person feels to the group. Small groups enhance people's feelings of group identity and common fate. As a result, greedy behavior can give way to cooperation and to concern for the group's welfare.

Seeking Outside Intervention: Mediation and Arbitration.   While direct communication is preferable, sometimes the tensions and suspicions between conflicting groups run so high that communication becomes impossible. In cases such as these a third party may be brought in to help resolve the conflict and to promote cooperation. A third party may be used to *mediate* a conflict by facilitating in the conflict-resolution process. A *mediator* is one who intervenes and negotiates between conflicting parties to promote reconciliation, settlement, or compromise. School administrators often act as mediators when they intervene between opposing school members—teachers, staff, students, parents, central office, or other community members. In a more extreme and formal situation, a lawyer may serve as a nonbiased external mediator.

A third party may also be used to *arbitrate* a conflict. The opposing parties must first agree to submit the matter to an *arbitrator*, who then proceeds to study both sides of the issue and impose a settlement. Arbitrators are often brought in to settle worker-management conflicts. In educational organizations, arbitrators are often used to resolve differences between teachers' unions and school district management.

Initiating Conciliatory Gestures.   According to Meyer (1987), "[W]hen a relationship is strained and communication nonexistent, it sometimes takes only a conciliatory gesture—a soft answer, a warm smile—for both parties to begin easing down the tension ladder, to a rung where communication can be reestablished and the conflict creatively resolved" (p. 603). Sometimes conflict is so intense that communication comes to an impasse. At such times conciliatory gestures (see Osgood, 1962, 1980) by one party may elicit reciprocal conciliatory acts by the other party. Conciliation begins when one side announces its desire to reduce tension and describes the conciliatory act prior to performing it. After the act is completed, the adversary is asked to reciprocate in an equal manner. This then elicits public pressure on the adversary to participate in the conciliatory process. The intent of conciliation is to edge both conflicting parties toward greater cooperation and less tension, and eventually conflict resolution. Repeated conciliatory acts breed greater trust and cooperation.

Selection of Conflict-Resolution Strategies

All conflict-resolution strategies are situational, modifiable, and combinable. Therefore, educators must carefully reflect upon their choices before selecting a strategy for conflict resolution. Reflection is important because it permits the simulation of possible outcomes based on the understanding of the context in which the conflict occurred.

Understanding the causal situations surrounding conflict will guide schools in selecting conflict-resolution strategies that coincide with the context of the problem. Figure 9-3 lists some of the questions that should be considered before selecting or engaging in any conflict-resolution strategy.

To institutionalize a proactive public relations program that acknowledges conflict and seeks resolutions that communicate a human touch, school organizations must first *understand* the context in which conflict occurs and from which it is communicated. Secondly, school organizations must *understand* how to structure cooperative communication through strategies that promote conflict resolution. Only through this dual understanding can peaceful and rewarding relationships be established.

◆ What is the source of the conflict? What additional conflicts are likely to arise as a result of this conflict?

◆ Do the conflicting groups or individuals have the necessary communication or problem-solving skills to work through their differences?

◆ Do potential losses outweigh possible gains?

◆ Who stands to gain—one party or all parties?

◆ How much time is available for resolving the conflict?

◆ Is the issue major or minor?

◆ Is additional research or information needed?

◆ Are tempers too hot for a productive resolution?

◆ Will a temporary solution suffice for the present?

◆ What communication failures are at the base of the conflict?

FIGURE 9–3
Reflections and Analysis: The Selection of Conflict-Resolution Strategies

---

SUMMARY

Defining an effective public relations plan is not easy. Skills in listening, in nonverbal communication, and in conflict resolution only facilitate the plan's development. The real commitment to making a difference for students and their parents must come from the individual educator. Providing the human touch and institutionalizing public relations is a personal commitment.

CASE STUDY

An Inner-City School Faces Crisis

The Greenhill School District is a large, inner-city district located in what is known as the "slums" of a large industrial city. As required by a new state mandate, the Greenhill School District had initiated a competency-testing program for graduating seniors. According to the mandate, students are required to score in the 70th percentile on the test in order to participate in graduation ceremonies and to receive their certificate of graduation. Upon completion of the competency tests in Greenhill High School, it was discovered that one-fourth of the seniors had failed to reach the minimum passing percentile. Parents of the failing students were notified by letter and were informed that their child would need to attend summer school for remedial instruction. Following summer school, the students would be given an opportunity to retake the competency test.

Two days following the notification of test results, the school was inundated with complaint calls from parents whose students had failed the test. Finally, the school's administrative staff, who had rarely heard from parents in the past, declined to take calls and sent home a memo restating the school's position: Students who had failed the competency test would not be graduating, regardless of the number of calls made to complain.

Memos were the usual way of communicating with parents of the Greenhill School District, and memos had earlier been sent home with students to explain the competency test. Interpersonal contact between parents and school staff was extremely rare. Parents never came to school and were never invited, unless it was to attend a sporting event. According to the administrative staff, it was useless to try to involve parents in school events and issues because parents lacked the knowledge to make useful contributions, were too busy just trying to keep food on the table and their children off the streets, and/or were indifferent and uncaring as to what went on at school.

Four days after the test results had been mailed, the superintendent of the Greenhill School District received a call from a B. J. Halihan, attorney at law. Halihan stated that he represented a newly formed parent group called "Parents for Fair Educational Opportunities." According to Halihan, the parents who had formed this group had students at Greenhill High School who had failed the graduation competency test, but a large number of other parents who were sympathetic to the cause had also joined the group. The parent group was attempting legal action against the district for educational negligence. In addition, parents were taking issue with the lack of communication from the school staff concerning the academic welfare of their children. Most parents stated that they had been unaware of the new competency-test requirement.

A preliminary meeting was set up between the parent group and the school's administrative staff. In attendance was a representative from the state educational agency. During the hearing B.J. Halihan, as lawyer for the parent group, quizzed the school's administrative staff on the accuracy and appropriateness of the competency test and the effectiveness of the district's teachers. Halihan also criticized school communications, stating that parents were not made aware of the competency test until two days prior to the testing. Furthermore, according to Halihan, if memos were indeed sent out, the memos had not made it home to parents. He further criticized the school for not providing the type of assistance that students needed in order to pass the test. In his argument, Halihan was quick to point out that many of the students who had failed the graduation competency test had successfully passed all of their classes throughout the school year. He questioned the type of instruction provided by teachers, the type of curriculum used by the district, and the lack or shortage of resource support provided by the school. In particular, Halihan mentioned the lack of equipment in the science and math labs; the shortage of desks, textbooks, and classroom space; poor lighting in the majority of classrooms; leaking roofs; and the outdated library.

The administrative staff was unprepared to deal with the accusations of the parent group. No record of the original memo sent to parents explaining the graduation competency test could be found. In the end, the school requested and was granted permission from the state educational agency to provide the failing students with tutorial assistance for three weeks in order to prepare the students to retake the test before the graduation deadline. Students who still did not pass the test would have to take a summer school session before taking the test again. While not completely satisfied, the parent group agreed with the decision.

While the hearing did not provide evidence of educational negligence, the state agency did feel that the high school had serious problems that needed immediate attention. The state agency ruled that in order to maintain its accreditation, the school was to develop and implement a plan that addressed all of the issues that the parent group had identified. The plan was to be developed with parental and community input. The agency further recommended a communication audit to determine the types, amounts, and implications of communication at Greenhill. It was the feeling of the agency that Greenhill lacked appropriate communication channels. According to the state agency, this lack of communication had resulted in a poisoned relationship between school personnel and parents.

QUESTIONS AND SUGGESTED ACTIVITIES

Case Study

1. It is now time to begin work on Greenhill's public relations improvement plan. Describe your thoughts and concerns as you begin working on the plan. What concepts can you apply from this chapter to help you? Where should you begin?
2. Create a detailed school improvement plan, one that will incorporate the input of the school staff, parents, community, students, and the state agency.

Chapter

3. As a listener, what first impressions do you make? Ask for feedback from a colleague and a few close friends to help you with your self-analysis.
4. On the basis of the results of your self-analysis, describe areas for improving your listening skills. Use key components of the strategic listening process to help you identify your listening strengths and weaknesses.
5. Walk the halls of your school, paying particular attention to various classroom arrangements. What nonverbal characteristics create a climate conducive for learning, and what nonverbal characterists detract from a favorable climate?
6. Evaluate your success at implementing the framework of visual communication skills covered in this chapter. Select two or three areas in which improvement is needed and develop an action plan.
7. Consider two recent conflict situations in which you were involved. Describe the context for each situation, the contributing factors, and the strategies you used (or which you had used) for conflict resolution.

SUGGESTED READINGS

Burgoon, J. K., Buller, D. B., & Woodall, W. G. (1989). *Nonverbal communication: The unspoken dialogue.* New York: Harper & Row.

Daly, J. A., & Wiemann, J. M. (1994). *Strategic interpersonal communication.* Hilldale, NJ: L. Erlbaum Associates.

Glickman, C. D. (1993). *Renewing America's schools: A guide for school-based action.* San Francisco: Jossey-Bass.

Hamilton, C., & Parker, C. (1993). *Communicating for results.* Belmont, CA: Wadsworth.

Hocher, J., & Wilmot, W. (1995). *Interpersonal conflict* (4th ed.). Madison, WI: Brown & Benchmark.

McIntyre, D. J., & O'Hair, M. J. (1996). *The Reflective roles of the classroom teacher.* Belmont, CA: Wadsworth.

O'Hair, D., Friedrich, G., & Shaver, L. (1995). *Strategic communication in business and the professions* (2nd ed.). Boston: Houghton Mifflin.

O'Hair, D., O'Rourke, J., & O'Hair, M. J. (In press). *HarperCollins business communication handbook.* New York: HarperCollins.

O'Hair, M. J., & Odell, S. J. (1995). *Educating teachers for leadership and change.* Newbury Park, CA: Corwin.

Spaulding, A. M. (1994, April). *The politics of the principal: Influencing teachers on school-based decision making.* Paper presented at the annual meeting of the American Educational Research Association, New Orleans.

Spaulding, A. M. (1994, October). The micropolitics of the elementary classroom. Unpublished doctoral dissertation. Lubbock: Texas Tech University.

Wolvin, A., & Coakley, C. G. (1988). *Listening.* Dubuque, IA: Wm. C. Brown.

REFERENCES

Argyle, M. (1988). *Bodily communication* (2nd ed.). London: Methuen.

Ball, S. (1989). Micro-politics versus management: Towards a sociology of school organization. In S. Walker & L. Barton (Eds.), *Politics and the processes of schooling* (pp. 218–241). Philadelphia: Open University Press.

Burgoon, J. K., Buller, D. B., & Woodall, W. G. (1989). *Nonverbal communication: The unspoken dialogue.* New York: Harper & Row.

Eibl-Eibesfeldt, I. (1972). Similarities and differences between cultures in expressive movements. In R. A. Hinde (Ed.), *Nonverbal communication* (pp. 297–314). Cambridge, England: Cambridge University Press.

Ekman, P., Friesen, W. V., & Ellsworth, P. (1972). *Emotion in the human face: Guidelines for research and an integration of the findings.* New York: Pergamon.

Fullan, M. G. (1991). *The new meaning of educational change.* New York: Teachers College Press.

Golen, S. (1990). A factor analysis of barriers to effective listening. *Journal of Business Communication, 27,* 25–36.

Gough, P. B. (1994). Shame on the press. *Phi Delta Kappan, 75*(4), 355.

Grant, C. A., & Secada, W. G. (1990). Preparing teachers for diversity. In W. R. Houston (Ed.), *Handbook of research on teacher education* (pp. 402–422). Englewood Cliffs, NJ: Merrill/Prentice Hall.

Hall, E. T. (1969). The hidden dimension. Garden City , NY: Anchor Books.

Hall, E. T. (1973). *The silent language.* Garden City, NY: Anchor Press.

Harper, R. G., Wiens, A. N. & Matarazzo, J. D. (1978). *Nonverbal communication: The state of the art.* New York: Wiley.

Hewes, D. E., & Graham, M. L. (1989). Second-guessing theory: Review and extension. In J. A. Anderson (Ed.), *Communication yearbook 12* (pp. 213–248). Newbury Park, CA: Sage.

Iacocca, L. (1984). *Iacocca: An autobiography.* New York: Bantam.

Leung, K., & Bond, M. H. (1984). The impact of cultural collectivism on reward allocation. *Journal of Personality and Social Psychology, 47,* 793–804.

Lynch, J. J. (1985). *The language of the heart: The body's response to human dialogue*. New York: Basic Books.

Merrill, L., & Borisoff, D. (1987, March). Effective listening for lawyers. *The Champion, 12*(2), 16–19.

Meyer, D. G. (1987). *Social psychology*. New York: McGraw-Hill.

Miles, M. B. (1993). Forty years of change in schools: Some personal reflections. *Educational Administration Quarterly, 29*(2), 213–248.

Molnar, A. (1993-1994). *Educational Leadership, 50*, 5.

Murphy-Berman, V., Berman, J. J., Singh, P. Pachauri, A, & Kumar, P. (1984). Factors affecting allocation to needy and meritorious recipients: A cross-cultural comparison. *Journal of Personality and Social Psychology, 46*, 1267–1272.

Nichols, R. G., & Stevens, L. A. (1957). *Are you listening?* New York: McGraw-Hill.

O'Hair, D., & Friedrich, G. (1992). *Strategic communication in business and the professions*. Boston: Houghton Mifflin.

O'Hair, D., O'Rourke, J., & O'Hair, M. (In press). *HarperCollins business communication handbook*. New York: HarperCollins.

O'Hair, M. J., & Bastian, K. (1993, October). *Physiological stress levels of urban elementary principals*. Paper presented at the annual conference of the University Council of Educational Administration, Houston.

O'Hair, M. J., & Ropo, E. (1994). Unspoken messages: Understanding diversity in education requires emphasis on nonverbal communication. *Teacher Education Quarterly, 21*(3), 91–112.

Osgood, C. E. (1962). *An alternative to war or surrender*. Urbana: University of Illinois Press.

Osgood, C. E. (1980). GRIT: A strategy for survival in mankind's nuclear age? Paper presented at the Pugwash Conference on New Directions in Disarmament, Racine, WI.

Peters, T. J. (1988). *Thriving on chaos: Handbook for a management revolution*. New York: Harper & Row.

Spaulding, A. M. (1994a, April). *The politics of the principal: Influencing teachers on school-based decision making*. Paper presented at the annual meeting of the American Educational Research Association, New Orleans.

Spaulding, A. M. (1994b, October). The micropolitics of the elementary classroom. Unpublished doctoral dissertation. Lubbock: Texas Tech University.

Spaulding, A. M. (1996). The political role. In D. J. McIntyre & M. J. O'Hair, *Reflective roles of the classroom teacher*. Belmont, CA: Wadsworth.

Steil, L. K. (1980, May 26). Secrets on being a better listener. *U.S. News and World Report*, p. 65.

Thurston, P., Clift, R., & Schacht, M. (1993). Preparing leaders for change-oriented schools. *Phi Delta Kappan, 75*, 259–265.

Weston, W. W., & Lipkin, M., Jr. (1989). Doctors learning communication skills: Developmental issues. In M. Stewart & D. Roter (Eds.), *Communicating with medical patients* (pp. 43-57). Newbury Park, CA: Sage.

Wolvin, A., & Coakley, C. G. (1988). *Listening*. Dubuque, IA: Wm. C. Brown.

Zunin, L., & Zunin, N. (1972). *Contact—The first four minutes*. New York: Ballantine Books.

CRITICAL TASKS

CHAPTER 10

Setting Goals and Developing Strategies

James D. Ricks

James S. Trent

Du024ring the past decade American public education has undergone profound examination by the public. Beginning with *A Nation at Risk*, published in 1983, a host of reports have characterized public education as failing a substantial portion of the population. Today, what began with reform is rapidly moving toward restructuring. Driven by economic interest, current efforts are increasingly focused on changing the basic arrangements under which education takes place.

During periods of rapid change the public relations functions of schools take on added importance. The exchange of information between the school and its many publics becomes critical to keeping needs in perspective and developing realistic expectations for change. Developing a systematic plan for public relations becomes essential to maximizing the positive effect of the communications process.

It is important to define school public relations as clearly as possible. Robert Crowson (1992) distinguishes between school public relations and community relations. In his view they are not synonymous. He prefers to emphasize the latter and suggests that three alternatives be considered in the development of a viable community relations program for schools of the 1990s.

The first alternative, *community-parental support*, is the more conventional view of school public relations and posits a facilitative strategy for administrators. The second alternative, *community-parental involvement*, an expanding trend, entails an interactive strategy, while the third alternative, *community-parental representation*, is an emerging trend with a negotiative strategy.

Crowson concludes by pointing out that much community support for the schools can derive as a side effect from strategies of participation.

The National School Public Relations Association (1985) substituted the word "educational" for "school" in identifying this branch of public relations, providing a much more extensive definition. NSPRA states that public relations must rely on a comprehensive two-way communications process involving both internal and external publics, with a goal of stimulating better understanding of the role, objectives, accomplishments, and needs of the organization.

Today, strategic planning represents the foremost planning technology available to educators. Based upon the supposition that constant external change has a profound impact on organizations, strategic planning is almost imperative, given the rapid pace of change characterizing educational reform in the '90s. This chapter defines and describes strategic planning and provides a strategic planning framework especially suited to school public relations programs.

EDUCATION IN TRANSITION

American society is in transition; that is nowhere more noticeable than in educational reform. Educators are striving to meet the expectations and demands of the public. Accountability—in the use of available resources and in the quality of the instructional program—has been a buzzword for over a decade. School district personnel, from the central office to the classroom, are under increasing scrutiny from parents, businesses, and the community. Educators are partly responsible for this because of their reactive, rather than proactive, response to challenge. Public relation efforts have been ineffective in communicating the reforms that have taken place. The same observation can be made of the business world, and some businesspeople who are pointing fingers at educators are equally culpable.

What is, or has been, the problem? First, educators need to look at the total society rather than at what is happening locally. Most educational systems and institutions have been too internally focused, too narrow in their approach to problem solving. We live in a global society that is connected by a technology that lends itself to effective communication, collaboration, and creative production. Not only have educators been slow to realize the importance of looking outside the local boundaries, but there have been very few attempts at providing students with a balance between learning concepts, acquiring information, and applying essential processes.

Secondly, educators have been expected to do more with less, trim and build, cut back and grow, add new programs, raise test scores, with fewer resources. Some special interest groups want an expanded voice and are demanding costly special programs that have an adverse impact on the budget while serving a small percentage of the population. State and national governments have placed mandates on the school systems and higher education while providing few new resources.

Finally, educators have been placed on the defensive too often. It is time to find the courage to make decisions about the future. According to Kaufman and Herman (1991), educational leaders must recognize the reality of the present, but must also have the courage to imagine the world they want their children to live in. Because of the pressure on educators today for restructuring, a window of opportunity has opened that offers an impetus for visionary thinking. Many educators, however, have been put in the position of having always to respond to criticism rather than being future-oriented. The most effective way to respond to criticism is by communicating to the public that the organization is thinking strategically, that it is looking to the future and creating educational programs that are flexible.

In 1962, Thomas Kuhn introduced the concept of the paradigm shift. Since that time, various professionals, including those in education, have begun to reevaluate the underlying assumptions upon which practices of the past were based. Although educators have been evaluating those assumptions, there has been little change as a result of their assessments, and educational practices are still being questioned by parents, students, administrators, boards of education, business and industry, religious people, nonparents, and the community at large. Although education is still suffering from being too internally oriented and being reactive rather than proactive, there is an important *paradigm shift,*—a change in a view and attitude—taking place that may have been triggered by society's paying more attention to education than ever before. The shift referred to here is an awareness that education can no longer stay with what has worked in the past and expect it to work in the future. The realization that today's students will need knowledge and skills that haven't been developed yet has gotten the attention of educators and society in general. Strategic planning, a process that looks to the future, is best suited to address this world in transition and provide the framework around which a public relations program can establish and maintain goodwill and mutual understanding between an organization and its public (Gray, 1991).

STRATEGIC PLANNING IN EDUCATION

Planning has long been a component of educational administration. Beginning in the late 1960s public calls for increased accountability led to the adoption of long-range planning models by educators. Reinforced through various processes, such as the management-by-objectives model, long-range planning became popular as educators sought ways to operationalize more systematic approaches to developing a positive future (Ricks, 1991).

Educators who recognize the paradigm shift now in the making—from traditional long-range planning to strategic planning—have an opportunity to look at new concepts, new initiatives, and new directions that will shape their programs for the future. And they have a chance to market the program through effective publication activities so that the public will realize the improving quality of service. Strategic planning moves the planners away from comfort zones of what has been to encourage projections of things to come.

How does strategic planning differ from traditional long-range planning and how can the process be utilized in the development of an effective public relations program? Strategic planning attempts to predict the external environment that the organization will have to deal with in order to accomplish its goals. Too often organizations are inwardly focused and fail to look outside their boundaries not only to see what is happening but to predict what might happen. Strategic planning recognizes that significant change will come from outside the organization (Ricks, 1992). Few parallels can be drawn between traditional public relations programs and the current practice of having more involvement from people outside the organization. Educators have too often "internalized" what the public wants or needs to know about the schools rather than asking that public what it needs or desires.

Lloyd Byars (1987) defined strategic planning as the process of clarifying the nature of the organization, making decisions about its future direction, and implementing such decisions. Organizations do not exist in a vacuum, but in both internal and external environments that continually change. As Byars observes, strategic planning attempts to anticipate change over time, project the future, and develop organizational direction based on agreed-upon visions of what the environment will look like. Public relations planners should use the same process of clarifying the present, deciding what should happen next, and implementing the plan.

Strategic planning and public relations are not mutually exclusive. Let's examine the nature of the two processes. Crowson (1992) provides help in this effort. He shows that the two processes can be complementary in context and application. Planning has the image of a highly rational, centralized exercise, something the staff of a chief executive engages in without much concern for public participation.

Planning, however, is experiencing new interest from all sectors. The current interest has been extended to public education at the local site amid initiatives to decentralize control from the central office to teaching professionals and parents. Strategic planning, where an awareness of the environment and of the importance of value differences—and broadened participation—are focal points, is replacing traditional planning. School public relations programs become the operational means to engage parents and the community, as well as the staffs at all levels of the school system, in the decision-making process.

The key to effective leadership is effective planning. The leader who is committed to strategic thinking and planning understands the difference in the two processes. Fenwick English makes the point that most practitioners get bogged down in the activity and see planning as the doing as opposed to the thinking (Kaufman, 1992). Thinking "strategically" requires a mind-set different from the typical of many planners, with flexibility being the key ingredient. The same shift in mind-set is needed in the development and implementation of a public relations program. Public relations involves much more than "doing" something. The traditional public relations activity has been to "tell" the public what educators think they should know or want to know. Effective public relations programs now reach out to parents, the community, businesses, and other constituents for total involvement in the planning, decision-making, and follow-through exercises.

Kindred, Bagin, and Gallagher (1990) provide a planning checklist that suggests a way to determine where to go and how to get there in school public relations planning:

1. A legally adopted policy in school-community relations is indicated.
2. The larger goals and specific objectives of the program must be consistent with the philosophy of the school system and the laws of the state.
3. To the extent possible, the larger goals and specific objectives must be stated in measurable terms.
4. The strategies for attaining the objectives must involve members of various special publics when such involvement is feasible.
5. A distinction must be made in the plan between short- and long-term objectives.
6. The objectives of the school-community relations program must reflect an assessment of need or the gap discovered between what is and what should be.
7. The program must be planned and tailored to the nature of the school and the community with which it is identified.
8. The communication channels selected for disseminating various kinds of information must be appropriate for the audiences involved.

9. The program must involve a continuing audit of the results it produces.
10. Each individual having responsibility in the program must know exactly what he or she is trying to accomplish.
11. The plan must include guides for resolving issues of emotional and intellectual concern to members of the community.
12. To the extent possible, provision must be made in the plan for long-range in-service education of the staff.
13. Program strategies and activities must be adapted to available human resources, funds, and facilities.

In order to plan strategically for a public relations program, it is important to understand the characteristics of strategic planning, which differs in several important respects from previous long-range planning models: It is systematic because it links the purpose and beliefs of the organization to the goals over time; it requires clear, collective understanding of internal and external environments as they presently exist to enable planners to objectively position the organization as future trends are projected; it projects a future based on the assumption that the internal and external environments continually change; it requires the reaching out beyond the boundaries of the organization to identify perceptions of external constituents; and, finally, it involves an ongoing, continuous process of reshaping the direction of the organization so that it can effectively respond to change.

Education's needs cannot be met unless the schools are positioned to meet the world of the future. An effective public relations program will assist with that positioning. Predicting the future should be an important component of any public relations or strategic planning, and it appears that organizations are connecting with that concept.

Strategic planning is proactive, as opposed to reactive. By forecasting the external environment and looking at the world ahead, planners are able to position themselves to address changes in variables that will impact us rather than reacting to unilateral trends and mandates that occasionally appear on the scene.

Strategic planning requires that a team of people of varying backgrounds and expertise come together for the development of visions of the future. Searches for top-level executives more often than not insist that the candidates have strategic planning experience before they will be considered for the position. But no one individual has the expertise to accomplish such an important task, and as changes occur in the environment it might be necessary to add people to the strategic planning team to assist in addressing a changing variable. Planning is continual and periodic, consistent review is essential, and total team involvement is necessary if the plan is to meet with success.

Roger Kaufman (1992) cites six critical success factors for thinking and planning strategically: being willing to move out of today's comfort zone to use new and broader limits for thinking, planning, doing, and evaluating; distinguishing between ends and means by focusing on what, not how; utilizing all three levels of results (mega, macro, and micro); using an ideal vision as the underlying reason for planning without being limited by current restraints or naysayers; developing objectives that will include measures that tell you what you have accomplished; and defining "need" as a gap in results, not as insufficient resources, means, or methods.

Strategic planning gives educators a chance to market their programs to their constituent publics. Marketing is one way for educators to take the offensive. Lynton Gray (1991) defines marketing as a management process responsible for anticipating, identifying, and then satisfying consumers' wants and needs. Consumers, of course, are identified as the students and those acting on their behalf, normally parents. Marketing is only one of several side benefits or spin-offs of strategic planning. In fact, strategic planning has a wide impact and results in many things other than mere development of a plan. If educators are to regain the confidence of the people whom they need as supporters, positive spinoffs of planning are important to the whole process. One critical spin-off is cited by Kindred, Bagin, and Gallagher (1990), who believe that it is a function of personnel at all levels in a school system to "improve and maintain optimal levels of student achievement and to build and maintain public support" (pp. 46-47). Cochran, Phelps, and Cochran (1980) indicate that one problem that has plagued public relations practitioners is that each group in the educational organization tends to view public relations as the responsibility of someone else; many opportunities are lost as a result of this thinking.

Many times there is a lack of responsibility for action. Every group—teachers, administrators, boards of education—agrees that effective planning is vital to the future of the school system. However, each group tends to think that the responsibility for planning rests with another group, or with someone else in the organization. Obviously, that is erroneous thinking. All people connected to the school system—and the general public—have to work together to extend common vision. Networks of concerned citizens, internal and external to the organization, must combine their efforts and their resources in planning for the future. Ways must be found to inspire greater community support and involvement.

Changing terminology is not enough. Simply substituting one term—"strategic planning"—for another—"long-range planning"—is easy enough, but educators need also to change their way of thinking and their attitude toward change. They have to react to immediate problems with which they are confronted, but reactive operation has become for many educators a way of life. They must relieve themselves of the reactive approach and become proactive in order to build the structure necessary for the planning process to move forward.

How strategic planning can assist in the planning of a public relations program is well stated by Kaufman and Herman (1991), who distinguish between "inside-out" planning and "outside-in" planning. The former makes the organization the primary client, "as if one were looking from within the organization outside into the operational world where learners graduate, and where citizens live, play and work" (p. 7).

The latter views society as the primary agent and beneficiary "as if one were looking into the organization from outside, from the vantage point of society, back into the realm of organizational results and efforts" (p. 8).

Kaufman and Herman indicate that the difference between the two perspectives is how one views the world. In the inside-out mode, the client (and beneficiary) is the organization; its survival and well-being will likely be paramount. The outside-in mode sees the basic client (and beneficiary) as society, and anything the organization can or should contribute is identified and considered in that light.

The authors affirm that

in reality both perspectives are important. Effective planning will integrate both by using the (proactive) outside-in mode. Through identifying what kind of world educational partners wish their children and grandchildren to live in, educational goals and objectives are derived for reaching that end. After setting the mission, developing the building-block objectives and related methods, the inside-out perspective may be used and a comparison of "what is" may be made against "what should be" in order to determine what to keep and what to change (p. 9).

It is becoming clearer that the traditional inside-out method of operation—"We'll tell you what you want to know"—is no longer a viable alternative, used alone. Public relations programs require total involvement of external and internal people. It is the responsibility of *all* the people of the community.

HALLMARKS OF AN EFFECTIVE STRATEGIC PLAN

Educational leaders seeking to develop and legitimize a school system's public relations program should strongly consider a strategic planning system that incorporates the following characteristics:

Simplicity: Most school systems simply do not have the resources to establish a full-time planning position. This being the case, an effective system will involve planners who hold other full-time professional positions. Time constraints will require a planning system that is simple, straightforward, and easily manageable.

Visibility: An effective plan should establish both the purpose and underlying principles that ground a public relations program. Visibility should be prime consideration in communicating key elements of the program and in shaping public expectations related to the public relations function.

Accountability: Outcomes of the plan should be tangible and measurable. Planning raises expectations that outcomes will be achieved. Planners must be sensitive to the need to visibly demonstrate planning outcomes.

Brevity: An effective plan should communicate to a wide variety of constituents. It should be succinct and to the point, with language structure appropriate to a wide audience.

A strategic planning format requires projection of future trends and development of a long-term vision for the program. Plans must be realistic and make sense to a wide variety of school constituents. These considerations suggest involving both members of the school family and members of the community in the planning process. Typically, a planning team should range between fifteen and twenty-five people, at least half of whom represent the community. Teams with these characteristics are broad enough to be representative but not so large as to make consensus difficult. Membership of the typical planning team often includes central-office administrators, building administrators, teachers, and noncertified staff. Community representatives may include both parents and nonparents. Representatives may also reflect constituencies that have a strong vested interest in education: business, government, human services, ministerial, and industrial constituencies. The planning team is led by the school system administrator responsible for planning and typically includes the superintendent of schools. The superintendent's presence lends credibility and reinforces high priority for the public relations planning function.

While it is not essential that all planning team members be experienced planners, it is desirable to select participants who have strong people skills and a commitment to working together. Planners must strive for consensus, which requires an ability to put aside individual biases and agendas and to base decisions on objective data.

THE STRATEGIC PLANNING PROCESS

In recommending a strategic planning process, it should be noted that processes must take into account the limited planning resources available to most school systems. Figure 10-1 recommends a process that is straightforward yet features essential strategic planning steps. These steps are detailed below.

Step 1: Database Development

As you will note, the process recommended here is data-based. As a first step, the school system's administration assembles hard data relative to the organization and its external environment. Database sources cited by Kindred, Bagin, and Gallager (1990) and Kaufman and Herman (1991) suggest that strong emphasis be placed on assessing both internal characteristics of the school system and external demographics. In addition, the authors recommend organizing community and school focus groups to better understand values, attitudes, and expectations regarding public relations. Focus groups may be organized by identifying constituent groups that interact with the schools and scanning their respective memberships to identify each group's perception of the public relations function.

Step 2: Strategic Analysis

Strategic analysis, the second step in the strategic planning process, represents the first activity of the planning team. Beginning with the assessment of the database and analysis of focus-group responses, planning team members develop findings for each category of data and each focus group's responses.

Analysis of data from both internal and external sources is undertaken to identify trends that will impact planning. Focus is placed upon reaching consensus through answering the following questions:

1. Finding: What do the data show has occurred over time? Specific pieces of data are examined over a five-year period to identify trends.
2. Projected future: Where does it appear that data will head in a three- to five-year future? What future trends may be predicted?
3. Comments/qualifications: What scenarios/events may intervene to impact the data? What does the projected future assume and depend upon? (Ricks, with Carr & Buroker, 1991, p. 66)

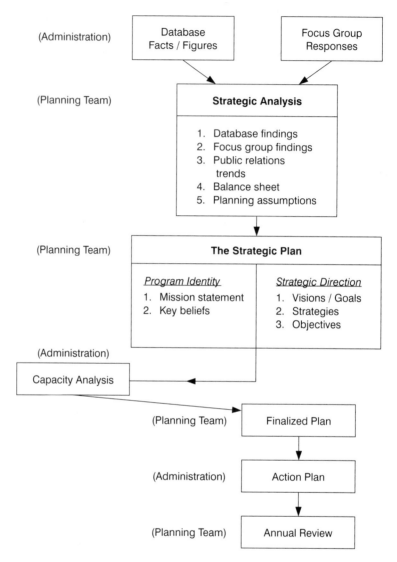

FIGURE 10.1
The Public Relations Strategic Planning Process

Figure 10-2 illustrates typical data analysis related to public relations.

Focus-group activity within the community is a second type of data utilized by planners. These data are gathered by asking open-ended questions of constituent groups related to the schools and then analyzing values, attitudes, and expectations reflective of group response. Values are defined as facets of the program deemed important. Attitudes toward the program may be positive or negative, and expectations represent what may be expected in the future. Figure 10-3 represents a typical focus-group analysis.

Database: Demographics

___

Finding (Summary)
Review of demographic data over a five-year period reveals a dramatic decline in the percentage of families in the community with children in school. From a high of 31 percent in 1993, 1996 data of 22 percent represents a 9 percent decline.

___

Projected Future
This trend is projected to continue in the future as the population ages. It does not appear likely that younger families will immigrate because of new business and industry.

___

Comments/Qualifications: Fewer families will have a direct stake in the educational process, particularly lessening support for the schools.

FIGURE 10.2
Analysis of Hard Data

___

Constituent Group: Chamber of Commerce

___

Question: What is the primary purpose of a school public relations program?

1. Sell the public on the value of school.
2. Keep the public informed about school events.
3. Promote school levies/bond issues.
4. Communicate about school life.
5. Promote extracurricular athletics.
6. Involve parents in school activities.
7 Communicate school policy.

___

Values/Attitudes (Summary)
Local businesspeople value public relations for a wide variety of reasons. Selling the public on the value of school, the number 1 priority, reflects business's desire to support excellence. Attitudes are positive, with substantial support present for a public relations program.

___

Organizational Expectations (Summary)
The business community will expect a diverse, multifaceted approach to public relations to effectively market the schools to the community.

(Duplicate this form for each group scanned)

FIGURE 10.3
Analysis of Focus-Group Response

Database analysis serves two important purposes in the strategic planning process. It provides planners with a common understanding of the organization and suggests trends that must be planned for or planned around.

After completion of database analysis, planners examine public relations trends and mandates imposed by the state department of education or the local board. More specifically, planners identify trends related to the database and project action to be taken, impact upon the organization, probability of occurrence, and projected duration. The potential impact upon planning decisions is also cited. Figure 10-4 illustrates a typical trend analysis.

Trend	[X]		[X]	National
Mandate	[ ]		[ ]	State

Description
Telecommunication holds promise for new media of communication to households. Public-access channels offer school systems an opportunity to better communicate with constituents.

Required Action
Innovative programming suitable for a wide audience needs to be developed to effectively compete with commercial channels.

Impact
Low   High

|————————————|————————————|————————————|———X————|————————————|

Probability
Low   High

|————————————|————————————|————X————|————————————|————————————|

Duration
Short Term   Long Term
                                                                                          X

|————————————|————————————|————————————|————————————|————————————|
2 years   4 years   6 years   8 years   10 years

Potential Planning Impact: _____

_____

_____

_____

(Duplicate this form for each Trend/Mandate)

FIGURE 10.4
Analysis of Trends and Mandates

Once trends and mandates are analyzed, it is essential to monitor future direction and to reassess it over time.

An analysis of important trends and mandates is followed by development of an organizational balance sheet designed to assess organizational strengths and weaknesses. The balance sheet provides planners with the opportunity to classify certain key factors:

1. *Assets:* Advantages enjoyed over time and likely to continue in the future
2. *Liabilities:* Temporary negative conditions that may be overcome in the short term
3. *Barriers:* Disadvantages experienced over time and likely to continue in the future
4. *Threats:* Predictable future conditions that may jeopardize the organization's capacity to meet its purposes
5. *Favorable probabilities:* Future advantages the organization may exploit to strengthen its position (Ricks with Carr & Buroker, 1991, pp. 88-90).

Figure 10-5 illustrates entries on a typical balance sheet.

A final step in strategic analysis involves development of planning assumptions. A *planning assumption* is a simple statement predicting a future condition that will need to be planned for or planned around. A planning assumption is not a goal or action

Present	
1. Assets Financial support has been and will be present to support a public relations program.	**2. Liabilities** A lack of public relations expertise exists in the school system.
	3. Barriers Historically, some segments of the public have been resistant to supporting a public relations plan.
Future	
5. Favorable Probabilities Technological advances in communications will open new awareness to better communication with the public.	**4. Threats** Educational restructuring may demand resources that might otherwise support public relations efforts.

FIGURE 10.5
Sample Balance Sheet

statement that addresses how a problem will be met. A planning assumption is a predicted condition, usually identified by examining data over time and projecting how related external and internal variables will impact future data. Examples of planning assumptions are given below:

Data: Five-year data show the number of families in the community without children is increasing.

Data: Demographic data and projections indicate a stable population base with insignificant in-migration.

Data: Community economic data project a significant growth of new industry.

Data: National and state data indicate a dropping birth rate (Ricks, with Carr & Buroker, 1991, p. 93).

Step 3: Developing the Strategic Plan

Completion of the strategic analysis phase leads planners to development of the actual plan itself. The plan consists of two components: identifying the program and determining the strategic direction:

Developing the Program Identity. Development of a program identity serves to establish both the purpose of and the key beliefs about the public relations function. This process is essential in establishing the program in that it serves to shape the expectations of the school's public and to set parameters that will guide in developing the strategic direction. Establishing an effective program requires a sustained effort on the part of the organization to communicate both the program's purpose and its key guiding principles to all involved. The development of a program mission statement and a belief system provides the primary communication channels in this process.

Development of a clear, concise *mission statement* is essential for organizational planning. The mission statement should provide:

1. A unifying sense of purpose
2. A sense of organizational direction
3. Parameters to guide decision making
4. Broad definition of operational scope
5. Parameters for the allocation of resources
6. Foundations upon which to develop strategic goals and objectives (Ricks, with Carr & Buroker, 1991, p. 102)

A mission statement should be structured in a fashion that will maximize its impact upon both the members of the organization and its external constituents. The following guidelines should be observed in developing an organizational mission statement:

1. Keep the statement as brief as possible. An effective mission statement should not exceed one or two paragraphs.
2. Use language that is understandable to the constituencies being addressed. The mission statement should be readily understood by members of the organization and people external to it.

3. Make sure the mission statement contains all required elements. Check the statement to see that it captures all dimensions of the organization.
4. Design and construct the statement for widespread dissemination. The statement should appear throughout the organization and should be predominantly displayed through organizational publications and posted in public areas.

A sample mission statement is found in Figure 10-6.

Development of a belief system represents a second step in clarifying the identity of the program. The primary purpose of a belief system is to establish the relationship between the program and its employees, clients, and external constituents. A belief system goes about meeting this purpose by establishing values and philosophies that provide the parameters for the way the program operates in practice. It serves to define the culture of the program while setting expectations for conduct. It also provides basic premises around which policies, rules, and regulations are developed.

Beliefs are not variable but serve as constants as the program responds to new challenges internally and externally. The reputation of the program is established through actualization of its belief system (Ricks, 1992).

In developing a belief system the program should be described *as it is* as well as the way *it aspires to be*. The behavior of employers toward all individuals should feature an underlying consistency. The belief system should set clear expectations *for the behavior of all who interact with the program*.

Typically, programs are encouraged to build their belief systems on a maximum of ten major tenets. A typical tenet is illustrated in Figure 10-7.

Determining the Strategic Direction.   A second activity in development of a srategic plan is a goal-setting process that involves drafting strategic visions, establishing strategic goals, devising strategies, and setting measurable objectives. The process relies on information found in the database and conclusions drawn through the strategic analysis. Information from both of these sources must be continually referenced throughout the goal-setting process.

The identity established for the program is equally important to the process. All outcomes of the strategic goal-setting process must be congruent with previously developed elements that define the organization's identity. In the strategic planning process each step builds on the other and moves sequentially in establishing and defining direction for the organization.

The public relations program of the Ashtown Community Schools is intended to involve, educate, and inform parents and community of the school system's purposes, program, and activities. Through the program, the public will develop greater understanding and insight into the schools, which will lead to greater appreciation of the school's contribution to the community. The program is structured to offer greater opportunity for expanded school-community communication to ensure community input in school activity.

FIGURE 10.6
Sample Mission Statement

FIGURE 10.7
One Tenet of a Belief System

> Effective public relations requires two-way communication between the school and community.

FIGURE 10.8
A Strategic Vision Statement

> Population trends in the nation and in our service area will continue to show an increase in the percentages of families without school-age children. Families of this type have less vested interest in participating in school life and in supporting schools.

The first task in the process for planners is development of strategic vision statements, which predict future environmental conditions that the program must respond to in meeting its purposes. A vision statement should be framed to address (1) desired educational outcomes and (2) conditions that must be met if the program is to retain its capacity to meet its purposes (Ricks, with Carr & Buroker, 1991). An example of a vision statement is seen in Figure 10-8.

Most strategic plans feature four to seven vision statements. Since vision statements drive development of the plan, it is necessary to limit them to what planners deem the visions most significant to the program.

Once strategic visions are formed and adopted, they are directly linked to the purposes of the program through the development of goals. Strategic goals constitute a broad general future for the program based as they are on projections of variables that will impact the program's future. Each goal should clearly indicate a priority direction for the organization that is based on a strategic vision (Ricks, Carr & Burker, 1991). A sample strategic goal is given in Figure 10-9.

Each goal should be driven by a strategy that, in turn, shapes objectives that define component activities related to the goal. In forming strategies, the organization concentrates on identifying alternative actions that hold promise for maximizing the organization's likelihood of reaching its goals. Strategy formulation may be accomplished by addressing the sequence of questions shown in Figure 10-10.

Strategies are alternatives the organization selects to best enable it to meet its objectives. These objectives are most often programmatic aspects of the total organizational effort, constituting the substance of what it will take to make the projected future a reality (Ricks, with Carr & Buroker, 1991).

Objectives should (1) be measurable and (2) feature clearly defined time references. (See Figure 10-11.) Typical time frames for objectives are from one to five years (Ricks, 1992).

FIGURE 10.9
Sample Strategic Goal

> The school system shall place increased emphasis upon keeping those without school-age children well informed about the schools, their programs, and their importance to the community.

What is our organization doing now?
The school district currently sends a newsletter to citizens of the
school system featuring school programs.

What are the deficits of our current activity?
Many residents do not read the newsletter because they do not perceive school news to
be important to them.

What needs to occur to overcome deficits?
The readership base of the newsletter needs to be significantly expanded.

Strategy
The district newsletter shall be expanded to include other information of vital community
interest as a means of expanding the readership base.

FIGURE 10.10
The Strategy Development Process

Projecting time lines and establishing ways to measure the achievement of objectives
involve a "best guess" consideration of how effective the previously developed strategy
will be in driving the desirable programmatic outcome. In setting objectives, you have to
project the impact of the strategy you will apply in shaping both standards for measuring
success and projected time lines.

Step 4: Capacity Analysis

Prior to final adoption of the strategic plan, consideration must be given to whether or not
the organization has adequate resources to carry it out. To this end the organization is
charged with the responsibility of conducting a capacity analysis to determine the plan's
viability.

The capacity analysis is a preliminary examination of the ability of the organization to
support objectives of the plan. "Capacity" comprises two elements: *Fiscal requirements* are
defined as the amount of money needed over time to accomplish each objective; *human
resources* is an estimate of personnel required to conduct plan activities. Each variable

FIGURE 10.11
Sample Objective

By 1997, the school system shall effectively communicate information
about district programs to 60 percent of all families without children in
school.

should be projected for each objective (Ricks, with Carr & Buroker, 1991). Figure 10-12 represents a typical capacity analysis.

Close attention to capacity analysis is critical in avoiding one major planning pitfall. Planning raises expectations in the community and in the schools. Credibility will be

---

Goal

The school system shall place increased emphasis on keeping those without school-aged children informed about schools, their programs, and their importance to the community.

Objective

By 1997, the school system shall effectively communicate information about district programs to 60 percent of all families without children in school.

Anticipated Activity

1. Evaluate newsletter content.	4. Bid graphics/printing.
2. Assess public views needs.	5. Assemble mailing list.
3. Reformat newsletters.	6.

Anticipated Outcome

Fiscal Requirements

Supplies	$ 5,000.00	Reallocated	50	%
Equipment/printing	$120,000.00	Reallocated	65	%
Personnel	$ 53,000.00	Reallocated	100	%
Construction	$	Reallocated		%
Maintenance	$	Reallocated		%
Total Cost	$ 178,000	Total New Monies	$ 47,550.00	

Human Resources

Director ___John Doe___   % Time ___100___

Other Participants (Describe) ___Secretary 100%; Newsletter editor 25%___

% Time Workday ___2-100%___ Additional costs (Estimate) ___$15,000___
___1-25%___

(Duplicate this form as necessary)

FIGURE 10.12
Capacity Analysis

damaged if the organization does not have the capacity to move its public relations plan forward. As a consequence, the community may lose confidence in the organization's ability to follow through.

Step 5: Action Planning

Each adopted objective in the strategic plan should be finalized and forwarded for action planning to the administrator responsible for public relations. Action planning consists of identification, in chronological order, of activities that must be initiated to satisfy the objective. Prior to initiating an action plan, the administration in charge should carefully examine the vision statement, goal, and strategy related to each objective. The action plan should be consistent with both the vision statement and the goal and should directly reflect the strategies around which the objective is based.

The development of action plans is best accomplished through the steps outlined in Figure 10-13.

Each step illustrated in the figure represents a specific activity taken over the course of approximately one year of the planning cycle. Evaluation of the cycle will drive annual review of objectives requiring more than one year of activity.

Step 6: Establishing a Planning Cycle

To maximize the effectiveness of a public relations strategic plan, the planning process should be ongoing. Unlike more traditional long-range plans, the components of a strategic plan are considered dynamic. As the future unfolds they must be revisited, readjusted, and updated. Changes in both the internal and external environments over time require

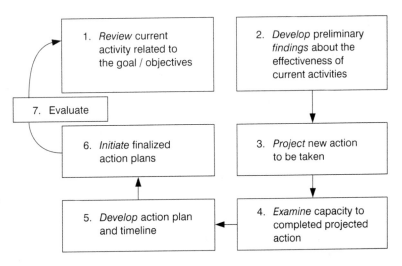

FIGURE 10.13
Steps in Developing an Action Plan

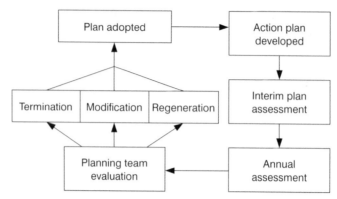

FIGURE 10.14
Annual Planning Cycle

flexibility. An annual planning cycle is necessary to ensure that the plan becomes a part of the culture of the public relations program.

In establishing an annual planning cycle it is considered most desirable to reconvene the original planning team annually to review progress on the plan and to reconsider its viability in the face of changing conditions. Figure 10-14 presents a simple flowchart illustrating the annual planning cycle. The figure illustrates a cycle that features flexibility in promoting termination, modification, or regeneration of objectives on an annual basis. Through this configuration the plan becomes dynamic over time, as changes in the environment will result in restructuring activity each year.

PITFALLS WHEN PLANNING

Even though the strategic planning system presented in this chapter is intended to provide planners with a simple, straightforward tool, users should be aware of pitfalls that may be encountered in its implementation. Even the best-planned efforts may become bogged down unless careful attention is given to avoid the following problems:

1. *Overreliance on data.* Databases utilized in strategic planning should be designed to lead to identification of general conditions that must be planned for or planned around. Adding extensive, detailed information to databases may not contribute to drawing accurate generalizations and may, in effect, bog down planners in trivia.
2. *Compromised analysis.* Planners often differ in their perceptions of what major priorities ought to be. All too often competing views may be adopted in the same plan because of the planners' inability to reach consensus. When this happens, plans soon proliferate and often exceed the capacity of the organization to complete.
3. *Strained resources.* Planners are urged to consider the importance of tailoring the scope of plans to available resources. Exceeding resources will lead to unmet objectives and goals and, as a consequence, unmet public expectations.

4. *Failure to consider mandates.* Educational reform often leads to mandates for change outside the control of local planners. Failure to project such mandates and incorporate them appropriately in plans may lead to overextension and competition for resources.

5. *Overly complex language.* Overly complex language may take several forms. Extensive use of "educationese" (complicated language only understood by educators) will confuse readers. Complex sentence structure and long, wordy sentences will discourage careful reading (Ricks, 1992).

Careful consideration of the pitfalls outlined above will help ensure a timely planning process that will generate a high-utility product.

SUMMARY

Public relations is an often-overlooked but very important component of any successful organization. School systems have not given it enough attention because of the lack of resources, knowledge, or skill levels—or because of failure to realize the impact that a good public relations program can have on the employees, clients, and external constituents. Boards of education and superintendents, because of the attention being given to education by the media, much of which is negative, have begun to focus on better ways of communicating with the public.

The development of a public relations program requires careful planning that not only takes into account current activities in the organization, but focuses on the future. It is important to understand the community internally and externally, as it now exists, but it is just as important to project the future environment that will have to be dealt with in order for the organization to meet its purpose. The image of the organization can be significantly enhanced through an effective and efficient public relations program.

Even at a time when educators are expected to do more with less, a public relations strategy will be invaluable to a school district. It is not a matter of whether one is needed or not, but a matter of getting started, moving forward in explaining to the constituents, employees, and clients where the system is, where it wants to go, and how it expects to get there. A positive image takes time, resources, and effort to establish, but the dividends are endless.

CASE STUDY

Pushing for the Development of a Strategic Plan

Dr. Ira Hoskins has just been appointed superintendent of the Ashton City Schools, a mid-sized school system located in a northeastern state. The city is going through a transition from a primarily white middle-class constituency to a multiethnic clientele.

After being in the superintendent's position for six months, Hoskins determines that the school system has a credibility gap with the people of the community. In previous years the middle-class constituency had voted for school funds without asking too many questions. With the transition from middle-class to multiethnic clientele, however, the passage of school issues has become difficult. The "new" constituency does not give education the priority that the "old" one did. The perception now is that the school system is wasteful and could do the same job with fewer resources.

Dr. Hoskins has determined that community relations needs to be a focus of the school system. With good community relations, the gap between perception and fact could be narrowed. With this reasoning in mind, he proposes that a strategic plan be developed to address the public relations problem and at the same time give the school system a chance to look to the future, to be visionary. He makes his proposal at a board of education meeting. The board decides to give the matter some thought and tables the superintendent's recommendation until the following month. As soon as some community leaders hear about the recommendation, however, they begin to complain. "The school system has five or six 'plans' on the shelf," one businessman says, "why not use one of them?" Another storeowner agrees, "All those school people do is plan," he says. "Do they ever put plans into action?"

QUESTIONS AND SUGGESTED ACTIVITIES

Case Study

1. Do you think Ira Hoskins moved too fast with his recommendation?
2. Would you, if you were in the superintendent's position, withdraw the recommendation? If so, why?
3. If you decided to leave the recommendation on the table, what would you do before the next board of education meeting? Be specific with your response.

Chapter

4. Do you think most school administrators engage in planning on a continuous basis?
5. Do most school districts have written plans and goals for their public relations programs?
6. Assume that you are a superintendent of a district with 3500 students. Would you involve principals in the public relations planning process?
7. Discuss potential barriers that may prevent school administrators from properly planning a public relations program. What actions can be taken to overcome these barriers?
8. Define a strategy. How does it differ from an idea?

SUGGESTED READINGS

Arnold, D., Becker, C. & Kellar, E. (Eds.). (1983). *Effective communication: Getting the message across.* Washington, DC: International City Management Association in cooperation with the ICMA Training Institutes.

Bagin, D. (1985). *Public relations for administrators.* Arlington, VA: American Association of School Administrators.

Bender, L., & Wygal, B. (Eds.). (1977). *Improving relations with the public.* San Francisco: Jossey-Bass.

Cochran, L. (1980). *Advisory committees in action: An educational/occupational/ community partnership.* Boston: Allyn and Bacon.

Gray, L. (1991). *Marketing education.* Philadelphia: Open University Press.

Grunig, J. (1983). *Managing public relations.* New York; Holt, Rinehart and Winston.

Hill and Knowlton, Inc. (1975). *Critical issues in public relations.* Englewood Cliffs, NJ: Prentice Hall.

Hilldrup, R. (1982). *Improving school public relations.* Boston; Allyn and Bacon.

Holcomb, J. (1993). *Educational marketing: A business approach to school-community relations.* Lanham, MD: University Press of America.

Kindred, L. (1990)). *The school and community relations.* Englewood Cliffs, NJ: Prentice Hall.

Kotler, Philip. (1985). *Strategic marketing for educational institutions.* Englewood Cliffs, NJ: Prentice Hall.

Ross, R. (1977). *The management of public relations: Analysis and planning.* New York: Wiley.

Ryan, C. (1986). *Strategic planning, marketing and public relations, and fund-raising in higher education.* Metuchen, NJ: Scarecrow Press.

Warner, C. (1994). *Promoting your school: Going beyond PR.* Thousand Oaks, CA: Corwin Press.

West, P. (1985). *Educational public relations.* Beverly Hills, CA: Sage Publications.

York, R. (1982). *Human services planning: Concepts, tools, and methods.* Chapel Hill; University of North Carolina Press.

REFERENCES

Bagin, D., Ferguson, D. & Marx, G. (1985). *Public relations for administrators.* Arlington, VA: American Association of School Administrators.

Bagin, D., & Gallager, D. (1990). *The school and community relations.* Englewood Cliff, NJ: Prentice Hall.

Byars, L. (1987). *Strategic management: Planning and implementation.* New York; Harper & Row.

Cochran, L., Phelps, L., & Cochran, L. (1980). *Advisory committees in action.* Boston; Allyn and Bacon.

Crowson, R. (1992). *School-community relations, under reform.* Berkley, CA: McCutchan Publishing.

Gray, L. (1991). *Marketing education.* Philadelphia: Open University Press.

Grunig, L., & Grunig, J. (Eds.). (1991). *Public relations research annual, Vol 3.* Hillsdale, NJ: L. Erlbaum Associates.

Harrigan, K. (1985). *Strategic flexibility: A management guide for changing times.* Lexington, MA: D. C. Heath.

Kaufman, R.L. (1992). *Mapping educational success: Strategic thinking and planning for school administrators.* Newbury Park, CA: Corwin Press.

Kaufman, R., & Herman, J. (1991). *Strategic planning in education: Rethinking, restructuring, revitalizing.* Lancaster, PA: Technomic Publishing.

Kindred, L. (1957). *School public relations.* Englewood Cliffs, NJ: Prentice Hall.

Kindred, L., Bagin, D., & Gallagher, D. (1990). *The school and community relations.* Englewood Cliffs, NJ: Prentice Hall.

Kuhn, T. (1962). *The structure of scientific revolutions.* Chicago, IL; University of Chicago Press.

National School Public Relations Association. (1985.) *Evaluating your school PR investment.* Arlington, VA: Author.

Ricks, J. (1992). Strategic planning. In J. Kaiser, *Educational administration* (pp. 151-182). Mequon, WI: Stylex Publishing.

Ricks, J., with Carr, P., & Buroker, C. (1991). Strategic planning for schools: A manual designed for school district organizational planning. *In Record in educational administration and supervision.* Dayton, OH: Wright State University.

CHAPTER 11

Working With the Media

Ann Hennessey
Theodore J. Kowalski

Contact with the media has always been a cogent topic for school administrators, but the issue has assumed much greater importance in recent years. Transition to an information age and protracted demands for school reform have forged new expectations for those who hold public office. In partisan politics, for example, individuals have often been elected and, once in office, evaluated on their ability to be "great communicators." In a very similar fashion, school superintendents or college presidents, especially at publicly funded institutions, are often appointed, and their performance judged, on the basis of their ability to create positive relationships between their organizations and the communities in which they function.

Regrettably, many school administrators are inclined to avoid reporters. In part, this posture is predicated on fear—fear of negative stories and fear of being treated unfairly. But even if such trepidation were warranted, administrators have little to gain by dealing with the media in this manner. Richard Wallace (1990) commented that while most administrators do not like to handle sensitive issues with reporters, they must realize that everyone benefits when education business is dealt with forthrightly and candidly. He added that proper information exchanges with the community were far more likely to occur when schools had developed a program for media relations. He cited three indices of a sound program:

- Administrators establish realistic expectations of the media.
- Media relations are personalized so that school officials know the reporters who are assigned to cover them.
- Administrators maintain some control over access to the media and messages that are transmitted.

Each objective requires leadership (deciding what to do) and management (deciding how things should get done). Each requires that educational administrators know something about journalism, journalists, and local media markets. This chapter addresses key issues that pertain to effective working relationships between school officials and reporters.

WHEN THE REPORTER KNOCKS ON THE DOOR

If there is anything that can make a school official wince, it is a pack of angry parents; add a lone reporter and you have the recipe for an ulcer. Any administrator who has had this experience will readily testify that it can be very unpleasant, but the degree to which it is pleasant or unpleasant often depends on readiness. That is to say, weathering the storm usually depends on the administrator's preparedness to deal with the situation.

Too often school officials attempt to avoid conflict by acting bureaucratically—ignoring telephone calls, refusing interviews, or failing to release information—or they attempt to concoct some semblance of a public affairs office as a public relations crisis mounts outside the school doors. Both tactics can prove fatal. The effects of having been unprepared become visible once the dust has settled. Some administrators may lose their jobs; the community may lose faith in the public schools; bond issues may become impossible to pass; support for necessary programs may be seriously eroded; volunteers and donors may seek other outlets for their time and money. But most tragically, a loss of public faith makes the students the real losers.

Not too long ago, the television program *60 Minutes* did a feature on custodial salaries and job performance in the New York City schools. In an interview on the show, Joseph Fernandez, then chancellor of the school system, tried to explain how union contracts and past practice made it nearly impossible for him to deal with the situation (Kowalski, 1995). While few school officials will ever be put in such an uncomfortable position on national television, most will encounter journalists in their local communities. And for some, the experience will be exceedingly stressful. It is what Hemet (California) Unified School District Superintendent Jack McLaughlin (1993) called "media phobia."

While some administrators may never feel comfortable being interviewed by the media, all should prepare to meet this responsibility. For those who do not possess the necessary self-confidence or communication skills, neither hiding nor knee-jerk reactions will suffice. McLaughlin (1993) suggested that those administrators who have made every effort to work with the media, but remain fearful and insecure, must create alternatives that allow some other person to serve as spokesperson for the organization. Bill Gephardt (1993), a Hollywood, California, television reporter, agrees. "If you don't think you're any good being yourself," he points out, "then go find someone who can be himself and let him represent you." When the reporter knocks on the door, the administrator's level of anxiety is usually determined by self-awareness, knowledge about journalism, and the degree to which this information has been used to forge a plan of action.

UNDERSTANDING JOURNALISM AND JOURNALISTS

Education officials are likely to encounter the media on a regular basis; for this reason alone, they ought to know something about journalism and journalists. From university presidents to assistant principals, administrators need some skill in dealing with reporters. Even in organizations where there are public information officers, administrators should know the reporters who are likely to cover them and their schools.

Misunderstandings often arise because educators have little insight into the practice of journalism. A superintendent may judge that local reporters are only interested in negative stories, in problems and scandals. Administrators may not understand why there is not an eagerness to do stories when things are going very well, or why reporters are not willing to praise schools when they educate students with less than adequate budgets (McQuaid, 1989). And more often than not, these perceptions cause administrators to steam silently or to complain to each other. Neither behavior increases the knowledge base they need in order to work effectively with the media.

McLaughlin (1993) offered several suggestions regarding ways in which administrators can enhance their knowledge of journalism. One is to follow his example and actually take a course in journalism. Another is that administrators should offer to do some writing for a local newspaper. And a third is to invite one or more reporters to a meeting with administrative staff to explain what newspaper, radio, and television consider news. Similarly, Kim Walker (1990) suggested that in the context of today's confrontational reporting practices media training for administrators is essential. She recommended a staff development approach for addressing the need.

In addition to knowing something about journalism, administrators need to know the people who report on them and their organizations. Experienced reporters and school officials agree that there are many benefits to being acquainted before a crisis situation or scandal evolves. A new school official might want to invite the reporter to lunch and have a friendly discussion of responsibilities. Each party can benefit. As with all professions, journalism has some good employees, some bad. Some reporters are prone to twist stories or sensationalize issues. While administrators may not prevent such things from occurring, they can deal with them more effectively if they understand the person who is responsible.

KEY ISSUES IN EFFECTIVE MEDIA RELATIONS

As in all professions, school administrators share accumulated wisdom commonly referred to as "craft knowledge." One pearl commonly passed from generation to generation is the caveat—a paraphrase of Mark Twain—that educational leaders ought not fight with persons who buy their ink by the barrel (Akers, 1983). While serving as executive director of the American Association of School Administrators, Paul Salmon developed a list of old-fashioned, commonsense guidelines for successful practice. Among them were the following two pieces of advice: (1) Recognize the importance of empowerment and effective communication; (2) develop a positive relationship with the media (Shannon, 1994). But seasoned administrators are quick to point out that such goals are far easier to articulate than they are to accomplish. Good relationships with the media must be fostered; they are most likely to occur when they are predicated on a mutual understanding of responsibilities.

Reporters and administrators who understand each other's responsibilities are in a position to maintain effective communication. For the administrator, this means possessing knowledge about fundamental facets of journalism and the role of journalists. What follows is a summary of critical dimensions of a reporter's world.

Working with Deadlines

One area that often creates tension between reporters and school officials relates to deadlines. Stories often must be submitted hours before publication or airing because the copy may require the preapproval of several editors. Time parameters necessitate expeditious information exchanges, and thus reporters are often perplexed when school officials either fail to return their telephone calls or return them after deadlines have passed. If inquiries are not answered promptly, reporters usually have no alternative but to publish the story without the administrator's perspective. Some administrators may believe that avoiding a reporter's inquiries will kill the story, but more likely, the story will run anyway and their silence will only serve to place them and their organizations in a precarious position.

Administrators should try to provide comprehensive and detailed responses to all media inquiries. Sometimes this is difficult or impossible to do spontaneously. Nick Pedro (1989) recommended that, when answering media questions, administrators be willing to admit ignorance if they cannot respond honestly. The administrator can always ask for time to look into the matter and prepare an informed answer. Doing so may reduce suspicions about why an answer is not forthcoming immediately. Even where deadlines do not permit consultation, a follow-up story may be planned to allow school officials to state their positions on the matter.

Encountering New Reporters

First and foremost, education leaders need to recognize that the press can be an ally in communicating the school's message to the public (Shaw, 1987). This consideration is especially crucial for school administrators. Reporters change beats and jobs often; education reporters change jobs more frequently than most. Surveying coverage of higher education institutions, Marilyn Posner (1994) found that even reporters for the nation's largest and most prestigious newspapers do not stay in their jobs very long. She found that smaller papers, those with circulations of less than 75,000, still tend to assign a reporter to several beats. This condition makes it more difficult for many reporters to concentrate on schools (and thus to learn about them) and more likely that they will seek promotions to assignments that have a single focus.

Change is also spawned by success. That is, good education reporters are often rewarded by being assigned to new beats—winning a prize for outstanding reporting in education can lead to a promotion away from the education beat (McQuaid, 1989). This pattern of being promoted away from education reinforces the proclivity of assigning the beat to novices.

School officials not only need to learn about journalists, many are faced with the unenviable task of having to educate newly assigned reporters. These journalists often know little about the inner workings of a university or school system, and they are even less likely to know the history of the challenges facing a specific institution. For example, one of the toughest assignments for a new reporter is to accurately cover a school board or board of trustees meeting. Topics discussed and the procedural nature of these meetings may be unfamiliar and confusing. In addition to these potential barriers, reporters almost always are required to write their stories on a tight deadline with little or no opportunity for follow-up interviews. Frequently they have only seconds to check name spellings and titles before submitting their work. Michael Fallon (1993) offered the following advice to administrators: "With new reporters, you may have to underscore the importance of an action taken at a meeting. To strengthen coverage of school board meetings, send out the agenda . . . with a note highlighting key issues . . . a few days in advance. On rare occasions, when a highly complex plan is to be presented, consider holding a news conference in advance. The intent is to allow a district to get its plan into print before the meeting." Such procedures can reduce the probability of errors and help to establish a positive working relationship with the media.

Even experienced reporters can benefit from contact with a public information officer who keeps abreast of educational issues. These administrators can point reporters in the right direction, suggest ways of documenting stories, and provide ideas for stories that may be of high interest for the local media. Rhoades and Rhoades (1991) offered several suggestions for aiding newly assigned reporters:

◆ Help the journalist better understand the pressing education issues of the day.
◆ Provide research and related information that the reporter can use as background material.
◆ Direct the reporter to individuals outside the school organization for additional or different perspectives on an issue.
◆ Show the reporter documents that clarify or add accuracy to their issues.

Dealing with Negative News

Administrators certainly like stories that put them in a good light. These are the articles that are posted on bulletin boards and showcased at public events. But not every story is a good-news story; some are highly critical of a school or its leaders. Unfortunately, when this occurs, administrators are prone to blame reporters for distorting events in order to increase newspaper sales or to gain more listeners or viewers. In reality, reporters see themselves as public watchdogs, not salespeople. Most would find it impossible to even describe how marketing and sales occur within their organizations.

While negative news about education is unavoidable, it can have a silver lining if properly managed. For example, consider the potential of doing a story that criticizes overcrowded conditions in a large city school system. Principals may go to great lengths to keep reporters away from the schools so that they will not see thirty-five or forty students crammed into a classroom or laboratory designed for far less than that number. They fear they will be unduly criticized if the public discovers that some students are forced to sit on the floor because there are not enough desks. Or, they do not want to answer questions regarding the failure to assign homework because there are not enough textbooks to go around. Disclosing such situations to the general public can certainly lead to outrage and anger; infuriated patrons may indeed respond to the news by writing negative letters to school board members and the editor of the local newspaper. But consider the alternative. If the truth is kept from the public, will these deplorable conditions ever be eradicated? Will school officials be able to muster the support to pass a bond referendum to get the needed resources? Deciding to do nothing with a negative story is as important a decision as preparing a specific response (Shaw, 1987).

There are three key facets to dealing with negative situations. First, admitting problems exist is better than the alternative. School officials who attempt to suppress problems, to keep them hidden from the public, are playing a dangerous game. Second, the impact of disclosing problems is usually softened when the administrator explains that there is a plan of action. Many citizens realize problems are inevitable, and they are impressed when leaders are prepared to deal with them. And third, administrators need to communicate their plans in language that can be understood by the reporter and readers. If an eighth-grade student cannot comprehend the solution being offered, it is likely that a large portion of the general audience will also be lost.

Negative news is a form of conflict. School officials who seek an ongoing information exchange with their wider environments realize that conflict can be source of change—a means for solving problems. In this respect, the ultimate value of negative news depends on the quality of management used by administrators.

Speaking Off-the-Record

Speaking off-the-record means different things to different people; more importantly, the rules regarding such communication vary among reporters. Thus, administrators should always exercise caution when deciding whether to communicate with journalists in this fashion. Certainly, the practice of doing so should never become a habit.

On occasions when officials feel the need to speak off-the-record, they should first ask the reporter to state his or her position on such communication. In particular, one should determine if the reporter intends to share the information (in any form) with others, for example, an editor. As a general rule, an administrator who does not want a reporter to know something ought not relay the information, even off-the-record. Accordingly, agreements about speaking in this manner should be made at the front end of the conversation, because a reporter is unlikely to let an administrator go off-the-record retroactively. Off-the-record conversations between an administrator and reporter should take place only when there is a trusting relationship between the parties and only when such conversations are absolutely necessary.

There are occasions when school officials find it advantageous to go off-the-record. Consider the example of a superintendent who is about to disclose a complicated financial plan. The superintendent wants positive media coverage; however, he will be out of town the entire week before the plan is to be unveiled. Thus he seeks to do an interview with the reporter before his trip, with the understanding that the story will be "embargoed," or held, until the plan is formally disclosed a week later. If there is a trusting relationship, the advance interview benefits both parties. The reporter has more time to do the story; the superintendent is able to communicate the nature and purpose of the plan despite his schedule.

The Option of "No Comment"

Clearly there are times when administrators are unable to answer a reporter's questions. For instance, the inquiry may pertain to a confidential or personnel matter. On such occasions, talking to the reporter is still preferable to saying, "No comment." The administrator can provide the reporter with reasons why the information cannot be shared, or the administrator can direct the reporter to another school official (for example, the school-district attorney) who may be in a position to provide answers. For example, an administrator may not be able to answer a reporter's questions about a child abuse case because state statutes prohibit this disclosure. In this situation, the administrator has an opportunity to educate the reporter and public about the statute and its intent.

Explaining why direct answers are impossible is far different from simply responding, "No comment." McLaughlin (1993) argued that refusing to comment only inflames the situation because reporters typically are encouraged to dig further. For many citizens, "no comment" conjures ideas of guilt. A preferable alternative is to indicate why direct responses are impossible. In the case of a breaking crisis, for instance, the administrator may be best served by saying something like, "I really can't respond until we are able to sort things out ourselves." This is especially useful if the reporter is promised information at a later date. The relationship between the administrator and reporter will remain intact if the reporter is convinced that there is no intent to withhold information.

Telling a Lie

One of the cardinal principles of public relations for administrators is to never lie to the media. School officials often find it tempting to mislead reporters, especially when the circumstances are personal. But experience has proven that lies come back to haunt those who tell them. For public officials, the gamble is especially great. If caught, they can lose public trust and destroy relationships with the media that took years to build—a tremendous price to pay for having gained the convenience of keeping reporters temporarily at bay.

Posner (1994) noted that a public relations person who lies or obscures facts will not prevent a good reporter from finding the real story. Thus the gain may only be a temporary obfuscation of the truth—and the potential price is high. Just one lie can forever taint the credibility of the administrator, and by extension, the entire educational organization.

Staying on Track

When reporters contact administrators, they almost always have a specific story or set of questions in mind. Further, they are probably operating under certain time parameters. Occasionally, school officials meander to other topics during the interview, either by avoiding questions or by raising new issues between questions. Diversions can create problems for the reporter. If there is another story that merits media attention, the administrator can make this suggestion to the reporter at the end of the interview (Ordovensky & Marx, 1993). Judy Parker (1991) has offered a general yet cogent suggestion: "Help, don't hinder the communication" (p. 5).

Getting the School's Story to the Media

As noted earlier, administrators often lament the lack of positive stories about their organizations. What they see as news may be rejected by the media, not because the story is positive but simply because it is not news. If administrators want their stories in the newspapers and on television, they have to perfect their pitch. They need to ask themselves a series of questions such as these:

- ◆ Would I want to hear this story?
- ◆ Who is the audience for this story?
- ◆ Why should taxpayers care about the story?
- ◆ Are there interesting photo opportunities that accompany the story? (This is a factor that can be crucial with television.)

Many times, stories that administrators want to see in print simply do not lend themselves to newspaper articles. A folk dancing group at a high school and a Thanksgiving skit at an elementary school exemplify activities that reporters may not see as newsworthy, but they could make their way into publication because they are suitable for standalone photos—that is, photos that are used without accompanying stories. Media coverage for schools is enhanced when administrators understand how news stories and features are used, but it is also enhanced when administrators understand that timing is important. Features that are not suitable for news stories can attract media attention if they are brought forward at an opportune moment. Bryan Patrick (1993), a photographer for *The Sacramento Bee* in California, said he likes school assignments that have some linkage to current events. Thus, a photo of science students setting off a rocket experiment typically may not get much attention, but when it is taken in conjunction with a story on NASA, it becomes more relevant.

Besides understanding the nature of news and the value of timing, administrators need to know their local media markets. Those who do are more apt to get their stories printed or on television. Consider, for example, the tremendous differences that usually exist between urban and rural areas. A small-town newspaper is usually more willing to cover "puff" pieces— stories that have no news value and little human interest but are published to keep good relations between the newspaper and the school district. Hence, reporters for these papers might do a photo and short story about a principal having lunch with the straight-A students, whereas a big-city paper is likely to reject the idea out of hand.

Michael Fallon, a former public information officer with the California School Boards Association noted there are many activities, such as presenting certificates to outstanding students, that are important to the school's mission but are rarely newsworthy (Fallon, 1993). He suggested that school officials concentrate on other areas where they have an opportunity to get news in print:

At the local school district level, some examples come immediately to mind . . . scores (good or bad) on standardized state and national tests, violence or drug abuse on a campus, the impact of budget cuts, school closures, attendance boundary changes, collective bargaining that goes awry. At the state level, trends in admission of students to state universities, the influence of the legislature in setting educational policy, and research reports on a range of topics . . . from students with a limited knowledge of English to student performance comparisons in other states. Surveys and research reports at the local level also can have a strong news value, particularly reports of educational innovations and new school programs that produce successful results.

In discussing ways to gain positive media coverage, he offered the following suggestions:

- ◆ Understand that there are slow and busy news days. This can make a difference in covering education stories.
- ◆ Realistically, schools should expect a combination of positive and negative stories. Unfortunately, positive stories are more quickly forgotten. But some negative stories can lead to positive stories, for example, a plan of action for a particular problem, or how a problem was eradicated. Always look for public relations opportunities—even in negative stories.
- ◆ Do not hesitate to make suggestions for future stories. Reporters like to receive ideas from administrators, and while they may not act on them immediately, they may place the ideas in their file for future reference.

Parker (1991) suggested that open and honest relationships require administrators to share both positive and negative news with reporters. Admitting setbacks or problems tends to reduce the "shroud of mystery so often connected with large institutions" (p. 5). She also observed that in many smaller communities, reporters are often the friends and neighbors of school officials. These contacts can serve to draw the reporter's attention to a desired story.

Using Press Releases and Press Conferences

Writing a press release is a simple process and a good way to eliminate misunderstandings. The release should be typed and include the full name and telephone number of the contact person the reporter can call for additional information. If the contact person, for example, a teacher, is not readily available during the workday, the reporter should be provided with appropriate instructions about making inquiries. Press releases should be sent about a week before the event—even sooner if it is anticipated that other institutions will seek coverage on the same issue. The releases may be mailed, faxed, or hand-delivered to assure that all media receive them in a timely fashion.

Ordovensky and Marx (1993) recommend that press releases be written in journalistic style and address the "five Ws" in the first paragraph (Who? What? When? Where? Why?) (p. 23). They also urge that any opinions contained in the press release be attributed to individuals as direct quotes.

Press conferences are usually more complicated matters for school officials. Perhaps this is one reason why they are used less frequently than press releases. There are three primary reasons for holding a news conference: (1) the need to communicate with multiple media outlets simultaneously, (2) the media's need to ask questions about breaking news, and (3) the need to make a knowledgeable source available to the media for a limited period of time (Ordovensky & Marx, 1993). Administrators should give ample notification to all media, including radio and television. In many communities, community-access cable television has become an outlet for school news. A press release should be distributed at the start of the conference, and it should include the exact announcement that will be read.

Successful press conferences don't just happen—They are planned. Among the key considerations are the following:

- ◆ Anticipate questions that will be asked and prepare appropriate responses.
- ◆ Know exactly what can be said at the conference.
- ◆ Be prepared to explain how reporters can get additional information.
- ◆ Avoid emotional behaviors that convey fear, nervousness, or anger.
- ◆ Identify measures for maintaining control of the conference—measures that ensure simplicity.
- ◆ Be sure that the purpose of the conference is newsworthy.
- ◆ Always know how the conference will end. The preferred method is to announce that only one more question can be asked. Never leave news conferences abruptly.

One argument for using news conferences sparingly is that reporters will fail to attend if they find the activity to be unworthy of their time. Good media relations are not nurtured when school officials gain the reputation of inviting reporters to frivolous conferences.

Making Corrections

As in all human endeavors, mistakes are made in media stories about schools. And errors are made on both sides of the fence—by reporters and by school officials. The key for the school administrator is to be prepared to act when an error occurs. As John A. G. Klose (1993), the former public information officer for the Stockton (California) Unified School District, advised, "You never let a mistake go. Even if a reporter gets someone's title wrong, let the journalist know."

Often good relations between the reporter and the administrator are best served when mistakes are pointed out directly to the reporter. Going to a supervisor may give the impression that the administrator is trying to get the reporter in trouble. There may be occasions when sloppiness or unfairness persist, and these circumstances provide a justification for the administrator to contact the reporter's editor—but it is advisable that this be done in a diplomatic, nonthreatening manner (Fallon, 1993).

Several years ago, a newspaper story mistakenly reported that a school district had paid $250,000 to a junior high school girl who had sued her teacher for sexual harassment. After the story broke, new court cases appeared, school officials filed their own complaints against the teacher, and disciplinary action took place. Countless stories followed in the city's two newspapers. Reporters came and went, relying on previous stories for historical background. Not until five years later did the superintendent tell an education reporter that the insurance pool, and not the school district, had paid the damages to the girl. Despite taxpayer complaints spanning four years, school officials had never set the record straight. As it turns out, the superintendent had not made the correction because he feared that it would damage the reporter and he wanted their positive relationship to remain intact.

Printing corrections ought to be determined jointly by the reporter and the administrator. In some instances, corrections will only repeat damaging or negative information that the educational organization prefers to avoid. But even in situations where the school officials do not pursue printed corrections, the error should be pointed out to the reporter. If not, it is likely to recur in subsequent stories.

SPECIAL CONSIDERATIONS RELATED TO TELEVISION

While the foregoing issues are relevant to dealing with reporters working in all types of media, there are other media-relations issues that are unique to television. For example, administrators who are asked to do interviews in this medium often find themselves asking a series of questions. What do I wear? Should I use makeup? How will I come across on television? Should I be casual or formal?

Bill Gephardt (1993), a television reporter in California who gives lectures on dealing with reporters like himself, offers the following suggestions:

- ◆ Dress depends on the nature of the story. If it's about outdoor education, jeans and flannel shirt are okay.
- ◆ Try to avoid the traditional scene of the school official sitting behind a desk in his or her office. Viewers don't remember interviews when the interviewees all look the same.
- ◆ Try to avoid televised news conferences. The public tends to equate news conferences with bureaucracy. Viewers are generally more interested in the human side of stories.
- ◆ Don't try to be too polished, since then viewers may not believe you. Credibility increases when administrators are seen as real people.

Commenting on personal appearance, Ordovensky and Marx (1993) warned that administrators ought not overdress for television interviews. Doing so may result in more attention being given to the individual than to the message. They urged administrators to dress just like they do every day, that is, wear what is commonly worn to the office. They also urged them to (1) prepare answers to anticipated questions, (2) suggest questions that could be asked by the reporter during the interview, (3) look at the interviewer while responding, and (4) thank the interviewer and the television crew for the opportunity to present a message.

Parker (1991) summarized her advice for administrators who will be on television by noting that they should be prepared, be calm, look great, take charge, and use good visuals. With regard to taking charge, she urged educators to

- ◆ Use related questions to make points
- ◆ Build a cutoff into an answer as a mechanism for dropping a topic
- ◆ Avoid repeating hostile questions
- ◆ Avoid appearing defensive
- ◆ Politely request that adequate time be allowed to answer a question

Television reporters who cover school board meetings usually look for short pieces that can be integrated into the nightly news broadcast. These spots provide opportunities for administrators to deliver a message, but the time is limited—maybe only forty-five seconds or less. Thus, words must be chosen very carefully (Parker, 1991). In this respect, planning is critically important. But being prepared for television encounters is essential for at least one other reason. Walker (1990) warned that administrators often find television reporters more confrontational than their peers in the print media. Administrators should therefore anticipate questions and have at least some broad conception of how to address them.

THE USE OF PUBLIC INFORMATION OFFICERS

Larger school districts often employ a public information officer, a specialist who is prepared to work with the media. But many educational organizations either ignore this responsibility or address it by routinely giving the duties to a current employee (who probably has not been adequately prepared for it). In some smaller organizations, the responsibility may even be given to a secretary who has no professional training in either journalism or education. Superintendents or college presidents who pursue these alternatives often see the duties of a public information officer as merely editing a periodic newsletter and making available general information about programs. But when crisis hits these organizations, top-ranking administrators soon realize that they have nowhere to turn.

John Klose (1993), himself a public information officer formerly with the Stockton (California) Unified School District, has little sympathy for school officials who put themselves in this position. As he noted, "That's tough biscuits . . . you shouldn't hire a nonprofessional to do a professional's job." Discussing an incident in his district in January of 1989 (commonly known as the "Stockton schoolyard shootings"), Klose said, "Your phone is going to ring off the hook. You've got to be prepared now for things to happen. Not 'if' they'll happen because they will happen." He warned that staff must be trained before a crisis, because once it occurs, there is no time to teach staff how to behave.

With regard to operating a public information office, Klose offered the following suggestions:

- ◆ School officials should direct all telephone calls regarding media relations to the public information officer. That person can either handle the matter or redirect the call to another administrator.
- ◆ If the school is in a bilingual area, be sure to have staff who are bilingual. Public information offices deal with parents as well as the media.
- ◆ School board members should speak for themselves because they are elected (or appointed) officials, though the public information office can provide guidelines and training for school board members in how to deal with the media—for example, in how to avoid making quotes on matters with which they have little familiarity.
- ◆ Always treat reporters with respect.

Clearly, small organizations may not be able to afford a specialist or to establish a public information office within the organization. This means that the responsibility has to be shouldered by some administrator as part of his or her total assignment. When this occurs, the organization should invest in staff development for the person to assure that the responsibilities can be met adequately.

TABLE 11–1

Working with the Media: Key Considerations of Administrators

Issue	Considerations
Building a positive relationship	Take charge; don't wait for the reporters to come to you. Make yourself known to them.
Understanding the work of reporters	Learn something about journalism and journalists; gain insight into their responsibilities.
Responding to telephone calls	Realize that deadlines are usually involved; return telephone calls and other inquiries promptly.
Working with a new reporter	Education reporters change beats and jobs often; be prepared to educate a newly assigned reporter.
Dealing with negative news	Don't run and hide; be prepared to offer a course of action in relation to the problem or crisis; look for positive aspects. (For example, Can the conflict lead to positive change?)
Speaking off-the-record	Don't—unless it is absolutely necessary; only do so with reporters with whom you have a degree of trust.
Answering questions	Never lie; avoid using the evasive statement, "No comment"; stick to the topic raised by the reporter; avoid using language that the reporter or general public may not understand.
Getting your story in the media	Judge whether the story is really news; evaluate timing of the material. (That is, Is the material more interesting because of current events?)
Issuing press releases	Try to use an accepted journalistic style; include pertinent and accurate information, especially about people whose names appear in the release; be sure that the objective of the release is clear.
Holding press conferences	Use them only when necessary; remain in control; be prepared to bring the session to closure.
Dealing with errors	Always bring errors to the attention of the reporter; determine if a correction or retraction is in your organization's best interest.
Appearing on television	Dress appropriately; anticipate questions you may be asked; suggest questions to the reporter; look at the interviewer when responding; express appreciation for the opportunity.

SUMMARY

Transition to an information age has increased expectations that school administrators be able to develop and maintain positive relationships with the media. Doing so requires that educators know something about journalism and journalists. More specifically, they need to know their local media markets and the degree to which education reporters understand the governance structure of schools and the pressing issues of the day. Good relations between administrators and reporters don't just happen. They occur when both parties are willing to learn and there is a mutual appreciation of responsibility. Table 11–1 provides a summary of key issues for school administrators with regard to media relations.

Administrators ought to recognize that media coverage will include both positive and negative stories, and over the long run, there is likely to be a balance between praise and criticism (Shaw, 1987). When confronted with negative press, school officials ought not bury their heads in the sand or run for cover. Nor should they concentrate on making excuses. Rather, they should attempt to manage the conflict, and they can do this by publicly discussing potential solutions. Even the most negative stories present an opportunity for change and improvement. When leaders confront problems by telling the public how they will deal with them, when they reveal a positive plan of action, they may be able to use the conflict to build support for their organizations and themselves.

| CASE STUDY | Mismanaging a Sensitive Situation |

School administrators are apt to face a variety of unforeseen situations, but none can be as anxiety-producing as those involving inappropriate relationships between faculty and students. Not long ago, a high school football coach was placed on paid leave after one of his players reported that the coach had asked him to have sex with the coach's wife. The story made its way to school officials who then acted to remove the coach from the school environment pending a legal investigation.

Knowing that rumors would fly as soon as reporters started asking questions about the coach's being placed on leave, the school's principal called a faculty meeting. Without releasing details of the problem, he emphasized to the staff that they should keep personnel matters confidential—in essence, he urged them to refrain from talking about the matter. Following the general faculty meeting, the principal met with the school's counselors and told them to be alert for relevant student problems.

Despite efforts to keep the matter private, the story was leaked to a local newspaper prior to the conclusion of a police investigation and the eventual arrest of the coach. On the very day the coach and his wife were taken into custody by law enforcement officials, a story confirming the investigation and the alleged sexual misconduct became front-page copy.

Faced with a media crisis, the school board decided to designate one of its members as the official spokesperson. This board member was to field all media inquiries, including those made to school district employees. But this action did not deter television crews and newspaper reporters from descending on the high school. Interviews were sought with students and teachers. Unable to control conversations with the media, school officials were stunned to watch students who had no real knowledge of the incident embellish tales on the nightly news; they were dismayed by anonymous quotes appearing regularly in the local newspaper.

Information in one of the articles was clearly wrong, but school officials decided not to call the matter to the reporter's attention. This decision was largely predicated on the fact that the newspaper that printed the story was a small local publication and they figured that making a correction may not be worth the effort. But shortly after the local story appeared, the Associated Press picked it up and ran it across the country. The error was now compounded.

Another major decision made by the school board was to hire a private investigator for $10,000 to determine whether any employees had prior knowledge of the sexual misconduct involving the coach and his wife. This decision sparked a good bit of criticism. Because the district was not in a good financial posture, taxpayers questioned whether such an expenditure was necessary. Their anger only increased when they learned that the private investigator had found nothing to show that any employee had had advance knowledge of the coach's misconduct.

Eventually, the coach and his wife pleaded guilty to the crimes. Two teenagers who were found to be victims in the crimes then sued the school district, alleging that school officials had failed to adequately protect them from the coach. When asked about the lawsuits, school officials and the board member designated as the official spokesperson uniformly responded, "No comment."

Many disgruntled patrons cited school officials for three failures. First, many concluded that proper supervision of employees could have averted the incident in the first place. Second, the problem should not have been compounded by spending money for a private detective. And third, the school district now faced more financial losses because of the suits filed by the students.

QUESTIONS AND SUGGESTED ACTIVITIES

Case Study

1. This chapter emphasized positive relationships with the media. To what extent do you believe that school officials in this case study had established such a relationship? Give reasons for your answer.
2. Should the principal have called a faculty meeting when he did? Why or why not?
3. Evaluate the decision to designate a school board member as the spokesperson.
4. What could school officials have done to control media access to students? To faculty?
5. If you were the superintendent in this district, what would you have done when the local newspaper printed the inaccurate story?
6. Assess the employment of the private investigator from the perspective of (a) the superintendent, (b) a school board member, (c) a teacher at the high school, (d) the principal at the high school, and (e) a taxpayer.
7. Would the school district have been in a better position to deal with this matter if it had had a public information officer?
8. If you were the superintendent in this case, what directions would you have given the principal about fielding questions from parents and students?

Chapter

9. Can school officials restrict access by the media to public buildings? Discuss the issue from the perspective of your state's laws.
10. Identify ways in which school officials in small districts can prepare principals to work effectively with the media.

SUGGESTED READINGS

Barbalich, A. (1994). The scoop on schools. *Case Currents, 20*(1), 12–13.

Frohlichstein, T. (1993). Dealing successfully with media inquiries. *NASSP Bulletin, 77*(555), 82–88.

Golden, S. (1992). The media and your message: Getting the coverage you want. *Community College Journal, 63*(2), 48–52.

Gorton, R. A. (1984). An administrator-reporter conflict. *Journal of Educational Public Relations, 7*(1), 8–10.

Hennessey, A. (1992). Getting the word out: Working with your local school reporter. *Phi Delta Kappan, 74*(1), 82–84.

Lyons, C. (1990). Getting the ink. *American School Board Journal, 177*(11), 37.

McCormick, C., & First, P. F. (1989). Press relations—Asset or liability: It's partially up to you. *School Business Affairs, 55*(12), 18–23.

Ordovensky, P., & Marx, G. (1993). *Working with the news media*. Arlington, VA: American Association of School Administrators.

Pohl, R. J. (1994). Beyond confrontation. *American School Board Journal, 181*(2), 54.

Posner, M. A. (1994). Read all about it. *Case Currents, 20*(1), 8–13.

Smith, A. (1991). How to be a great communicator. *American School Board Journal, 178*(8), 31–33.

Taber, B., & Halverson, R. (1985). *How to deal with the news media professionally and effectively*. (ERIC Reproduction Service, Document No. ED 271 848)

Townsend, R. (1993). Coping with controversy. *School Administrator, 50*(9), 24–27.

REFERENCES

Akers, J. T. (1983). *Don't fight the man who buys his ink by the barrel*. (ERIC Reproduction Service, Document No. ED 246 553)

Fallon, M. (1993, November). Written interview.

Gephardt, B. (1993, July). Telephone interview.

Klose, J. A. G. (1993, October). Telephone interview.

Kowalski, T. J. (1995). *Keepers of the flame: Contemporary urban superintendents*. Thousand Oaks, CA: Corwin.

McLaughlin, J. (1993, February). Oral interview.

McQuaid, E. P. (1989). The rising tide of mediocre education coverage. *Education Digest*, pp. 7–10.

Ordovensky, P., & Marx, G. (1993). *Working with the news media*. Arlington, VA: American Association of School Administrators.

Parker, J. (1991). *Accessing the media*. (ERIC Reproduction Service, Document No. ED 339 337)

Patrick, B. (1993, October). Telephone interview.

Pedro, N. J. (1989). Be prepared to meet the press. *Executive Educator, 11*(5), 18.

Posner, M. A. (1994). Read all about it. *Case Currents, 20*(1), 8–13.

Rhoades, L., & Rhoades, G. (1991). Helping the media add depth to education news. *Clearing House, 64*(5), 350–351.

Shannon, T. A. (1994). Salmon's laws. *Executive Educator, 16*(4), 52–54.

Shaw, R. C. (1987). Do's and don'ts for dealing with the press. *NASSP Bulletin, 71* (503), 99–102.

Walker, K. B. (1990). Confrontational media training for administrators: Performance and practice. *Public Personnel Management, 19*(4), 419–427.

Wallace, R. C. (1990). Greet the press! *School Administrator, 47*(7), 1–17, 19.

CHAPTER 12

Responding to Crisis

Edward H. Seifert

$\mathbf{A}$s principal of Bethany Elementary School you cannot feel it. You cannot touch it or taste it. But you do smell it. The smell, however, is alien to your senses. You ask yourself if you might be inhaling something that is harmful, even life-threatening. Your eyes start watering, but you are not sure if this symptom is connected to the smell or to your nervous state. You start to wonder if the building is safe. You think to yourself, "Please let there be no problem!" Should you order the evacuation of the 500 students and their teachers? Should you call the superintendent? How do you contact parents? Should you call the media first? Call the Bethany fire department? What's the number? Where do you take the children? It seems a hundred questions are racing through your mind.

When facing crisis, an administrator is bombarded by dozens of stimuli. They often send conflicting messages and serve to further cloud one's thinking. But despite these adverse conditions, the administrator knows that decisions must be made quickly. More importantly, there is the realization that these decisions may affect the welfare of hundreds of other people.

Situations such as the one at Bethany Elementary School are not uncommon. Principals and superintendents across the country can attest to the fact that crises occur with regularity; for some administrators they occur so frequently, they are actually anticipated. For seasoned school officials, panic and fear have been replaced by psychological coping mechanisms that treat crisis as an inevitability, as something that happens in schools across this nation on a daily basis.

Each year, crises take their toll on schools. Consider these statistics:

◆ Approximately 9000 teens are killed in car accidents annually.
◆ Suicide has become the second leading cause of death in 15- to 24-year-olds.
◆ More than 3 million crimes are committed on school grounds each year, with nearly 184,000 students and teachers injured.
◆ Each year about a dozen natural disasters occur.

◆ Every thirty-six minutes a child is killed or injured by a gun.
◆ Approximately 100,000 students bring guns to school each day (Harper, 1989).

Administrators have no choice but to make sense out of this chaos. They cannot turn their backs and pretend that such circumstances do not exist. Unfortunately, there is no concise, universally effective answer for dealing with crisis situations. Accordingly, school administrators ought to develop contingencies that permit them to continue operations even in the midst of severe psychological and physical disruptions.

DEFINING CRISIS

When attempting to conceptualize *crisis management*, it seems appropriate to define *crisis*. Merriam-Webster's Collegiate Dictionary (1993) defines crisis as "the turning point for better or worse," as a "decisive moment" or "crucial time," and goes on to describe crisis as "a situation that has reached a critical phase." R. E. Hayes (1985) defines crisis by stating, "Crisis arises when there is a major incongruence between the expectations of an organization and what happens in the environment" (p. 36). Karl Weick (1988) notes that crisis is surrounded by low probability–high consequence events that are in direct competition with or opposite to the goals of the organization. Most of the time these events are unanticipated and require immediate administrative response.

Crisis is, by its very nature, unpredictable, and it may not always be bad. Steven Fink (1986) observed that outcomes are almost equally divided between those that are desirable and those that are not. He suggested that the key to shifting the percentages in favor of desirable outcomes is adequate preparation. Such preparation entails three elements: (1) designing a crisis-management system, (2) teaching the system to employees, and (3) reinforcing the system's effectiveness through rehearsal. The intent is to make the system an integral part of the organization so that management control over crisis is maximized.

A crisis-management system is composed of self-correcting, interrelated parts that direct employees toward desired actions. It is predicated on the assumption that there will be future events that are potential turning points for the school and that when such situations occur, the maintenance of organizational homeostasis requires purposeful, planned action. Administrators who develop such plans and monitor the environment in an effort to predict crisis situations are more likely to influence outcomes positively (Fink, 1986).

In the example presented at the beginning of this chapter, you, as principal, have no management system in place to give you direction. It is possible that you will make appropriate decisions and protect the welfare of those under your supervision even without a plan of action. However, it is foolhardy and dangerous to rely on good fortune; and even if outcomes are not damaging to the school, students, and employees, the process of facing crisis unprepared may take its toll on your well-being.

All too often, administrators first think about plans of action *after* they have already reached a potential turning point. Typically, this is too late. The management system should be molded in periods of tranquility when administrators have the opportunity to identify contingencies and reflect on their potential effectiveness. This chapter provides strategies for developing and implementing such plans.

DEVELOPING A SYSTEMATIC CRISIS-MANAGEMENT MODEL FOR SCHOOLS

Crisis comes in many forms and is viewed by the various stakeholders in the school organization from their individual perspectives. In order for the school organization to respond in a consistent and meaningful manner, a crisis-management policy must be put in place providing direction, consistency, and information. This policy ought to be sufficiently comprehensive to assure that it (1) helps direct the organization regardless of the situation, (2) guides the training program for faculty and staff, (3) defines the school's role, and (4) guides school personnel toward appropriate resolutions.

Policies provide direction for operation but do not dictate procedures (Palmo, Langious, & Bender, 1988). Because events are sporadic and often beyond conjecture, administrators frequently fail to use any systematic approach to resolve the crisis. These individuals seem to deal with crisis by acting and then observing what happens rather than by using prior experience and knowledge to guide practice (Weick, 1988).

People in an organization influence an event by their understanding of the event, and they can actually make things worse. Weick (1988) believes that commitment, response capacity, and expectation affect the individual's view of crisis and thus how the organization responds to the crisis. This supports the idea that a system for crisis management is necessary if the organization is intent on reducing the negative effects of crises on the organization.

In developing a systematic approach for managing crisis in schools, some general guidelines need to be observed; though general, the guidelines should reflect the uniqueness of each school campus. According to Fink (1986) the reason for creating an emergency plan is to assure that the mechanical parts, aspects that rarely change, are implemented as a matter of routine, allowing the crisis-response team to concentrate on the content of the crisis. These guidelines help teachers, students, administrators, parents, health care professionals, and community resources to work cooperatively. To maximize effectiveness, such plans ought to be developed campus by campus, recognizing that each institution is unique.

General system guidelines suggested by Fink (1986); Kelly, Stimeling, and Kachur (1989); Markwood (1988); Palmo, Langious, and Bender (1988), Serafin (1990); and the North Carolina State Department of Public Instruction (1988) for implementing a crisis-management system include the following:

- ◆ Define the kind and limits of the crisis.
- ◆ Communicate to the faculty and staff about the crisis as quickly as possible.
- ◆ Communicate to the persons needed to correct the crisis.
- ◆ Create a communications center for the purpose of information coordination.
- ◆ Ask faculty and staff to refer all questions to the communications center.
- ◆ Contact the central administration and apprise them of the situation.
- ◆ Communicate with the media, letting them know the facts surrounding the crisis.

- Release information when facts are known and make sure the school's position is made clear.
- Prepare news releases and read the statements.
- Have designated staff handle information releases.
- Release crisis-team members from daily duties.
- Provide time and a place for faculty and staff working in the communications center to relax and get food.
- At the culmination of the crisis, thank all workers for their help.

Perhaps even more important than a district plan is a campus plan. Most crises occur on a single campus rather than affecting an entire district. A campus plan needs to be updated each year and shared with the faculty, staff, and community agencies. Before the crisis-management system is actually developed, the following topics ought to be considered (North Carolina Department of Public Instruction, 1988):

- Faculty and staff need to discuss the various types of crises that might occur and decide the types to which they would feel capable of responding.
- Faculty need to be trained in CPR—if not all faculty, several key persons such as coaches, nurses, secretaries, special education personnel, administrators, and selected teachers.
- At the secondary level several students should be trained in delivering critical messages.
- Principals, assistant principals, and secretaries need to know how to contact emergency assistance agencies in the community. They should be trained in how to inform these agencies about the crisis occurring at their campus: the nature of the crisis, who it involves, where it is, and how long it has existed.
- The principal or someone comfortable in working with the media must be trained in what information to release, how to communicate it, and how much information to release. This person becomes the designated spokesperson for the crisis. The best policy is to be honest and yet protect the integrity of the individuals involved in the crisis.
- All staff and faculty should be trained in the ethical and legal aspects that involve staff, faculty, students, and student families during a crisis.
- Perhaps the most frequent systematic failure in the crisis-management operation is postassessment of the plan. Aftermath assessment is essential if the system is to be updated and improved.

Training Faculty and Staff

According to Palmo, Langious, and Bender (1988) and Weinberg (1989), most individuals feel uncomfortable working through catastrophic situations. Faculty and staff apprehension may result in avoidance anxiety. This is especially true when they must deal with situations such as student or teacher suicide, automobile accidents, or attacks on children. For this reason faculty and staff ought to receive annual in-service instruction and training in preparing them for crisis situations. This point was reinforced in a document prepared by North Carolina Department of Public Instruction (1988): "When crisis occurs," the agency warned, "it can be magnified or minimized depending on how well the school staff follows the appropriate policies and procedures. For that reason, the school system should have annual inservice about the policies and procedures that relate to various crisis situations (p. 4)."

Precrisis planning and faculty and staff training are key elements to successful implementation of any crisis-management system. Training and more training will allow for successful plan implementation. Training will not prevent crisis, but it will reduce the likelihood of a panic mentality taking over during the initial stages of the crisis.

Training in small groups with an excellent presenter who is sensitive to faculty and staff responses to crisis situations helps assure a positive result (Ruof, Harris, & Robbie, 1987). Crisis-management training, according to Jane Serafin (1990), should cover:

- The district's and campus's rationale for developing a crisis-management system
- The duties of each member of the crisis-management system
- The referral process to be used by all members of the system
- The various aspects of the grief process
- The process of networking with the community
- Legal issues surrounding liability and student confidentiality
- A method of review and assessment
- Specialized training in working with the media
- Specialized training for secretaries in handling telephone-related threats, media referrals, and issues of confidentiality
- Specialized training for students who will be involved in peer counseling or student-staffed hot lines

Members of the crisis-response and aftercare teams should be the recipients of the major amounts of staff training time, but all faculty and staff should be instructed in some aspects of crisis management. Peterson, Andress, Schroeder, Swanson, and Ziff (1993) state that the crisis-response and aftercare teams should meet a minimum of six times a year in order to create continuity, review situations, make recommendations, and plan training. At the beginning of each year, all faculty and staff should be reminded of their roles and responsibilities in the event of a crisis. This is a time when new and changed procedures in the management system should be described to crisis-response and aftercare teams and all faculty and staff.

One way to assure that all faculty and staff know their expected roles in the event of a crisis is to conduct simulations (Harper, 1989; Phi Delta Kappa Educational Foundation, 1988). This enactment of a crisis ought to be as realistic as possible, and all aspects of the crisis-management system should be tested, including those aspects that involve community agencies.

Staff development and training are imperative for a successful crisis-management system. Most school personnel do not enter employment with the skills or training necessary to work in crisis situations. And even if they did, they would still require opportunities to interface those skills with a specific management plan. Most school faculties and staffs do not understand how tragedy affects people and what it takes to deal with people who have been traumatized.

Creating the Crisis-Response and Aftercare Teams

The key to an effective crisis-management system is structure. Kelly, Stimeling, and Kachur (1989) wrote that when an organization is in turmoil, with rumors running rampant and emotions running high, it's imperative to have a structure that defines who is in control. They also argue that the system needs to be simple, concise, and flexible. The very first thing that needs to be attended to is the creation of a response team and an aftercare team. The makeup of each team is dependent on the resources available to each campus; but even in situations where there are only limited resources, such teams need to be formed.

Administrators should exercise caution in selecting individuals for these teams. Those selected will have to confront students and employees who may be quite emotional or psychologically vulnerable. It is helpful to first develop criteria to guide the selection of team members.

According to Kelly, Stimeling, and Kachur (1989), the crisis-response team and the aftercare team should be small groups of individuals who have the knowledge and skills to act during an ill-structured situation. The typical response team and aftercare team would consist of

- ◆ Campus administrators
- ◆ Selected teachers
- ◆ A secretary
- ◆ Community members (parents)
- ◆ A police officer
- ◆ A member of the clergy
- ◆ A social worker
- ◆ A mental health care worker—that is, a counselor or a psychologist

Response-team members should be well trained in working through all types of crisis situations. Members should be emotionally under control, responsible, and level-headed. They should also have rapport with students. Team members should have strong clinical skills, understand the operation of the school, and be trained in crisis-intervention strategies. Carol Nation (1988) suggested that a cadre of translators be available if the school population has a high percentage of non-English-speaking students.

The aftercare team becomes active once the crisis has been stabilized and members of the response team feel the need to be relieved because of the length of time on duty or the sustained psychological stress. The aftercare team should be composed of a higher concentration of mental health care workers, clergy, community members, and media spokespersons. By this time, students, faculty, and staff will have received the information concerning the situation and may need the services provided by the aftercare team members.

Each member of the crisis-response and aftercare teams should have a wallet-sized card listing his or her roles and responsibilities. Each card should also include the unlisted emergency telephone number, the local emergency fax number, telephone pager numbers for team leaders, and the names of the crisis-response and aftercare team leaders. The following are examples of the emergency cards:

Principal—Crisis Team Leader
Emergency Tel. 245-2575   Emergency Fax No. 245-3107
Pager Numbers: 245-2345, 245-2678, 245-3968, 245-2579
Crisis-Response Leader: Judy Boswell, Pager No. 245-3030
Aftercare Leader: William Kurtz, Pager No. 245-4040
1. Declare a crisis and activate the crisis-response team.
2. Notify community agencies, as appropriate.
3. Notify the central administration.
4. Collect facts for accurate information dissemination.
5. Notify emergency agencies, as necessary.
6. Arrange for the spokesperson to meet the media.
7. Arrange for faculty and staff notification.
8. Remain calm and keep your emotions under control.

Counselor—Mental Health Care Specialist
Emergency Tel. 245-2575   Emergency Fax No. 245-3107
Pager Numbers: 245-2345, 245-2678, 245-3968, 245-2579
Crisis-Response Leader: Judy Boswell, Pager No. 245-3030
Aftercare Leader: William Kurtz, Pager No. 245-4040
1. Make referrals to necessary agencies.
2. Work with students and faculty needing emotional care.
3. Serve as a consultant for the crisis-response team.
4. Participate in crisis-response team decisions.
5. Contact community mental health care agencies.
6. Help identify at-risk students.
7. Help activate peer counselors, as appropriate.
8. Assist teachers when they are informing students.

ACTIVATING THE CRISIS TEAMS

When the principal or the principal's designee determines that a crisis has occurred, the crisis-response and aftercare teams should be notified and the management system should be activated. All members of the crisis-response team should meet to discuss implementation of the management system in a specific situation. According to Hunt (1987), Nation (1988), and McQuinn and O'Reilly (1989), the purpose of this first meeting is to (1) review facts pertinent to the situation, (2) review specific tasks to be assumed by team members, (3) establish an agenda for the current day as well as subsequent days, and (4) put into operation rumor-control strategies. The aftercare team leader should receive all internal communication transmitted to and provided by the crisis-response team.

Facts surrounding a given situation should be shared with the crisis-response and aftercare teams. The severity of the situation should be determined and decisions made about contacting outside agencies. Attempts to gather information should continue via interviews of individuals at the scene of the crisis in order to understand what and how the incident occurred.

Once the crisis-response team has met and made its decisions, the information needs to be shared with the entire faculty, students, administration, community, and media. The goal of the crisis-response team is to assure that the school continues to function as normally as possible. One of the most difficult and important tasks is controlling rumors. Getting timely information to the stakeholders and information-distribution organizations in the community is the key to rumor control. Students and faculty should also be informed, because they are potential spreaders of rumors. As a matter of course, it makes sense to get information to faculty and students before releasing information to any other group.

When the situation is stabilized, the aftercare team begins meeting to review the circumstances and individual tasks. Members of this team provide suggestions to the response team as the situation begins to resolve itself. They determine the need for additional help and attempt to secure those resources if required for further action. The aftercare team may be kept in place for an extended period of time if students, faculty, staff, or the community need their services.

INFORMING FACULTY, STAFF, STUDENTS, AND PARENTS

Various groups need to be notified when the crisis-management system is activated. In most cases, the principal is the key communicator, but someone else at the campus should be designated as a backup person. This person should be present at the school during periods when the principal is absent.

The first group that should be informed during a crisis is the faculty. Telling the teachers first allows them to adjust to the situation and to prepare themselves emotionally to meet with students, parents, and colleagues. According to Petersen and Straub (1992), the principal should never use the intercom system to relay critical information because teachers and students would receive the information at the very same moment. Teachers react to crisis information differently, and some will actually take longer than students to move from the shock stage. Students also differ in their responses, but most will react with shock and then move to the fight-or-flight stage. If teachers are still in shock, they will be unable to help control student emotions. Faculty notification should be made personally if at all possible. This could be accomplished through a general faculty meeting, a meeting of all grade-level or department chairs, a telephone tree, or one-on-one meeting between a teacher and the principal (or his or her designee).

According to Petersen and Straub (1992), maintaining maximum control of rumors can best be accomplished by first communicating with faculty—if possible, at a general meeting. This action assures that information is accurate and consistent, and it gives the faculty and staff an opportunity to deal with their own grief and take care of each other. It also gives the principal a chance to remind faculty and staff of their responsibilities and to let them know how students are going to be informed. It is often prudent to have a counselor from one of the community agencies to work with faculty and staff who are unable to cope with their emotions. This meeting also allows the administrators and the counselor to assess which faculty and staff are not capable of working further with students. Additionally, the crisis-response team leader should be prepared to make decisions about changing the day's schedule if such action becomes necessary.

Nonteaching staff should be informed at the same time as the faculty. The best way to accomplish this is through a general meeting of employees. Staff members also need to be reminded of their roles and responsibilities during the crisis. Petersen and Straub (1992) note that staff are an important part of the school organization, and they play an important part in rumor control, working with students and parents.

Informing students is a major concern during a crisis, especially when the task involves telling a child or teenager bad news. Harry L. Powers (1987) created guidelines for this critical task:

- ◆ Students should receive information from someone they trust and believe as an authority figure.
- ◆ Often the task of informing the student is assumed by a teacher, counselor, or fellow student who is close to the individual being informed.
- ◆ The information should be transmitted in a private area.
- ◆ Students should be informed quietly, simply, and directly. Unnecessary details should be avoided.
- ◆ The person informing the student should be prepared for varied reactions.
- ◆ The student should not be left alone after being informed. Some students need expressions of sympathy.
- ◆ Silence is perfectly normal, but the student should know that it is also fine to express emotions.
- ◆ The student's teachers also need to be informed of the situation.

Wall and Viers (1985) believe that school officials should be open and honest about a tragedy, because such an approach helps ensure a higher level of trust among students and parents as they begin the coping and healing process. The authors cite concerns about informing the student body: (1) What should the timing of the announcement be? (2) What information should the announcement contain? (3) What strategy should be used in making the announcement? and (4) What can be anticipated regarding student reaction? They also cite the need for identifying students who might be the most distressed by the news and suggest giving these students the information prior to sharing it with the general student population.

The preferred method of announcing tragic news to the general student population is through a carefully prepared, factually based written statement that is read in individual classrooms. Emphasis should be placed on providing all students with the same, accurate information simultaneously. Providing information to smaller groups (such as classes) gives students the opportunity to grieve and share feelings in a more intimate environment. It also gives students greater opportunity to ask questions and have them answered.

Petersen and Straub (1992) have suggested some sample announcements:

In-Classroom Loss

Billy Bob will be absent from class today because his mother and father were tragically killed in an accident. Billy Bob will not be back in class for several more days. When he *does* return he will feel very sad. We should discuss some ways that we can help Billy Bob.

SchoolWide Loss

As many of you know, Principal Montemajor has been very sick lately. We have been told that his illness took his life last night at McKenna Hospital. We will be celebrating Principal Montemajor's contributions to this school and community next week. Please think about ways your class might celebrate his life. Please share those ideas with your class leaders and teachers.

Students should be made aware of counseling services that are available, and they should be told how they can access these services.

Parents should be informed when a tragedy occurs at school that has the potential for traumatizing large numbers of students. Petersen and Straub (1992) point out that parents should be considered one of the school's greatest resources. Invite them to suggest activities; be willing to accept parental help. The parent-teacher organization may have a person or committee that can help coordinate parental involvement. Using a telephone tree through the PTO might serve as a rumor-control mechanism, while providing accurate information.

The more the individuals in an organization are kept informed, the more likely they will be to support the organization and to respond in caring ways—and the more likely the organization will exhibit the characteristics of a family (Overman, 1991).

HANDLING MEDIA RELATIONS

A major component of every crisis-management system is the development of a strategy for working with the print and electronic media. The media component should be an integral part of the development process from the beginning. According to Scott Tilden (1980), every school organization ought to have a well-thought-out media policy in place. The policy should clearly spell out who will be the spokesperson and where the media headquarters will be located. Arrangements for a member of the crisis-response or after-care teams to be on duty around the clock if necessary should also be made. Regardless of the extent of the crisis, the media center should be open extended hours in order to answer questions and provide accurate information.

Newsom and Scott (1985) and Kelly, Stimeling, and Kachur (1989) outlined the activities of the spokesperson who will be working with the media. Their guidelines include the following:

- ◆ A speedy reply should be provided to all questions.
- ◆ The spokesperson should be a calm distributor of information, even when pressured by reporters.
- ◆ The person should not be afraid to say, "I don't know," but should assure the media that the answer will be provided as quickly as possible.
- ◆ The person should never ask to see reporters' stories before they are printed.
- ◆ The person should give permission to be quoted by name.
- ◆ The person should never spend time arguing with a reporter.
- ◆ The person should give the same information to all media outlets.
- ◆ The person should never flatly refuse to give information unless it's an issue of liability or confidentiality.
- ◆ The person should tell the truth. Honesty is essential.

- The person should never color or slant information.
- The person should be aware of photographers on campus. Determination should be made about allowing photographs. The school has every right to control photographers on its property. Consider pool photos if necessary.
- The person should be quick to point out heroism if such action has occurred.
- The person should always articulate the positive aspects of the situation, if at all possible.
- The person should be brief. It is not advisable to engage in information overload.
- The person should keep all faculty and staff informed of news releases.
- The person should have a special unlisted telephone number if the crisis is going to extend over many days.

The media center or headquarters provides a place where all media personnel and visitors can gather to receive briefings. According to Kelly, Stimeling, and Kachur (1989), the media center provides a place where (1) volunteers can meet to get their individual assignments; (2) emergency planning meetings can take place; (3) press releases can be created; and (4) crisis-team members can get data and information. The size and extent of the crisis determines the need for a headquarters away from the campus; but a media center should be established for even the smallest of crises. Newsom and Scott (1985) advise that the person in charge of the media center should

- Maintain contact with reporters
- Focus on the questions and the feedback from the reporters
- Be responsible for guiding reporters through the campus if such activity is warranted
- Be responsible for providing facts about the campus and the crisis
- Keep a log of all information given to the media
- Be responsible for assuring that the names of victims are not released until the next of kin have been notified
- Provide information for all internal communication to faculty, staff, and students
- Be aware of nonverbal language, which could send the wrong message

James V. Jones (1983) noted that both print and electronic media feel that they have a social responsibility to report truthful, comprehensive, factual accounts. The perception among many people is that half-truths, made in multiples of two, equal truth. It is up to the crisis spokesperson to make sure the facts surrounding the situation become known.

Normally a "no comment" statement to the press is interpreted as a lie or a negative response. Robert Detwiler (Jones, 1983) has suggested that there is a time when a "no comment" answer is appropriate. He believes that occurs when the person being questioned is not qualified to answer. One should not speculate when answering, even though he or she may be trying to be helpful. "No comment" also may be judicious when one is angry or does not have proper clearance to make comments in behalf of the organization. Detwiler goes on to say that the "no comment" response is necessary when one does not have all the facts or does not know how those facts affect all of the publics in the community. A "no comment" is also most appropriate when issues have legal or regulatory implications. However, it should be used sparingly because, regardless of circumstances, it often generates distrust. It is acceptable to say, "I can't release the information now," or "I don't know, but I will try to get the information and get back to you" (Slahor, 1989).

The communicator ought to try to anticipate questions that will be raised by the media—even go so far as to prepare a list of questions that might be asked. The crisis-response team may be helpful in identifying such questions. This same group can be a vital resource in helping to shape answers to these questions.

Responses to media questions should be written and read to the reporters. Listed below are some basic questions that Jones (1983) thinks reporters might ask:

- ◆ What happened?
- ◆ Who was injured and how badly were they injured?
- ◆ Is the crisis under control and has it been terminated?
- ◆ Can you give us the names and numbers of people affected by the situation?
- ◆ What was the cause of this situation?
- ◆ Is it possible for us to see the situation firsthand?

DEALING WITH VIOLENT EVENTS

According to Frisby and Beckham (1993), it is only a matter of time before some violent event occurs in a school; only a toss of the dice distinguishes those who have experienced violent school crisis from those who have not. In the most recent past, schools have had to work through school bombings, children being shot by people walking onto the campus, children being taken hostage, teachers being killed in front of children, and administrators being gunned down in their offices.

It is becoming increasingly apparent that a school-police liaison should be part of a crisis-management system. Many school administrators and teachers have resisted the inclusion of law enforcement personnel on their campus or in the development of their crisis-management system. Moriarty, Maeyama, and Fitzgerald (1993), however, believe that school administrators and boards of education must be willing to face the realities of society. They have to recognize their role in providing safety for students. In violent situations the primary focus is on the delineation of responsibilities between the police department, fire department, emergency medical service, and the school. Without a well-coordinated plan detailing the responsibilities of participating agencies, chaos may occur. Various agencies may attempt to take charge, and such disagreements redirect energies from the crisis itself.

Moriarty, Maeyama, and Fitzgerald also believe that schools are vulnerable to a crisis-system failure during a violent incident because (1) administrators seldom have the training to work with a violent situation; (2) administrators have little experience in working with the type of violent incidents that police, fire, and emergency medical service personnel deal with daily; (3) the existence of a crisis-management plan may rouse fear in individuals or groups who assume that the school is in turmoil; and (4) dread of violent events alone may make it psychologically convenient to avoid drafting a plan of action. Frisby and Beckham (1993) encourage the employment of police-trained security personnel on the campus in order to prevent crises. They assert that competent and well-trained security officers have the knowledge to respond appropriately in violent situations.

In developing the crisis-system response to violent incidents, both Frisby and Beckham (1993) and Moriarty, Maeyama, and Fitzgerald (1993) recommend that the plan include

TABLE 12–1
Categories of Crises

Crisis Level	Definition	Example	Agency Responsible
Level I	Resistance intended to or likely to cause injury	Attack with a weapon or firebomb	Law enforcement or fire department
Level II	Resistance to authority	A push or a blow	School or law enforcement
Level III	Resistance to request to leave the premises	Trespassing	School or law enforcement
Level IV	Resistance that is active and purposeful in nature	Running or pulling away	School
Level V	Resistance that is passive and static	Refusal to follow a reasonable request	School
Level VI	Resistance that is spoken	Verbal defiance	School

categories of crisis levels, a list of responsible agencies, and examples of action. Table 12–1 provides an example of such a plan. A quick glance at a chart such as shown in the table can provide guidance for administrators, police, fire, and emergency medical service personnel during violent incidents in a school building or on a campus. But this type of systematic crisis management can only occur when good relationships are cultivated among the participating agencies. Each agency should have one liaison person who assumes responsibility for working with the school and is a member of the crisis-response and aftercare teams.

The North Carolina State Department of Public Instruction (1988) has suggested that a signal system be employed to warn faculty and students of violent situations in progress. For instance, a voice or bell would signal a crisis. This signal would then be followed by a voice code number giving the nature and location of the crisis:

Code 1 Door lockdown: unauthorized person in the building, perhaps with a weapon; do not leave the room for any reason.

Code 2 Illness: for example, a heart attack, stroke, or choking.

Code 3 Suicide attempt or threat.

Code 4 Tornado evacuation.

Code 5 Accident.

When the alert for Code 1 is sounded, each teacher would take swift action, instructing the students to move quickly, to get on the floor, to crawl toward the outside wall of the building. The teacher would position the students in this way so that anyone looking through windows would not see them. In most cases, concrete block or brick walls serve as the best protection against bullets. Placing students against an interior wall puts them in danger of being hit by bullets coming through structurally less substantial walls. Doors with windows should have blinds installed so that during a Code 1 lockdown no one could see into the room.

During Code 2, 3, or 5 incidents, all school corridors should be kept clear until the situation is handled. This may require someone to sweep the corridors to make sure everyone is in a classroom or other appropriate area. This may mean delaying bells that signify class changes if the campus is operating on a departmentalized schedule.

Code 4 incidents require teachers to move rapidly, since tornado alerts are not always made in advance. Students should be moved to the nearest solid interior wall and instructed to kneel facing the wall, with their hands and arms covering their heads. If students become frightened or hysterical, teachers will need to help them get into the safety position.

Because of the type of construction, some areas of a school building may be more dangerous than others. In some instances, gymnasiums should be avoided during tornados because of the construction of the roof. Perhaps interior rooms, like dressing rooms, might be the most secure areas adjacent to the gymnasium. It is the responsibility of the crisis-response team to tour the building and determine the best areas for students during Code 4 situations. The response team may wish to request the services of structural engineers to evaluate the safe areas of the building.

According to Suzanne Harper (1989), the following equipment may prove very useful during a crisis situation: (1) a cellular phone; (2) an unlisted telephone line; (3) a fax machine with a dedicated line; (4) a bullhorn; (5) a battery-operated intercom system in case the electricity goes off-line; (6) a floor plan of the building showing room numbers, windows, and exits; (7) a well-stocked first-aid kit. Other types of equipment such as weather radios and radios to contact law enforcement, fire department, and emergency medical service personnel may also be helpful.

ASSESSING THE SYSTEM

Assessing the crisis management system is of utmost importance in determining how well the system functions. In the absence of an actual crisis, this can be accomplished through simulation. An assessment team, consisting of community members, agency members, and team members, should be involved. This group has the responsibility of recommending ideas for changing the crisis-management system.

Serafin (1990) suggested that the crisis-management system be reviewed on a yearly basis, or more often if deemed necessary. Kelly, Stimeling, and Kachur (1989) believe that an assessment should be undertaken every time the crisis-response team is activated. This assessment should be done formally and in writing. An assessment form should be developed in order to assure that all aspects of the system are reviewed. The following questions may serve as a beginning for creating an assessment instrument:

◆ What was the nature of the crisis?
◆ What steps did the crisis-response team undertake?
◆ What additional steps could the crisis-response team have taken?
◆ Did the system function as it was designed? If not, describe the malfunction(s).

The time spent reviewing the process pays dividends when the next activation of the system occurs.

DEVELOPING THE CRISIS-PREVENTION TEAM

The on-going solution to crisis management is preparation and prevention. To this point the chapter has focused on the activities that must occur when a crisis actually happens. The next step in the crisis-management system is the development of a crisis-prevention team (Gorney, 1990). Incidents such as student suicide, teacher suicide, alcohol abuse, drug abuse, and student-on-student attacks might be reduced if strategies and a prevention plan is implemented. This plan should include activities that provide information and make available individuals with helping skills when a student or teacher needs assistance. The crisis-prevention group should be composed of teachers, staff members, parents, mental health care workers, and students.

The major goal of this group is to collect and provide information about students— in some cases, teachers—who undergo observable shifts in behavior: depression, withdrawal, and other types of personality changes (Dempsey, 1986). The gathering of information can be accomplished by asking faculty and staff to make referrals to the crisis-prevention group concerning abnormalities in observed student or teacher behavior. Each referral should be reviewed by the team and a plan of action put into place to work through the situation. The plan should include strategies for bringing together the person in question and another who can help the individual. This helper could be a teacher, counselor, coach, secretary, nurse, or member of the community with the skills to work with students and teachers (Dempsey, 1986). The team may elect to meet weekly or only when referrals have been made.

All teachers need to be reminded yearly about the activities and availability of the prevention team. New teachers need to be instructed in the referral process and in observable traits of depression, suicide, alcohol abuse, drug abuse, and other behavioral changes (Dempsey, 1986). Faculty and staff should realize that overreacting is better than saying nothing when a potential problem exists. Extending this information to parents also helps. Evening presentations should be offered to parents and other interested community members. Information concerning these staff development opportunities need to be made known to all campus stakeholders through school newsletters, print media, and/or electronic media.

Richard A. Dempsey (1986) strongly supports the idea of peer counselors in working with students demonstrating depression and other behavioral changes. However, students who assume such roles require extensive training. Perhaps the most crucial aspect of a peer counseling program is the selection of peer counselors. This program may not work if all of the peer counselors are considered to be the "good kids" on the campus. Peer counselors should come from all segments of the student population. The goals of peer counseling, according to Dempsey (1986), should be to

◆ Train and develop students in helping relationships
◆ Develop lines of communication among students from very different backgrounds

◆ Develop lines of communication among parents, faculty, and administration
◆ Help students cope with crisis situations so that they might grow into productive citizens

Claire Hunt (1987) made the case that peer counselors could help bolster student self-esteem and confidence, while also helping students develop coping skills. Two effective prevention strategies are the "buddy system" and a "new student club." Another idea that may prove helpful is the development of wallet-sized cards with telephone numbers of agencies that provide help with such problems as drug and alcohol abuse and of agencies focusing on suicide prevention, pregnancy prevention, legal counseling, runaway services, and psychological counseling.

SUMMARY

Designing a crisis-management system may seem like an exercise in fear, but the fact remains that it is better to be in a state of readiness than in a state of panic. This is especially true when facing a panel of reporters from various media outlets. Kelly, Stimeling, and Kachur (1989), Bernstein (1990), and Cultice (1992) have all recommended procedures for designing a crisis-management system. These eight procedures encompass strategies outlined in the preceding paragraphs of this chapter.

1. **Select qualified individuals to serve on crisis-response and aftercare teams.** The selection and development of these two teams is critical to the functioning of the crisis-management system. These two groups of people should have the skills and knowledge to handle problems that arise and should be able to consult with members of the faculty, staff, and students. Individuals selected should be both reliable and rational. Both teams should be involved in the development of the roles, policies, and procedures that govern system operation.

2. **Establish a headquarters for the response and aftercare teams.** In an attempt to provide the most accurate information possible and to eliminate rumors, it is vital to establish a distribution center for information. Response and aftercare team members can use the center to review data and develop information for distribution. If a telephone hot line is established, the information center should be its location.

3. **Select an individual to be the official spokesperson during a crisis.** The media should be apprised of the person who will speak for the district during a crisis. This individual should be comfortable working with all media and should be prepared to answer anticipated questions. The spokesperson should not be the campus principal since he or she will be busy managing the system. If the district has a public relations person, it is logical that this person assume the role of spokesperson. If no public relations person exists, two members of each team need to be trained as spokespeople.

4. **Establish a procedure for activating community support services.** This includes preparing a list of mental health care workers, clergy, and social workers who can be contacted in the event of a crisis. Persons on this list should be contacted at the

time the procedure is established, and their continued availability should be reviewed yearly. When selecting members of the community to participate in crisis situations, be sure to review the individual's credentials for performing a helping role.

5. **Establish a procedure for developing channels of communication.** Community size and the number of media outlets dictate the type of communication that can be used. Often reporters who normally do not cover education will be involved in crisis situations. These individuals may be more likely to try to sensationalize the situation. Any reasonable method that provides information should be used—faculty meetings, internal memoranda, community meetings, letters to parents, a key communicators' network, and press conferences.

6. **Establish a procedure for controlling rumors.** Rumor control is very difficult, but it is possible to reduce damage. The key is to provide accurate information to the community in quantities that make rumors difficult to establish. Establish in the minds of all stakeholders that the only accurate information will come directly through a campus spokesperson.

7. **Establish a procedure for assessing the crisis-management system.** The goal of assessment is to make the plan function better in the future. Even if the system is never used, it is advantageous to engage in simulations annually. Information gained through simulations should be used to improve the system.

8. **Establish a procedure for bringing closure to the crisis.** Once the crisis-response team turns the crisis over to the aftercare team, it is time to bring the situation to a close. Depending on the type of crisis, closure can be attained by a final press release, a memorial service, or the writing of a report to be released to the community. It is mandatory that some act be performed to end the crisis so that all students, faculty, and staff can begin the final stages of their personal healing (Dempsey, 1986; Kelly, Stimeling, & Kachur, 1989). Hunt (1987) observed that it takes about four days for school to reach normalcy after a crisis.

These eight steps form the skeleton for developing a crisis-management system on the campus. Expanding each step with roles, responsibilities, training, practice, and assessment will provide the campus with a desired level of self-confidence. Practice and more practice, along with training are the necessary ingredients for successful implementation of a crisis-management system. The systems aspect of this intervention strategy is critical because of the need to function in a holistic manner.

CASE STUDY

Crisis at Cameron Middle School

When Principal Sandra Rodriguez arrived at Cameron Middle School at 7:15 A.M., she was startled to find three Cameron City Police cars and a Cameron Emergency Medical Service unit sitting in front of the building. What could the problem be? A building break-in? Perhaps the fire alarm had malfunctioned once again. Maybe the security alarm had been activated. As she moved quickly to the main entrance, Rodriguez heard the sound of distant sirens. In her office she found José and Mary, the building custodians, talking to Detective Mario Palos, whom she knew from activities in her church. As the principal approached the three, she knew from the looks on their faces that something must be very wrong.

Taking Rodriguez into her inner office, Detective Palos told her that the custodians had called 911 about 6:35 A.M. after finding the body of Billy Block, a science teacher, hanging from one of the rafters in the gymnasium. The principal could hardly believe the news. Block was one the best teachers on the faculty—and very popular with the students. The preliminary investigation indicated suicide, for there was no evidence of foul play.

The principal was unsure how to deal with the crisis. Everything was so confusing. Students and teachers would be arriving soon. Suicides weren't supposed to happen in Cameron. She had no crisis-management system at hand and she couldn't recall the system that had been used in the district where she'd been an assistant principal.

In the midst of her anxiety, Rodriguez tried to remember Block's attitude last Friday when she'd met with him about the life science curriculum. She remembered nothing strange or different about his behavior. She wondered if she had contributed to this awful tragedy. And she wondered what was so wrong in his life that he would leave his wife and children this way.

As Rodriguez began to get her emotions under control, she realized it was 7:45. Students would be arriving on the first bus in ten minutes. They'd normally go to the gymnasium to wait for the first bell at 8:30. Panicked, the principal rushed to the bus unloading zone. By this time the arriving teachers were abuzz about the emergency medical service and police units in front of the building. The buses pulling up, the teachers arriving for work, her staff in a state of shock. Rodriguez faced a situation she'd never faced before.

QUESTIONS AND SUGGESTED ACTIVITIES

Case Study

1. What information does Sandra Rodriguez need to deal with the immediate problem at Cameron Middle School?
2. Which faculty and staff members should she meet with immediately?
3. What should she do with the arriving children? How can she keep this tragedy from becoming traumatic for all children, especially Mr. Block's students?
4. What must she do to solve the long-range problem of no crisis-management plan at Cameron Middle School?
5. What research should she do in beginning to develop a crisis-management plan?

Chapter

6. What process would you, as a principal, use to develop a crisis-management plan?
7. As principal, how would you develop faculty and staff ownership of a crisis-management system?
8. As the campus leader, what steps would you take to involve the community in dealing with violent situations and potentially violent situations on your school campus?

SUGGESTED READINGS

Bernstein, J. (1990). The ten steps of crisis management. *Security Management, 34*(3), 75–76.

Frisby, D., & Beckham, J. (1993). Dealing with violence and threats of violence in the school. *National Association of Secondary School Principals Bulletin, 77*(552), 10–15.

Kelly, D. G., Stimeling, W. F., & Kachur, D. S. (1989). Before worst comes to worst, have your crisis plan ready. *The Executive Educator, 11*(1), 22–23.

Moriarty, A., Maeyama, R. G., & Fitzgerald, P. J. (1993). A clear plan for school crisis management. *National Association of Secondary School Principals Bulletin, 77*(552), 17–22.

North Carolina State Department of Public Instruction (1988). *Guidelines for handling crisis situations in the schools.* Raleigh: North Carolina State Department of Public Instruction. ERIC Document Reproduction Services No. ED 297 233.

Petersen, S., & Straub, R. L. (1992). *School crisis survival guide.* West Nyack, NY: Simon & Schuster.

Serafin, J. (Ed.). (1990). *Be aware be prepared: Guidelines for crisis response planning for school/communities.* Denver, CO: Office of Federal/State Programs and Services.

REFERENCES

Bernstein, J. (1990). The ten steps of crisis management. *Security Management, 34*(3), 75–76.

Cultice, W. W. (1992). Establishing an effective crisis intervention program. *National Association of Secondary School Principals Bulletin, 76*(543), 68–72.

Dempsey, R. A. (1986). The trauma of adolescent suicide. A time for special leadership by principals. *Monograph of the National Association of Secondary School Principals,* pp. 1–25.

Fink, S. (1986). *Crisis management.* New York: American Management Association.

Frisby, D., & Beckham, J. (1993). Dealing with violence and threats of violence in the school. *National Association of Secondary School Principals Bulletin, 77*(552), 10–15.

Gorney, C. (1990). Crisis management: How to plan ahead for potential crises. *American School and University, 62*(5), 20–23.

Hayes, R. E. (1985). Corporate crisis management as adaptive control. In S. J. Andriole (Ed.), *Corporate crisis management.* Princeton, NJ: Petrocelli.

Harper, S. (1989). *School crisis prevention and response.* Malibu, CA: National School Safety Center. ERIC Document Reproduction Services No. ED 311 600.

Hunt, C. Y. (1987). Step by step: How your schools can live through the tragedy of teen suicides. *The American School Board Journal, 174*(2), 34–37.

Jones, J. V. (1983). Crisis management and media relations. *NASPRA Journal, 21*(2), 36–40.

Kelly, D. G., Stimeling, W. F., & Kachur, D.S. (1989). Before worst comes to worst, have your crisis plan ready. *The Executive Educator, 11*(1), 22–23.

McQuinn, J., & O'Reilly, R. (1989). Adolescent suicides and high schools: Recommendations for administrators. *National Association of Secondary School Principals Bulletin, 73*(514), 92–97.

Markwood, S. E. (1988). When the television cameras arrive. *NASPRA Journal, 25*(3), 209–212.

Merriam-Webster's Collegiate Dictionary. (1993). Springfield, MA: Merriam-Webster.

Moriarty, A., Maeyama, R. G., & Fitzgerald, P. J. (1993). A clear plan for school crisis management. *National Association of Secondary School Principals Bulletin, 77*(552), 17-22.

Nation, C. (1988). *Managing crisis.* Alexandria, VA: National Association of Elementary School Principals. ERIC Document Reproduction Services No. ED 293 222.

Newsom, D., & Scott, A. (1985). *This is public relations* (3rd ed.). Belmont, CA: Wadsworth.

North Carolina State Department of Public Instruction (1988). *Guidelines for handling crisis situations in the schools*. Raleigh: North Carolina State Department of Public Instruction. ERIC Document Reproduction Services No. ED 297 233.

Overman, S. (1991). After the smoke clears. *HRMagazine, 36*(11), 44–47.

Palmo, A. J., Langious, D. E., & Bender, I. (1988). Development of a policy and procedures statement for crisis situations in the school. *The School Counselor, 36*(2), 94–102.

Petersen, S., & Straub, R. L. (1992). *School crisis survival guide*. West Nyack, NY: Simon & Schuster.

Peterson, B., Andress, P., Schroeder, L., Swanson, B., & Ziff, L. M. (1993). The Edina, Minnesota, school crisis response team. *Journal of School Health, 63*(4), 192–194.

Phi Delta Kappa Educational Foundation. (1988). *Responding to adolescent suicide*. Bloomington, IN: Phi Delta Kappa Task Force on Adolescent Suicide. (ERIC Document Reproduction Service No. ED 301 813).

Powers, H. L. (1987). Death and grief: A plan for principals to deal with tragedy affecting the school community. *ERS Spectrum, 5*(4) 24–26.

Ruof, S. R., Harris, J. M., & Robbie, M. B. (1987). *Handbook: Suicide prevention in the schools*. La Salle, CO: Weld BOCES.

Serafin, J. (Ed.). (1990). *Be aware be prepared: Guidelines for crisis-response planning for school/communities*. Denver, CO: Office of Federal/State Programs and Services.

Slahor, S. (1989). Media relations during a crisis. *Supervision, 50*(8), 9–12.

Tilden, S. W. (1980). Working with the media. Basic school PR guide. *Monograph of the National Public Relations Association*, pp. 1–36.

Wall, F. E. & Viers, L. A. (1985). The process and the technique of managing schoolwide tragedy. *National Association of Secondary School Principals Bulletin, 69*(478), 101–104.

Weick, K. E. (1988). Enacted sensemaking in crisis situations. *Journal of Management Studies, 25*, 305–317.

Weinberg, R. B. (1989). Consultation and training with school-based crisis teams. *Professional Psychology: Research and Practice, 20*(5), 499–501.

CHAPTER 13

Collecting and Analyzing Decision-Oriented Data

James McNamara
Maryanne McNamara

Truly effective school and community relationships require two-way communication. Accordingly, school administrators must actively seek information from the wider environment and use this information to make critical decisions. Both the act of collecting data and the process of analyzing them require knowledge and skills related to functions such as needs assessments, survey research, and data interpretation.

The purpose of this chapter is to examine that portion of public relations practice that involves gathering and analyzing information. Both quantitative and qualitative procedures are reviewed. Since the purpose of gathering and interpreting information is to enlighten administrative decision making, the chapter begins with this topic.

ADMINISTRATIVE DECISION MAKING

Herbert A. Simon (1977) divides administrative decision making into four principal phases:

1. *Intelligence activity*, which consists of searching the environment for occasions (problems) calling for decisions
2. *Design activity*, which centers on inventing, developing, and analyzing courses of action
3. *Choice activity*, which encompasses actually selecting a particular course of action from those available
4. *Review activity*, which consists of evaluating past choices

Simon's model clearly implies that an administrator is involved in all stages of decision making, not simply the act of choice.

Each of the four principal phases in Simon's administrative decision model provides opportunities for an organization to collect and analyze relevant decision-oriented information. In modern organizations, there is a large inventory of tools that can be used to formalize the collection and analysis of relevant information. McNamara and Chisolm (1988) have suggested that it is helpful to think of these tools as systematic procedures used to complete tasks associated with one or more of the major phases in Simon's decision model. When used as intended, these tools improve our capacity to make more effective managerial and policy decisions.

Public relations is viewed here as an organizational entity whose purpose is to provide relevant information that assists policy makers and practitioners in all phases of decision making. From this perspective, public relations plays an instrumental role in *creating* a shared vision among all organizational stakeholders, *designing* a plan of action, and *evaluating* the organization's progress toward reaching its agreed-upon goals.

In examining the ways in which a public relations specialist can use decision tools to collect, analyze, and share relevant decision-oriented information, we'll look first at how social scientific surveys (a decision tool based on *quantitative* research strategies) can be used effectively to inform planning and evaluation decisions. Then we'll see how case studies (a decision tool based on *qualitative* research strategies) can be used effectively to improve both problem-defining and problem-solving activities encountered in managerial decision making.

QUANTITATIVE RESEARCH STRATEGIES: SOCIAL SCIENTIFIC SURVEYS

In the early stages of planning a school restructuring effort, it is not uncommon to conduct a preference survey of one or more key stakeholder groups. For example, the planning group for a school district that is considering a year-round schooling program might be interested in knowing the preferences of students, parents or guardians, teachers, and voters in the district for starting such a program. Clearly, all of these stakeholders are likely to experience significant changes if a year-round school policy is approved by the district's board of trustees.

How might one go about conducting a social scientific survey that yields accurate stakeholder preference information?* Since accuracy in social scientific surveys is directly related to sample size, the district would have to begin by focusing on three questions relating to specific sample size:

1. Is there a simple table of recommended sample sizes one might use to determine the actual sample size for a policy preference survey?
2. Are there valid ways to reduce the actual sample sizes recommended in these tables?
3. What special problems should be considered in reaching a final decision on the actual sample size for the survey?

Taken collectively and in the order specified above, answers to these three sampling design questions reveal a straightforward three-step process that provides a correct sample

---

*See Research Design Note 1, p. 264.

size solution for a school preference survey. Along the way, we'll find out how to build in the margin of error that is needed to prepare an accurate report of survey findings.

Step 1: The Initial Solution

The initial solution, a response to question 1, can be illustrated by focusing on a single stakeholder group and just one preference question. Thinking again in terms of the school restructuring effort referenced above, let's assume that the members of the planning group wish to estimate the percent of the district's classroom teachers who would prefer to explore the year-round school alternative. In this case, the questionnaire item for the preference survey might be the following: *This school district is considering a year-round school program. Would you prefer this alternative to our existing nine-month school year?(Yes or No)*

Sampling Design.   An appropriate format here is a simple random sampling design. One would begin by constructing a list of all classroom teachers in the district. Numbering the entries in this teacher list would reveal the size of the population (N). Once N is known, a published sampling table (for example, see Krejcie and Morgan, 1970) can be consulted to indicate the required sample size (n). Finally, a table of random numbers or a computerized random number generator can be used to select n random numbers between 1 and N. Teachers whose numbers were selected would then be asked to respond to the survey question specified above.

When all n respondents have indicated their preferences, the proportion of "yes" respondents identified in sample data (p) would provide the estimate of true proportion (P) of all classroom teachers who prefer the year-round school alternative.

Sampling Tables.   An abbreviated (but typical) random sampling table is given in Table 13–1. Its interpretation is straightforward. For example, if a school district has 200 classroom teachers, the required sample size would be 132 (Table 13–1). Thus, N is 200 and n is 132, which represents 66 percent of the classroom teacher population. If the school district of interest in our case study was a very large urban school district, then N might be 5000. For this school district, the required sample size (from Table 13–1) is $n = 357$. In this case, the sample size is just 7.14 percent of the population.

A careful examination of the table clearly indicates the efficiency of probability sampling. Specifically, the larger the population, the smaller the percent of the population needed in the sample. Moreover, the *maximum* sample size for any population—no matter how large it is—is just 384.

Let's assume that the actual classroom teacher population for our case study school district is $N = 1000$. Using Table 13–1, we find that the required sample size is $n = 278$, which represents 27.8 percent of the total population of classroom teachers in the district. Accordingly, 278 randomly selected classroom teachers would be requested to complete the district's questionnaire, and these 278 responses would be used to estimate the true proportion of all classroom teachers in the district who prefer the year-round school program.

Preprogrammed Decisions.   The use of a typical published sample size table to determine the initial (or maybe the final) recommended sample size involves agreement with

TABLE 13–1
Typical Table for Determining Sample Size

Population (N)	Sample (n)	Sample Percent of Population 100 (n/N)
50	44	88.00
100	80	80.00
200	132	66.00
500	217	43.40
1,000	278	27.80
5,000	357	7.14
10,000	370	3.70
20,000	377	1.89
75,000	382	0.51
1,000,000	384	0.04
2,000,000	384	0.02
4,000,000	384	0.01

Note: This table is an abbreviated version of a typical published sample-size table for a simple random sampling design. The table is constructed to yield a 95 percent confidence interval for a margin of error not to exceed 5 percent. It assumes that no reliable prior information is known about the true proportion of "yes" responses in the population of interest. For all populations having more than 4 million members, the required sample size (*n*) will be 384 and the sample percent of the population will always be less than 0.01, the last entry in column 3 above.

three preprogrammed survey design decisions. The three preprogrammed decisions, the symbols used to represent them, and the actual preset formula values used to get the recommended sample size of 278 are as follows:

1. The *precision value* (B) has been preset at 0.05 to guarantee a margin of error no larger than 5 percent.
2. The *confidence value* (A) has been preset at 3.84 to indicate the use of a 95 percent confidence interval for reporting the margin of error.
3. The *prior information value* (P) has been preset at 0.50 to indicate that there is no reliable presurvey estimate of the true proportion of "yes" responses in the population of interest, which in this case is all 1000 classroom teachers in the district.

Each of these three preprogrammed design decisions was used to construct Table 13–1. Agreement with these three decisions (a position taken when one wishes to end the search for a recommended sample size at step 1) guides the analysis and reporting of the actual survey responses provided by the classroom teachers. This consequence is discussed below.

Survey Findings.   For every sample-size table, there is a second table to indicate the actual margin of error that results from the analysis of the survey responses. Table 13–2 is the corresponding table for our case study where N = 1000 and n = 278. Consistent with the predetermined values used in Table 13–1, the survey findings are to be reported using a 95 percent confidence interval for the margin of error.

TABLE 13–2
Precision Values for Possible Sample Results

Sample Proportion (p)	Sample Percent (100p)	Margin of Error (%)	Confidence Interval Low (%)	Confidence Interval High (%)
0.50	50	5.0	45.0	55.0
0.55	55	5.0	50.0	60.0
0.60	60	4.9	55.1	64.9
0.65	65	4.8	60.2	69.8
0.70	70	4.6	65.4	74.6
0.75	75	4.3	70.7	79.3
0.80	80	4.0	76.0	84.0
0.85	85	3.6	81.4	88.6
0.90	90	3.0	87.0	93.0
0.95	95	2.2	92.8	97.2
0.99	99	1.0	98.0	100.0

Note: This table was constructed for a simple random sample of 278 from a population of 1000. Entries can be interpreted as follows: If the sample percent of "yes" responses is 55 percent, the margin of error is 5 percent, and the 95 percent confidence interval for the true proportion of "yes" responses in the population is between 50 and 60 percent. For sample values less than 50 percent, use the same distance above 50 percent. For example, if the sample percent is 10, use the 90 percent entry. In this case, the margin of error is 3 percent and the 95 percent confidence interval ranges from a low of 7 percent to a high of 13 percent.

Table 13–2 also has a straightforward interpretation. If the actual percent of "yes" responses for this classroom teacher survey is 55 percent, then we take the position that the correct percent for the population that includes all classroom teachers in the district is between 50 and 60 percent.*

While only one percentage value will result from conducting a survey, it is important to recognize that the actual sample percent of "yes" responses can be any value between 0 and 100. Thus p, the corresponding sample proportion, could range from 0 to 1.

Table 13–2 is constructed to cover all of these possibilities. For example, if the actual percent of "yes" responses for classroom teachers in the sample is 85 percent, the margin of error is 3.6 percent and the confidence interval to estimate the true percent of "yes" responses for the classroom teacher population would range from 81.4 to 88.6 percent.†

A careful examination of Table 13–2 reveals a very important sampling design consequence. Specifically, the margin of error for implementing the simple random sampling design where $N = 1000$ and $n = 278$ will never exceed 5 percent. However, as the actual percent of "yes" responses in the sample increases, the corresponding margin of error decreases.

---

*See Research Design Note 2, p. 264.
†See Research Design Note 3, p. 265.

Sampling Error.   It is important to recognize that a margin-of-error table is needed for any probability sampling survey one chooses to implement. Thus Table 13–3 provides a step-by-step procedure the school district planning committee can use to determine the margin-of-error values reported in Table 13–2.

Application of this procedure is illustrated in Table 13-4 for the situation where the actual proportion of "yes" responses for the 278 classroom teacher responses is 55 percent. Notice that this table yields a margin of error of 5 percent, which is the actual Table 13–2 value reported on line 2 for $p = 0.55$.

Reflections on Step 1.   The use of a published sample-size table in step 1 provides a quick and valid solution to the sample-size problem. However, if standard guidelines for

---

TABLE 13–3
Estimating the Margin of Error Using a 95 Percent Confidence Interval

Step 1	Evaluate pq = the product of p and q.
Step 2	Determine $U = pq$ divided by n.
Step 3	Calculate $F = (N - n)$ divided by N.
Step 4	Evaluate V = the product of U and F.
Step 5	Determine S = the square root of V.
Step 6	Evaluate M = the product of 1.96 and S.

Legend

p	=	the actual proportion of "yes" responses in the sample.
q	=	$(1 - p)$.
U	=	the unadjusted variance of the estimator p.
F	=	the finite corrected factor *(fcf)*.
N	=	the size of the population.
n	=	the size of the sample.
V	=	the adjusted variance of the estimator p using *(fcf)*.
S	=	the standard error of p.
M	=	the margin of error with 95 confidence coefficient.

Note: If 99 percent confidence interval is desired, replace 1.96 with 2.57. If 90 percent confidence interval is desired, the replacement value in step 6 is 1.64. All three of these values are the square roots of A, which is the tabled value of chi-squared for 1 degree of freedom at the desired significance level. For 95 percent confidence interval, the corresponding significance level is 0.05.

TABLE 13–4
Calculating a Margin of Error

Step 1	pq	$= 0.55 \times 0.45 = 0.2475$
Step 2	U	$= 0.2475 \div 278 = 0.000890$
Step 3	F	$= (1000 - 278) \div 1000 = 0.72200$
Step 4	V	$= U \times F = 0.000643$
Step 5	S	= square root of $V = 0.0253$
Step 6	M	$= 1.96 \times 0.0253 = 0.05$ (or 5 percent)

Note: Since proportions rather than integers are used, accuracy to at least six decimal places is required in steps 2 through 4. Values in the last step are usually rounded to two or three decimal places. This table is to be read in conjunction with Table 13–3.

TABLE 13–5

The Basic Sample-Size Formula to Estimate a Binomial Proportion

Formula

$$n = NPQ \div [(N - 1) D + PQ]$$
$$D = C \div A$$

Legend

N = the population size

n = the recommended sample size

P = the population proportion (which is preset at 0.50 when no prior survey estimate can be given)

Q = $(1 - P)$

A = the table value of chi-squared for 1 degree of freedom at the desired significance level (which is usually preset at 3.84 to yield a significance level of 0.05 and a corresponding confidence coefficient of 0.95 for the confidence interval)

B = the desired precision (bound) for the margin of error expressed as a proportion (which is usually preset at 0.05 to yield a confidence interval estimate of $\pm$5 percent)

C = the square of B

reporting survey research findings are to be followed, there is still the need to report a margin of error for the school preference survey.*

Thus, one who wishes to solve the sample-size problem using a published table must not only understand the predetermined survey sampling design decisions but must also be able to use this design information to construct a corresponding estimation table for correctly interpreting and reporting the school preference survey findings.†

Step 2: Alternative Solutions

Assume this urban school district wishes to explore ways to reduce the actual classroom teacher sample size of 278 recommended in step 1. The district must then alter the three preprogrammed decisions used in constructing Table 13–1.

To understand the consequences of altering the preprogrammed decisions used in step 1, it is essential to know how the three decision values are related. These relationships are determined by the basic sample-size formula given in Table 13–5. The formula elaborated in the table is used to construct any published sample size table for a simple random sample focusing on the percent of "yes" responses in a population of interest.

This sample-size formula was used to construct Table 13–1. It can be verified by setting P at 0.50, A at 3.84, and B at 0.05. Substituting these values into the formula, along with N = 1000, yields a recommended classroom teacher sample size of 278, which is exactly

---

*See Research Design Note 4, p. 265.

†See Research Design Note 5, p. 265.

TABLE 13–6
Application of the Basic Sample-Size
Formula

Initial Calculations	
Step 1	$NPQ = 1000 \times 0.50 \times 0.50 = 250$
Step 2	$C = 0.05 \times 0.05 = 0.0025$
Step 3	$D = C \div A = 0.0025 \div 3.84 = 0.000651$
Step 4	$(N - 1)D = 1000 - 1 \times 0.000651 = 0.650349$
Step 5	$PQ = 0.50 \times 0.50 = 0.25$

Recommended Sample Size (n)
$n = NPQ \div [(N - 1)D + PQ]$
$n = 250 \div (0.650349 + 0.25) = 278$

Note: Since proportions rather than integers are used, accuracy to six decimal places is needed to get D in step 3. This exact D value is then used in step 4.

the value entered in Table 13–1. These calculations are presented in Table 13–6 using a step-by-step procedure.

Exploration 1: Prior Information. When no prior information is available, *P* is usually set at 0.50. This represents a *maximum* sample size. However, if prior knowledge—that is, data from previous studies or informed conjectures—is available, *n* can often be reduced appreciably. Consider the formulae for this case study given in Table 13–7. Let A remain constant at 3.84 and B remain constant at 0.05. However, let *P* be free to vary.

TABLE 13–7
Explorations Using the Basic
Sample-Size Formula for N = 1000

Exploration	*P*	*B*	*A*	*n*
1. Vary only P	0.50	0.05	3.84	278
	0.60	0.05	3.84	270
	0.70	0.05	3.84	244
	0.75	0.05	3.84	224
	0.80	0.05	3.84	197
	0.85	0.05	3.84	164
2. Vary only B	0.50	0.05	3.84	278
	0.50	0.06	3.84	211
	0.50	0.07	3.84	164
	0.50	0.08	3.84	131
3. Vary only A.	0.50	0.05	2.71	214
	0.50	0.05	3.84	278
	0.50	0.05	6.63	399

Note: All input values (P, B, and A) and the formula used to get the recommended sample size (n) are described in Table 13–5. Table 13–6 illustrates how to use this formula for a population N = 1000. In each exploration, the typical sample size recommended in published tables is given in bold.

Following the calculation guide given in Table 13–6, we find that the solutions for the first exploration, where only P is altered, yield an interesting result. Specifically, these Table 13–7 solutions clearly indicate that the further one moves away from the predetermined P value of 0.50, the smaller the recommended sample size becomes. For example, if P is moved to 0.85, the recommended sample size n is 164 rather than 278, which was the *only* solution in step 1.

Exploration 2: Precision.   Assume the planning committee might be willing to relax the precision requirements as a means to reduce sample size. With this alternative in mind, consider the Table 13–7 solutions where P remains constant at 0.50, A remains constant at 3.84, and B is free to vary. This numerical specification represents our willingness to relax the precision requirements.

Solutions for the second exploration indicate that only minor increases in the preprogrammed B value of 0.05 yield large reductions in n. For example, if B equals 0.08 rather than 0.05, the recommended classroom teacher sample size is 131 rather than 278. Thus, altering only this one of the three predetermined values used in Table 13–1 to get our initial solution can result in a sample-size reduction of 147 teachers.*

Exploration 3: Confidence Coefficient.   The step 1 sample size can also be reduced by changing the confidence coefficient used to report the margin of error. Consider the Table 13–7 formula solutions where P remains constant at 0.50, B remains constant at 0.05, and A is permitted to vary. This numerical specification represents our willingness to alter the confidence coefficient.

Solutions for this third exploration indicate that reducing only the confidence coefficient will also reduce the recommended sample size. For example, if the alternative confidence coefficient is to be 90 percent ($A = 2.71$) rather than 95 percent ($A = 3.84$), the sample size of classroom teachers is reduced from 278 to 214 teachers.†

Exploration 4: Time Constraints.   Assume the district's planning committee encounters the following problem. The school trustees plan to make a policy decision regarding year-round schools at their next meeting, which is two days away. Moreover, each trustee has received a small number of phone calls from teacher representatives who either enthusiastically endorse the twelve-month school year or vehemently oppose this alternative. However, no stakeholder group has been surveyed to date. Thus, little is known about the true preferences of the district's classroom teachers.

If one is willing to simultaneously alter all three of the preprogrammed decisions from step 1, a reduced sample size that allows completion of the survey to meet the two-day deadline could be determined. To do so requires the following numerical specification. First, set P at 0.75. Next, set B at 0.07. Finally, set A at 2.71. This specification will result in a margin of error with a 90 percent confidence interval not likely to exceed 7 percent.

---

*See Research Design Note 6, p. 266.
†See Research Design Note 7, p. 266.

Using the basic sample-size formula, we find that the solution in exploration 4 is 104. If each of twenty-one persons was responsible for completing just five brief telephone calls to determine five teacher preferences, this survey could easily meet the two-day time constraints given above.*

More important, those who present the survey findings to the school district trustees can speak directly to the validity of their survey results, noting that they used the same scientific sampling procedures required in such major national polls as the Gallup poll or the New York Times/CBS poll.

Reflections on Step 2. The procedure elaborated in step 2 can be used in any school preference survey where N is given and those responsible for the survey (the school planning committee in this case study) are willing to examine in more detail their survey expectations and their three survey sampling decision rules.†

Step 3: Special Considerations

Two special research design considerations are often encountered in conducting school policy preference surveys. These two problems and their solutions are treated in Step 3.

The Multiple-Stakeholder Problem. The school district planning committee considering a major policy change, such as the movement from a nine-month to a twelve-month school year, will likely be interested in the preferences held not only by classroom teachers, but also by other school district stakeholders. If this is the case, a stratified random sample involving *all* stakeholder groups as individual strata will need to be conducted. To accomplish this objective, one would repeat steps 1 and 2 for a simple random sampling design for each stratum.‡

Implementing a stratified random sampling design will allow the planning committee to compare the preferences of all stakeholder groups for the year-round school alternative. To ensure adequate statistical power, which is the ability of the survey to detect true preference differences if they do exist among the survey populations of interest, *at least* 100 randomly chosen survey respondents are recommended for each stakeholder group.§

The Multiple-Item Problem. The school district planning committee would probably use more than the one questionnaire item referenced above. To enhance the information used to explore the idea of year-round schools, the committee might construct additional "yes" or "no" response items. Such items might address individual preferences about year-round program alternatives or beliefs that stakeholders have about how such a program

---

*See Research Design Note 8, p. 266.

†See Research Design Note 9, p. 266.

‡See Research Design Note 10, p. 266.

§See Research Design Note 11, p. 266.

will improve learning, enrich teaching, reduce costs, or provide families a more flexible school schedule.*

The sample-size solution for the multiple-item problem is also straightforward. It follows the procedures elaborated above for steps 1 and 2. Three specific examples are given below to show how sample-size solutions are generated for a questionnaire having two or more yes/no preference items.

Example 1

If no prior information is known about the proportion of the population likely to offer a yes response for any of the preference items included in the study, then set P equal to 0.50 for each item. If no changes are required in the predetermined A and B values, the recommended sample sizes in Table 13–1 for step 1 provide the correct solutions.

Example 2

If, in the first example, there is some interest in reducing the step 1 solution, then let P remain fixed at 0.50 and examine alternative values for A or B, or both A and B using the basic sample-size exploration strategy detailed in Table 13–7.

Example 3

Assume that no prior preference information is available for some questionnaire items, but prior preference information is available and is deemed to be reliable for other items in the same questionnaire. Strictly speaking, one would need to set P equal to 0.50 so that the margin of error would not exceed the desired level (B) for any item in the questionnaire. This solution was offered in Example 1 above.

In practical work, however, there is an excellent compromise solution for the multiple-item problem. It is to set P equal to 0.75 and proceed to determine what values to use for A and B.†

In our case study district (where N equals 1000), the numerical specification could be $P = 0.75$, $A = 3.84$ and $B = 0.05$. The recommended sample size for the multiple-item questionnaire in practical terms is 224. Notice that this is the same sample size we encountered in the first exploration in Table 13–7 when P was set at 0.75 and the other two predetermined decisions of Table 13–1 were left unchanged.

Advantages of Probability Sampling Method

Whenever a policy preference survey (or for that matter any needs assessment or program evaluation survey) is to be undertaken as part of a school restructuring effort, serious con-

---

*See Research Design Note 12, p. 267
†See Research Design Note 13, p. 267.

sideration should be given to using the probability sampling procedures elaborated above rather than using a quota sampling design, a less formal sampling strategy, or a blanket survey that is either forwarded to all members of a stakeholder group or made available to them as a questionnaire published in a local newspaper.

There are several reasons for this. First, probability samples such as those detailed in this chapter are almost always no more expensive to implement than nonprobability sampling alternatives—and in many cases, they are far less expensive.

Second, as the three-step procedure demonstrates, the basic sample-size formula for probability sampling provides a wide range of recommended sample sizes that can accommodate the specific needs of any planning group.

Third, it is extremely difficult, and in some cases almost impossible, to identify the nonresponse bias that follows from implementing a nonprobability sampling design. In a probability sampling design this bias is defined and, in many cases, can be accurately estimated.

Finally, and most important, only probability samples can yield true margins of error to guide inferences about a population using data from samples. These margins of error are not only informative but are also required to meet the standard ethical guidelines for reporting survey findings.*

QUALITATIVE RESEARCH STRATEGIES: THE CASE STUDY

In keeping with the rich historical overview provided by David Lancy (1993), most social science researchers and program evaluators acknowledge the case study to be an integral part of the qualitative research tradition. Along with Lawrence Stenhouse (1985) and Michael Patton (1990), Lancy argues that case studies conducted in educational research share a common purpose: They all address directly the improvement of practice. Accordingly, case studies in education are designed to influence important educational policy decisions.†

Robert Yin (1984) suggests that the case study has at least four applications:

1. *Explaining* the causal relationships in real-life interventions that are too complex for the survey or experimental strategies
2. *Describing* the real-life context in which an intervention has occurred
3. *Creating* a rich illustration or journalistic account of a specific intervention
4. *Exploring* situations where a promising intervention has no clear, single inventory of outcomes.‡

Now we'll see how one might go about conducting a case study that yields accurate decision-oriented information to help practitioners and policy makers improve educational programs. Specifically, we'll examine the use of the case study as a decision tool to assist

---

*See Research Design Note 14, p. 267.
†See Research Design Note 15, p. 267.
‡See Research Design Note 16, p. 268.

school and university colleagues in designing a governance structure and identifying cooperative research projects for their new school/university research collaborative.

In terms of Simon's (1977) decision model, the case study developed here concentrates on collecting, analyzing, and reporting data to be used in the first two phases of administrative decision making: *intelligence activity*, which focuses on problem-defining tasks, and *design activity*, which focuses on problem-solving tasks.

Setting Up the Case Study

Results from the eighth *Research about Teacher Education Report* released at the 1994 meeting of the American Association of Colleges of Teacher Education (see Bradley, 1994) indicated that nearly half of the eighty-four schools of education who hold membership in the association were regularly engaged in "partner schools," where large numbers of student-teachers are placed, faculty members and classroom teachers conduct joint research-and-development projects, and faculty members are assigned to work.

Over the past decade, school/university collaborative arrangements such as the AACTE efforts referenced above have been undertaken as a means to bridge the gap between theory and practice, as well as the gap between the public schools and teacher training.* While it has become commonplace for public schools and universities to say, "Let's collaborate," getting started on a productive venture requires answers to several key questions: How do people come together? Who provides the leadership for a collaborative? Who initiates and who responds? What problems can best be solved using collaborative strategies? How are prospective collaborative research projects identified? How are proposed new collaborative research projects approved?

Let's assume that these policy questions were raised in a newly formed collaborative where graduate education school professors and public school practitioners in a single innovative school district wished to conduct joint research-and-development projects. Let's also assume that the university collaborators were asked explicitly by their school district colleagues to take the lead in two areas: *designing* the organizational governance structure for the partnership and *identifying* promising cooperative research-and-development projects.

One way the university collaborators could be responsive, but not prescriptive, would be to use the case study as a decision tool to uncover *how* school partners would prefer to interact with key players in the collaborative and *what* real-world problems these school district practitioners would like to research together.

In the case study offered below, the superintendent was chosen to be the school partner whose views were to be collected, analyzed, and shared with all involved in building a productive collaborative. Obviously, other school partner case study efforts could be (and more than likely would be) conducted following the four-phase strategy elaborated below. Put briefly, these phases are collecting the data, analyzing the data, verifying the findings, and sharing the report.†

---

*See Research Design Note 17, p. 268.
†See Research Design Note 18, p. 268.

Using the Case Study in Decision Making*

Phase 1: Collecting the Data.   The collaborating school district superintendent was interviewed on a Friday morning, June 18, 1993. The interview started at 9:15 and was concluded at 10:15. It was conducted using a semistructured instrument having a few general questions designed to elicit the superintendent's perspectives on school/university collaboration in her school district. The obvious overall issue in the protocol dealt with collaboration. What follows is a transcript of the one-hour interview.†

> *Question: What role do you (as superintendent) play in school/university collaboration in your district?*
> First, I want to make it clear that any collaboration between the school and university must have good fit with our district's mission. I want to assure you that *all* of our students receive the best education—not just a select few.
>
> *Question: How do you interact with key players in the collaboration? What communication strategies do you use?*
> My role involves setting up communication channels that are formal. For example, it is my understanding that there is a subgroup—namely, the Administration Council (ten key players in our collaborative) that is co-chaired by my Assistant Superintendent for Instruction. He informs me about the goings-on of the collaborative, and I, in turn, keep the Board of Trustees updated.
>
> *Question: How do you do this—communicate with the Board, that is?*
> Yes. I brought this idea with me from my last superintendency in [another city]. I personally write a formal update of issues to be shared with the Board in a weekly written report called *Board Notes.*
> *Board Notes* are separated into two categories. One category includes ongoing activities that the Board needs to know about—such as details about what is happening at our partnership middle school. Another category focuses on separate issues that require Board action.
> I have a senior administrative staff that helps me on this. This is my way of informing *all* Board members. In other words, *no* single Board member receives information that others are not privy to. This is a kind of one-on-one almost face-to-face communication strategy. It avoids the common problem that many superintendents have when some Board members receive more information than others do.
> I also have a CONFIDENTIAL stamp that I use for information that should not go beyond their purview. This way we have a common level of understanding about confidentiality.
>
> *Question: Do you have a screening procedure for collaboration with the University?*
> Yes, we are now involved with another collaborative at a second partnership school (an elementary school which is operating as a professional development school). This partnership will involve a host of projects that must be screened. My Assistant Superintendent for Instruction will be responsible for this. Again, let me say that collaboration ventures are messy and I understand and welcome that.
>
> *Question: What do you mean by "messy"?*
> Yes. Any effort to change the way things have always been done is messy. If we expect innovation, then we have to be able to tolerate ambiguity, and I have a high tolerance for

---

*See Research Design Note 19, p. 268.
†See Research Design Note 20, p. 268.

ambiguity. However, I know when to draw the line. If I believe that any of these programs are counter to our mission, then I put a halt to it.

Question: What are your thoughts on the University's ultimate goal—to involve other professionals from health care and human services in the collaboration?

I feel that this will take time, and I'll tell you why. There is some confusion among parents and Board members about issues like condom distribution. That's the bottom line.

Sadly enough, whenever parents hear about health services coming into the school, they believe that their morals will be compromised. This is unfortunate because our goal is to have students coming to school ready to learn—and they can't do this when they aren't healthy—physically or mentally healthy.

In my last superintendency . . . we had a health center located on our high school campus. It worked beautifully. The students who used it were for the most part—and I mean about 95 percent—students who had stomachaches, sore throats, toothaches, etc. Normally they would stay home for at least a day, and in the case of sore throats, they'd be out for a week [if] strep infection set in. This way, with a health center, they came to school knowing that they'd get help. They'd miss only an hour or so of school.

Schools need to take the position that a health center facilitates bringing service to where the customer is. We can serve kids best by keeping them in school. This is why stores like Randall's have film developing and flower delivery services located right in the store. It's good business!

Question: Do you see moving toward full-service schools anytime soon?

This will take time. We need to work on our constituency. Educate them. Get them to understand the need. They must understand that schools are not insular. [The city where I previously had a superintendency] already has networks with AFDC, WIC, HHS, and other groups. I realize, though, that this community is conservative and will reject this move. We need to build trust. Explain that only a small number of cases deal with the issues that they fear most.

Question: Do you have any other concerns that you want to discuss about the Superintendent's role in collaboration?

Yes. The district and the university need to get together and sit down and say we won't have things done the way they're being done in the language arts area. Our students deserve a better program—not one where reading and writing and grammar are separated into different classes.

I see this as urgent and critical. It's a travesty that these subjects are taught separately. We must put a stop to it. This idea of separate subjects is one of the keenest instructional issues I've had to face.

Question: Why is it so difficult to change? Can't you just demand a change?

Again, here is something that will take time and training. I was shocked at the initial response I received when I proposed an instructional change with teachers. One teacher actually said—pompously—"We see ourselves as grammarians not as remedial teachers." They confuse reading classes with remediation—a carryover from the past.

We are giving one more year to allow teachers to adjust to the idea of teaching in another way. We'll provide training. We'll seek a waiver for certification problems, and we'll provide a safety net for teachers. But change they must!

Question: Do you see collaboration with the university as a help with this?

Yes. Together maybe we can change teacher attitudes. We need to sit down together—all of us—[this city], the University, *and* [another major city in the region that also has its own independent school district]. We need to show teachers and principals evidence that these areas—

reading, writing, literature, grammar—are interdependent. They must be taught together—not in unrelated packages.

We want our schools to produce clear thinkers, and one way to do this is to provide students with more than we presently offer. This is our challenge. [End of the formal interview]

Phase Two: Analyzing the Data.   In analyzing the data from the superintendent's interview, the case study researcher uncovered six emergent themes that help clarify how the superintendent views her role in school/university collaboration arrangements. Each of these themes is elaborated below.

Promoting the district's mission. The superintendent was clear about the necessity for a good fit between university goals and the mission of the district. As superintendent she believes her role is to ensure that the district's mission is the driving force behind collaborative activities.

Respecting community values. The superintendent respects the values and beliefs of all stakeholders in her community. She understands that community values cannot be compromised. Implementing collaborative programs involving health care and human services in the schools will work *only if* the community believes that the effort is meaningful.

Communicating with the school board. The superintendent's role includes following an organized strategy for informing board members about collaborative activities. In addition to meeting with them monthly, she sends each board member a weekly copy of *Board Notes*, which includes issues and activities for their perusal. If relevant policy issues regarding collaboration arise in her school district, these issues are very likely to appear in *Board Notes*.

Defining problems. The superintendent's role as problem definer is reflected in her description of instructional changes that she hopes to implement in the district. While welcoming input from the university, it is clear that she will *not* allow the university to dictate to the district what changes are necessary in school district classrooms.

Empowering key players. The superintendent's role in collaboration includes sharing power with her assistant superintendent for instruction, her special council members, principals, and teachers. In accordance with this role, the superintendent promotes staff development and other workshops for training teachers. Her goal is to encourage teachers to assume ownership and leadership in efforts toward change. She is sensitive and responsive to their concerns.

Reaping Benefits. It is clear from the interview that the superintendent sees school/university collaboration as a way to effect positive change in teaching and learning in the schools. For example, she suggested that a school/university collaborative effort would be an excellent way to solve the school district's instructional problem regarding the need to integrate reading, literature, writing, and language arts. It is also of interest to note that she believes school/university collaboration efforts can involve several school districts working together with the university to solve problems of mutual interest. For example, in the interview she suggested that both her school district and the other major school district in the regional area might both join with the university to work on a curriculum project devoted to integrating instruction in reading, literature, writing, and language arts.

Reanalysis of these six themes indicates that they are consistent with the literature on successful collaboration. Most important among these themes is the superintendent's insistence that school/university collaboration must be based on a shared vision of what needs to be accomplished in a specific collaborative venture.

Phase 3: *Verifying the Findings.*   Once the initial draft of the case study report is prepared, the next step is to share this written record with the superintendent, who should verify the accuracy of both the interview text and themes that were uncovered in the phase 2 analysis of the data.* Also to be accomplished in phase 3 are two additional important concerns. First, the superintendent and the case study researcher should discuss any special circumstances (ethical and legal issues) that might require revision before the report is shared in a public meeting. †

Once the case study report is revised and meets the approval of both the university researcher and the school district superintendent, the researcher should exercise professional courtesy and formally request the superintendent's permission to go public with the final draft of the report. "Going public" is taken here to mean sharing the case study report in a policy planning work session involving school district and university collaborators.

Phase 4: *Sharing the Report.*   When the case study is used as a decision tool, it is absolutely essential that the report be written and shared with the intended audience. In many circumstances, the format used to report case study results can vary. For example, Sharan Merriam (1988) suggests that one might consider executive summaries or specialized condensations. Yin (1984) offers another suggestion: Replace the narrative with a set of open-ended questions and answers drawn from the data.‡

For this case study on the superintendent's position regarding school/university collaboration, we believe the report should remain in the format presented here. Accordingly, the first part of the report is in question-and-answer form (using the actual semistructured questions raised in the interview) and the second part provides brief analytic summaries of the themes uncovered in data analysis. To maximize the value of this information in a planning work session, the case study report would be distributed to work session participants about a week prior to the actual session. Moreover, having the superintendent present as a participant in the session would also have several advantages.

Essential Characteristics of a Case Study

In this part of the chapter, the intent was to advance the position that the case study is an excellent option in gathering, analyzing, and sharing relevant decision-oriented infor-

---

*See Research Design Note 21, p. 268.
†See Research Design Note 22, p. 268.
‡See Research Design Note 23, p. 269.

mation. The unique value of the case study as a decision tool can be recognized by reflecting on its essential characteristics. Merriam (1988) has pointed out four such properties: The case study is particularistic, descriptive, heuristic, and inductive .*

Particularistic implies that the case study focuses on a particular situation, event, program, individual, or group. It can suggest to the reader what to do or what not to do. It can concentrate on a specific instance but illuminate a general problem or outcome.

Descriptive implies that the case study yields a rich description of the event or entity being investigated. It can illustrate the complexities of a situation. It can identify differences of opinion on an issue and suggest how these differences might influence—or might have influenced—the actual decision reached by policy makers and practitioners. Most important, the case study can describe the views of a wide array of organizational stakeholders.

Heuristic implies that the case study extends the reader's understanding of the issue or entity selected for inquiry. Accordingly, it can explain the reason for a problem, it can lead to the discovery of new relationships, it can verify (or negate) an informed speculation, and most important, it can often explain why an innovative program worked or failed to work.

Inductive implies that the case study relies on inductive reasoning. As such, it begins with collection of data (empirical observations of interest) and then identifies theoretical categories and patterns (trends or propositions) from relationships uncovered in data analysis.

Two additional points deserve mention. First, the case study does not claim any particular method for either data collection or data analysis. However, qualitative methods are most often chosen in conducting case studies because researchers or policy analysts are primarily interested in insight, discovery, and interpretation rather than in testing hypotheses or estimating parameters. Second, it should be kept in mind that the case study is just one of many qualitative decision tools that can be used to inform administrative decision making.†

SUMMARY

This chapter advanced the idea that both the selection and application of either the social scientific survey (a quantitative method) or the case study (a qualitative method) as a decision tool can be linked directly to one or more of the four principal phases identified in Simon's (1977) administrative decision-making model. Two additional ideas were central to the recommendations advanced in this chapter.

First, it should be noted that *collecting* and *analyzing* data are necessary activities but not sufficient in themselves to inform decision making. They must be followed by a formal effort to prepare and share a written report that effectively communicates the findings of the inquiry with the intended audience.

---

*See Research Design Note 24, p. 269.
†See Research Design Note 25, p. 269.

Second, public relations specialists can use these decision tools to play an instrumental role in *creating* a shared vision among all organizational stakeholders, *designing* a plan of action, and *evaluating* the organization's progress toward reaching its agreed-upon goals.

To public relations practitioners interested in taking the lead in the use of modern decision tools in educational organizations, it should be mentioned that the risks of innovation were well understood by Machiavelli. "There is nothing more difficult to take in hand, more perilous to conduct, or more uncertain in its success," he said in *The Prince*, "than to take the lead in the introduction of a new order of things, because the innovator has for enemies all those who have done well under the old conditions and lukewarm defenders in those who may do well under the new law."

RESEARCH DESIGN NOTES

Note 1. When researchers and policy analysts introduce the topic of social scientific surveys, two questions naturally arise. The first question is as follows: What is the difference between a *survey* and a *poll?* In their book *Polls and Surveys*, Bradburn and Sudman (1988) state that these two terms are interchangeable. For the record, educational researchers and school practitioners are more likely to prefer the term "survey." Public opinion researchers are more likely to prefer the term "poll."

A second question is the following: What is the difference between a *social scientific survey* and a *probability sampling survey?* Put briefly, these two terms are also interchangeable. In his book *Survey Research Methods*, Babbie (1990) suggests that social scientific surveys use probability sampling to ensure that the sample is an accurate representation of the population to which the survey researcher wishes to generalize. Also it should be noted that a *margin of error* (an essential feature of social scientific surveys) can be constructed *only* when a true probability sampling plan is implemented. (See O'Shea, 1992, and Williams, 1978.)

For the reader who is interested in learning more about basic survey operations see James McNamara (1993b). In addition, a practical overview of survey sampling operations written for consumers of research is *What Is a Survey?* (Ferber, 1980). A single copy of this twenty-page nontechnical publication is available free of charge from the American Statistical Association, 1429 Duke Street, Alexandria, Va 22314-3402. (This publication is also available in Spanish and several other languages.) We have found this booklet to be an excellent document that can be shared with school district trustees and administrators conducting surveys. In several school/university collaborative survey research projects, superintendents have found it very helpful to share the publication with trustees and administrators a week before a proposed survey is presented in their school board meetings.

Note 2. In reporting these survey findings, the actual statement for this 5 percent margin of error should follow the standard reporting formats used in national polls. Modeling the New York Times/CBS poll, for example, the margin of error statement might read as follows: In theory, in nineteen out of twenty cases, the results based on samples such as this one will differ by no more than 5 percent from what would have been obtained by interviewing all classroom teachers in the school district.

Technically speaking, there are two estimates of interest in our example. First, the 55 percent "yes" response is called a *statistic*, which is a summary measure for a set of sample responses. This statistic is a *point estimate* because it provides the best single point to estimate the population *parameter*, a summary measure that can be calculated *only* when the requested information is available for *every* member of the population.

In addition to a point estimate, a probability sample provides a second estimate called an "interval estimate." An *interval estimate* indicates a range rather than a single point. This range is used to acknowledge that the information in a sample reflects sampling error regarding the true value of the parameter.

In terms of our example, the lower bound of the interval estimate is equal to the point estimate minus 5 percent. This difference is 50 percent. Similarly, the upper bound of the interval estimate is equal to 55 percent plus 5 percent, or 60 percent. Thus, the range of the interval estimate is twice the value of the margin of error. To verify that this is true, one can inspect the difference between the upper bound (60 percent) and the lower bound (50 percent). This difference is 10 percent, a value that is exactly twice the 5 percent margin of error.

For the record, it is of interest to that the New York Times/CBS margin-of-error statement and the actual sample percent are all that is needed to construct the interval estimate. Moreover, given the theoretical information about nineteen out of twenty cases in this statement, one also knows that the interval estimate represents a 95 percent confidence interval.

Note 3. Every probability sampling design has both a *selection process* (the rules by which the actual sample is selected) and a corresponding *estimation process* (the rules by which the sample estimate of the population parameter and its margin of error are determined). For example, Table 13–1 is a selection-process table. Table 13–2 is an estimation-process table. Similarly, Tables 13–3 and 13–4 are estimation-process tables. Tables 13–5 and 13–6 are selection-process tables. Table 13–7 is also a selection-process table. It offers several selection alternatives for the recommended sample size to be used for the population of 1000 classroom teachers.

This two-part strategy for probability sampling work is well treated in an easy-to-read basic survey sampling text by Schaeffer, Mendenhall, and Ott (1990). Chapter 4 of this source addresses simple random sampling designs, the design used in this present chapter. For a more mathematical source, deemed by most survey sampling statisticians to be one of the very best sources for demographers and social science practitioners, see Kish (1965). Educators may also want to examine Jaeger (1984) to get some basic insights on how survey sampling can be applied effectively to a wide array of typical problems encountered in educational organizations.

Note 4. Technically speaking, the American Association for Public Opinion Research (AAPOR) has set both ethical guidelines and scientific standards for reporting survey research findings. In addition to reporting the margin of error, there are seven other items the AAPOR believes must appear in a publication reporting survey results. These are *sample size, sponsor, response rate, dates when data were collected,* an *accurate definition of the population, how respondents were contacted,* and the *precise wording of questions* used in the survey.

An excellent overview of both ethical and scientific considerations to be addressed in conducting and reporting survey findings is given in Chapter 19 of Babbie (1990). These considerations are also elaborated in McNamara (1993a).

Those who wish to conduct a school preference survey should also see Chapter 20 of Babbie (1990) for an insightful checklist to evaluate all aspects of a published survey. Another useful checklist for both producers and consumers of survey research is given in McNamara (1993c).

Note 5. The procedures for determining the school preference survey margin of error elaborated in Tables 13–3 and 13–4 can be applied to any simple random sampling design where N, n, p, and A are available. Accordingly, this procedure can also be used by consumers of research to create an accurate margin of error for any published survey findings.

If A is not reported, the consumer can choose his or her own value for the confidence level to be used in constructing the margin of error. Most often, consumers will choose the square root of A which is equal to 1.96, to yield the traditional 95 percent confidence interval. This square root value was used in step 6 of Table 13–3.

Note 6. Setting B equal to 0.08 rather than 0.05 means the *maximum* margin of error will never exceed 8 rather than 5 percent. However, since the actual sample proportion p can range from 0 to 1, it is quite possible the actual margin of error (with a 95 percent confidence coefficient still in place) will be significantly less than 8 percent. For example, if the *actual* survey findings proportion is 0.90 (a 90 percent "yes" response from our teacher sample), the actual margin of error (using Table 13–4 procedures with a sample size of 131) is only 4.8 percent.

Note 7. Changing just the confidence coefficient will still preserve the preprogrammed value of a maximum bound no more than 5 percent. However, as a result of reducing A, the actual bound for the unchanged margin of error has a 90 percent rather than 95 percent confidence coefficient.

Careful examination of the third exploration reveals another interesting feature. The last entry in this exploration is used to increase just the confidence coefficient. Accordingly, A is set at 6.61. This change will also preserve the maximum bound request. It will now yield a 99 percent confidence coefficient. However, this change is not without some cost. Specifically, the increase from 95 to 99 percent confidence requires a corresponding increase in sample size from 278 to 399.

Note 8. For this proposed sampling design, the actual margin of error will have a 90 percent confidence coefficient and a maximum bound of 7 percent. If the survey is implemented and the findings yield an 85 percent "yes" response from the 104 classroom teachers in the random sample, the actual margin of error (using the Table 13–4 procedure with n equal to 104 and the square root of A set at 1.64) is only 5.7 percent. Recall also that the binomial distribution is *symmetrical*. Thus, the margin of error for a 15 percent "yes" response from classroom teachers would also be 5.7 percent.

This example clearly indicates that a researcher can simultaneously vary either two or three of the preprogrammed decision rules. Also, the explorations undertaken in step 2 of the three-step procedure should provide sufficient evidence to suggest that a survey group is never left with just the one sample-size solution given in published sample-size tables such as Krejcie and Morgan's (1970).

Note 9. If a school public relations group is interested in reducing the sampling-size requirement in their policy preference survey, they should construct a Table 13–7 survey sampling plan using their specific population size (N). To think in terms of time constraints in their survey, they should also repeat the fourth exploration described in the text, using the same N they specified in their Table 13–7 calculations. This second suggestion should alert the group to the actual flexibility associated with social scientific surveys.

Note 10. A stratified random sampling design can be viewed as a series of simple random sampling designs where each person in the population appears on only one list. On the use of stratified sampling in policy preference surveys, see McNamara (1992b). For an easy-to-read treatment of all essential features of stratified random sampling see Chapter 5 of Schaeffer, Mendenhall, and Ott (1990).

In a policy preference survey of members in each of several stakeholder groups, some names will appear on more than one list. For example, a teacher may also be a parent. This poses no real problem. If a teacher's name is selected from a population list of teachers, the response requested would be from a teacher's perspective. If the teacher's name is also selected from a population list of parents, the parent's viewpoint would be requested.

Note 11. If the planning committee wished to compare the preferences of two or more stakeholder groups using formal statistical tests such as a t-test of proportions from two independent groups or an F-test of proportions of two or more independent groups entered in an analysis-of-variance model, then sample-sizes should be based on sample-size formulae used in hypothesis-testing designs to ensure adequate statistical power. Differences in the decision rules between formulae used here in estimation and those used in hypothesis testing are treated in McNamara (1992c).

The specific reason for recommending at least 100 respondents in each stakeholder group is to ensure that the survey sampling design and the corresponding test statistics are able to detect real and meaningful group differences. For a brief overview of statistical power and its sampling requirements, see McNamara (1991, 1992b).

Note 12. Excellent ideas for questionnaire items are given in the *Phi Delta Kappan's* Hot Topics Series on year-round schools, assembled by their Center on Evaluation, Development, and Research. (See Williams, 1990.) Those seriously interested in conducting a school preference survey might wish to examine the following excellent questionnaire design sources. On constructing either telephone or postal questionnaires see Berdie, Anderson, and Niebuhr (1986), Dillman (1978), and Sudman and Bradburn (1982); on designing and conducting questionnaire surveys as a school/university collaborative venture consult Smith, McNamara, and Barona (1986); on reporting findings to policy makers and practitioners examine Haensly, Lupkowski, and McNamara (1987) and Borg and Gall (1989, Chapter 21). For a very informative discussion of how opinion surveys have been used effectively by businesses, government agencies, and associations, see Chapter 2 of Bradburn and Sudman (1988).

Note 13. In practical survey sampling designs, it is not unusual to preset P equal to 0.75 rather than to the traditional preset value of 0.50, even though no reliable prior information is readily available. In our own survey sampling work, we almost always use this rule of thumb when survey research resources are limited or when there is a very short time allocation for conducting and reporting survey findings.

Technically speaking, this is done for two reasons. First, differences in the two resulting standard errors are almost always very small. For example, if n is 278 (as was the case in the initial solution presented in Step One), the maximum standard errors are 0.0222 for P (a population parameter) equal to 0.50 and 0.025 for P equal to 0.75. Notice that the difference cannot be determined until we move to the third digit to the right of the decimal point. Even then, the difference is almost trivial.

Second, if we start with a preset value of P equal to 0.75 rather than 0.50, the required sample-size reduction is usually significant. In our case study, the recommended classroom teacher sample size for P preset at 0.50 is 278. However, if we preset P at 0.75 for the same case study, the recommended sample size is only 224, a reduction of fifty-four teachers.

It should be kept in mind that the practice of moving P preset at 0.50 to P preset at 0.75 yields even larger sample-size reductions when the population size (N) is larger. For example, assume we wish to survey a school district parent and guardian population (N) of 10,000 households. In this case, moving the preset P from 0.50 to 0.75 yields a sample-size reduction from 370 (see Table 13–1) to 280 households. This is a reduction of 90 sampling units (households). If relevant data was collected in lengthy household interviews, this sample-size reduction would save a significant amount of time and money.

Note 14. These guidelines are given in the *Code of Professional Ethics and Practices* of the American Association of Public Opinion Research (AAPOR), an interdisciplinary association of both academic and commercial survey researchers. A convenient source for the guidelines is Babbie (1990, Chapter 19).

The reader may also wish to note that all six 1992 and 1993 *International Journal of Educational Reform* articles referenced in the first thirteen notes have been conveniently reprinted in McNamara (1994b). Several of these reprinted articles contain specific research design suggestions pertaining to the use of the AAPOR guidelines by educational organizations.

Note 15. An excellent starting point for the beginning researcher or school policy analyst to get an accurate overview of the use of qualitative research methods is Lancy (1993). Those wishing to conduct action research in the schools might also examine Erlandson, Harris, Skipper and Allen (1993).

In Chapter 5, Lancy (1993) suggests that the case study, used alone or as part of a larger quantitative study, is the method of choice for studying educational interventions or innovations. For

Lancy, interventions and innovations include school improvement strategies such as "trying out" new curricula, technology, staffing arrangements, student assessment procedures, and community volunteer programs.

Note 16. Case studies (usually conducted using open-ended interviews with individuals and/or groups) are also often used as an initial step in the design of a standardized instrument or a custom-made questionnaire to be used later in a social scientific survey. On this application see the discussion of focus groups in both Morgan (1988) and Stewart and Shamdasani (1990). For the record, focus-group interviews (in contrast to unstructured public sessions) are becoming a popular action research strategy in a wide variety of public-sector organizations.

Note 17. Over the past two decades an extensive literature has emerged on the productive use of the case study to conduct both formative and summative evaluations. Given the easy access to this literature, we elected to bypass program evaluation applications in this chapter and decided to highlight how to use the case study to gain a superintendent's perspective regarding the potential of school/university collaboratives. We believe that public relations specialists will soon be expected to communicate both the value and progress made by individual schools and school districts who join either the popular professional development school movement or other productive school/university collaboratives such as partner schools.

Note 18. Another significant reform effort for bridging the gap between the public schools and administrative training in the university is the Principals' Center movement. Both the organizational design of these centers and their potential for improving schools are clearly elaborated in Barth (1990). Chapter 9 in his book provides several excellent practical suggestions for making the relationship between school and university more fruitful.

Note 19. In reading the case study, the reader should keep three ideas in mind: First, while a semistructured interview method is used to collect the data, this inquiry is not merely a quick and casual interview that just anyone can conduct. Clearly, excellent interviewing skills are required in phase 1. Additional research skills are also needed to complete each of the remaining phases of the case study if it is to be used as an effective decision tool.

Second, while frequently overlooked, phase 3 is an absolutely essential part of the process when the case study is used in decision-oriented rather than academic research. On this point, the interested reader may also wish to examine the positions that the case study is not strictly a method but rather a research strategy (see Lancy, 1993, Chapter 5) and that there is a clear distinction about how a policy research analyst is expected to operate in a decision-oriented rather than an academic research project. (See McNamara, 1992b.)

Third, it is helpful to remember in designing the decision-oriented case study the time-honored Pythagorean adage that a problem well defined is half-solved. On this and other essential administrative decision-making concerns, see McNamara (1993d, 1994a).

Note 20. This case study uses the information from an actual case study having the intents we assumed in the text. Real names and specific locations have been removed or retitled. All other data collection and data analysis text are reproduced here exactly as they appeared in the original case study report.

Note 21. In naturalistic inquiries, the phase 3 verification activities described here are seen as "carrying out a member check." The purpose of a member check is not only to test for factual and interpretative accuracy, but also to provide evidence of credibility (a criterion of quality research analogous to internal validity in conventional quantitative studies such as scientific surveys). On member checks, see especially Lincoln and Guba (1985, Chapter 11) and Erlandson, Harris, Skipper, and Allen, (1993, Chapter 7).

Note 22. On dealing with the issues of validity, reliability, and ethics in qualitative case study research, see especially the easy-to-read but comprehensive treatment of these issues in Merriam (1988, Chapter 10).

Note 23. Other suggestions include preparing analytic summaries with supporting data in appendices and using a *chart essay*, a formal question-and-answer system that reports on four basic questions: What was the problem? What was the research design? What were the research findings? What were the implications? On the use of the chart essay in decision-oriented studies, see Haensly, Lupkowski, and McNamara (1987).

We have found the chart essay to be a general-purpose report format likely to be understood by most stakeholder groups, including trustees, school practitioners, parents, students, and professionals from other social agencies who often work cooperatively with schools. Because it is often easier to understand than other report formats, the chart essay can be a very effective device in stimulating meaningful interactions between and among these stakeholder groups. For the record, Borg and Gall (1989) have indicated that the chart essay is also an excellent communication strategy for summarizing and sharing all types of research findings with professional groups.

Note 24. This section draws extensively from Chapter 1 in Merriam (1988). Readers are encouraged to explore this excellent synthesis on other case study sources.

Note 25. Other qualitative decision tools include (1) scenario writing, policy-focused Delphi, relevance tree analysis, and environmental scanning from forecasting and futures research and (2) team building, role analysis, job enrichment, consulting pairs, and intergroup problem solving from organizational development. All of these qualitative decision tools, along with their counterparts from the quantitative-methods domain are described in McNamara (1994a). An overview of the current use and future potential of these decision tools in information resource management in educational organizations is given in McNamara, Dickson, and Guido-DiBrito (1988). Of special interest in this article is the use of information systems to support interinstitutional research in a system of public school districts and the use of decision support systems to solve administrative problems at Stanford University.

CASE STUDY

Good Intentions Aren't Always Enough

Having to spend extra time hunting for a parking space at the John F. Kennedy Elementary School was not in Jane West's plan for this April evening. As director of communications for the Lancaster School District, Dr. West was ending a two-week marathon of scheduled meetings in each of the district's seven elementary schools. The purpose of these meetings was to share information with parents about a proposed new year-round calendar to be piloted in the district beginning in September.

Persons attending each elementary school campus meeting had been asked to fill out and return a questionnaire related to their interest in having their children participate in the new year-round school pilot program. Questionnaire responses from previous elementary school meetings indicated that, in general, parents were supportive of the program. However, West was cautious about these findings because she realized that (1) attendance at the previous meetings had been low, (2) those in attendance had come from what is considered to be the more affluent sections of the district, and (3) many of those attending had not returned their questionnaires.

After searching several minutes for a parking spot, West was convinced that low attendance would not be an issue at tonight's meeting. As she entered the cafetorium, she saw that all seats were taken and that a few parents were standing. She was surprised to see the large numbers of preschool children accompanying their parents.

The audience was largely Hispanic and West was pleased that she'd had the good sense to arrange to have a translator at the meeting, since many of the residents in this area of the school district were new immigrants.

When West turned on the overhead projector and began her presentation, she heard shouts coming from several areas of the room. "No! We don't want to hear about something that you've already decided for us." "We can't afford to have our children out of school at odd times of the year. How will we find babysitters?" "We've heard rumors that you're going to force all of the children in *this* neighborhood to go to school this summer." "Why is it that no one has asked *us* what *we* think about a year-round school program?"

West, though startled, recovered quickly: "Your children brought information home last month, and the local newspaper published two articles on this pilot program just last week. We're now asking you to fill out this questionnaire so that we'll *know* how you feel." But her enthusiasm to share more information about the program was quickly eroded as she realized that the angry questions and comments were not going to stop.

At the close of the meeting, a frustrated West had her assistants pass out the questionnaires. "Before you go home could you please fill these out?" she asked. "We'll pay close attention to your responses."

Several parents had already left the building before the questionnaires were distributed. A few people crumpled the sheets when they saw that the forms were written in English. Most people, however, simply left the questionnaires on their empty seats. As the last of her audience filed out, West leaned over and dejectedly picked up a few of the questionnaires that had floated to the floor.

Early the next morning, Jane West sat in her office thinking about the series of meetings she'd conducted on the year-round school pilot program. Last night's meeting at the John F. Kennedy Elementary School had made it clear that something more needed to be done to get clarity on whether or not families with children in district schools were interested in exploring year-round schools as an alternative to the current nine-month school year. Moreover, if families declared an interest in participating in a twelve-month pilot program, what should she do to get accurate information on how the pilot program could best work for them? And would "working best for them" be different for different types of families?

QUESTIONS AND SUGGESTED ACTIVITIES

Six specific activities are offered below to link the quantitative and the qualitative strategies detailed in this chapter with problems encountered in practice. Each of these suggested activities can be conducted by individual students or carried out by one or more groups.

Case Study

1. You are the director of field studies at a local state university that has an excellent record of collaborating with school districts in your region. Jane West from the Lancaster School District has expressed an interest in having your field studies research group conduct a needs assessment for her district.

In your meeting with Dr. West you learn that the needs assessment must answer two policy questions. First, the school district wishes to determine what percent of its families with school-age children would be interested in participating in a year-round school program. Second, for those families who wish to participate in the year-round program, the district would like to know what specific arrangements would work best for them. In addition, Dr. West lets you know that she is agreeable to using both a social scientific survey and a set of case studies to explore these two policy questions in detail.

With this information in hand, you agree to prepare a two-page needs assessment proposal elaborating a specific research plan for the Lancaster School District and forward it to Dr. West. Prepare the proposal..

Chapter

2. Invite an educational research methods professor to join one of your public relations classes. Prior to the professor's visit, each student should read the section on survey research in a basic social science or educational research methods text (for one example, see Borg and Gall , 1989, Chapter 11) and list any questions he or she might have about the design and use of a survey on a 3-by-5 index card. This inventory of cards should be shared with the visiting professor at the start of class or a few days before the scheduled visit.

3. In Chapter 3 of her excellent practical guide for designing and carrying out a qualitative case study in an educational setting, Merriam (1988) suggests that not everyone will feel confident conducting a case study. She believes that case studies, like any other research strategy, demand certain skills. The first half of her chapter provides a discussion of the characteristics and skills needed to do qualitative case study research.

First prepare a list of characteristics and skills you believe are essential for designing and carrying out a qualitative research case study in a school or a school district, then read Merriam's treatment of needed characteristics and skills. Compare your list with hers and discuss any differences you encounter in the two perspectives.

4. In the latter part of her Chapter 3, Merriam (1988) notes that qualitative case study research usually begins with a problem identified from practice. Next, broad questions are raised, questions that provide the insights necessary to identify a general problem of interest. Finally, the unit of analysis, or "the case," is defined and the specific sample is selected. The case can be based on an individual, a program, an institution, a group, an event, or a policy. The key issue for determining "the case" is to decide what it is you want to say about the problem of interest at the end of the study.

First read Chapter 3 in Merriam (1988), then follow her guidelines to design a hypothetical qualitative research case study for a real-world problem you have encountered in either a school or a school district. Use the four-phase model from the case study of the school district superintendent presented in the last half of this present chapter to illustrate how your hypothetical case study would move beyond the first phase (data gathering) to create information that could be used to improve managerial and policy decisions.

5. An urban school district wishes to conduct a household preference survey that is identical to the one described in this chapter. Specifically, this school district wishes to design a simple random sample survey to estimate the proportion of its 5000 households (N) that would give a "yes" response to the following questionnaire item: This school district is considering a year-round school program. Would you prefer this alternative to our existing nine-month school year? (Yes or No).

The survey research design decisions established by the school district are as follows: (1) The precision value B is preset at 0.50; (2) the confidence value A is preset at 3.84; and (3) the prior information value is preset at 0.50. (These three preprogrammed values, or decision rules, are explained in step 1 of the three-step procedure to determine the recommended sample size.) Use the procedure in Table 13–5 to get the recommended sample size n for this preference survey. Your solution to this problem should be a Table identical in form to the one given in Table 13–6.

6. Assume that the household preference survey was conducted using the required sample size n you identified in your solution to the preceding activity. Also assume that the proportion of "yes" responses in this survey was 0.85—that is, 85 percent of the households in the sample gave a "yes" response to the questionnaire item on the preference for a year-round school program. Your task is to determine the margin of error for this household preference survey using the six-step procedure detailed in Table 13–3. Your solution to this problem should be a table identical to the one given in Table 13–4.

SUGGESTED READINGS

Several noteworthy sources for readers who wish to conduct social scientific surveys or qualitative research case studies are given in the Research Design Notes section. Additional suggestions for relevant readings are elaborated below, using seven specific topics.

Decision Making.   Surveys, like other scientific and technical tools, can be well or poorly made and can be used in appropriate or inappropriate ways. In Chapter 3 of their widely referenced book, Bradburn and Sudman (1988) discuss a wide range of uses of surveys and give some excellent examples of uses that to them are clearly appropriate, clearly inappropriate, and questionable. A special easy-to-read section in this chapter entitled "Use of Opinion Data by United States Presidents" is one of the very best overviews for illustrating how surveys and polls can be used to inform managerial and policy decisions.

Ethical Guidelines.   Since ethical concerns of survey research are not part of scientific methods, researchers and practitioners must look to another set of guidelines. These guidelines are given in the *Code of Professional Ethics and Practices* published by the American Association of Public Opinion Research, an interdisciplinary association of both academic and commercial survey researchers. A reprint of the AAPOR Code is given in Chapter 19 of Babbie (1990). This chapter also gives seventeen realistic illustrations that identify ethical issues and steps one might take to ensure that AAPOR norms are met without endangering the scientific quality of the survey. On the use of ethical guidelines for survey research in educational organizations, see also McNamara (1993a), which is reprinted as Chapter 5 in McNamara (1994b).

Consumer of Survey Research.   In professional work it is often helpful to distinguish between producers of research and consumers of research. Practitioners who wish to be informed consumers of survey research should examine the excellent consumer's checklist given in Chapter 20 of Babbie (1990). Use of consumer checklists in school improvement research is given in McNamara (1993c), which is reprinted as Chapter 7 in McNamara (1994b).

Questionnaire Design.   While there are many sources one can turn to for help in developing a questionnaire, one of the very best sources for both practitioners and researchers is still Dillman (1978). Chapter 3 of this source provides a very straightforward elaboration of sixteen basic types of questions used in surveys and polls. Dillman's book is also recognized for its clear elaboration of a data-collection strategy that consistently yields survey return rates exceeding 90 percent. Two additional nontechnical questionnaire design sources frequently recommended by our colleagues are Sudman and Bradburn (1982) and Berdie, Anderson, and Niebuhr (1986).

Sampling in Qualitative Research. Since generalization in a statistical sense is not a goal of qualitative research, probabilistic sampling (used in social scientific surveys) is not necessary or even justified in qualitative research. With this in mind, case study researchers often use purposive sampling based on the assumption that one wants to discover, understand, or gain insight. Accordingly, one needs to select a sample from which one can learn most. Excellent overviews of purposive sampling and other nonprobability sampling strategies are given in Chapter 3 on defining the case in Merriam (1988) and in Chapter 5 on gathering data in Erlandson, Harris, Skipper, and Allen (1993).

Telephone Surveys. The telephone survey is now one of the more popular types of survey methods used in the United States. Its use in school districts as a means to improve two-way communication is also increasing. Both the ability to train telephone interviewers (often community volunteers) in a single location and the need to use fewer interviewers than required for conducting personal interviews are two key reasons why administrators and policy makers prefer telephone surveys to other data-collecting methods. If your organization is interested in exploring the use of telephone polls, an excellent first source to consult is Chapter 6 in Dillman (1978). Early on one might also wish to review Chapter 6 in McNamara (1994b).

Focus Groups. Both school practitioners and educational researchers interested in using less formal (but effective) action research strategies to improve two-way communication are encouraged to investigate the use of the focus group as a means to gather information from a wide array of school and community stakeholders. Two easy-to-read (and very informative) sources to review before turning to more technical references are Morgan (1988) and Stewart and Shamdasani (1990).

REFERENCES

Babbie, E. (1990). *Survey research methods* (2nd ed.). Belmont, CA: Wadsworth.

Barth, R. S. (1990). *Improving schools from within: Teachers, parents, and principals can make the difference.* San Francisco: Jossey-Bass.

Berdie, D. R., Anderson, J. F., & Niebuhr, M. A. (1986). *Questionnaires: Design and use* (2nd ed.). Metuchen, NJ: Scarecrow Press.

Borg, W. A., & Gall, M. (1989). *Educational research* (5th ed.). New York: Longman.

Bradburn, N. M., & Sudman, S. (1988). *Polls and surveys: Understanding what they tell us.* San Francisco: Jossey-Bass.

Bradley, A. (1994, March 2). Education school links with K-12 on the rise, survey finds. *Education Week, 13*(23), 3–4.

Dillman, D.A. (1978). *Mail and telephone surveys: The total design method.* New York: Wiley.

Erlandson, D. A., Harris, E. L., Skipper, B. L., & Allen, S. D. (1993). *Doing naturalistic inquiry: A guide to methods.* Newbury Park, CA: Sage.

Ferber, R. (Ed.) (1980). *What is a survey?* Alexandria, VA: American Statistical Association.

Haensly, P. A., Lupkowski, A. E., & McNamara, J. F. (1987). The chart essay: A strategy for communicating research findings to policy makers and practitioners. *Educational Evaluation and Policy Analysis, 9* (1), 63–75.

Jaeger, R. M. (1984).*Sampling in education and social sciences.* New York: Longman.

Kish, L. (1965). *Survey sampling.* New York: Wiley.

Krejcie, R. V., & Morgan, D. A. (1970). Determining sample size for research activity. *Educational and Psychological Measurement, 30* (6), 607–610.

Lancy, D. F. (1993). *Qualitative research in education: An introduction to the major traditions.*New York: Longman.

Lincoln, Y. S., & Guba, E. G. (1985). *Naturalistic inquiry.*Newbury Park: Sage.

McNamara, J. F. (1991). Statistical power in educational research. *National Forum of Applied Educational Research Journal, 3* (2), 23–26.

McNamara, J. F. (1992a). Sample size for school preference surveys. *International Journal of Educational Reform, 1* (1), 83–90.

McNamara, J. F. (1992b). Statistical power in school improvement research. *International Journal of Educational Research, 1* (3), 313–325.

McNamara, J. F. (1992c). Research designs and sample size requirements in school improvement research. *International Journal of Educational Reform, 1* (4), 433–445.

McNamara, J. F. (1993a). Ethical guidelines in survey research. *International Journal of Educational Reform, 2* (1), 96–101.

McNamara, J. F. (1993b). A study guide for developing survey research skills. *International Journal of Educational Reform, 2* (2), 213–223.

McNamara, J. F. (1993c). The informed consumer of survey research. *International Journal of Educational Reform, 2* (3), 346–353.

McNamara, J. F. (1993d). Administrative decision making: Part one. *International Journal of Educational Reform, 2* (4), 465–474.

McNamara, J. F. (1994a). Administrative decision making. Part two. *International Journal of Educational Reform, 3* (1), 113–121.

McNamara, J. F. (1994b). *Surveys and experiments in education research.* Lancaster, PA: Technomic Publishing.

McNamara, J. F., & Chisolm, G. B. (1988). The technical tools of decision making. In N. J. Boyan (ed.). *Handbook of research on educational administration* (pp. 525–567) New York: Longman.

McNamara, J. F., Dickson, M. A., & Guido-DiBrito , F. (1988). Decision science perspectives for information systems and data administration. In J. Rabin and E. M. Jackowski (eds.). *Handbook of Information Resource Management* (pp. 107–173) New York: Marcel Dekker.

Merriam, S. B. (1988). *Case study research in education: A qualitative approach.* San Francisco: Jossey-Bass.

Morgan, D. L. (1988). *Focus groups as qualitative research.* Newbury Park, CA: Sage.

O'Shea, D. W. (1992). Survey design. In M. C. Alkin (ed.). *Encyclopedia of educational research* (6th ed.) (pp. 1323–1331). New York: Macmillan.

Patton, M. Q. (1990). *Qualitative evaluation and research methods* (2nd ed.). Newbury Park, CA: Sage.

Schaeffer, R. L., Mendenhall, W., & Ott, L. (1990). *Elementary survey sampling* (4th ed.). Boston: Duxbury.

Simon, H. A. (1977). *The new science of management decision* (rev. ed.). Englewood Cliffs, NJ: Prentice Hall.

Smith, R. G., McNamara, J. F., & Barona, A. (1986). Getting good results from survey research. *Public Administration Quarterly, 10* (2), 233–248.

Stenhouse, L. (1985). A note on case study and educational practice. In R. G. Burgess (ed.), *Field methods in the study of education* (pp. 263–271) London: Falmer.

Stewart, D. W., & Shamdasani, P. N. (1990). *Focus groups: Theory and practice*. Newbury Park, CA: Sage.

Sudman, S., & Bradburn, N. A. (1982). *Asking questions: A practical guide to questionnaire design.* San Francisco: Jossey-Bass.

Williams, B. (1978). *A sampler on sampling*. New York: Wiley.

Williams, S. (Ed.) (1990). *Year-round schools: Do they make a difference?* Bloomington, IN: Phi Delta Kappa.

Yin, R. K. (1984). *Case study research: Design and methods*. Newbury Park, CA: Sage.

CHAPTER 14

Public Relations in a Funding Campaign

Glenn Graham
Gordon Wise

One of the most critical tests of public relations activities conducted by and for public schools comes at those inevitable times when the schools must turn to the community of voters for financial support. In most of the United States, the level of state financial support has failed to keep pace with increases in the cost of public education. In recent years, many states have made substantial cuts in financial support. Increasingly costly and rigorous mandates of programs and facilities are commonly thrust upon local schools—typically without accompanying budgets to fund them.

All of this leads to more frequent trips by the schools to the public funding well. In most states such a trip is successful *only* if voters in the district approve some form of tax levy and/or bond issue. It is in this all-too-common and frequently dreary scenario that the public relations activities (both long-term and short-term) are vital.

Let it be said up front that a school district that reaches for its public relations tools only at times when a funding election approaches is not worthy of the support of its community. A basic theme of this entire book, and certainly of this chapter, is that an effective public relations effort must be *ongoing*. The promotion and public relations efforts undertaken during funding campaigns will ideally reinforce, support, and supplement the regular links already in place between the community and the schools.

MARKETING VERSUS SELLING

The ongoing public relations effort, including those activities used during funding campaigns, should be an integrated part of a broader marketing commitment of the schools. In the past (and, sadly, too often at present) schools have tended toward a more traditional selling approach in their promotional efforts, which may include some nod toward the public relations area.

Schools that are the most successful at funding campaigns are also the most successful at discerning the difference between a marketing approach and a selling approach. When you are "selling," you are attempting to "get rid of what you have"—for example, the grocer who has a surplus of produce needs to "sell" it to the buyer to get it off his hands. "Marketing" is having what you "*know* you can get rid of."

This distinction may sound overly simple, but the difference is profound. In the former (selling) posture, the focus is on the *product* (the program, the curriculum, the levy campaign) in an effort to convince the "market" (students, parents, voters) that they must accept/vote for that product. In the latter (marketing) posture, the focus is on the *market*. Here the primary efforts are devoted to determining what constitutes "value" to that market: What are its needs, wants, desires? What perceptions and expectations does that market have? Then—and only then—does the school that practices a marketing approach attempt to put together its "product." This revised focus allows the astute marketer to combine the resources he or she controls into a bundle of satisfactions that has the best chance of gaining acceptance from the market.

THE FOUR P'S OF MARKETING

The tools of a marketing approach used by a school are very similar to the marketing tools used by a business firm. They include the following:

1. The *product*, or the "bundle of satisfactions" developed from the resources the organization controls.
2. The *price*, or the sacrifice of scarce resources required to access that bundle of satisfactions. This may be found in fees and taxes but also in time, effort, and energy provided to the school by the person who chaperones the band bus or the prom or who serves at a PTA function.
3. The *promotion*, or the application of both personal and nonpersonal efforts to expand awareness, interest, and support for the product. This area of marketing encompasses the public relations effort.
4. The *place* (physical distribution), or the actual delivery of the bundle of satisfactions. Schools find "place" activities in such areas as boundaries, districts, bus routes, and the grouping of students or classes. (Should the sixth grade be in the elementary school or in the middle school/junior high?)

The successful ongoing marketing program of a school uses these tools in appropriate and often-changing proportions to develop and direct its *controllable* marketing efforts in response to those *uncontrollable* variables it must confront. Included in those uncontrollables are such things as changing populations and demographics; the emergence of "competitors" (private schooling, home schooling, open enrollment, as well as anything that competes for the time and resources the school would normally attract from its students, parents, and taxpayers); and the wide range of environmental variables (economic, social/cultural, legal/public policy) that can thwart the objectives of the schools. (The authors have treated this subject in greater depth in a specialized article addressing the need for school administrators to adopt an ongoing total marketing approach. (See Graham & Wise, 1990.)

THE SCOUTING REPORT AND GAME PLAN

Consider approaching a campaign for a school tax levy or bond issue as a coach approaches an upcoming game. You scout the opposition, ascertain their strengths and weaknesses, and from this scouting report develop a game plan to achieve victory.

The Market Survey

The "scouting report" here is a survey of the market—the voting-age population of the school district.

The market survey that works best is the door-to-door, structured, personal interview method. This format is preferred over mail or phone surveys for several reasons:

1. With mail surveys you risk hearing from the extremes of an issue but not from those in the middle, and it is they who are critical to the success of a campaign.
2. The response rate of mail surveys is notoriously low—20 percent, if you're lucky.
3. With both mail and phone surveys it is much more difficult to tell if respondents are being honest.
4. Many people are antagonized by phone surveys, and this might carry over into a negative vote.

A structured interview has all the questions written out for the interviewer, who then reads them to the interviewee and records the responses. Because the campaign strategies and tactics—that is, the "game plan"—depend on the information obtained from these interviews, they must be carefully planned.

Initially, meetings should be held with a committee of school administrators and board members to determine components of the interview: Are specific school programs to be evaluated? Are attitudes to be evaluated? What are the issues that influence people to vote yes or no? What demographics should be obtained?

Following this, three or four focus groups should be established from a cross section of the voting-age population of the school district. Each focus group should have from six to twelve members. (Be sure to include negative people.) There should be two focus-group leaders to take notes and keep the discussion going (Wise & Graham, 1993). To encourage honest, open dialogue, no tape recorders or video recorders should be used; with two people taking notes, you won't miss much. Some questions for a focus group might include: (1) What are the strengths of the schools in this district? Weakness? (2) The operating levy was defeated last election. Why? (3) Of the people you come in contact with, what reasons do they give for voting for or against the upcoming levy?

An hour to an hour and half of open-ended discussion should generate many positive and negative concerns from the focus group. These concerns and issues will then provide the basic ingredients for the structured interview.

The question format for the structured interview should utilize forced-choice items: The interviewer reads a statement to which the interviewee responds according to a scale such as Strongly agree, Agree, Neutral, Disagree, Strongly disagree. This type of question is good for obtaining attitudes toward the schools and school programs. In the next section of this chapter we'll discuss how two other types of forced-choice items are used to deal with positive and negative perceptions.

Once the first draft of the interview has been prepared, it should be shared with the school committee, and revisions made as necessary. The next step is to select about ten people and *field-test* the interview. Give them the instrument and discuss the questions to be sure they are clear and not biased. From the field test the final version of the interview is obtained. The interview should take about fifteen to twenty minutes. A piece of advice: *Always field-test your market survey.*

Before administering the survey, interviewers need to be trained so that they are thoroughly familiar with it. They should *not* interview anyone they know since this will potentially bias the results. They must take care to be courteous at all times, yet not give verbal or nonverbal cues. The names of the interviewers should be given to the local police department, and interviewers should wear a name badge at all times. Should anyone be concerned about their purpose, interviewers can suggest that the police be called for verification. This will help them gain access to people who might otherwise refuse the interview.

Interviewees should be determined as randomly as possible. Divide the school district by voting blocks (precincts or townships). Using the results of the last two or three school votes, which you can get from the board of elections, determine what proportion of the total vote came from each voting block. If, for example, 4 percent of the vote came from precinct 1A, then 4 percent of the sample should come from 1A. Next, number all the streets and roads in *each* precinct, staring at 1 each time. Using a table of random numbers (which can be found in most statistics texts or can be computer-generated), select the streets and roads for your sample. Each time the street number comes up in the table, select one residence from it. A residence can be a house, apartment, or trailer. For example, if Plum Street is number 15 on your list, and 15 occurs as you go through the random number table, then take a residence on Plum Street; should 15 occur again, pick a second residence. Which *specific* residence gets picked is up to the interviewer, for if no one is at home at one location or if a person refuses to be interviewed, the interviewer will need to go to another residence on the same street. If no interview can be obtained on the street selected, the interviewer should go to the next-closest street.

The size of the sample to be interviewed depends on the population of the school district and the amount of error with which the district is comfortable. Typically, in school districts of 5000 to 100,000, sample sizes will range from about 250 to 400 people, for an error rate of ± 5 percent (Arfim & Colton, 1971). (See also the previous chapter for sampling techniques.)

Identifying and Dealing with Positive and Negative Perceptions

Identifying the Issues That Influence a Vote. Using the focus groups as the source, you can identify the issues that have the potential to be a positive influence (encourage a vote for the levy or bond) or a negative influence (encourage a vote against the levy or bond). These issues are then incorporated into the market survey by means of a statement such as:

> In any levy (bond) election there are certain issues that may influence you to vote for it, there are other issues that may influence you to vote against it, and there are some issues that would have no influence on how you vote. For each of the following, please tell me if it would:
> 1. Influence you to *vote for* the levy (bond).
> 2. Have *no influence* on how you would vote.
> 3. Influence you to *vote against* the levy (bond).

The interviewee is then handed a sheet with the above response options, and each of the issues is read. Once the list of issues has been covered, each issue can be classified as positive, negative, or a nonissue.

But if you stopped at this point you would miss a crucial part of the information necessary to drive a campaign. That is, what is the *relative strength* of each issue? Which will have the *most influence* on a vote for and a vote against? So after the list of issues has had its initial reading, the interviewer proceeds to give these directions:

> I am going to show you the issues from this list that you picked as influencing you to vote for the levy (bond). Of these issues which is the *single most important* in influencing you to vote for the levy (bond)? [Pause] Which is the *second most important?* [Pause] Which is the *third most important?* [Pause] Now I'm going to show you those issues you picked as influencing you to vote against the levy (bond). Of these issues which is the *single most important* in influencing you to vote against the levy (bond)? [Pause] Which is the *second most important?* [Pause] Which is the *third most important?*"

Weight each of the ranks, giving issues ranked as "most important" three points; "second most important," two points; "third most important," one point. Total the points for the positive issues and for the negative. From these, the top five or six of both positive and negative become those issues that will drive the campaign.

Dealing with the Positive and Negative Issues.   In the words of the old song, you must now "accentuate the positive and eliminate the negative." To eliminate the negative does **not** mean to ignore the negative issues and hope they'll go away. Those issues influencing a vote against need to be explained carefully and honestly in order to weaken their impact. For example, while people don't want to pay more taxes, they typically like increased property values. Linking the quality of schools to increased property value may well ease the impact of the tax bite.

The lists of top issues should serve as a screen for any campaign materials, whether they be ads, brochures, or letters to the editor. If at least one of the top positive or top negative issues is not addressed, then that campaign material should not be used.

Projecting the Election Outcome

Many school systems have run campaigns based on a false optimism that is trampled by harsh reality on election day. Afterwards district leaders will hear comments such as "But they told us they'd vote for it!" The problem is the questions were asked the wrong way.

Take the question, "Will you vote for or against the levy (bond)?" This question requires a socially acceptable answer; most people will not admit to voting against the schools. Therefore, a question designed to help project the voting outcome must allow for the respondent to say "no" in a socially acceptable way. Phrase the question this way:

If an election were held *today*, and you were asked to vote on a five-mill levy to increase property taxes to support operating expenses of our school district, how would you most likely vote:

1. I would *certainly vote for* the levy.
2. I would *almost certainly vote for* the levy.
3. I would *probably for* the levy.
4. I am *uncertain* as to how I would vote.
5. I would *probably vote against* the levy.
6. I would *almost certainly vote against* the levy.
7. I would *certainly vote against* the levy.

People who respond that they will "certainly vote for" have put themselves on the line, and in most cases they will be supportive. It is the authors' experience in projecting the vote, that 90 percent of those who give this response can be believed. If they choose the "almost certainly vote for" option, they are hedging a bit; 60 or 70 percent of these responses can be believed. (If over 30 percent of those asked to take the interview refuse to do so, use the 60 percent value.)

Those who respond "probably vote for" will probably vote against. This is one of the socially acceptable "no" options. Such persons have passed over two more-positive options to give this response. When projecting the vote, 30 or 40 percent of these responses can be considered as voting for the tax. (Use the lower percentage if over 30 percent have refused to be interviewed.) Those who respond "undecided" really aren't undecided; they will almost certainly vote "no." When projecting this vote, only count 10 or 20 percent of these responses as voting for the tax. Obviously, those who say they'll vote against are to be believed.

The projection of those voting for is found by adding 0.90 × the number of people responding "certainly for," 0.60 or 0.70 × the number responding "almost certainly for," 0.30 or 0.40 × the number responding "probably for," and 0.10 or 0.20 × the number responding "uncertain." This sum is then divided by the total number of *all* responses to give the proportion projected as voting for (Graham, Wise, & Bachman, 1990).

While there is no highly scientific or mathematical defense for the percentages used, on the basis of the authors' experience, there is support for their validity. The procedure rarely projects less than 30 percent voting for, which is consistent with election results. Also, in those elections where little or no campaign was conducted, the voting outcome on each of these has been within ± 5 percentage of points of the prediction.

Since a good campaign can easily turn on 10 percent of the voters in the middle, any projection of 40 percent or more means the bond (levy) has a good chance of passing; a projection of 35 to 39 percent means there's a moderate chance; 30 to 34 percent connotes a high risk; and anything less means the bond (levy) has almost no chance of passing (Graham, Wise, & Bachman, 1990). If the latter projection should occur, this does not mean that the bond or levy should be taken off the ballot. It is quite common for a bond or levy to fail in several elections before passing. The issues simply need to be thoroughly debated before some voters are convinced of the need.

Developing a Plan and Strategies for the Campaign

A funding campaign is brought closer to success through thorough, timely planning. A version of a marketing plan, with identification of appropriate strategies, tactics, and timetables, can and should be employed.

Development of a marketing plan for the campaign includes such elements as:

1. *Identifying the objective*, which is generally as simple as figuring out the proportion of votes needed for passage of a school levy (50 percent, 60 percent, . . .) plus a sufficient margin to survive a recount.
2. *Identifying strategy options*, that is, the range of possible overall strategies (running a positive campaign versus a negative campaign, using heavy personal contact versus media only, . . .).
3. *Evaluating all strategy options*—costs, feasibility, strengths and weaknesses—which leads to the selection of the appropriate strategy.
4. *Developing tactics* to support the strategy option or combination of strategies chosen. Several examples of campaign tactics will be presented later in this chapter. This area of the plan must be specific in identifying *who* is to do *what* and *how* it is to be done.
5. *Developing a timetable* for use in the campaign. This segment will be the major element of control that assures that campaign events and activities will be sequenced for maximum impact.
6. *Developing a budget* for funding the campaign. This will identify the general areas of expenditure (media advertising, printing, postage, space rental, salaries, . . .). This budget amount must be coordinated with fund-raising efforts so that the planned spending does not exceed the revenues available for campaign use.

Organizing Public Relations for the Campaign

Campaign Leadership: The Organizational Chart.   The failure of many school tax issues can be attributed to a lack of organization and planning time. The campaign organization must be in place and functioning four to six months before the election. Figure 14–1 provides a suggested organizational chart.

The steering committee provides direction for all aspects of the campaign. This committee is composed of the campaign co-chairs; treasurer; consultant(s) (if any); the four division chairs; and representatives from the school board, school administration, teachers and staff, students and parents, and the local media. Having representation from the local media might surprise you, but the campaign should have nothing to hide, and if you get them on your side, it can be of great benefit. They won't always accept the invitation, but do offer it to them. Many successful campaigns have included a member of the clergy. Having access to church bulletins, newsletters, and sermons provides additional avenues for the campaign message. The steering committee should meet biweekly at the outset and

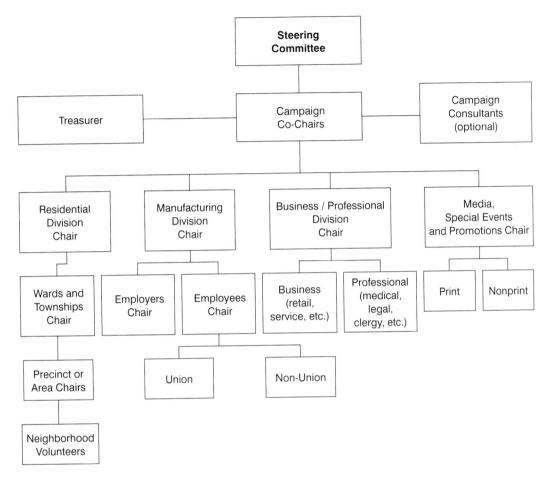

FIGURE 14.1
Organizational Chart for Funding Campaign Leadership

weekly during the final two months of the campaign. A noon or evening dinner meeting (the pay-your-own-expenses type) works well.

The campaign co-chairs are responsible for the day-to-day direction of the campaign. These people need to be dedicated, competent, and credible, but most importantly they must have the time and schedule flexibility necessary to involve themselves in

1. Recruitment of chairs for the other positions
2. Recruitment and training of volunteers
3. Development of a campaign theme and slogan
4. Approval of all media copy
5. Scheduling of ads and promotional events
6. Chairing the steering committee
7. Speaking at public and organization meetings

With these duties in mind, using politicians, CEOs, or media and sports celebrities in this position is *not* recommended; they simply won't have the time to perform. Instead, use these persons for endorsements.

The treasurer should record all financial transactions and expenditures, sign all checks for the campaign organization, and complete all forms and reports mandated by state law.

Campaign Consultant(s), while an optional part of the organizational structure, can provide professional and *experienced* assistance. The consultant may even be the ingredient that produces success. Be certain to check his or her track record and to contact some previous clients before hiring this person.

The residential division chair is, other than the campaign co-chairs, the most important person in a campaign. Through this individual's leadership, the residential division has the following tasks (highlighted here, but discussed in detail later) to accomplish:

1. Recruit, train, and motivate the volunteer army necessary to accomplish tasks 2–5
2. Ascertain who the positive voters will be and get them registered if necessary
3. Arrange for absentee ballots to be sent to *those identified as positive* who will not be in town on election day
4. Deliver, through personal contact, campaign literature to as many households as possible
5. Cover the polls on election day, make phone calls to remind those identified as positive to vote, and provide assistance such as babysitting and transportation to get the positive voters to the polls

The individual who chairs this division must be well connected throughout the school district and have excellent organizational and interpersonal skills.

The manufacturing division chair interacts with two groups, employers and employees. This position requires an individual with accomplished negotiating skills. Obtaining the endorsements and financial support of both groups can be a delicate matter.

The business/professional chair holds responsibilities similar to those of the manufacturing division chair.

The media special events and promotions chair must handle all advertising, letters to the editor, endorsements, videotapes, parades, and other promotional activities.

The Volunteer Army.   Several hundred persons may be needed as the volunteer support for the campaign. Clearly, the chair of the residential division cannot contact all these people, but he or she can organize a pyramid system to accomplish the contacts. First, each ward and township chair is recruited by the residential and campaign chairs. The charge to each ward and township chair is to recruit the necessary precinct or area chairs and to assist each of these chairs in recruiting their respective volunteers.

The volunteers should be in place at least one month before the last day of voter registration. This permits time for them to canvass their assigned area to locate positive voters and register them if necessary. Each volunteer should be assigned ten to twelve residences in their neighborhood; assigning more may make recruitment difficult. But there will be those who'll take more.

Building Potential Support through Positive-Voter Identification

Locating and Registering Positive Voters.   Before starting out, the volunteers should be trained in how to determine who is a likely positive voter and how to register that person. Tell the volunteers to approach their neighbors with a comment such as "I'll be the neighborhood volunteer for the levy (bond) campaign. Is there some information I can get for you, or are there are some questions you have? What do you see as the issues?" Neighbors who bring up negative concerns—"I don't see how we can afford this, since we're on fixed income"; "Don't the teachers make enough already?"; "They never told us how they spent the money from the last levy"—are likely to vote against the levy or bond. The volunteer should write down their questions and concerns, thank them, and say, "I appreciate your sharing these with me. I'll be back in a few weeks with some information to help you make a decision." The volunteers should be instructed to then leave *without any further discussion or argument.* They need to know that this visit is to find positive voters; the campaigning comes later.

If, in answer to the volunteer's question, the neighbor gives a positive response—"It's about time we fixed the old building for the kids"; "I'm worred about losing business and industry if we don't improve our schools"; "How can I help with the campaign?"—it is likely that this is a potential positive voter. If the volunteer is still uncertain that the person is positive, he or she should ask, "Would you be willing to have a yard sign during the campaign?" Once the volunteer has determined that the person is positive, the question can then be asked; "Are you registered?" If the person is not registered, the volunteer can explain the registration procedures or perhaps actually register the person at that time.

It was mentioned previously that volunteers should write down the questions and concerns they hear voiced. At the training sessions each volunteer should be given a stack of "Voter Contact Cards." These are 3-by-5 notecards, printed if possible, that have spaces for the name, address, ward, precinct, township, and phone number of the person contacted; the volunteer's assessment of whether that person is positive, negative, or undecided; and the questions asked and/or information requested. As these cards are completed, volunteers make one copy for themselves and return the other copy to campaign headquarters where they will be arranged by precinct or township polling place. We'll say more about these cards later.

Following Up.   Once the campaign is underway, the volunteers return to their neighborhoods with the promotional materials. They should make every effort to **contact** personally each person for whom they have a voter contact card. Those identified as positive need reassurance of the importance of their vote; the negative should have their questions answered.

There is a chance that a negative person who has an open mind and is willing to listen to the information can be persuaded to vote "yes." A challenge to give the volunteers is for each to convert one negative to a positive. For each conversion, the campaign actually acquires *two votes*—one is removed from "against" and one is added to "for."

Getting the Positive Voters to the Polls.   In many states, a list of those who have voted must be posted at each polling place, usually by 4:30 p.m. A volunteer is assigned to visit each poll at this time and, using the list of positive voters obtained from the voter contact cards, identify all who have voted. Anyone on the list who has not voted should be called by one of the volunteers. The call should be in the nature of a friendly reminder. "Hello, this is [name] from the levy committee. I wanted to see if you have voted yet. We really need your support." Offers of babysitting and transportation can be made at this time.

ELEMENTS OF A SUCCESSFUL CAMPAIGN

Once an overall strategy is chosen, all elements of the campaign should contribute toward implementation of the strategy. Input from the market survey should be considered the "marching orders" for all phases of the campaign. There are many general forms of campaign tactics that can be fine-tuned into specific activities. The list that follows is suggested only as a menu from which campaign leadership can select the tactics that are feasible and affordable. Some of them are pure public relations in scope and structure. Others are broader forms of promotion and marketing activities. All have been campaign-tested by the authors (Graham, Wise, & Bachman, 1990). They are not presented in any order of importance, cost, or effectiveness.

Testimonials

Prominent people in the community—clergy, doctors, dentists, business and civic leaders, and celebrities—can provide testimonials for use in the media advertising program. All it takes is the asking. Although accustomed to writing and speaking, these very busy people may be amenable to lending their name to a testimonial that is ghostwritten, as long as they have the right to approve the copy. When this can be arranged, it gives the campaign leaders an opportunity to address the major issues by speaking through the mouths of people who command respect in the community.

One of the most successful types of testimonial is the "I've changed my mind" testimonial. This is solicited from someone who has been negative about the levy in the past but realizes now how important it is for the schools or the community. Voters who are on the fence can identify with someone who has the courage to admit publicly a change of heart.

Presentation of the Price

There is a price attached to passage of a levy or bond issue—usually in the form of a tax increase. Voters tend to overestimate what they will have to pay, which only serves to heighten their resistance. To counteract this resistance, it is important to provide some perspective about tax increases.

An effective tool is a tax table that compares one's increase in property taxes with the present level of *taxes paid* rather than with the current market value of their home. This table should be simple to interpret but include enough detail so voters will be able to determine the actual tax increases for a wide range of tax amounts. The tax increase should also be broken down into cost per day. In this way the cost is made to seem relatively small when compared with other daily expenditures. Accuracy is extremely important in contructing such a table. Input from the county auditor or treasurer will be needed to ensure that accuracy.

Such a table can be used in different components of the campaign program. Certainly it should be included in any brochure developed for campaign use as well as in media advertising, with an appropriate concluding message such as: "For such a reasonable price, we must say 'yes' to our schools!"

The Audiovisual Presentation

An effective audiovisual presentation can be a major tool for communicating the campaign issues. It can be used to present a consistent message to the community and serve as a virtual speakers' bureau for the campaign committee.

The presentation should be produced well in advance of the campaign. Preparing the slides or videotaping the footage, plus writing and editing the narrative, is a time-consuming process. It undoubtedly will require the technical assistance of a media specialist. The presentation should address all the issues that were identified in the market survey.

Once the presentation has been developed, it should be shown first to campaign chairs and volunteers to ensure they have a full understanding of its contents, to answer any questions they may have, and to correct any technical errors. Once formal approval is gained from the campaign committee, the appropriate community groups should be made aware of its availability.

A Campaign Song

A campaign song is a good project for students working on the campaign. It serves as a creative activity and involves them in a tangible way. The song could be recorded by the school choir and used as background for TV or radio ads. Additional opportunities to sing the song may come if students are asked to present programs at community activities. Be sure to obtain publisher approval if adapting a song that is still under copyright.

The Question of the Day

Well before the campaign begins, approach newspapers, radio stations, and cable TV to see if they would, without cost, publish or announce as a public service a question and answer to be provided by the campaign committee for each day of the campaign. If they agree, set up a schedule so that the same question is used on the radio and newspaper on the same day. The schedule could be structured so that the critical questions get repeated several times during the campaign.

The Campaign Brochure

A good brochure should be the centerpiece of campaign strategy. It must be planned and produced well in advance and be ready for distribution about three weeks before the election. The brochure should be attractive but not so slick that the voters see it as an extravagant use of taxpayers' money. The text should be easy to read in five to seven minutes. It should include the tax tables and a question-and-answer section that addresses the major positive and negative issues.

Radio and TV Call-in Programs

Call-in programs on local radio stations and community cable television are other outlets for getting across the campaign message. These programs will need to be staffed by a panel that is well informed about the campaign issues, including representatives of the board of education, campaign leadership, and school administration. Also consider including teachers, students, and parents who will add a different perspective. If there is a campaign song, use it to introduce and close the program. Show the campaign videotape if the program is televised.

To ensure that important issues are addressed, arrange to have designated persons call in with specific questions, which the panel will be prepared in advance to answer. If possible, reserve the right to screen questions that are irrelevant or inappropriate. It is best to schedule call-in programs toward the end of the campaign when specific issues need to be clarified or refuted.

Newspaper Coverage

The local newspaper offers several avenues for carrying the campaign message. Consider using the following:

General coverage: Most newspapers cover school district news on a regular basis. Some even assign a reporter full time to cover the schools. If the school district previously has established good relationships with the education reporter and/or the editor, then the newspaper is likely to be cooperative in covering general campaign news.

Letters to the editor: During the course of the campaign, there should be a sequence of letters to the editor, from different constituencies, addressing key questions and emphasizing the benefits that the levy or bond issue will provide. Some of these letters will come unsolicited, but do not wait for them. Designate respected persons in the community to send letters to the editor. Of course, there will likely be negative letters from those opposing the levy. Certain individuals from the campaign committee should be prepared to respond to negative letters immediately, especially when they contain false or erroneous information.

Editorial endorsement: If you can obtain it, editorial endorsement of the levy or bond issue can be a powerful weapon in the campaign. Be prepared to provide the editor with information about school finances and other issues related to the levy.

School page: In many communities, the newspaper has a section devoted to student activities and student opinion. This presents an excellent opportunity for students to express their views about the campaign issues. Students can be very persuasive when it comes to extolling the benefits they will derive from the levy passage.

Question of the day: Mentioned earlier, this feature in a newspaper keeps the issues before the public on a regular basis during the campaign.

Paid advertising: Postelection surveys have shown that paid advertising in newspapers is effective in influencing voters (Wise, Graham, & Bachman, 1986). A common type of paid advertising is an endorsement from business and civic leaders in the community. Another approach is to ask businesses to include a "slug" in their own ads near election time—for example, "Vote yes for our school's future."

Radio and TV Coverage

Like newspapers, local radio and public-access TV stations can be used to good advantage for the levy campaign. Call-in programs and "question of the day" formats are possibilities. If the school district has a weekly program, that time can be devoted to discussion of various campaign issues. Other possibilities are:

Special programming: Local radio and TV stations may be willing to carry special programs that have been prepared in advance on audio or videotape. One program might introduce the campaign leadership to the community. Another might discuss the vital issues in the campaign. Still another might focus solely on economic issues.

Public service announcements: Many cable television operations have a "weather screen" channel, which in addition to reporting the weather carries other short messages on the screen. The campaign committee should investigate to see if the TV station would consider running a campaign message at no cost as a public service announcement.

Paid advertising: Buying TV time is expensive. If a decision is made to use it, be sure that the ad is of professional quality in terms of graphics, sound, and narration. The ad copy should highlight the issues identified in any earlier market analysis. If there is a campaign song, it might be used as a lead-in or conclusion for the ad.

Town Hall Meetings

A town hall type of meeting provides an open forum for anyone in the community to ask questions about the levy or bond issue. Members of the board of education, school administration, and the campaign committee should be on hand to answer questions, to reaffirm the positive benefits to be derived from the levy, and to refute any misinformation being circulated. Such a meeting offers a way to neutralize any "We haven't been given all the facts" criticism. As with call-in programs, it is useful to have "plants" ask questions that the campaign committee wants to address publicly. Be sure to invite the media to cover the meeting, since their reports will reach those who were not in attendance.

School Tour and Model Display

Those who have recently been inside a school building are more likely to be positive voters (Wise, Graham, & Bachman, 1986). A good way to get voters into the school is to give them an opportunity to see a model of the proposed new facility or the school renovation project that the bond issue will fund. Architects are usually willing to construct a model since their contract depends on the passage of the bond issue. Also request that they prepare a floor plan that shows the number and size of rooms, the activity areas, labs, gymnasium, and so forth.

Combine the showing of the model and floor plans with a tour of the building that features different aspects of the school's programs and displays of students' work. Conclude the tour by showing the campaign videotape and handing out campaign literature. Involve parent organizations and students in publicizing the model display and school tour. Students can also serve as tour guides.

Main Street Projects

Letters to Employees.   Consider approaching local business leaders to see if they would be willing to send a letter to their employees discussing the merits of the levy or bond issue and how it will likely affect the local economy and their specific business and encouraging employees to vote yes. A variation on this is to request permission to place a campaign poster on the company's bulletin boards. (These approaches may not be appropriate if the business has had a history of labor problems and employee morale is low.)

Statement Stuffers.   Banks and utility companies often include stuffers on a variety of topics as a public service in their monthly statements. Inquire to see if they will include a stuffer on the levy or bond issue election. The stuffer should be prepared well in advance and must be designed to fit into the size of envelope used by the bank or utility.

Table Tents.   Seek permission from businesses and firms in public buildings that have a lot of in-and-out traffic to set up a table tent to display campaign materials. Remember to assign someone on the campaign committee to keep the table supplied with materials.

Student Projects

Windshield Washing.   A unique way to involve students in a campaign is to ask service station operators to allow students to wash the windshields of customers, free. After cleaning the windshield, the student would give the driver a card that says, "We are pleased to clean your windshield. We hope you can see your way clear to vote YES on _____." The pun will win a smile and perhaps even a vote.

Parades.   If the time of the year is appropriate, consider holding a parade on the Saturday before the election. A parade might include the high school band, drill teams, and student groups who pass out campaign brochures to people along the parade route. The parade could conclude downtown with brief remarks from campaign chairs and others who can give one last push to convince people to come out and vote "yes."

Menugrams

Many schools distribute a weekly lunch menu, which students take home and post prominently on the refrigerator door. In many homes it is the most frequently referred-to piece of literature the school publishes. Reserve space on the menugram to place a brief message about the levy campaign that urges parents to vote "yes" on election day.

Lapel Badges

A distinctive lapel badge or pin carrying the campaign logo or slogan can be worn by campaign workers as they make their rounds in the neighborhoods. Many companies make these pins with only a short lead time. Ordering in large quantities keeps the unit cost low.

Announcements at Athletic Events

Campaign information or inserts can be included in the printed programs for athletic events. Many schools now have electronic scoreboards that can carry messages as well as the team scores. Use this technology to present a brief message to a large audience. Another approach is to have campaign workers pass out brochures as people come through the gates.

EXAMPLES OF SUCCESSFUL CAMPAIGNS

The authors have employed the procedures discussed above in consulting work with public schools since 1977. A thorough application of the marketing approach to the presentation of levies and bond issues has produced numerous success stories, and one of those stories is the basis for the case study concluding this chapter. Other cases have brought similarly encouraging results:

1. A bond issue campaign had failed in four earlier efforts that had used more-traditional "selling" activities. After a market analysis revealed the real issues surrounding the situation to be economic rather than educational, a market-based campaign was successful with a margin of victory of 68 to 32 percent. The issue passed in every precinct of the district, and the new high school became a reality.
2. An operating levy had failed badly on two previous occasions. A "scouting report" identified issues that had never been addressed, and the new campaign addressed those issues, publicizing an accurate estimate of taxpayer cost and a thorough explanation of how funds were to be spent. The result was a resounding 62 to 38 percent victory at the polls.
3. District leadership was uncertain of their next step following the crushing defeat of a broad-based issue. A market analysis tested for positive and negative issues involved in several different options the district was considering. A market-acceptable option was selected, presented to district voters, and easily passed.

POTENTIAL PITFALLS

There is no such thing as a sure thing in funding campaigns. The activities presented here are campaign-proven to be effective, but since no two situations or campaigns are identical, it is impossible to *guarantee* that certain specific steps/strategies/tactics will always result in victory. Some pitfalls can generally be identified and overcome by timely and adequate planning, funding, and volunteer effort.

The most serious pitfalls to a successful campaign include the following:

1. A late start in getting input from the market (the "scouting report")—or no time to gain such input, which inevitably leads to "flying blind" in developing campaign strategy and tactics.
2. A lack of campaign workers. These "troops in the trenches" are at the heart of a successful campaign. Given a choice between unlimited funds for advertising and an adequate supply of willing-to-train-and-work campaign volunteers, the authors will always select—and usually win with—the latter.
3. A campaign organization composed solely of the elite of the community. A grassroots campaign team will generally create the best image, deliver the most credible message, and turn out the hardest-working volunteers. In most communities a significant presence of blue-collar workers is to be preferred over an organization staffed by only the upper socioeconomic segment of the district.
4. The presence of organized opposition. A formidable foe, their presence gives many undecided voters an excuse to withhold their support.
5. A split in support for the campaign among members of the school board. Again, such a situation gives many persons who may not have strong or compelling reasons to vote "yes" a reason to rationalize a "no" vote.

Although the pitfalls noted above stand out in general, there will almost always be specific negatives encountered in a local campaign. These will frequently include:

1. Perceptions of high fringe benefits for teachers—or administrators
2. Perception of too many frills, a top-heavy administration
3. A past closing of a treasured school building
4. A past consolidation of schools within the district, resulting in the loss of identity for one or more neighborhood schools
5. Past abuse, scandals, or perceived sins of earlier school boards, superintendents, or teachers

SUMMARY

The point has been made earlier, but it bears repeating here for additional emphasis: Public relations *must* be a continuing effort for the schools. It must *not* be trotted out just before a levy or bond issue campaign. Much of the content of this book is directed toward the application of public relations concepts and tools on a *continuing basis*.

In the increasingly skeptical, often hostile, environment in which the schools exist today, the need for effective, ongoing public relations skills is enormously important. Regardless of the title given to the activities or to the position within the organizational structure of the schools, it is vital that schools pay far more than lip service to public relations efforts.

CASE STUDY

Learning from the Market

Residents of a suburban school district defeated a $10.5 million bond issue by a vote of 64 percent against, 36 percent for. The bond had included the following components:

1. An addition to the present middle school, which would permit all sixth-, seventh-, and eighth-graders to attend one facility
2. Removal of asbestos from the elementary buildings and the middle school
3. Locker and training rooms for boys and girls at the high school
4. Remodeling of elementary buildings to add classrooms and increase energy conservation
5. Addition of a gymnasium/multipurpose room at the high school
6. Additional instructional facilities—library/media center, art room, music room, science labs—at the high school

Before putting any further bond issues back on the ballot, the school board decided to conduct a market survey and use the results to guide a new campaign. A survey instrument was developed and a sample of 300 households was chosen for door-to-door interviews. The survey question and results are shown in Table 14–1.

TABLE 14–1
Survey Question and Results

Which of the components from the previous bond campaign did you consider Indispensable, Very important, Somewhat important, or Not important?

Component	% Indispensable	% Very Important	% Somewhat Important	% Not Important
Addition to middle school	18	35	32	15
Asbestos removal	59	23	10	7
Locker and training rooms	7	25	42	26
Remodeling elementaries	22	43	28	7
Gym/multipurpose	3	13	36	48
Additional instructional facilities	14	38	32	15

TABLE 14–2
Projecting the Vote

Component Combinations	Cost in $	% For
All six components as before	10.5 million	28.6
Build new middle school	6.5 million	36.3
Build new middle school and asbestos removal	7.8 million	37.9
Remodel elementaries, build addition to middle school, asbestos removal	5.3 million	40.6
Remodel elementaries and build addition to middle school	4.0 million	39.7

In analyzing the survey results, the district found that the top five factors encouraging a vote for were

1. Explain *why* money is needed and *how* it will be spent.
2. Allow elementary school children to attend a neighborhood school.
3. Eliminate overcrowding at the elementary schools.
4. Prepare for growth in enrollment.
5. Avoid cost increases that will accompany a wait-and-see stance.

Analysis also revealed that the top five factors encouraging a vote against were

1. Building now will increase property taxes.
2. The information from the last campaign was not sufficient.
3. New industrial property has been tax-abated.
4. Renovation of the board of education building last year was unnecessary.
5. Operation of new or expanded schools is bound to increase property taxes.

When the district projected the for vote for different combinations of the six bond components, they came up with the figures given in Table 14–2.

QUESTIONS AND SUGGESTED ACTIVITIES

Case Study

1. Which combination of components would you put on the ballot? Explain.
2. Design the strategies and tactics you would use in the campaign.
3. Prepare five ads to be used for TV, radio, and print.
4. Prepare ten "questions of the day" to be used in a brochure and in the newspaper.
5. Prepare three letters to the editor addressing the positive and negative issues that were identified.
6. Prepare an outline for the scenes and write the script of a videotape presentation.

Chapter

1. Form a focus group (or two) from your community and discuss school issues and concerns. Use the results of the discussion(s) to prepare a market survey.

2. Give the survey prepared from the activity above to a sample of community members. Analyze the results.

3. Use the survey results to design promotional materials and/or activities.

SUGGESTED READINGS

Conyers, J. G., & France, T. (1989, October). We turned to Madison Avenue for tips on selling our $64 million bond issue. *The American School Board Journal, 176*(10), 27–28.

Fowler, F. J., Jr. (1993). *Survey research methods* (2nd ed.). Thousand Oaks, CA: Sage Publications.

Hansen, B. J. (1985, Winter). Marketing educational change to school boards. *Educational Horizons, 63*(2), 84–85.

Hanson, C. B. (1969, July). How to pass a bond issue. *School Management, 13*(7), 67–69.

Harrison, C. H. (1972, March). In bond campaign, publicize the need, not the proposal. *Nation's Schools,* pp. 77–78.

Konick, E., Jr. (1978, October). A miracle—one can perform—passed this board's referendum. *The American School Board Journal, 165*(10), 46–47.

Kotler, P., & Andreasen, A. (1991). *Strategic marketing for nonprofit organizations* (4th ed). Englewood Cliffs, NJ: Prentice Hall.

Lane, J. J. (Ed.) (1986). *Marketing techniques for school districts.* Reston, VA: Association of School Business Officials.

Panas, J. (1971, March). But some districts still do win school referendums. *The American School Board Journal, 158*(9), 40–42.

Tonigan, R. (1971, July). How to pass the bonds to get the plants to keep maintained. *School Management, 15*(7), 41, 48.

Weir, R. W., Jr. (1981, February). Four key suggestions for winning bond elections. *The American School Board Journal, 168*(2), 37–38.

Whitman, R. L., & Pittner, N. A. (1990). *Planning, promoting, and passing school tax issues,* (rev. ed.). Columbus, OH: Ohio School Boards Association.

REFERENCES

Arfim, H., & Colton, R. R. (1971). *Tables for statisticians.* New York: Barnes and Noble College Outline Series.

Graham, G. T., & Wise, G. L. (1990). Marketing for the school administrator: Tracking the variables that ruin the best laid plans. *Record in Educational Administration and Supervision, 11*(1), 64–69.

Graham, G. T., Wise, G. L., & Bachman, D. L. (1990). *Successful strategies for marketing school levies* (Fastback No. 310). Bloomington, IN: Phi Delta Kappa.

Wise, G. L., & Graham, G. T. (1993). Using the "scouting report" in a market-centered development of policy and programs for the schools. *Record in Educational Administration and Supervision, 14*(1), 54–56.

Wise, G. L., Graham, G. T., & Bachman, D. L. (1986). *Marketing levies and bond issues for public schools* (University Monograph No. 7). Dayton, OH: Wright State University.

CHAPTER 15

Evaluating Public Relations Programs
Doug Newsom

In a budget-driven economy, whether an educational organization is a public or private entity is inconsequential. Nor does it matter whether it is a college or university or a lower-level school. Results from expenditures have to be demonstrated in tangible and credible ways. The myth that public relations activities are not measurable may result in their not being funded. The primary role of the public relations professional is to offer counsel in strategic planning that delivers measurable results.

Strategic planning begins with the organization's own mission statement, which is at the core of all decision making. Most accrediting agencies recognize that when they do their evaluations. An ongoing monitoring and evaluation program by the public relations office can generate the documentation wanted by accrediting agencies—and give direction to policy makers by identifying problems and opportunities as they arise.

EVALUATION OF THE MISSION STATEMENT

An organization's mission statement should undergo frequent review as discussed in Chapter 10. If the organization *and* its socioeconomic and political environment are relatively stable, then every five to seven years is acceptable frequency. But if an organization undergoes dramatic change, then the mission statement should be quickly reevaluated. It should be reviewed first by *every* internal public. While this adds to the time and expense of the review effort, it is a valuable learning experience for participants and it can build morale.

One way to initiate a review is to send the mission statement to each unit for study and feedback to top-level administrators. However, this may not be very effective because of resistance to change in some units, especially if their authority is threatened. Another way is to appoint committees in each unit, such as administrative staff, staff, faculty and support groups, including student government and faculty governance groups.

These committees need a structure by which to examine the viability of the mission statement. Each word needs to be examined to see how every part of the mission statement can be translated to specific activities of the organization. Sample questions that need to be asked are What does this statement mean? How is it now being interpreted? What is the organization doing now that demonstrates this statement of the mission?

When these reports are in, a central committee formed of members from each unit group, preferably selected by the units themselves rather than appointed by the administration, can write a consensus critique that goes back out to the units for affirmation or dissent with explanation.

Yet another way to arrive at a qualitative/quantitative evaluation of the mission statement is to use focus-group interviews (FGI), followed by a questionnaire. The results of FGIs are sometimes accepted as substitutes for legitimate research, which is a serious methodological mistake. FGIs should be used only to gain insights into questions to be included in a questionnaire and into how those questions should be asked. Effective FGI techniques require careful selection of homogeneous groups within units and inclusion of enough groups to represent the diversity of the unit. The selection of participants should be dictated by an organization's characteristics. Panels should have no more than twelve participants nor fewer than five. The ideal is eight to ten. To build good dialogue in an FGI usually takes from two to three hours. The moderator needs to be skilled in conducting FGIs so that responses are not biased by his or her questions or behavior. All participants must be drawn into the discussion.

Videotaping the focus groups allows for more definitive analysis of the discussion, since nonverbal behavior may contradict what is being said. However, in some organizations, members of a focus group prefer to remain anonymous. If the review of the mission statement is controversial, it is better to use only an audiotape of the proceedings. The key issue is to analyze results for adjectives and adjectival phrases that tend to reveal points of view as well as the language used by the participants to describe common concepts. These become semantic road maps leading to questions that are more easily understood.

The survey that follows FGIs should use bipolar scales, thus allowing for degrees of intensity of response. The survey instrument must be pretested with a few respondents representative of the same units participating in the focus groups, yet members of the focus groups should not be included in the pretest. The pretest is used to check validity and to spot problems that can be corrected.

There is also a strictly quantitative way to review mission statements: the DELPHI process. Participants may be chosen randomly or by quota sample. (A quota sample may also be selected randomly.) Usually cost and acceptable sampling error are considerations. Questionnaires that elicit open-ended responses are sent directly—not through supervisors—to participants. The questions asked—Is it our mission to make students good citizens of the world?—might prompt whole paragraphs in response. Participants' responses are compiled *without editing* and sent back to them. After they have read everyone's response to the questions, they are asked to rate the responses on a numeric scale. They might rank their own response below another's to the same question. (Perhaps, for example, one might prefer "First let's be sure they develop a sense of self-esteem and social responsibility" to his or her own response: "We need to make them good citizens of their immediate community first.") The respondents' rankings are then totaled and a collective order given to edit the responses. The response that receives the most first-place rankings is placed at the top of the list, and so forth. This collective rank ordering makes it possible to edit the responses and arrange ideas into categories or statements. These statements then are sent back to the participants. The two-way process can go through several phases until ideas are clarified. Eventually, the results can help mutually redefine or reaffirm an organization's mission.

EVALUATION OF POSITIONING STRATEGIES

Although a mission statement should be the focus for all of an organization's activities, the statement itself does not define how an organization wants to be seen by all its publics. That is the purpose of a positioning strategy, which is also expressed as a statement. For example, a strategic positioning statement for a university in an oil-and-gas-producing area might be that it wants its publics to see it as *the* university for research breakthroughs. A high school might want to be known as a leader in combining vocational and liberal arts, or it might want to be seen as offering the best opportunities for students with learning disabilities.

The positioning strategy is drawn from an interpretation of the mission statement. It is usually written by top management, then sent out for evaluation by internal publics, but more support for and agreement with the positioning strategy usually comes from inclusion of those internal publics, especially faculty and administrative staff, in the development process. Be aware that fashioning a positioning statement is likely to be a more contentious process than drafting the mission statement because some constituencies within an organization may see the strategic position targeted as excluding them.

Existing position strategies should be reviewed qualitatively in the same way as mission statements are, especially if priority external publics are included. While it's imperative for internal publics to agree about the mission, the primary advantage of having a strategic positioning statement is to focus the opinions of external publics.

Proposed or existing positions can be reviewed quantitatively by a telephone survey of internal and external publics. This process not only validates the positioning, but also gives some evidence of the effectiveness of the organization in communicating its self-image.

USE OF EVALUATIONS IN PLANNING, REPORTING, AND COUNSELING

The way publics see the organization living up to its self-defined role is critical to the financial and moral support the organization gets. Evaluating public *perceptions* of how well the organization has achieved its goals and objective—inspired by its mission statement and focused by its positioning strategy—is as important as documenting its achievements. Many accrediting reviews attest to this in that they ask for the *opinions* of both internal and external publics as well as hard evidence on such matters as promotion and testing results at the lower levels and retention and graduation statistics at the college level.

Planning

Decisions about emphases, which is what positioning is all about, always have budget implications. Because funding is important at all levels of education—only the funding mechanism differs—it's necessary to monitor the publics to locate problems that might have funding implications. The opinions of one public might correlate with the opinions of another. For example, faculty complaints about broken, worn-out equipment may correlate with student complaints about classroom resources. The weight of such attitudes may result in a counselor's steering students away from a certain educational institution or in complaints from parents about priorities.

Results of internal and external evaluations can help set priorities and establish systems for maintaining what is working well for a school. They can also validate aggressive leadership or risk taking on the part of administrators. Evaluations should not only anticipate problems that can be addressed in planning, they should also help substantiate decisions.

Reporting

Evaluations give authority to reporting requirements of all institutions. Organizations must justify actions to a plethora of oversight groups, from regulatory and accrediting agencies to special interest groups. Monitoring and evaluating on a regular basis offers credible benchmarks for progress made and justifies actions taken. Monitoring and evaluating activities also provide opportunities to communicate an organization's effectiveness to different constituencies. Survey results often generate responses from publics and influence opinions.

Counseling

Counseling is a reasoned recommendation based on sound *evidence*, not necessarily *experience*. Counseling—a primary public relations function—is not an "I think" process. Acceptable evidence must come from ongoing monitoring and evaluation. Counseling is most critical, of course, when there is a crisis. Crisis counseling, sometimes called "reputation management," is often needed in a situation where the reputation can no longer be "managed" because of prior action or inaction. However, sound counsel can come from evidence of how priority, and sometimes nonpriority, publics are likely to respond.

INDENTIFYING AND MONITORING AN ORGANIZATION'S PUBLICS

Every organization has easily identifiable publics. Consider at least eight categories, with multiple levels in each: media publics, member publics, employee, community, investor, government, consumer, and special publics (Hendrix, 1992, 13–16).

Media publics include print and broadcast mass and specialized media—national, state, and local. *Member* publics for a school include all of the special organizations within the institution, from honoraries to professional groups, many with outside constituencies.

Employee publics include the management and nonmanagement staff, and may include labor unions. *Community* publics include community media—mass and specialized—and community leaders and organizations. *Investor* publics for educational institutions are all private parties involved financially with the institution, either as individuals or as foundations. *Government* publics include all levels—federal, state, and local—and all branches—executive, legislative, and judicial. These obviously include taxpayers. *Consumer* publics for schools includes students, parents, and all institutions that contract with the school for services such as research. *Special* publics are organizations like religious, political, civic, cultural, business, service, or youth groups or activist groups like textbook watchdog organizations—and the media used by these special groups.

It is important to develop and maintain a complete list of an organization's publics. But it is unreasonable to monitor all of them carefully all of the time, which is why organizations prioritize their publics according to normal business needs. While prioritizing ordinarily works fairly well, it can create blind spots. Trouble may be brewing with a nonpriority public and go unobserved until it becomes a problem. It's a good idea to schedule nonpriority publics for occasional monitoring. If national trends in education seem to indicate an interest on the part of some of these publics, these groups should be given priority standing until the trend is understood.

One way of prioritizing publics is to use a PVI index (P = VI), which is an informal measure of a *public* in terms of the organization's ability to *influence* or *impact* that public (on a scale of 1 to 10) and the *vulnerability* of the organization to action by that public. Although not a true "index," a PVI index can provide a rank for each public in relationship to the organization.

THE RESEARCH BASIS OF MONITORING A PUBLIC

Informal Research Methods

Three basic informal methods of measurement are available: unobtrusive measures, audits, and publicity analysis. (Newsom, Scott, & Turk, 1993, pp. 112–113).

Unobtrusive measures are observations that don't intrude on the process of gathering data. One such measure might be color-coding tickets to a performance or lecture so you can see which publics are most responsive to that offering. Sometimes this helps determine whether the activity is worth doing again. Such measures are indicators but not very reliable indicators. For instance, a ticket may be given to someone else.

Audits are much more structured and reliable, especially if they employ formal research methods. Audits can help discover the opinions and attitudes of various publics toward an organization, its actions, and its policies. They are most likely to include survey research, although not necessarily. Communication audits are a common public relations tool because organizations must evaluate the effectiveness of their communication with their publics. The communication audit weighs what an organization *intends* to communicate and what its communicators *think* they are communicating against what outside publics think the organization is saying and their reactions to those communications. Disparities between the two perceptions are then examined, and recommendations for improvement are made.

In analyzing publicity, organizations use print media clippings and transcripts from broadcast publicity to see how effective their efforts are in gaining recognition for the organization. The *publicity analysis* can be done according to audience, medium, message, frequency, and, sometimes, context. Publicity about the organization is also examined for its positive and negative content. Often the analysis makes an effort to weight the value of the publicity according to the prestige of the medium, the amount of time or space, and the significance of the medium to priority audiences.

Table 15–1 lists the pluses and minuses of the three basic informal methods of evaluating a public's perception of an organization.

Formal Research Methods

Formal research methods are *qualitative* or *quantitative* in technique. *Qualitative* measures include the use of focus groups and panels; in-depth interviews that are fairly self-explanatory; and case studies, diaries, and historiography. *Quantitative* techniques are varied, but the methods most commonly used in educational public relations are content analyses and surveys. Whether the method used is qualitative or quantitative, researcher bias is always an issue (Newsom, Scott, &Turk, 1993, p.113). Advantages and disadvantages of the various methods are shown in Table 15–2.

TABLE 15–1
Advantages and Disadvantages of Various Informal Research Methods, All Qualitative

Method	Advantages	Disadvantages
Unobtrusive measures	No "intrusion" affects the publics. They yield physical evidence. They can be less costly and more convenient.	There can be investigative error. There can be record error. They yield fixed data. They yield some physical evidence not appropriate to psychological or sociological study.
Audits	They make it possible to locate problems in the making. They can detect breaks in the communication chain. They help develop images held by different publics.	They involve special sensitivity to the "guinea-pig" effect—that is, awareness of the measure itself. They can be insensitive to confidentiality. People with less formal schooling may give only socially acceptable answers. They can encourage response to visible cues from the interviewer.
Publicity analysis	It shows evidence of efforts. It suggests other opportunities.	It has the same disadvantages as do unobtrusive measures. It yields incomplete documentation. It is difficult to put in context. It is not a measure of audience impact.

Note: Adapted from Newsom, Scott, & Turk, Belmont, 1993, p. 107. Reprinted with permission.

TABLE 15–2
Advantages and Disadvantages of Various Formal Research Methods

Method	Advantages	Disadvantages
Qualitative Focus groups	Feedback can be quick and less expensive than with other research methods.	They are often used as giving conclusive evidence when they are merely tools used for subsequent research.
	They are flexible in design and format.	They can be mishandled by the moderator so that not all participants express opinions.
	They elicit more in-depth information and often point out "whys" of behavior, as well as showing intensity of attitudes held.	They are often not representative of the research universe.
Panels	The advantages here are the same as with focus groups.	They involve the same disadvantages as focus groups.
	They may be chosen to represent a specific population.	Panelists over time may "learn" some of the reasons for difficulties and cease to be representative.
In-depth interviews	They allow ways to follow up on new lines of questioning.	They are difficult to transcribe and code for content analysis.
	They permit respondents to describe in detail, thereby making more information available.	The interviewer sometimes "leads the witness," or otherwise influences responses.
	They permit questions that are broader, more comprehensive in scope.	Responses often include basically meaningless information.
Historiography, case studies, and diaries	They give insights into situations. They suggest further research to examine the "whys" that it indicated.	They are difficult to generalize from. They often lack the rigor of the scientific method.
	They provide detail that can put other research into perspective.	They are time-consuming and require boiling down a lot of data that are sometimes selectively presented.
Quantitative Content analyses	They show what appeared, how often, where, and in what context.	They can be expensive and time-consuming.
	They allow comparison with other data, especially about publics.	They provide no information about the impact of a message on an audience.
	They can be useful in tracking trends and in monitoring change.	Some information may not be in the media.
Surveys	They are flexible.	Respondents may not tell the truth because they don't remember accurately or because they want to appear different from their behavior.
	They can be varied—administered by mail, telephone, computer, personal, or group interview.	They are inflexible, allowing for no expression of intensity of true feelings.
	They capitalize on the enjoyment of expressing one's opinion.	The wrong questions may be asked of the wrong people in wrong way.

Note: Adapted from Newsom, Scott, & Turk, 1993, pp. 112–113. Reprinted with permission

Ethical and Legal Ramifications of Research

Ethical and legal problems can occur during the research process. Ethical issues include honesty in the gathering of data and in consideration of subjects—not adversely affecting them nor misrepresenting to them who wants to know what and why. Confidentiality must be preserved, if that is a factor, and there must be no misrepresentation of the results, or "cooking the data," which can occur with both qualitative and quantitative measurements.

These are concerns whether the research is being done in-house or by a vendor. When the research is bought from an outside contractor, it's imperative that the public relations person understand the methodology well enough to judge its validity and to determine if the conclusions drawn are legitimate.

Breaches of confidentiality can cause harm to respondents and invite legal problems. For example, people identified in focus groups or through survey responses may be fired or transferred as a result of disclosure of their identities. It's also important to be sure that in reporting results, such as candid responses to an audit, respondents are not damaged in a way that might produce a libel suit.

The accumulation and storage of data can open up possibilities for both ethical and legal problems, so research results must be protected. If results are shared in industry, trade, or professional publications, the name of the organization as well as of all respondents should be masked unless specific, written permission for disclosure is given.

MONITORING PROGRAMS FOR DECISION MAKING AND FINE-TUNING

The critical importance of monitoring is as a preventive device. For everything planned, some measure of evaluation must be built in or there is no accountability.

Adjusting and Meeting Expectations of the Publics

Publics are generally defined as people who share a common interest. For convenience, publics are often referred to as internal or external, but these are artificial boundaries. Through ongoing involvement, for example, many alumni make themselves members of internal publics and have to be considered as such. Thus, while alumni are usually classified as an external public, an alumni group may include many who are also members of a school's internal public.

Likewise, the parents and grandparents who give public schools their time as volunteers and are at the school almost as regularly as teachers and staff see themselves as an internal public. Faculty and staff are often members of a school's donor public, as well as being employees of the institution. It's very important to keep the vagueness of these classifications in mind when dealing with publics and certainly in prioritizing and monitoring them.

Public relations people use research to identify publics and their characteristics. This helps practictitioners prioritize these publics. They also evaluate the ongoing relationships these publics have with an organization, especially in particular situations such as crises. They then use the media to reach these publics. Media alternatives must be researched thoroughly to determine which one or combination is most effective as a delivery system. It is also necessary to monitor these media to see their effects on publics. (See Tables 15–3 and 15–4.)

A public has to be clearly identified before it can be conceptualized. There is no such thing as a "general public." A public doesn't exist unless a mailing list can be created for it. Even the mass media know exactly who their publics are and can give very clear descriptions of those they are reaching. That's how they sell time and space. They are selling audiences made up of real people.

An educational institution's publics generally have high expectations, which makes delivery sometimes difficult. Determining exactly what each public's expectations are is an important purpose of monitoring. Another is finding how satisfied a public is with the match of expectations and reality.

Some universities have used exit interviews very effectively to detect why students leave before graduating. Graduates are asked how much value they place in the degrees they have earned. Seniors are asked to demonstrate the level of their appreciation (a match of expectation with experience) through senior giving programs. But these types of surveys have all the flaws of other unobtrusive measures. Exit interviews are informal and not subjected to content analysis, which would make evaluation more significant. Alumni are sometimes surveyed, but usually only for accreditation purposes. Why should they be surveyed only occasionally? There's much to be gained from carrying out regular surveys of all important publics.

TABLE 15–3
Prioritizing Publics

Internal Communication	External Communication	
Publics	Direct (marketing communications)	Indirect (institutional communications)
Management: Top and middle	Customers: Students	Potential customers
Staff/employees: Faculty, union, nonunion, employee organizations	Sales representatives: Admissions	Potential investors
Stakeholders	Traders and distributors Recommenders	Financial community
Directors, trustees, regents	Suppliers	Special community of the institution
	Competitors	Government (all levels) Community (total environment)

Note: Adapted with permission from Newsom, Scott, & Turk, 1993, p. 168.

TABLE 15–4
Media Alternatives

Internal Communication	External Communication
Personal One to one and one to group	Personal
Audiovisual Specialized media: films, slides, videotapes, closed-circuit TV, computer networks	Audiovisual Specialized media available to external audiences
Publications Specialized media: books, newspapers, magazines, newsletters	Publications Mass and specialized media: controlled and uncontrolled publicity; institutional and commercial advertising
Direct mail	Direct mail Personalized, institutional, and promotional
Exhibits Posters, bulletin boards, personalized items	Exhibits Mass and specialized
Critics Individual and institutional	

Note: Adapted with permission from Newsom, Scott, & Turk, 1993, p. 168.

Determining Levels of Acceptance for Policies

Even before a policy is put in place, the likelihood of its acceptance by various publics can be evaluated. If publics have been carefully described by their demographics and psychographics, a statement about the policy can be pretested on a sample to get reactions. A more common way among educational institutions is to form a panel of affected publics to review the proposed policy. The method used is often dictated by organizational culture and an institution's relationship to the publics involved.

A survey of a college's faculty can determine what their reaction might be to keeping specific, posted, weekly office hours or their reaction to using discretionary funds to hire minority faculty. It's better to find out that a proposed policy may be opposed than to have to fight for an unpopular policy once it's put into force — or, even worse, to have to withdraw a failed policy.

These hypothetical policy issues have gradations of levels of acceptance. Focus-group interviews can provide the basis for a questionnaire to be sent to the larger public. Responses can help determine what sort of policy would meet the most resistance and be likely to cause serious problems.

Budgeting Aspects of Monitoring and Evaluation

Monitoring all publics all of the time in great detail is generally not cost-effective for any organization. Educational institutions generally have fewer resources for such operations, so they must be selective. However, an audit can be done once a year for each high-priority public, just as audits are done for other aspects of the institution. This produces longitudinal documentation for decision making. The audit of nonpriority publics on a revolving basis can then be budgeted.

Every communications project should have a monitoring and evaluation component built into its budget. Budget levels can vary dramatically, depending on the size and elaborateness of a project—ranging from a simple homecoming event to a capital fund-raising or bond issue campaign. Monitoring and evaluation costs should be at least 3 percent of the overall budget. This allows for extensive monitoring of the primary publics and a sound evaluation of all tactics used to implement strategies. One way to save money is to design monitoring systems that will help build toward a final evaluation. Unobtrusive measures combined with more formal monitoring processes can pull together evidence so that by adding some in-depth interviews the evidence may be put into perspective for evaluation.

Assessing and Recommending Policy

Public relations practitioners have to function as internal counsel to management. If there is no opportunity to affect policy, then what they are doing is *publicity*, not public relations. The evaluation of policy is a part of the public relations counseling process. Policies should be considered as a fundamental part of the auditing process. What are publics saying or doing that would cause some sort of new policy to be considered? What are publics doing that may suggest the level of policy effectiveness? Some policies may not be working. Others may be working but having a detrimental effect on attitudes and opinions among some publics. That could suggest a change.

Information already accumulated for other reasons may be a rich resource for public relations people. Information from routine record keeping sometimes reveals trends with policy implications. One school district discovered, for example, that most of its teachers did *not* live in the district. Knowing that the city had once considered a mandate that all employees live within the city limits—or at least that a salary consideration be given those who did—the school public relations official suggested that hiring from within the city, all other considerations being equal, be instituted as a policy. The school board accepted his recommendation after considerable debate, and while not precluding the hiring of those living outside the district, new policy gave preference to those who did. And every new hire was encouraged to locate in the city rather than the suburbs. A side benefit of the new policy was that minority recruiting improved.

In order to make policy recommendations, the public relations practitioner must use existing records to determine what information the institution should collect to supplement what it is currently gathering. Basic record keeping and fact finding is something that the public relations person may have to do independent of other departments. In any case, an efficient retrieval system must be in place because the public relations person sometimes needs information at a moment's notice.

In the public relations department, it is necessary to keep easily accessible files on all forms of communication from the institution. These range from news releases and annual reports to speeches by officials. The department is also expected to keep information on what is written and said about the institution.

Combining all of this intelligence makes it possible to get a reasonably good picture of what the priority publics of the educational institution think about it—personnel, programs and facilities. A review of this information is likely to indicate some gaps that additional research may need to fill.

Assessing Results in Relation to Goals

Research should be ongoing and structured. As shown in Figure 15–1, routine research moves into developing and testing hypotheses, then revising and following up with additional research to fill in the gaps. The plan, once put in place, is monitored in all its aspects; the ongoing evaluation process is also monitored so that the final evaluation is complete enough to offer some suggestions for planning and policy making, and the cycle starts all over.

This cyclical pattern can help any institution see if it is meeting its own goals and objectives. Most organizations attempt to do this. However, what they often don't do is to see how their publics are reacting to the way goals and objectives are being accomplished. It's necessary for an organization to have such knowledge if it is to fulfill its mission statement and meet the intrinsic goals of its positioning strategy.

Evidence is sometimes available from unobtrusive measures. Chambers of commerce seek evaluations of their cities' public schools to entice companies to relocate. Real estate agents in a school district seek information about particular schools to use in selling

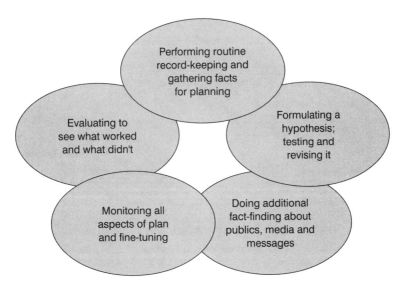

FIGURE 15.1
The Cyclical Pattern of Research (Adapted from Newsom, Scott, & Turk, 1993, p. 102)

homes in that school zone. At the university level the number of applications to a school's graduate programs is often useful information. If the university has as a goal to become the premier institution in either a region or in a field, the quality of its applicants is one indicator of whether it is meeting that goal. Another is how it is ranked among its peers. Law and medical schools attach particular significance to peer ranking. Libraries may be ranked by their overall holdings or holdings in a specific area. The problem is that in spite of documentable evidence, such as holdings, many rankings are purely opinion-based. A system must be developed, therefore, to measure how publics, especially priority publics, are perceiving the institution.

Monitoring Collective Perceptions

Collective perceptions about an organization by its publics are based on what it says and what it does. These collective perceptions constitute the organization's image. If all of these fit together so that what the organization says is consistent with what it does and fits with the mission statement, which has given people some expectations of what it *should be*, then public perception generally fits the reality fairly closely. When this is true for most of the organization's publics, the image of the institution or organization is generally clear and accurate. That image may not fit a new positioning strategy, and it may not match the

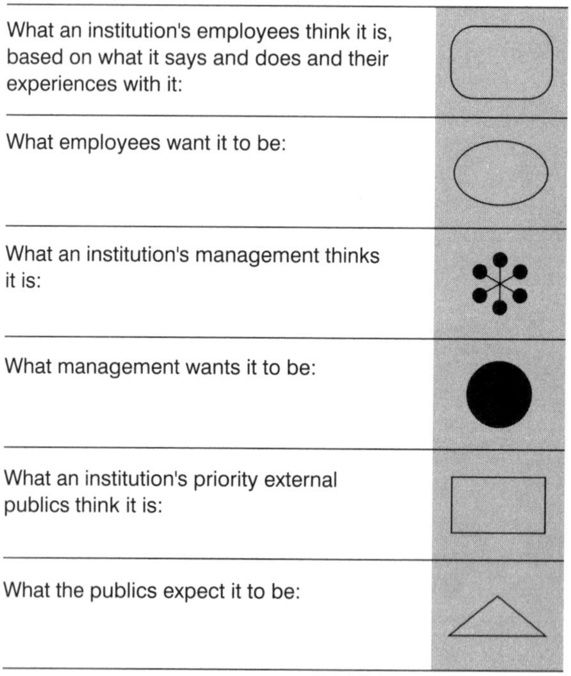

What an institution's employees think it is, based on what it says and does and their experiences with it:	
What employees want it to be:	
What an institution's management thinks it is:	
What management wants it to be:	
What an institution's priority external publics think it is:	
What the publics expect it to be:	

FIGURE 15.2

Problem Profile (Adapted with permission from Newsom, Scott, & Turk, 1993, p. 171)

organization's strategic goals—but the image will be clear and measurable. If an organization wants to change the image to reflect new positioning or new goals, it will be relatively easy to see when the image begins to change.

On the other hand, if an organization has an image that is *not* clearly defined, it may indicate two problems. One is that the organization is not communicating very well with its publics. Another is that what it is saying doesn't match what it is doing or what various publics are experiencing in their relationships with the institution. When that happens, a problem profile for an organization may began to appear.

A *problem profile* results when different priority publics hold very different views of the organization. (See Figure 15–2.) The solution is to discover through research where the discrepancies are and correct them, either through communication or through policy changes that are then clearly communicated.

Anticipating responses from all publics, especially priority publics, is key to evaluating and monitoring the climate of public opinion, another responsibility of the public relations officer. Yet this cannot be done effectively unless the officer has good evidence of the perceptions of relevant publics about the organization. The public relations practitioner (or anyone else in the institution) cannot create an image for the institution. But he or she can be effective in improving the way publics perceive an organization, a goal achieved only by monitoring public opinion, which is always in flux and is highly sensitive to events and experiences.

USING EVALUATIONS IN REACHING OUT

Sound program evaluations tell an organization how it is seen by different publics, thus supporting the identification of and an analyses of shortcomings. These evaluations are especially critical when building a precrisis constituency. They also help to determine the persuasive level at which continuing campaigns are functioning. Evaluations can also be used to estimate the persuasive level at which new campaigns should be launched. When a campaign is over, a sound evaluation indicates what succeeded with whom and why and the quality and depth of the residue of goodwill that is left for the future.

Building a Constituency before a Crisis

When an organization—educational or commercial—is involved in a crisis, it's too late to shore up relationships with its publics. That's unfortunate because in a crisis, an organization must draw on all of its resources, including good relations with its publics.

Priority publics are likely to shift somewhat in a crisis, and there's no way to predict the direction of the shift. A low-priority public in normal operating times might suddenly become critical to crisis survival. Evaluations can help guide the development of a strategy for strengthening relationships when they are not as strong as they might be.

Special publics are ones to watch when auditing relationships. These publics often have some intense, though peripheral, relationship with an educational institution. Consider animal rights groups and a university that gets funding for research involving the use of animals. Once the funding is announced, either by the funding source or the university, then the animal rights group is alerted. The university may not perceive this to be a critical point in its relationship with a public, but it is.

Through monitoring and ongoing evaluations, an organization can maintain continuing dialogue with its publics so there are no surprises on either side. An educational organization can also get a clearer understanding of how much its publics appreciate its goals and objectives, critical information in launching any campaign.

Determining Strategy According to the Persuasion Process

There is seldom a situation where an organization has only one campaign going on at once. While there may be something that has a priority, such as a school or community college's bond drive or a university's capital funding drive, there will also always be a recruiting campaign, a retention campaign or some athletic effort.

The typology of campaigns mirrors the six levels of the persuasion process. Therefore, it's critical to know the persuasive level of any priority publics *before* structuring a campaign.

A campaign to create *awareness*, the first level of the persuasion process, may be required if priority publics are not aware of the issue, problem, or need. Monitoring and evaluation processes can identify this for each public. On the other hand, since awareness campaigns are perhaps the most expensive to launch and maintain, resources can be saved if the priority publics for the campaign are already aware of the problem even if they are not really paying attention to it—perhaps because they are not convinced it is important.

A campaign to convey strong *information*, the second level of the persuasion process, is totally different in structure from an awareness campaign, both in using media and in crafting messages. Monitoring and evaluation of publics helps indicate where to start.

Suppose the knowledge of an issue among priority publics is such that there is no need to get their attention or inform them about its significance. This does not necessarily mean the publics understand what they can do about this issue, or, more important, what the educational organization *wants* them to do about it. Thus the campaign should be structured to gain the publics' *comprehension*, the third level of persuasion.

Yielding is the next level. Pitched at this level of the persuasion process, a campaign is likely to emphasize shared values as a way of gaining compliance or participation. Such a campaign is a facilitating effort aimed at getting priority publics to *act* on whatever it is they have already accepted and are ready to do. Say a university's library has been damaged by fire, the damage is widely known, and the extent of it understood; Many constituencies may be ready to help rebuild the collection; they need only be told specifically how they can help.

Publics must be encouraged to *retain* a desirable position, especially if that public has been encouraged to do something new. Suppose, for example, the burnt-out library attracts some first-time givers to the university. It would be easy to write them off as "one-timers" and be grateful for that. But it would be even better to change their attitude and behavior and convert them to regular donors.

It is possible that priority publics are already at the persuasive level of acting. But what they do now may not be exactly what is desired. If so, a campaign to modify behavior is called for. A university might, for example, ask regular donors to designated funds to consider a special undesignated gift for a capital fund drive.

The ongoing campaigns of an organization are likely to be at all of these different levels, depending upon the issue, or the need, the priority publics, and their level of understanding.

Determining the Level of Success

All campaigns should have specific purposes derived from goals and objectives that are the tangible expressions of the mission statement and positioning strategies. But evaluating a campaign is more than determining whether the purpose was achieved. A capital fund-raising campaign can meet its goal and leave a path littered with hostile publics who not only never will help again but will make negative comments about the organization every chance they get.

Evaluations should examine two outcomes: (1) what the organization did and how much it cost to do it and (2) what the results were for each effort, tangible and intangible.

First the focus is on determining the actual productivity involved in the campaign and the real costs of each effort. Then the cost-effectiveness of the various efforts is determined. Sometimes carefully contrived formulae are used to figure out something like the dollar equivalents of donated publicity if the same space or time had been bought. That sort of fiction is not very useful. What you want to know is who saw it and what they thought about it. Or if a campaign has focused on the introduction of a new core curriculum, no matter how much meeting time it took or how many publications were produced, the bottom line is whether students and faculty understand it and see it as an improvement. It's also important to know whether other evaluators, such as accrediting groups and professional associations, say good things about the university for making the change.

Glorious campaigns have introduced dismal failures. The commercial marketplace often makes quick assessments, but the marketplace of ideas sometimes takes a little longer. Evaluations must judge results and offer predictive information for planning.

CASE STUDY   ## Public Relations in a Crisis

You are the public relations director at a private university enrolling 10,000 students. The urban campus, located only six miles from a major metropolitan area's downtown, is bordered on all sides by interstate highways. Until recently, the location had always been touted as one of convenience and accessibility. The city's crime statistics have mounted, however, and the area's public schools reflect that fact. Because several murders have occured in their schools, the city's independent school district has put metal detectors in all of its buildings. There are four public schools in your university's immediate neighborhood: two elementary schools, one middle school, and one high school.

To make matters worse, another school in town—a small, private college—is also located in a high-crime area, and crimes on its campus have directed attention to the safety of all campuses. Two state universities and three other private colleges in your area (all within 150 miles) have also reported rising crime rates.

Adding to the public perception that your area is an increasingly dangerous one for college students are reports from six two-year colleges in the area. Three of these are especially vulnerable to crime because they are directly off interstate highways and one is actually downtown in a nearby city.

In fact, some of that college's students have been involved in criminal activity because, according to the police department, "They don't have much to do between classes, and they get into mischief." That "mischief" has included holdups of downtown retailers and a bank, and there is increased concern that criminals are actually a part of the college population, that they do not just come on campus to commit crimes. This is confirmed by national statistics which show that 80 percent of campus crimes are student-perpetrated.

The local metropolitan daily puts all school crime on the front page and has made much of the statistics from the *Chronicle of Higher Education* that reported 7500 violent crimes in 2400 schools for 1992, the first year of data collection. The newspaper also carries *USA Today* rankings of the nation's "safest campuses," rankings based on that newspaper's own statistics.

As a private university enrolling students from all over the nation, your school competes with some of the schools ranked by *USA Today* as "safe." These colleges are using their ranking in promotional literature. You suspect that since the reporting of campus crime is on the "honor system," statistics being reported by some schools are not exactly accurate and that the public is being misled.

As a private school, your university had been able to keep information about crimes on campus confidential until the Campus Security Act of 1990 required colleges to report all serious crimes occuring on the campus—statistics that have to be made available to current and prospective students. In reporting campus crime that first year, your president said "All schools are microcosms of society, and this university is not exempt from crime. However, we have taken special measures to protect our students."

In response to that statement, the student daily newspaper interviewed the campus police chief about the exact nature of the crimes reported and of the "special measures" taken. In the story the police chief said that a campus security consultant had been hired and that as a result of his recommendations additional security staff had also been hired and lighting added in areas that had been "troublesome." The chief also said that most of the university's crimes involved petty theft, a statistic the federal law exempts from reporting. He gave the reporter the figures though, saying that they were lower than those of most schools.

Now the student paper is planning a special edition for Friday, the beginning of Parents' Weekend. As public relations director you've purchased a quarter-page ad in the special edition, thanking the parents for their support of their students and the university. Now, on Wednesday, you discover that that same edition will carry a story listing and describing all campus crimes reported over the last semester, with an emphasis on date rape and parking-lot robberies that resulted in injuries to students. Furthermore, there is to be a "roundup" story about crime on all campuses in the area, taking a sort of *USA Today* ranking approach.

Fearing fallout, you call the university advisor to the paper who refers you to the editor. The editor confirms that the story will run. She indicates that some "art" will accompany the story, but doesn't tell you what that will be. She says she thinks it is the newspaper's responsibility to inform parents of what's going on on campus. She also plans an editorial on the subject for the same edition. She tells you that she is encouraged; she has heard—but has not been able to confirm—that the admissions office is going to start requiring information about prospective students' police records. You tell her that that decision has not been made yet because of internal conflict at upper-management levels about the plan's effect on recruiting. The editor thanks you for the information and says she will stay in touch with you—and with the admissions office.

QUESTIONS AND SUGGESTED ACTIVITIES

Case Study

1. You only have one and a half working days before the publication appears. Your best bet is to try to get some action on the admissions policy, but that's not likely. You know you're going to have to alert your president and the admissions office so they won't be surprised, and you know that you are going to be asked to evaluate the public relations "damage" caused by the Parents' Weekend edition of the newspaper. Who are the publics involved in this evaluation and how will you measure the impact of this edition on them?
2. Looking to the future, how would you suggest to admissions that the university measure the impact of disclosure of crime statistics on prospective students and their parents?
3. How would you evaluate community perception of the safety of your university versus that of other area colleges and universities?
4. Knowing that your internal publics—current students and the faculty and staff—are your public relations "front line," how would you measure their perceptions of their own safety? How would you find out what they would be likely to say to others outside the university about the relative safety and security of the campus?
5. What sort of ongoing monitoring of the "climate of public opinion" about campus security would you recommend?

Chapter

6. How can publics be monitored and evaluated for planning? reporting? counseling?
7. How are evaluations useful in reaching out to special publics?

SUGGESTED READINGS

Culbertson, H. M., Jeffers, D. W., Stone, D. B., & Terrell, M. (1993). *Social, political, and economic contexts in public relations: Theory and cases.* Hillsdale, NJ: L. Erlbaum Associates.

Fernandez, A., Lizotte, A. J. (1993, November/December). What's happening to rates of campus crime? *The Public Perspective*, p. 29.

Graham, E. (1993, October 25). Fortress academia sells security. *The Wall Street Journal*, pp. B1, 8.

Hunt, T. & Grunig, J. E. (1994). *Public relations techniques*. New York: Harcourt Brace College Publishers.

Jaksa, J. A., & Pritchard, M. S. (1994). *Communication ethics: Methods of analysis*. Belmont, CA: Wadsworth.

McElreath, M. P. (1993) *Managing systematic and ethical public relations*. Dubuque, IA: Wm. C. Brown Communications.

Newsom, D., Scott, A., & Turk, J.V. (1993). *This is PR: The realities of public relations*. Belmont, CA: Wadsworth.

Wilcox, D. L., Ault, P. H., & Agee, W. K. (1993). *Public relations: Strategies and tactics*. New York: HarperCollins.

REFERENCES

Hendrix, J. A. (1992). *Public relations cases*. Belmont, CA: Wadsworth.

Newsom, D., Scott, A., & Turk, J.V. (1993). *This is PR: The realities of public relations*. Belmont, CA: Wadsworth.

CONTEXTS FOR PRACTICE

CHAPTER 16

Practice in Public Elementary and Secondary Schools

Terry Wiedmer

Public relations programs in public schools are as different as the districts they serve. Teeming multicultural districts such as New York City's, Chicago's, and Miami's are in sharp contrast to those that draw their students from far-flung farms and ranches of the Dakotas or Wyoming. Such differences can include school configuration, programming, curriculum, the public each district serves, and the school's relationship with that public. Public relations personnel must meet a school's unique needs, but by learning about common factors that exist among districts in different geographical areas and about successful programs in some specific districts they can build effective programs.

The objective of a school public relations program is for the district and each school within it—through responsible communications, marketing, and interpersonal relationship-building—to help every community member accept responsibility for the education of the community's children. To develop a caring and committed community school support system, concerted effort must be allocated to inform, involve, and invest in all of the citizenry of a community. The best kind of public relations program is one based on open dialogue with the public regarding the strengths, weaknesses, and problems of the school, thus creating and maximizing opportunities for community groups and individuals to give information, advice, and assistance to the school (Gorton, 1976).

MAJOR GEOGRAPHICAL TYPES OF SCHOOL DISTRICTS

The standard metropolitan area is composed of three subareas: the rural area (outside both the central city and the suburb), the urban area (the central city or center core), and the suburban area (the urban fringe, which is somewhat densely built up and located outside the central city). School districts in each of these areas have conditions and needs that are unique to them as well as common features that enable them to employ similar types of programs to promote schools successfully (Knezevich, 1975). For the most part, these schools have fixed attendance area boundaries. But the community may be extended or dispersed by use of voucher systems, open-school attendance, choice, magnet schools, and busing to eliminate segregation. These conditions make it increasingly difficult to determine who composes the school community, which in turn complicates communication and rapport with constituent groups (Drake & Roe, 1986, p. 44).

Rural, urban, and suburban schools are also affected by changing demographics. In 1991–1992, 41.8 million students attended 86,287 public schools in the United States. The distribution of students in rural, urban, and suburban districts changes constantly. Some areas have fewer students each year, while others experience rapid growth, especially with certain populations—like Asians and Hispanics—which are increasing disproportionately in some places. The nation's ethnic youngsters are expected to increase by 4 million by the year 2010, reaching a total of 23 million, while the number of white youths is expected to drop by 6 million (National School Public Relations Association, 1991b, p. 5).

Schools serving the rural-urban fringe have experienced the greatest growth. The out-migration from the central city and the changing social composition of the central city brought about by the new minorities have created new problems for administrators.

Rural Areas

Rural schools, as compared with suburban and urban schools, typically have lower student enrollments, which limit specialization in instruction, forcing a less diversified curriculum. Rural conditions may also limit social and cultural opportunities, and there often is very little money to purchase materials and provide funding for program development. Transportation is often a problem because of the expanse of the district and the remoteness of some areas, taxing busing programs and resources to the limit. To enhance curriculum, rural schools often rely on distance learning, school-business partnerships, and cooperative efforts to reduce costs, save schools, and integrate technology.

Urban Areas

Urban problems make education of children difficult and strain and challenge school public relations efforts. Compared with suburban and rural areas, urban areas have significantly higher levels of unemployment, low-skill jobs, poor housing, rundown schools, and poverty; they also have ethnically more diverse populations, and those populations are generally limited in access to medical care. Large sectors of the job market are often closed to urban residents with limited skills, poor education, and inappropriate manners and speech (Ravitsch, 1983, p. 147). Urban schools generally have low achievement, high dropout rates, poor discipline, truancy, and high teacher turnover. Children from poor urban areas generally have less access to toys, books, games, or objects to stimulate visual and auditory senses; inadequate food, rest, and medical care; and fewer opportunities for social and academic stimulation.

Suburban Areas

James B. Conant has reported that the per capita expenditure in wealthy suburban schools was more than twice that of big-city high schools. In the suburban schools, 80 percent or more of the students go on to college; in the urban schools as many as 50 percent drop out before graduating (Ravitsch, 1983, p. 149). Children from suburban areas have a better chance to experience education in spacious modern schools, staffed with greater proportions of professionals per 1000 pupils; to graduate from high school and attend college; and to live in neighborhoods of modern and attractive homes. They tend to have parents who have more leisure time and education and who make time to read to, talk to, and interact with them in ways that enhance language skills and encourage curiosity (Ravitsch, 1983, p. 151).

THE ROLE OF PUBLIC RELATIONS PROGRAMS

Attitudes toward public schools are very different from what they were twenty years ago. In the past, most adults had children or grandchildren in the public schools. They were in touch with the school program and their attitudes were generally positive. Today only 23 to 27 percent of people in a school district service area are parents (Erwin, 1993). Fewer adults have direct knowledge of and experience with the public schools. Attitudes are further influenced by the flurry of reports in the last decade detailing the problems of education. These factors, reinforced by stories of gun-toting students, metal detectors, security cameras, gangs, and assaults on students and teachers, have led to general mistrust of public schools. In addition, the expectations of what services schools should provide have also increased. Although the public does not blame the schools for current problems (Gallup, Elam, & Rose, 1990), it does expect schools to deal with an increasing array of problems, an attitude shared by most teachers (NSPRA, 1991a, p. 4).

Schools are subject to the stresses and strains of every organization within the community, and they are under parental and general adult scrutiny at every point (Drake & Roe, 1986, p. 40). As public agencies with publicly elected officials, schools must tell taxpayers how their tax dollars are spent in order to maintain or increase current levels of support.

To change attitudes, inform the public about school activities, and increase financial support there is a very great need today for adequate public relations in the public schools. Successful public relations is more than simply publishing and distributing a newsletter or some other form of written message. It requires planning, two-way communication, honesty, common sense, and the ability to deal with perceptions. Barbara Erwin (1993) has said that, when dealing with the public, "Perception is reality." A district's public relations program must guarantee that public perceptions do reflect reality.

The challenge of relationship-building and marketing is in identifying what is important to the market segment and then identifying the channel through which a clear, responsive message can reach the proper audience at the correct time, from a credible source, in a way the audience can understand, accept—even if there is disagreement—act on, respond to, and be heard. Effective plans call for using a variety of listening strategies, recognition and training programs, and collaborative efforts with all segments of the community. Numerous communication channels must be employed so that a community's diverse population will have a variety of ways in which to be informed and involved.

Administrators in small districts are usually responsible for their own school's public relations program, which may be significant or quite limited, depending on the individual administrator's attitude toward public relations. In larger districts, a public relations or public information officer directs the program and in many cases is a member of the superintendent's cabinet, speaking on behalf of the superintendent, board of education, and district on many issues (Gorton, 1976). Some districts hire outside agencies to handle their public relations efforts, while in some states policy analysis organizations provide taxpayers with information about the schools.

Regardless of size, geographical location, or number of persons involved in the school or district, personnel working in successful school public relations programs develop a public relations policy, conduct research, establish goals, promote candor, attend to internal and external public relations, establish good media relations, foster enthusiasm, and evaluate results (Toy, 1981).

COMMUNICATION: THE KEY COMPONENT OF THE PROGRAM

Society is in the midst of a communication revolution. The types and frequency of communication determine how we govern, respond, and live. Communication affects leadership throughout the world *and* at the local level. Advanced technology has made this an instant-response society. The intensity of the media spotlight can distort events, yet schools also realize that the media can highlight events to gain support for the schools. Unfortunately, educators often do not take best advantage of the media to tell the whole story. Often they become involved only in responses to events. But people are indeed interested in school news, and so the quality and quantity of media coverage of school events has improved (Knezevich, 1975). There is great pressure on school officials to relate the educational program to the community effectively and to help people interpret its significance.

District-Level Communication

A policy of open and frequent communication should provide the entire school system with leadership from the board of education and the superintendent. To be effective, a school communication plan must involve the staff, volunteers, students, community members, legislators, and media. All members of the public require honest, attentive, clear, and consistent communication.

Communication audits are often implemented by school districts to determine the current status of the existing public relations program and to make recommendations for improvement. In an audit principals are encouraged to define the mission of the program in consultation with the superintendent, tying it to the overall district mission and beliefs. Program objectives, also tied to the overall mission, must be defined, must be specific, and must have measurable outcomes. Program priorities must be set according to the size of the staff and available resources. Key publics, representing all areas within the district, must be identified and involved in a key-communicator program. Key communicators should be provided in-service training to help them understand and support district communication objectives so they can provide input for program improvement to meet the changing needs of the school district and its constituents.

School-Level Communication

How a school conducts parent-teacher conferences, greets visitors, and even answers its telephones can affect its image (Gorton, 1976). Students are also important public relations agents for the school. It is often through students that parents and the larger community gain their strongest impressions of the school.

The success of the public relations effort hinges on the principal's ability to clearly and persuasively convey the programs, accomplishments, and concerns of the school. The principal must use every avenue available to get out positive messages about the school to various constituencies in the community, and the messages must be tailored to different audiences: parents, senior citizens, and business groups, for example (Pawlas & Meyers, 1989). Other staff members are important too. Erwin (1993) reported the results of a national poll conducted to determine whom the public perceived to be credible sources of information in public schools. At the top of the list was the school secretary, followed closely by the custodian, bus driver, and cafeteria worker. Teachers were ranked fifth, followed by principals in sixth place. These results emphasize the need for involving all employees in the public relations program. Parent involvement is also important. Research has shown that when parents are involved in school affairs the overall level of student achievement increases.

The individual school is typically where an understanding of the district's mission and goals begins, so it is important for every school to identify public relations and marketing goals. Current interest in districtwide strategic planning and site-based management reinforces the notion of involving individual schools in the district program. Public elementary and secondary school public relations programs are most successful when they are initiated at the building level rather than being imposed from central administration down (Ross, 1994). While the district has to have an overall communications plan, buildings within the district must have individual plans in place. In reality, the director of the public relations program depends on the building principal's support and on the commitment and backing of the central office, staff, students, and community at large.

A Special Form of Outreach

Urban communities are often criticized for not being attractive, safe, and supportive of education. Santee Ruffin (1989) referred to these urban conditions as "a national emergency." He advised urban school leaders to set high expectations for students, build less bureaucratic administrative structures, initiate a comprehensive renewal program, and create a support network beyond the school. To respond to this "emergency," he charged schools with the responsibility of collaborating with community groups, businesses, governmental agencies, and parent groups; through varied and multifaceted programs, he advised, they should establish long-range strategic plans, determine objectives, and initiate action.

Urban schools frequently capitalize on opportunities to establish school-business partnerships with local entrepreneurs, business enterprises, and various agencies. Often viewed as school district "allies" in efforts to improve education, businesses forge partnerships for the purpose of improving educational opportunities for students, frequently disadvantaged youth in urban areas.

There are many configurations for school and business partnerships. Three popular models for these collaborations were described by McMullen and Snyder (1987):

◆ The pairing of a business with a single school
◆ Collaborative efforts that focus on entire educational systems
◆ Collaborations intended to increase employability through the provision of special classes and/or part-time jobs

A study of nine school-business programs concluded that (1) school disticts and students benefited by having youth involved in programs that link schooling and employment, (2) there was a wide range of program success—some serving only public relations functions while others were rigorous and intensive, (3) participants increased their employability while growing personally, and (4) many of the schools realized physical and academic improvement through partnership activities (McMullen and Snyder, 1987).

Private- and public-sector agencies have joined forces in many states to create umbrella organizations—school-business partnerships—to provide leadership in public education. Since 1985 school-business partnerships have received tremendous attention. In fact, business-education partnerships increased from 17 percent of U.S. public schools in 1983–1984 to 40 percent in 1987–1988. The rise of these partnerships, in great part, is in response to the needs of public education and society for a future supply of a qualified workforce to enable the country to complete favorably in a global economy.

In the near future, if the current trend continues, a majority of school districts will be involved in some form of business partnerships. A key to building successful partnerships is to see that both the business and the school benefit from the association. Through careful planning by both parties, fragmentation and disruption caused by possible school-business goals can be avoided. As the demand for public service continues to grow and resources continue to shrink, the sharing of human and material resources will likely become even more critical.

In addition to providing schools with hand-me-down technology, business leaders can provide insights into the needs of business in the coming years, instruction in special areas not covered by the school's staff, and assistance with technical aspects of management. Interactive partnerships can get key people engaged in the important work of educating children, helping community leaders better understand the complexities of educating youth and involving them in the process of restructuring the educational system. Business partners who want to see better results commit themselves to working with educators to challenge traditional beliefs, to advocate changes, and to support new ideas. Some of the rewards of partnerships are community involvement, direct interaction between students and employees of businesses, enhanced student career awareness, improved community attitudes, and broadened community support.

EXAMPLES OF SUCCESSFUL PROGRAMS

The following descriptions of school public relations programs show how they incorporate many of the features described above in the successful handling of both difficult problems and everyday matters.

Rural Schools

America has many small elementary and secondary rural schools, which, like other community school configurations, have unique needs, problems, strengths, and successes. In describing rural school conditions, Bethann Berliner (1989) pointed out that rural school communities are more homogeneous than are urban schools, although they are gradually becoming more ethnically diverse.

Funding in states where a funding equalization formula has not been imposed, combined with the variability in school size and the economics of allocation of funds on a per-pupil basis, works against rural schools in their fixed operating costs. The 1980–1986 economic decline in many parts of rural America had a serious impact on public school finances and programs. The recession had serious effects on land values and property taxes, which in turn affected rural school funding, since about two-thirds of farm property taxes goes to schools (Richter, 1986).

Beginning with the establishment of one-room schools, which were the norm in colonial America, rural schools have continued to foster substantial and outstanding relationships with their communities (Oswald, 1983). Jon Wefald, former president of Kansas State University, credited rural America with developing what we know today as the American way of life, including emphasis on values of equality, private enterprise, decentralization, agriculture, and potential for economic and educational development (Horn & Parmley, 1986). Yet Glen Shaw, a rural Minnesota school administrator, contends that economic and technological changes have threatened rural jobs and the rural way of life, while Roy Forbes, former director of the Rural Education Institute in North Carolina, emphasizes the need for combining existing rural strengths with new technology to foster a developmental "restructuring" of rural areas (Horn & Parmley, 1986).

Rural schools possess unique conditions that directly impact teachers, administrators, and overall school programs. For educators, the limited number of staff members, multiple assignments, resource sparsity, climate, and remoteness of living arrangements produce both positive and negative results. Joan McRobbie (1990) described the role conflicts encountered by rural school teaching principals and the multiple tasks they are expected to perform. Stress, anxiety, social isolation, lower salaries, limited mobility, lack of personal privacy, difficulty of interpersonal and managerial role conflict, overload due to mandated paperwork, the need to make and take various roles within the school, the need to educate members of the board of education, difficulty in recruiting and retaining teachers, and limited opportunities for staff/professional development were cited as detractors from rural school employment.

Still, rural schools provide opportunities for educators that would not be possible in suburban and urban settings. From a positive perspective, rural schools provide teachers and administrators greater freedom to make curriculum changes; opportunities for daily contact with numerous publics; the ability to win community support through credibility, professionalism, and outreach; opportunities to write articles for the local newspaper and edit newsletters; and unlimited opportunities to involve students in community work (McRobbie, 1990). Each of these situations is a public relations opportunity that can enhance the success and overall image of the school.

Public relations programs of rural schools revolve around such projects as establishment of school cooperatives; implementation and use of distance-learning practices; establishment of school-business partnerships; use of technology to enhance instruction; and cooperation to manage low and declining enrollments, reduce costs, save schools, avoid consolidation, and maintain autonomy. Strong public relations programs can serve to swing public opinion toward cooperation, which can otherwise be very difficult for parents and the community to accept. The bottom line is, if students are pleased, then even skeptical parents become supporters.

Zions First National Bank in Utah adopted a local school in Garrison (Utah) with a student body of eleven and invited them to participate in their Christmas tree program and a field trip to Salt Lake City. The program was so rewarding for the children and bank staff that more field trips were funded, and later, when the school burned down, the bank donated money, books, a television set, and videocassette equipment. The bank obtained the name of four additional small rural schools to sponsor as a result of the success of this program and the positive relationships it fostered (Taggart, 1983).

In 1982, New Mexico State University introduced a program to inform teachers and students about computer technology. This program took microcomputers into rural classrooms (in a van that traveled throughout the state) to introduce technology and its potential for instructing students in outlying communities. The program was supported with donations from the International Space Center, the International Hall of Fame Foundation, New Mexico State University, and Texas Instruments Corporation. Cost were about $150 per day. The program components included computer awareness, computer literacy, and hands-on machine time. The project improved university relations with public elementary and secondary rural schools and with the related businesses (Amodeo, 1982).

A small rural Idaho school district gained public support for a school levy by producing and distributing a videotape of school activities and district needs. The videotape, a clear, concise presentation of information, circumvented the confrontations that often occur with other methods of communication (Diaz Grandox, 1991).

In Pittsfield, Illinois, the public library worked with the schools and parents to provide a variety of children's programs. Through a preschool story hour and summer-session activities for children through the fourth grade, positive public relations were developed with the children, community, and schools (Henry, 1988).

Pojoaque Valley (New Mexico) Schools. Jerry Floyd of the National School Boards Association identified the Pojoaque Valley Schools, Pojoaque Station, Sante Fe, New Mexico, as having an exemplary rural school public relations program (Floyd, 1994). Superintendent Art Blea attributes the success of the Pojoaque Valley Schools (PVS) to having a "very committed and unselfish board of education that is very proactive and visionary in policy making" (Blea, 1994). From a pool of eighty-eight school districts in New Mexico, PVS has been recognized twice by the New Mexico School Boards Association (1986 and 1993) as the School Board of the Year. This recognition was due in part to the district's clear and effective policies that are continually updated to meet the needs of the ever-changing educational and social climate.

The district is located twenty miles north of Santa Fe and nineteen miles from Albuquerque. It has a student population of 1818 students served by one elementary school located on three campuses (grades K through 5), one middle school (grades 6 through 8), and one high school (grades 9 through 12). The diverse student population is composed of approximately 69 percent Hispanics, 10 percent Native Americans, 19 percent white, and 1 to 2 percent blacks and Asian-Americans. Four Indian pueblos are served by the district, and 12 percent of the enrollment is from outside the district's boundaries. The PVS 1992–1993 accountability report filed with the New Mexico State Department of Education reported an 84 percent graduation rate, with 41 percent of the students applying for admittance to two- or four-year post–high school institutions.*

The PVS instructional staff consists of 118 professionals, including teachers, counselors, nurses, and support personnel. Their ethnic composition is 70 percent Hispanic, 27 percent Anglo, 2 percent Native American, and 1 percent Asian-American. These professionals live in Pajoaque, Los Alamos, Espanola, and Santa Fe.

Because of the small size of PVS, public relations activities are handled by Superintendent Blea in cooperation with the staff and board of education. Employee input is always a prerequisite in crafting policies that affect the staff. Public input is also sought for significant policies that may change long-standing practices—or, in some cases, new policies that may have impact on the educational community. Examples of recent policy changes and additions include the prohibition of weapons in schools, allowance for student removal from school, institution of smoke-free campuses, the first student sexual harassment policy in the state of New Mexico, employee criminal background checks, admission of out-of-district students, deferred sick leave pay, drug testing for bus drivers, prohibition of substance abuse, a reduction-in-force (RIF) policy, establishment of a sick leave bank, naming of facilities, and recognizing accomplishments of individuals within the district.

Site-based and participatory management principles are encouraged and supported in the school district. Decision-making authority is delegated to the levels impacted by the decisions. School principals and their staffs have broad authority in areas such as the school calendar, budget, curriculum, and textbook selection.

PVS board members receive $15 per regular meeting that they attend. They use this money to provide two scholarships, one for a male and one for a female senior, and they purchase service-recognition plaques for retiring employees. Thus they perform their service to the community for no personal financial compensation.

The expanding service responsibilities of the schools have been recognized by the community. The schools actively participate with external organizations and agencies to provide auxiliary services for students and the community. Examples of such participation include:

1. A before- and after-school program for grades K through 5 through a contract with the Children, Youth, and Families Department. The program served more than sixty students in the 1993–1994 school year, when it was in its third year of operation.

---

*Data given here are based on 1994 figures.

2. A summer recreation program for students in grades K through 5, which was operated during the 1992 and 1993 summers through a contractual agreement with Santa Fe County, which helped subsidize costs. Breakfast and lunch are part of the program that provides recreational, educational, and sports activities to students.

3. Use-of-facilities agreements that allow groups such as the YMCA, athletic leagues, community service organizations, churches, and private individuals access to PVS facilities free of charge or for minimal fees.

Academic awards assemblies are sponsored in May of each year. Students are recognized for academic excellence, either for a straight-A record or for standardized-test achievement. There are also athletic and scholarship award assemblies, as well as recognition letters and awards for other types of individual and group achievement throughout the course of the year.

Media relations have been very good with the two local newspapers that cover the board meetings and school events. Blea described school reporters as always being fair and giving PVS the benefit of doubt.

Andover (Kansas) Unified School District No. 385. This district was identified by Dr. Jerry Floyd of the National School Boards Association as being an exemplary rural district with a well-established and successful public relations program (Floyd, 1994). Mary E. Bentley, the assistant superintendent, coordinates the district's public relations efforts.

Andover Unified School District (AUSD) is located approximately ten miles from Wichita, Kansas, and serves 2001 students from two counties. During the 1993–1994 academic year, AUSD experienced a 10 percent gain in students (200+), and the growth cycle was expected to continue. A housing development program, which was progressing at an amazing rate, had had direct impact on all aspects of the district. Bentley attributed the growth to an exodus of students from the Wichita (Kansas) schools to a district that was recognized as having quality teachers who were creative and forward-thinking and who performed at superior levels with their students.

At the heart of the AUSD public relations program is the belief that a multitude of problems can be headed off with the establishment of an open, honest, direct, and ongoing communications program that enables all constituent parties to stay informed. The AUSD communications program includes the following publications:

◆ A monthly district newspaper, *Trojan Accent,* with a circulation of 5400
◆ The superintendent and assistant superintendent's bimonthly publication, *Trojan Communicator*
◆ Individual school newsletters
◆ The assistant superintendent's weekly column, "School Happenings," in the city newspaper, the *Andover Journal Advocate.*

In each publication, educational jargon and use of acronyms are kept to a minimum; a plain and direct approach is incorporated to bring attention to significant happenings, key individuals, and district concerns.

Because of the influx of population, AUSD is most concerned about securing adequate space and appropriate facilities to serve the district's growing number of students.

Plans are under way to propose a bond election to meet the current and anticipated needs of the district. A secondary issue is how to split the grades between the school buildings into some configuration that will be acceptable to the community. Extensive dialogue and numerous opportunities have been provided for communitywide discussion. The third major issue, an ongoing concern, revolves around the need to become current with technology and provide adequate training, hardware, and software to meet the district's needs. The district is *not* experiencing funding problems nor does it experience problems with violence or gangs. Still, with growth, the district is undergoing tremendous change.

The overwhelming support of the community for AUSD was demonstrated by the board of education's unanimous decision to expand the district's program offerings during 1994–1995 to include principles of technology, applied communications, and advanced computer programming in the high schools. Foreign language offerings were also extended to the primary levels.

Urban Schools

In urban settings, public relations efforts must address the broad spectrum of issues associated with an entire urban geographic area, multiple cultures, and diverse socioeconomic groups.

Each urban school district has its own problems, issues, and concerns; however, there are elements of commonality in problems that big-city school districts share. A review of the literature reveals a variety of issues with which urban school districts and their respective public relations programs typically contend:

- Significant curricular changes to include issues of global economy to infuse technology, and to cover environmental concerns
- Reform efforts incorporating site-based management, local school councils, and democratic decision making
- Multicultural and interracial education
- Student discipline related to gang violence
- Bilingual education, special education, gifted and talented education, vocational education, and tech prep
- School dropout prevention programs
- Safe communities and urban renewal programs
- Management of magnet and alternative schools
- Busing and transportation programs
- Programs for at-risk and disadvantaged students
- Master plans to improve the physical environment, community relations, school attendance, and academic performance

Among the most pressing concerns of urban schools is the necessity to provide equal education for all children while remaining sensitive to the vitality and viability of their many cultures. Urban schools work to implement multicultural education programs designed to bring about genuine integration. Historically, however, research has shown that such attempts often fall short, leaving neighborhoods segregated by race and ethnicity and marked by a record of troubled intergroup relations (McHugh, 1993).

In response to such concerns, the Pittsburgh (Pennsylvania) Public Schools established Prospect Center to facilitate appreciation of diversity. Working through the district office of multicultural education and Prospect Center, the district's public relations efforts concentrated on establishing respect and understanding, community confidence, program ownership, and student psychosocial development. Key to the program's implementation and success was the involvement of parents and community members.

The Wichita (Kansas) Public School System implemented its own multicultural education plan in 1991-1992. This broad-based public relations plan was developed by an administrator and twelve teachers. The program focus was to establish a year-long Culture of the Month program, beginning with a September emphasis on human relations and interactions. Each month that followed featured programs highlighting a particular culture. Included was an in-service workshop and opportunities for the district's staff to share ideas. The program was well received and accomplished the program's goals (Wichita Public School System, 1991).

Spanish Harlem's Community District 4, known as one of New York City's most disadvantaged school districts, developed a system of alternative educational programs, coupled with controlled parental choice. Begun in 1974, with the creation of a single alternative elementary school, by 1990 the system was serving nearly one-fifth of all junior high school students. Public relations efforts were expanded to address school organization, including imposing consistency in management between buildings and schools and easing the traditional boundaries between administrative and teaching roles. Although student achievement data were not determined, there was evidence that students were receiving significantly more individualized attention under the new system. Alternative programs were also highly focused on academic learning for disadvantaged children. Efforts of the district public relations department had to be further extended to address parental and community concerns that a substantial portion (80 percent) of elementary students lacked access to alternative programs that were at the center of the instructional improvement plan. The district dealt extensively with the public perception that the creation of new programs was driven by teacher initiatives and standards of quality, not by the objective of serving all students (Elmore, 1990).

The Detroit Public Schools (DPS), through strategic planning and involvement of key stakeholders, conducted a survey to determine economic, social, political, technological, and educational factors that would impact the future of DPS. Key to the study were the perceptions of various groups (consisting of students, parents, and community members) about program areas, educational services, strengths and weaknesses, goals, and groups DPS should serve (Detroit Public Schools, 1985).

The New York City (New York) Public School System (NYCPSS) established the Fund for New York City Public Education, composed of business leaders, which increased and channeled community concerns about education toward lasting improvements in the New York City School System. The program focused on comprehensive school restructuring, professional development and incentives, improved school-community relations, and better communication of school issues to the schools' publics (Leif, 1992).

Urban districts face myriad problems. Solid public relations efforts are crucial not only to their success, but often to their survival.

Duval County (Florida) Public Schools. The National School Boards Association identified Duval County Public Schools as an urban school district that exemplifies superior public relations. DCPS has a public relations plan designed to help it thrive; the program is massive, comprehensive, and responsive to the demands and interests of the community it serves. Jim Lashley, communications director for the district, says the focus "is not to call attention to our program but to call attention to our schools, which is at the heart of what we should all be about" (Lashley, 1994).

The district serves all of Jacksonville County, which has a consolidated government that fits nicely with the configuration of the school district. The county covers 821 square miles, is the fifteenth largest in the country, serves more than 120,000 students in approximately 150 schools, and has more than 12,000 employees.

The communications department, under the direction of the superintendent and assistant superintendent for administrative support services, develops and implements an ongoing communications program using all appropriate media and techniques to foster understanding, involvement, and support of the public schools. Department staff maintain contact with the news media, school system employees, and citizens to provide accurate and current information about the school system upon request or on its own initiative. Principals and central staff are encouraged to consult the communications department concerning procedures and practices affecting the release of information.

Information materials published by the school system for distribution to the public are prepared under the supervision of the department. Responsibility for district printing includes forms, tests, instructional guides, and other materials generated by the school system staff.

The community involvement and television services section of the department initiates and coordinates school district efforts in these two areas. A renewed emphasis on volunteer services and school-business partnerships includes encouraging, assigning, training, and supporting individuals and organizations who play an increasingly significant role in educating children. Business partnership activities are coordinated, as appropriate, with efforts of the Education Foundation of the Duval County Public Schools district.

Television services include combining the latest technological developments with existing resources to support the mission of the school district. This involves producing informational and educational video presentations, managing the elementary broadcast and teleconference schedules, and assisting schools in purchasing video equipment and designing production and distribution systems. Also included is the contractual and supporting relationship between the school district and WJCT-TV (Channel 7).

The district communications office employs three full-time staff members, including the public relations director and two specialists. One specialist is primarily responsible for design and graphics (using computer graphics), while the other specialist is more of a public relations generalist who, for the most part, works with ongoing communication projects such as monthly newsletters but is also responsible for special projects (for example, the governor's participation in school projects). The director handles what are often referred to as "lightning rod functions" such as media questions, concerns of the superintendent or board of education, or other issues that generate problems or concerns that need to be handled immediately. Many of the ongoing communication activities are also handled by the director, including the planning and execution of internal and external communications programs. Such products or projects include staff newsletters, annual reports, pamphlets, brochures, audiovisual presentations, and news media liaison; the director is also responsible for community relations and assists the superintendent and staff in any matter concerning communications and/or public relations.

The district communications program is a reflection of the superintendent. Prior to Larry Zenke's assuming the superintendency in 1989, primary interest had been directed at generating pride in the schools and county by seeking national recognition for the school system. Under the direction of Superintendent Zenke, communication efforts have not overlooked national perceptions, but the primary focus is now on communicating with the staff through a ground-level systematic program to build relationships, support, and involvement. Communications Director Lashley believes there is a place for both foci but he also believes that there is a lot that needs to be done simply to help people understand what schools are doing and to help schools understand what the people want them to do. As Lashley has said, "The heart of a good communications program is to draw attention to the schools and what they are doing and to foster the relationships that organizations and schools need to become the best that they can be."

The National School Public Relations Association says school communication should be a systematic, two-way, ongoing process, which is what the Duval County system attempts. Listening is emphasized along with action.

Programs undertaken by Duval County incorporate "select-targeting"—identifying target audiences, then determining the message to convey, the medium to use, and the desired impact. The communications are thus tailored to fit the audience.

Duval County is increasingly turning to nonprint media—video and computers—for its presentations at board meetings and to various groups. Computer communication also has straightened and shortened many of the district's internal communications pathways. With 150 schools in the system, there had been no efficient way to get a newsletter of any frequency to the entire staff and employees. *Acclaim*, a monthly newsletter for all employees, is not produced often enough to be a "news carrier." To establish a more immediate means of communicating with all the schools and employees, the Duval County district implemented a computer network connecting the schools. This enables the director of communications to key a newsletter in his office which then appears on the computer screens in each school, and in many of the offices. The newsletter can be printed off the computer screen, duplicated, and disseminated to employees in a timely fashion. This is done on a weekly basis and has enhanced internal communications between staff and administration.

The same computer newtork is utilized for a daily bulletin board, "Superintendent's Daily News," which is received by every school. It is used for short administrative announcements or for emergencies, such as a hurricane evacuation announcement. The system also produces *Teamwork*, a weekly newsletter for principals. It is printed in the central office, has materials attached to it, and is delivered to the 150 principals. Another newsletter is prepared each Friday for school board members and the superintendent.

Mass media efforts have met with varying results. In reality, the media sets the agenda more than the school system does. Diligent efforts are undertaken to foster relationships and retain credibility. Television stations assist the school system with a regular series of offerings. One feature is "Top of the Class," which focuses on positive happenings in the schools. Another TV station, during its 5:30 P.M. news program, includes "News 101," an innovative student-produced news brief. Topics may include a report on a performing artist or rock star or any issue of the students' choosing.

Newspaper coverage is handled by the only newspaper in the county. The community news section every Saturday carries an "answerline" column wherein a question of community interest, often about education, is addressed.

Each year, the sixty-seven countywide school districts in Florida are required to submit a school improvement plan, from which the *Florida School Report* is produced. The report includes data from every district in the state, including achievement scores, mobility rates, graduation rates, and dropout rates by school, district average, and state average. State law requires that the *Report* go to every family and every home in every district. The Duval County district's printing office prepares these for all of the district's schools.

This report serves as the baseline for school improvement plans, coupled with each school's own council's input. This process has generated a tremendous opportunity for communications. The school council plan is currently being used to assist in deciding how best to meet problems of overcrowding in some of the district's schools, even as some inner-city schools have empty classrooms. The superintendent has asked each school advisory council to come up with recommendations, alternatives, and priorities (for example, capping enrollments, changing boundaries, building new schools, or modifying the school year). Each community in the district, working through its school advisory council, is charged with the responsibility to submit plans and recommendations. Superintendent Zenke studies the councils' reports and will ultimately make a recommendation to the board based on communitywide input.

Charlotte-Mecklenberg (North Carolina) Public Schools.   Shep Ranbom, of the Washington, D.C., public relations firm Widmeyer Public Relations, identified another southern school district, the Charlotte-Mecklenberg (North Carolina) Public Schools (CMPS) as having an exemplary public relations program (Ranbom, 1994).

Like Duval County, Charlotte-Mecklenberg is a countywide district, creating a complex and diverse public relations need. The district encompasses Charlotte, the largest city in North Carolina, and the remainder of the county, which ranges from extremely rural to very upscale, highly developed areas. The county's population has nearly doubled in the past ten to fifteen years, and Charlotte is now recognized as the banking capital of the Southeast. There is a high level of international trade, and a significant proportion of residents are from overseas.

Charlotte-Mecklenberg serves approximately 82,000 students who are housed in 121 school buildings, with 78 elementary schools, 23 middle schools, 11 high schools, and 9 special-program facilities. Special programs include schools for students with significant discipline problems who are deemed rehabilitative, teen pregnancy programs, and opportunities for severely handicapped students who cannot be mainstreamed.

According to Melissa Madurn-Altman (1994), one of the district's public relations supervisors, public relations activities are conducted by nine staff members and the switchboard operator. The director of public relations is assisted by three supervisors who specialize in print, video, and general public relations media, respectively. The inclusion of the switchboard operator in the public relations configuration was based on the belief that the person who answers the telephone is truly the front line of public relations.

As with other large businesses, the Charlotte-Mecklenberg program is successful because public relations is approached from numerous levels. The district implements a wide variety of techniques and approaches. There are two weekly newsletters, with one distributed to all employees that provides information from the system (meetings, events, grant application deadlines, kudos for employees, and so forth). The second, *Feature Grab Bag and Photo-Ops,* is distributed to the local media and all the schools but is primarily geared toward the media. It includes all positive happenings in the schools, including photo opportunities, grab bag ideas, grandparent luncheons, and so forth, to which the media might turn on a slow news day. An outgrowth of the *Feature Grab Bag and Photo-Ops* newsletter is a four- to five-minute story carried by a local television station each Monday that features a handful of school happenings. This serves as a public awareness campaign and has greatly strengthened school and community relations.

Charlotte-Mecklenberg also makes a concerted effort to improve internal communications between the schools themselves and the central administrative office. A wide range of resources and assistance is available to individual schools from the central office. Examples include assistance with designing, producing, and printing brochures for individual schools and/or programs and helping teachers instruct students on the use of desktop publishing programs for course assignments.

An increasingly important responsibility for the district public relations department is implementation of a crisis-management program to handle such issues as shootings, suicides, and bus accidents. In emergency situations of this nature, the public relations staff members attend to the needs of specific publics (hospitals, media, parents, and citizen groups).

A unique component of the district program is a parent-concern telephone line that rings directly into the public relations office. A parent or community member who has exhausted all other means of resolution to a problem can seek closure through the parent line. A designated staff member handles all these calls and works until a solution is reached.

The establishment of magnet schools in twenty-eight of the district's buildings has increased the need for additional public relations efforts to promote the notion that magnet schools are better for some students while neighborhood schools are better for others. Community sentiment that not every Charlotte-Mecklenberg student has an equal opportunity to attend magnet schools has generated additional public relations efforts. Because of the significance of the magnet school concept, the district conducted a full-blown campaign that included use of billboards, flyers, building tours, and demonstrations at shopping malls.

The Charlotte-Mecklenberg public relations department is closely coupled with the video department and print shop. This arrangement serves to facilitate the district's overall program efforts.

Like all school districts, Charlotte-Mecklenberg does have special needs. Many of those needs are due to its expansive geographic area and large number of students served. Special efforts are undertaken to enhance communications between the schools and among staff members of different schools. A real challenge for the department is that of working to make everyone feel comfortable and feel that they are equally served. Conflict in dealing with the "haves" and "have nots" does exist in the district. Affluent parents sometimes feel that they or their schools are not receiving their fair share because attention is being given to inner-city students. Inner-city parents often feel that their schools do not have the same kinds of equipment and quality of teachers as do schools in the suburbs. The public relations department must stay attuned to the issue to ensure that a balanced and accurate picture is reported.

Special CMPS public relations efforts include preparation of videos of school board meetings, aired once a month on a local television station. There is also a quarterly call-in show on the local public television station with the superintendent, who hosts a variety of guests. An annual fall kickoff parade is sponsored by the public relations department at the beginning of each school year for the purpose of advocating family involvement in the schools. Every school is represented in the parade. A fair that shows parents how they can become more involved in the education of their children follows the parade.

Suburban Schools

Suburban schools deal with many of the same concerns and issues faced by rural and urban schools.

Beaverton (Oregon) School District 48.   Beaverton (Oregon) School District 48 (BSD) was identified by the National School Public Relations Association as having an exemplary public relations program (Much, 1994). In a telephone interview and through printed materials, Jennifer Much, BSD communications specialist, provided an overview of the district's comprehensive communications program.

The district serves a population base of 166,260 people with a student enrollment of 28,361 housed in thirty-eight schools—twenty-eight elementary (K through 6), six intermediate (7 through 9), three high schools, and one options school (10 through 12). The district employs 2000 personnel and provides bus service for 12,000 students. Beaverton is a relatively young community. Children younger than 18 compose nearly one-third of the population, and nearly half of the residents are between 19 and 44 years old.

The marketing and public relations program for Beaverton focuses on building effective partnerships with all segments of the community, with the common goal of ensuring success for all children in the district. The district emphasizes employing a variety of listening strategies, recognition and training programs, and collaborative efforts with all segments of the community. The diverse and changing population of Beaverton is served through numerous communication channels to inform and involve all citizens.

The Beaverton public relations department has three staff members (an executive administrator, a communications specialist, and a secretary) who coordinate the school-business partnership program, parent involvement and volunteer services, government interagency relations, and communications. Public relations is viewed as a program that belongs to every employee of the Beaverton School District, rather than the sole responsibility of the public relations department.

The district's mission is to meet the educational needs of each student in its schools and to provide a quality education that prepares each student to become a productive member of the community. Through responsible communications, marketing, and interpersonal relationship-building, the objective of Beaverton's public relations is to help all members of the community accept responsibility for the education of its children.

To that end, a listening campaign was initiated to enlist input from and support of the public. A variety of techniques were implemented, including providing information through forums and opinion research. The forums were conducted at district-sponsored breakfasts and afternoon meetings. Discussions were held with various administrative groups, focus groups met and discussed school-related issues, and surveys were administered to district residents. An internal advisory committee was also established to deal with internal communications. Student representatives were asked to serve on the board of education.

Recognition programs were expanded to bring attention to the many positive happenings and outstanding individuals and groups in the district. Patrons were provided a history of the Beaverton employee contributions that had served to favorably position the district in the state of Oregon. A monthly luncheon was implemented to facilitate communitywide attention to special events and outstanding individuals. District honorees were announced at the board meetings, and, wherever possible, their names were cited in notes, publications, and announcements.

Numerous workshops were offered for staff, parents, local school councils, and the board of education. Topics included marketing your school, working with critics and pressure groups, the customer-driven school, parent-involvement strategies, and publishing the school newsletter. Other projects include Team Building 2000—A Process for Change and training programs for key communicators, volunteer coordinators, computer lab volunteers, and parent-club presidents.

In the area of interpersonal communication, the school district has facilitated the establishment of a neighborhood network, has held board zone meetings, and has instituted quarterly local school council meetings with the board of education. A special event, "Success for All Children," was sponsored to involve patrons throughout the district. The superintendent has sponsored luncheons for community and business leaders and moderated meetings with key community and political groups. Other special events have included a "New Residents Fair," a "Child's Expo" for preschool parents, and scheduled school tours.

Mass communication efforts have been expanded to include a variety of forms of media—print, radio, television, and a speakers bureau. Print items include comprehensive brochures about the district, board of education, and community volunteers. A school calendar is printed and distributed throughout the district. Newsletters are prepared and distributed to students, parents, key communicators, and targeted audiences. *Key Communicators* is a publication ($8\frac{1}{2}$ by 11, printed front and back) that serves to update 450 identified community members on district educational issues. Monthly *Hot-Tip* sheets are prepared for local school councils to update them about issues of local concern. Weekly media packets are prepared and distributed to media contacts; school-related articles are published in the *Valley Times*, the *Oregonian*, and the chamber of commerce *Advocate*. A monthly radio show is produced, along with audiotapes that are made available to district patrons. The local cable television station covers the meetings of the board of education. Other special efforts include distribution of a map that serves to "introduce Beaverton Schools" and establishment of a speakers bureau for district spokespersons to meet with community and civic groups to talk about the school district. A twenty-four-hour newsline has been established to provide up-to-date school news, agendas for upcoming school board meetings and highlights of recent meetings, announcements, and other information about Beaverton Schools. As well, a budget information hot line has been installed for patrons to call and leave questions for a school official's response.

Central office communications have been expanded to include distribution of board packets and the "Friday Report"; communication channels include e-mail and a cable television hookup. These efforts were designed to facilitate more-efficient and comprehensive communication.

Most recently, the district has had to adapt to massive budget cuts and shifts mandated by the Oregon legislature to eventually restructure the state's school system from top to bottom. The district's public relations staff have been actively involved in explaining the new requirements to the various school constituencies and seeking input from those constituencies to assist in the decisions that are to come.

SUMMARY

Regardless of size or location, every school needs an effective plan and a shared agenda. Districtwide coordination of effort and message is critical at every level. Even the smallest district needs the support of its publics—the students, the teachers, the voters, the local power structure—or it will fail in its most critical mission, the nurturing of young American students.

Larger districts most often have public relations offices, staffed by one or more full-time people. In suburban settings, public relations functions are often left to a middle manager—the curriculum director or associate superintendent. In rural districts, it is often the superintendent, individual building principals, or even school board members, each with his or her own agenda, who manage public relations efforts.

A commitment to a clearly defined and implemented public relations program is essential to the success of all schools if they are to survive and prosper under public scrutiny. Today, every school district faces funding problems, limited resources, and heightened levels of public involvement and scrutiny.

Rural schools are more prone to have a limited number of staff members who, as a result, perform multiple roles; to face limited resources; and to pay lower salaries. But they also have greater freedom to make curriculum changes and provide opportunities for staff to interact daily with numerous publics. Rural school public relations programs often center on the establishment of distance learning and school-business partnerships, on upgrading technology, and on reducing costs while saving schools and maintaining autonomy.

Urban school public relations programs generally strive to set high expectations for students, build less bureaucratic structures, and create support systems beyond the school. Urban school public relations efforts tend to focus on busing and transportation problems, programs for at-risk and disadvantaged students, school dropout prevention programs, multicultural education and desegregation efforts, and problems related to school funding, safe communities, and urban renewal.

Suburban schools contend with many of the same concerns and issues faced by rural and urban schools. These include school reform, site-based management, funding issues, curricular changes, student discipline, diversity issues, bilingual education, gifted and talented education, and tech prep.

In all these settings, school public relations is receiving the greatest level of attention and support it has yet known. In many school districts, the director of public relations is a member of the superintendent's cabinet and is recognized as a critical component in the overall success of the school's work.

Often the public does not know how schools are doing and must glean their information from media reports. For most, the status quo is no longer acceptable; if a public feels it is not being informed about how schools are doing, it generally responds negatively. No longer are the three R's of education reading, writing, and 'rithmetic; now they are reform, revise, and refocus. And voters in school districts whose publics do not know the condition of schooling respond to bond elections and school referenda through revolt, refusal, and reductions. In contrast, budgets and referenda pass where the public is informed, where it knows the goals and objectives of the district and the level of student performance, where it is kept aware of how the taxpayers' dollars are being spent.

Schools that succeed in dealing with their many publics have found that they must provide clear explanations—free of educational jargon—of how programs impact individual students. Successful schools are responsive to parents and community, involve parents in the schools, and give them a direct voice in school governance, even while working to preserve professional discretion and autonomy. The growing sense of shared responsibility and shared decision making is an outgrowth of recent school reform movements and a movement toward decentralization.

CASE STUDY	Directing the Winds of Change

When the Missoula Public School District hired Dr. Madgie Hunt as superintendent, she was the third person to fill this position in five years and its first female administrator. Dr. Hunt was a unanimous choice by the five-member board of education to replace Toby Rolshoven, who had accepted a like position in a much larger school district in a neighboring state. Hunt's ten years of experience in building a strong and productive school district with limited funds and community support had won her the favor of the board.

Irene Hiller, current board president and member for thirteen years, had outlined the tasks before Hunt upon her appointment as superintendent. Missoula is a rural area that serves as the hub of five valleys; its countywide public school system serves 7200 prekindergarten through grade 12 students. There are eight elementary, three middle, and two high schools.

The economy has historically been based on the lumbering industry, but with rising interest rates, the district has fallen on hard times for its financial base. Conditions have continuously worsened over the past seven years. And for the first time in more than twenty-five years, the school bond election had failed the previous April.

To add to the problems, two of the elementary schools will be forced to close at the end of the academic year because of their inability to meet state building codes and safety requirements. The already overtaxed busing system will be called upon to transport the displaced students to the remaining six elementary schools, which have limited ability to incorporate the students; some of the teachers and building principals from the condemned schools will have to be released. The district does not have a reduction-in-force policy in place.

Historically, the concept of neighborhood schools has been held near and dear to the hearts of the Missoula citizens, and as Hiller advised Hunt, it will take a magician to persuade and win the support of families to successfully implement a program to house and educate district students in schools not in their immediate neighborhoods.

During the first month of her superintendency, Dr. Hunt met with building principals, faculty, support staff, community service groups, and the general citizenry in a variety of forums. Many of the residents are fourth- and fifth-generation products of the Missoula Public School system and want things to remain the way they have always been—in spite of financial cutbacks and the condition of facilities falling into disrepair.

In that first month, Hunt also identified the components of the existing district public relations program: a semiannual newsletter distributed to parents of students enrolled in the school district, parent councils in four of the buildings, a parent handbook that was last updated six years prior, and a reporter from the local newspaper who found favor with emphasizing the worsening condition of the school system and failed bond election.

In spite of the obvious problems, the superintendent was quick to determine the strengths of the district and the resources available to her to meet the board of education's expectations. Students scored on average in the 76th percentile on state and national standardized tests; there was a 92 percent graduation rate, with 61 percent of the graduates going on for postsecondary education; more than 58 percent of the teachers held master's degrees or higher, and their salaries ranked in the middle of those in the state; six students had been named National Merit Finalists in the past two years; and the athletic teams were ranked in the top three places in the state for both boys and girls track, volleyball, football, and basketball. Plans were in place to begin a talented and gifted program and to replace instruments for the band and orchestra programs at the middle and high school levels, but lack of funds had caused these plans to be put on hold.

In her second month Hunt called a communitywide meeting to address the faculty, parents, board of education, and Missoula citizenry. There, she provided a status report of the district that emphasized its strengths and perceived needs. She called upon each individual in the community to assist with the challenges that stood before them within the next ten months.

QUESTIONS AND SUGGESTED ACTIVITIES

Case Study

1. In your opinion, what should Madgie Hunt do to improve existing public relations practices? What should be done immediately and what should be considered part of a long-term plan?
2. To what degree and how should Hunt involve the newspaper reporter, parent councils, principals, citizenry, students, community service groups, and television personnel to address the many issues before them?
3. In a school district like Missoula, how can boards of education entice superintendents to stay long enough to make a lasting difference? Should superintendents be encouraged to stay for more than two or three years?
4. What can Hunt do to facilitate a smooth closing of two schools, increased busing, and terminating a minimum of seven teachers and two elementary principals?
5. To what degree and how should Hunt work with the school board in making the necessary plans and implementing change to meet their expectations?

Chapter

6. Does a school need a public relations program if it is a *good* school? How would this compare with the need of a successful business to have an advertising program?
7. Regarding public schools, how are the opinions and attitudes of parents and nonparents influenced and shaped?
8. What is meant by having a "proactive" rather than "reactive" school public relations program?
9. What are critical components of successful school-media relations?
10. Interview one or more school district public relations officers about their roles and responsibilities. Determine if the school corporation is rural, suburban, or urban. Ask them about their perceptions regarding the ideal and the reality of their roles relative to the type of school district served.
11. Study school public relations practices in two different public schools—an elementary school and a high school. Identify and compare ways the schools implement internal and external communications. Are there distinct differences? Why or why not?
12. Identify and study a school-business partnership in your community. Delineate the advantages and disadvantages for students, schools, businesses, and the community.
13. Identify public relations components of several recent school events in your community. Select one event and describe the approach that was taken by the district, identifying successful and unsuccessful endeavors. What formal and informal communication channels were used?
14. Trace the development of school public relations in your school district.
15. Interview a public relations officer in private industry and a public relations officer in a school district to ascertain their perceptions of the efforts needed to promote their employers.
16. Study a recent decision in your school. What was the process used to arrive at the decision? Who was involved in the process? What factors were taken into consideration in making the decision? How were internal and external publics involved in the process?
17. To what degree is technology incorporated in your school public relations program? What is the future for technological incorporation?
18. Assume you are hired to create a public relations program for your school. Develop a list of program components you would implement.

SUGGESTED READINGS

Atkin, J., & Bastiani, J. (1988). *Listening to parents: An approach to the improvement of home-school relations*. London: Croom Helm.

Barth, R. S. (1990). *Improving schools from within: Teachers, parents, and principals can make the difference*. San Francisco: Jossey-Bass.

Campbell, R. F., Cunningham, L. L., Nystrand, R. O., & Usdan, M. D. (1990). *The organization and control of American schools* (6th ed.). Englewood Cliffs, NJ: Merrill/Prentice Hall.

Cavazos, L. F. (1989). *Educating our children: Parents and school together*. Washington, DC: U.S. Department of Education.

Coleman, J. S. (1985, April). Schools and the communities they serve. *Phi Delta Kappan, 66*(8), 527–532.

Craft, M., Raynor, J., & Cohern, L. (Eds). (1980). *Linking home and school: A new review* (3rd ed.). London: Harper & Row.

Davies, D. (1987). Parent involvement in the public schools: Opportunities for administrators. *Education and Urban Society, 19*(2), 137–145.

Davies, D. (1991, January). Schools reaching out: Family, school, and community relationships for student success. *Phi Delta Kappan, 72*(5), 376–382.

Deal, T. E., & Peterson, K. D. (1990, September). *The principal's role in shaping school culture*. Washington, DC: U.S. Department of Education, Office of Educational Research and Improvement.

Epstein, J. L. (1985, Winter). Home and school connections in schools of the future: Implications of research on parent involvement. *Peabody Journal of Education, 62*(2), 18–41.

Epstein, J. L. (1991, January). Paths to partnership: What we can learn from federal, state, district, and school initiatives. *Phi Delta Kappan, 72*(5), 344–349.

Fuller, W. E. (1982). *The old country school: The story of rural education in the Middle West*. Chicago: University of Chicago Press.

Kindred, L. W., Bagin, D., & Gallagher, D. R. (1990). *The school & community relations* (4th ed.). Boston: Allyn and Bacon.

Kirst, M. (Ed.) (1989). *The conditions of children in California*. Berkeley: Policy Analysis for California Education (PACE).

Kowalski, T. J., & Reitzug, U. C. (1993). *Contemporary school administration: An introduction*. White Plains, NY: Longman.

Lareau, A. (1989). *Home advantage: Social class and parental intervention in elementary education*. London: Falmer.

Lightfoot, S. L. (1984). *The good high school*. New York: Basic Books.

Lober, I. (1993). *Promoting your school: A public relations handbook*. Lancaster, PA: Technomic.

Lutz, F. W., & Iannaccone, L. (1978). *Public participation in local schools: The dissatisfaction theory of American democracy*. Lexington, MA: Lexington Books.

Marburger, C. L. (1990). Education reform: The neglected dimensions, parent involvement. In S. B. Bacharach (Ed.), *Education reform: Making sense of it all* (pp. 82–91). Boston: Allyn and Bacon.

Mauriel, J. J. (1989). *Strategic leadership for schools*. San Francisco: Jossey-Bass.

Milwaukee Public Schools. (1992). *Impact of school desegregation in Milwaukee public schools on quality education for minorities . . . 15 years later*. Milwaukee, WI: Author (ERIC Document Reproduction Service No. ED 351 427)

Mitchell, B., & Cunningham, L. L. (Eds.) (1990). Educational leadership and changing contexts of families, communities, and schools. *Eighty-ninth yearbook of the National Society for the Study of Education, part II*. Chicago: University of Chicago Press.

Moles, O. (1987). Who wants parent involvement? Interests, skills, and opportunities among parents and educators. *Education and Urban Society, 19*(2), 130–136.

National School Public Relations Association. (1986). *School public relations: The complete book.* Arlington, VA: Author.

Ogbu, J. U. (1978). *Minority education and caste: The American system in cross-cultural perspective.* New York: Academic Press.

Pawlas, G., & Meyers, K. (1989). *The principal and communication.* Bloomington, IN: Phi Delta Kappa Educational Foundation.

Preshkin, A. A. (1978). *Growing up American: Schooling and the survival of community.* Chicago: University of Chicago Press.

Ruffin, S. C., Jr. (1989). Improving urban communities and their schools: A national emergency. A *Bulletin* special. *NASSP Bulletin, 73*(517), 61–70.

Saxe, R. W. (1984). *School-community relations in transition.* Berkeley, CA: McCutchan.

Swap, S. M. (1987). *Enhancing parent involvement in schools.* New York: Teachers College Press.

REFERENCES

Amodeo, L. (1982). *The computer experience microvan program: A cooperative endeavor to improve university-public school relations through technology.* (ERIC Document Reproduction Service No. ED 241 517)

Beaverton (Oregon) School District. (1992). Working together for our children's future: Public relations marketing plan for the Beaverton School District 1991-92. Beaverton, OR: Author.

Berliner, B. (1989). *Rural schools in California: A demographic, economic, and educational state profile.* (ERIC Document Reproduction Service No. ED 325 273)

Blea, A. (1994, January). Personal communication.

Detroit Public Schools. (1985). *Strategic planning resource document (Rev.).* Detroit, MI: Detroit Public Schools. (ERIC Document Reproduction Service No. ED 287 915)

Diaz Grandox, F. (1991). Try a videotape for communicating with district patrons. *Journal of Rural and Small Schools, 4*(3), 20–21.

Drake, T. L., & Roe, W. H. (1986). *The principalship* (3rd ed.). Englewood Cliffs, NJ: Merrill/Prentice Hall.

Elmore, R. F. (1990). *Community District 4, New York City: A case of choice.* (CPRE Report Series TC-002). (ERIC Document Reproduction Service No. ED 332 347)

Erwin, B. F. (1993, September). Marketing your schools: Perception is reality. Paper presented at the meeting of the Indiana School Board Association, Indianapolis, IN.

Floyd, J. (1994, January). Personal communication.

Gallup, A., Elam, S., & Rose, L. (1990). The 22nd annual Gallup/PDK poll of the public's attitudes toward the public schools. *Phi Delta Kappan, 72*(1), 35–47.

Gorton, R. A. (1976). *School administration: Challenge and opportunity for leadership.* Dubuque, IA: Wm. C. Brown.

Henry, S. (1988). Tips to the success of a rural children's public library. *Illinois Libraries, 70*(1), 38–40.

Horn, J., & Parmley, P. (1986). Rural education: A proud heritage and a bright future. *Proceedings of the 8th Annual Rural and Small Schools Conference,* Manhattan, KS.

Knezevich, S. J. (1975). *Administration of public education* (3rd ed.). New York: Harper & Row.

Lashley, J. (1994, January). Personal communication.

Leif, B. (1992). A New York case study: The private sector and the reform of public education. *Teachers College Record, 93*(3), 523–535.

Madurn-Altman, M. (1994, January). Personal communication.

McHugh, B. (1993). Meeting the challenges of multicultural education. *The Second Report from the Evaluation of Pittsburgh's Prospect Multicultural Education Center* (Report No. CDS-R-41). (ERIC Document Reproduction Service No. ED 358 201)

McMullen, B. J., & Snyder, P. (1987). *Allies in education. Schools and businesses working together for at-risk youth.* (ERIC Document Reproduction Service No. ED 291 821)

McRobbie, J. (1990). *The rural teaching principal: Meeting the challenges of multiple roles* (Knowledge Brief No. 7). (ERIC Document Reproduction Service No. ED 350 134)

Much, J. (1994, January). Personal communication.

National School Public Relations Association (NSPRA). (1991b, May). U.S. population and school enrollment growth. *NSPRA Network,* p. 5.

National School Public Relations Association. (1991a, May). Metropolitan Life survey of teachers. *NSPRA Network,* p. 4.

Oswald, D. M. (1983). *Rural studies in teacher education from innovation to stabilization.* (ERIC Document Reproduction Service No. ED 235 946)

Parmley, F. (1987). Rural education: A hope for the future. *Proceedings of the 9th Annual Rural and Small Schools Conference,* Manhattan, KS.

Pawlas, G., & Meyers, K. (1989). *The principal and communication.* Bloomington, IN: Phi Delta Kappa Educational Foundation.

Ranbom, S. (1994, January). Personal communication.

Ravitsch, D. (1983). *The troubled crusade: American education, 1945–1980.* New York: Basic Books.

Richter, A. J. (1986). *The impact of the rural recession on public school financing and programs.* (ERIC Document Reproduction Service No. ED 287 648)

Ross, V. (1994, January). Personal communication.

Ruffin, S. C., Jr. (1989). Improving urban communities and their schools: A national emergency. A Bulletin special. *NASSP Bulletin, 74*(517), 61–70.

Taggart, D. (1983). *School adoption program.* (ERIC Document Reproduction Service No. ED 233 831)

Toy, S. (1981). Use this ten-point plan to bolster community rapport. *Executive Educator, 7*(6), 23–25.

Wichita Public School System. (1991). Wichita High School West: Multicultural education plan 1991–92. Wichita, KS: Author. (ERIC Document Reproduction Service No. ED 349 356)

CHAPTER 17

Practice in Private Elementary and Secondary Schools

Jerry A. Jarc
Theodore J. Kowalski

Several aspects of school reform have rekindled interest in private elementary and secondary schools in the United States. Among them has been the ability of private schools to focus on specific purposes, to maintain discipline, and to attract parental support through a framework of values that bond schools and families. Their popularity is attested to by the fact that in the early 1990s, about 15 percent of all enrollees in elementary and secondary education were attending nonpublic schools. And that figure is expected to increase in the next few decades (Kowalski & Reitzug, 1993).

The topic of private schools is also drawing more attention within the study of school administration. There are several reasons for the growing interest, including these three:

- There are estimates that one-fourth to one-third of future administrators will be working in private school settings (Kowalski & Reitzug, 1993).
- Within the arena of public policy, support for ideas such as school choice and voucher systems is expanding. The prospect of increasing competition for public schools has made private schooling a more relevant topic.
- Comparative studies between public and private schools are becoming more common. These studies focus on areas such as administrative behavior, climate, culture, discipline, and learning outcomes.

Over the years, the continued existence of public schools has virtually been assured by state governments. Private schools, on the other hand, have had to rely more on attractive programs, values, and aspects of climate and culture to encourage parents to enroll their children. Success for these institutions, usually measured by the ability to recruit the desired number of students, has often required the delivery of a challenging, personalized, academic curriculum in a socially defined atmosphere. Hence, private schools function in a competitive environment—a factor that makes the development of public relations programs an essential element of administration.

THE NATURE OF PRIVATE SCHOOLS

A common classification scheme for private schools divides them into (1) high-tuition schools, (2) religiously affiliated schools, (3) fundamentalist schools, and (4) other private schools (Erickson, 1983). But more generally, private schools are divided into only two groups: those that have a religious affiliation (parochial schools) and those that do not. Historically, the former group has constituted a majority of private elementary and secondary schools. And within the category of parochial schools, Catholic schools have constituted a majority. In 1965, Catholic schools educated 88 percent of the students attending private schools in the United States; from that year to 1983, the number of Catholic schools declined by 30 percent; in 1983, only 46 percent of the students enrolled in private schools were attending Catholic schools (Cooper, 1984). Responding to declining enrollments and rising costs, Catholic schools across America launched a marketing campaign in the early 1990s called "Discover Catholic Schools 1992" (Rist, 1991).

While Catholic schools were declining in number, other segments of the private school category were growing. Much of that growth was due to new fundamentalist Christian schools. In recent years, however, interest and enrollments in virtually all types of private schools have been escalating. In large cities, for example, a growing number of minority families is opting for Catholic schools—even in situations where family religion is not a factor. Interest in private education has been fueled by perceptions that many public schools are less effective in terms of discipline and academics. Today the prime motivator for enrolling children in Catholic schools is academics—only about 20 to 30 percent of parents list religious convictions as the prime reason for choosing these schools (Convey, 1991).

Since the early 1980s, interest in the creation of entrepreneurial schools also has grown. These proprietary institutions are likely to proliferate if vouchers or tax credits become reality in some states. (These schools should not be confused with operations that entail a private company holding a contract to operate a public school system.) Myron Lieberman (1986) argued that entrepreneurial schools can create levels of competition with public schools that have not been achieved by other types of private schools. He noted, for example, that competition between Catholic and public schools is often "genteel" (p. 216), because Catholic leaders do want to risk alienating church members who send their children to public schools by labeling public schools as ineffective. He believes that officials in entrepreneurial schools will have fewer inhibitions in this regard. Hence, the marketing and recruitment strategies in for-profit schools are likely to be far more aggressive than those in other types of private schools.

THE FINANCIAL REALITIES OF PRIVATE SCHOOLS

Private schools receive no direct tax dollars to support operations. They rely primarily on the following funding sources:

◆ Tuition and fees
◆ Capital campaigns and other forms of annual fund raising

◆ Major private gifts and endowments
◆ In the case of parochial schools, various forms of fiscal support from parishes, congregations, or religious orders (for example, the order of priests, brothers, or nuns operating a school)

Compared with public schools, funding for the private school is less assured and more sporadic.

Administrators in private schools typically have more flexibility in making decisions about the use of resources. For instance, they are not bound by legal restrictions in using funds to the same extent as are public school administrators (for example, in using funds for advertising). They are also able to initiate and control fund-raising activities more easily than are public schools officials. Although some larger public school systems have moved to create foundations, this action is still relatively rare for these institutions across the country.

Virtually all private schools are experiencing cost increases. Catholic schools, for example, once relied heavily on men and women in religious orders, individuals who received little compensation for their service as teachers and administrators. But declines in religious vocations forced many parochial schools to employ lay teachers—a situation that significantly increased operating budgets. Since many parish schools are funded heavily by weekly collections, pastors and principals had to face difficult decisions about continuing to operate their schools. Many parishes discovered that it was virtually impossible to divert 70 or 80 percent of church revenues to operate a school, and tuition increases became the only plausible alternative to ceasing operations. Tuition increases, however, had the tendency to spark enrollment declines, and many Catholic schools soon found they were in a seemingly hopeless cycle of budget-enrollment problems.

Many nonreligiously affiliated schools—for example, boarding schools and country day schools—fall into the "high-tuition" category of private schools. Found primarily in urban and suburban areas, these schools usually serve distinct student populations—populations generally defined in terms of economics and/or ability. That is, they cater to wealthy families and high-ability students. These schools often have their own endowments, and their foundations are the depository for revenues raised through periodic capital campaigns and annual alumni contributions. Also in the high-tuition category are the emerging entrepreneurial schools. These institutions, however, usually lack tradition and endowments, and they are much more reliant on direct tuition revenues.

THE ATTRACTION OF PRIVATE SCHOOLS

A number of writers (for example, Greeley & McManus, 1987) have pointed out that many private schools, especially those with a religious affiliation, use climate as a selling point. "Climate" refers to the general characteristics of a school, including its physical attributes, social structure, organizational design, and culture (the values and beliefs held in common by those who constitute the school community). Parochial schools, in particular, are often able to create a "family atmosphere" congruent with the philosophical convictions of their intended patrons.

As noted earlier, the focus on school reform has helped to proliferate convictions that private schools are academically superior and safer and more orderly, especially when compared with large inner-city schools. In part, these beliefs stem from perceptions that private schools set higher expectations for students, tolerate less misbehavior, and require students to spend more time on academic tasks. Thus it is not surprising that instruction and discipline now often outweigh religious considerations when parents elect to send their children to private schools (Convey, 1991). This does not mean, though, that culture does not remain an important consideration, especially for parochial schools. As Kowalski and Reitzug (1993) note, "Many scholars have found that strong, positively perceived organizational cultures contribute to effectiveness. Private schools have several natural advantages in ensuring the development of positive organizational culture. Private schools are formed to promote a central (frequently spiritually oriented) mission or set of values" (p. 141).

Regardless of expressed parental motives, increases in private school enrollments are probably linked directly to a growing dissatisfaction with public schools. At the very center of this disenchantment is the question of purpose. That is, what are the primary objectives of public education? Noted school reform expert, Philip Schlechty (1990) observed, "Few leaders in education, and fewer critics from outside the education establishment, have addressed the fundamental question of purpose" (p. 7). Many parents observe that public school officials continue to be pushed and pulled in multiple directions, and as a result, long-standing tensions between the goals of *equity* and *excellence* keep growing. The result is frequent, and often radical, shifts in policy. For example, a state legislature may set mandatory testing for high school graduation (in pursuit of excellence) only to find that their dictate significantly increases school dropout rates. Soon they are inundated with complaints from citizens who see testing mandates as unduly harsh on certain types of students—for example, those living in poverty. New policy directives are then likely to be developed (in pursuit of equity)—mandates designed to keep students in school. While such meandering may affect all schools having state accreditation, they tend to create more instability in public schools than in private schools.

Table 17–1 provides a list of general considerations relative to comparing public and private schools. These considerations help to frame the special importance of public relations programs in private schools.

MARKETING THE PRIVATE SCHOOL

Positioning is a technique used in the commercial sales world to associate a product with consumer needs. Much of the success of private schools (that is, the ability to maintain desired enrollment levels) is associated with this process. Put simply, school officials are able to position their institution so that parents, grandparents, and alumni decide that tuition is a wise investment in the future of their children. Virtually all private schools engage in some form of marketing that attempts to span age groups and interest levels. Brochures, newsletters, buttons, wearing apparel, bumper stickers, and even athletic teams become instruments of the effort to sell an all-inclusive image.

Some scholars (for example, Hanson, 1992) have observed that the ability of public school officials to counter the current confidence crisis has been attenuated by the fact

TABLE 17–1
Public and Private Schools: Key Considerations

Factor	Comparison
Structure	Public schools rely on laws and state regulations; private schools usually rely on cultures and climates to attract clients.
Funding sources	Public school funding is regulated largely by state legislatures and local school boards; private schools rely heavily on tuition, gifts, and foundations.
Clientele	Because of mandatory attendance laws, public schools have an assured clientele but must serve all eligible students; private schools must compete with both public schools and other private schools for students but can be selective in admissions.
Market status	Public schools are considered quasi-monopolies; private schools function in a competitive market in which the future is not assured.
Purpose	Public schools have always suffered from the inability of society to focus on several major purposes; private schools are often erected around a specific set of values and purposes.
External communication	Public schools are expected to have a positive relationship with their wider environment (communities), which is often very heterogeneous; private schools attempt to maintain a close relationship with alumni, parents, and donors and a looser relationship with the general community.
Programming	Public schools must serve a range of student needs and thus curricular and extracurricular programs are usually quite broad; private schools are more likely to focus on specific student needs and serve a more homogeneous student population.
Parents/volunteers	Involvement varies markedly among public schools; involvement is generally high in private schools.
PR structure	Public schools are organized into districts, which makes it more likely that a specialist will be employed to handle public relations; private schools often assign the task to a staff member or employ consultants on an as-needed basis.
PR programming scope	Public schools tend to concentrate on information exchanges between the schools and the community; private schools spend much more of their resources on marketing, recruitment, and fund raising.

that public schools have not developed an effective marketing strategy for themselves. If the failure to properly engage in marketing has negatively affected public education, imagine how critical this issue is to private schools, where ineffective marketing often leads to extinction. This reality forces many private schools to expend much of their public relations resources (already typically insufficient) in the marketing arena.

Marketing efforts define the school to potential consumers. Whereas thirty years ago parents may have chosen parochial schools solely on the basis of religious convictions, today they are more likely to consider a broader range of issues. For example, tuition, distance from home, financial aid, athletic programs, social standing of the student population, and average ability and achievement scores may influence school selection. Accordingly, marketing programs must be broad in both content and dissemination to be effective.

Defining the School

Experience has shown that a private school is most apt to be successful if it can create a unique niche in the market. This means identifying those attributes that set the school apart—not only from public schools, but also from other private schools. To accomplish this goal, officials must define their school in terms that are simultaneously realistic and accurate. The defining description of a school should not merely represent the dream of the principal or the faculty; rather, it should reflect the actual experiences of consumers (current and former students). A number of private high schools, for example, define themselves through alumni testimony. They pay for newspaper ads that feature the testimony of successful graduates. A highly respected surgeon in the community, for instance, may indicate that he learned to study at this school or that the school helped him to develop self-discipline.

The importance of being able to connect to potential consumers has prompted private school officials to rely less on their own judgment and more on techniques such as focus groups. This approach brings parents and students directly into the process of defining the school. Parents, for instance, are asked to talk about what they like best about the school; they are urged to identify problems and other elements of the school that may alienate other parents and students.

The defining process is absolutely essential to private schools, because it puts forth those qualities that make the school unique. Proven educational benefits, properly articulated by the school's staff and alumni, often override parental concerns about cost. As is the case with all consumer decisions, parents usually weigh their options by considering the cost-benefit ratio. And since these considerations vary from one family to another, private schools find it advantageous to identify a range of assets so that they can appeal to a wide audience.

Values are one of the strongest selling points for private schools. In the face of severe financial problems and declining enrollments, some inner-city parochial schools are able to show that high student performance is a product of vision, autonomy, and traditional values (Meade, 1991). Also, moral values and discipline are seen by many parents as features distinguishing public and private schools.

Interrelating Public Relations, Marketing, and Recruitment

Public relations, marketing, and recruitment are interrelated in private schools. This happens, in large measure, because these institutions have no guaranteed audience. School officials must simultaneously monitor the environment, interpret existing needs and wants, define the school, market the product, and select a desired pool of students. Accordingly, the work of staff in these three areas should be coordinated.

Private schools obviously cannot exist unless they have sufficient students—and thus, sufficient income. But for most of these schools, recruitment entails more than raw numbers. It also involves attracting the right types of students. One school may place importance on family income; another may emphasize high ability and achievement scores; and yet others are focused on religious beliefs and affiliation. So for private schools, the issue is almost always recruiting a sufficient number of desirable students.

Relationships with parents are critical in private schools. Just as in public schools, parental involvement in homework, discipline, and attendance constitutes a positive contribution that reinforces the work of teachers. But because parents have chosen this school freely, and because they are paying tuition, even minor levels of dissatisfaction or mistrust can cause them to place their children in another school. The convictions that led parents to enroll their children in a private school in the first place must be continuously reinforced. Hence, school officials must know the reasons why parents selected their school and be able to validate those reasons once the students are enrolled.

ORGANIZING THE PUBLIC RELATIONS FUNCTION

Since the average private school is small in comparison with public schools, the allocation of resources for public relations is a difficult decision. Should one person handle public relations, marketing, and recruitment? Should these tasks be assigned to teachers or administrators who have other duties? Ideally, the answer to both questions is no. Properly executed, public relations can be a full-time job requiring an individual with special expertise. Even in schools with enrollments as small as several hundred students, preparing newsletters, doing periodic needs assessments, preparing press releases, scheduling promotional activities, and seeking community input can require fifty to sixty hours per week.

In reality, however, most private schools function with limited resources. Administrators may be forced to combine responsibilities or to assign them to employees who already have too much to do. One of the current trends is to create an office that integrates public relations, marketing, fund raising, and recruitment. Individuals who direct such offices hold varying titles—director of public relations, director of admission, director of development, or director of external affairs. Regardless of the structure selected, administrators need to recognize that additional investments must be made in staff development for those who are assigned these responsibilities. Even if the person who runs the public relations office is a well-educated journalist or school administrator, he or she needs to keep abreast of emerging trends in the field.

One of the least desirable yet still prevalent patterns is to have the principal of the school do all the public relations, marketing, recruitment, and fund-raising activities. If this person is doing these functions reasonably well, then little time is left for those duties that are most essential for the principalship—working closely with teachers to assure the proper delivery of the academic and extracurricular programs. More often than not, all responsibilities get less attention than they need.

BUILDING AND USING A PUBLIC RELATIONS CALENDAR

Inappropriate funding for a public relations office in a private school often results in less-than-adequate planning and scheduling. One measure that can prevent this from occurring is the development of a public relations-marketing-recruitment calendar. The calendar is a guide for daily, weekly, and monthly activities. A sample calendar is illustrated in Table 17–2.

TABLE 17–2
Sample Public Relations-Marketing-Recruitment Calendar

Program/Event	Date	Start/End Time	Target Audience	Objective
Alumni reception	9/22	6:00–9:00 P.M.	Alumni in local area	Communicate goals for annual fund drive
TV program	9/23	4:00–4:30 P.M.	Potential students	Promote the school
Parent advisory meeting	9/23	7:00–9:00 P.M.	Parents	Get information about problems, positive experiences, etc.
Deadline for newsletter copy	9/24	5:00 P.M.	Potential contributors	Get materials on time

All events and responsibilities pertaining to public relations, marketing, and recruitment should be placed on the calendar, and it should be updated almost daily. This includes deadline dates for submitting materials for newsletters, getting material to printers, and so forth.

There are internal and external audiences to be considered when preparing such a calendar. Internally, the entire calendar should be shared with the administration of the school and members of the school's governing body (for example, the parish council) so that officials are continuously aware of scheduled activities, programs, and communication efforts. The calendar, or at least parts of it, should also be shared with teachers and support staff. Externally, private school officials need to keep multiple publics informed. Thus parts of the calendar ought to be shared with parents, city officials, local public school officials, fund-raising groups, selected community leaders, the media, and other relevant individuals and groups.

The calendar also serves another vital purpose. It becomes a guide for assuring that some form of communication is coming from or going to certain parties. For instance, the public relations officer can determine if adequate communication will occur with college recruiters or whether alumni will receive a sufficient number of contacts in a given year. In this respect, the calendar helps those in the public relations office to balance activities and to allocate resources more effectively.

COMMUNICATING WITH EXTERNAL PUBLICS

Private schools need to connect continuously with key individuals who support and sustain the organization. These contacts should be both professional and regular; most individuals are put off by poorly prepared materials—for example, a newsletter filled with grammatical errors or misspelled words—or by the experience of receiving communiques only when school officials want something. The objectives of these contacts may include sustaining interest in the school, providing information about accomplishments or activities, or calling attention to planned actions— a fund drive, an athletics event, a need for volunteers. Each communication can reinforce how well the school is doing and the school's role in the community.

A comprehensive public relations approach in a private school entails the development of a list of targeted audiences. Included are those individuals and groups with whom school officials wish to exchange information. Some avenues to communicating with external publics are rather standard, such as newsletters and recruitment brochures, but the spectrum of alternatives is quite expansive. Press releases, public service announcements on radio and television, outdoor advertising, open houses, community service projects, lectures, cultural events, and open forums on community issues exemplify other options that schools can employ.

Often overlooked is the need for school officials to listen—to gather information rather than disseminating it. This is especially crucial for private schools because of their competitive market status. Changing economic, social, and political conditions can affect the status of a private school in a relatively brief period of time. For example, a downturn in a local economy may negatively influence parental decisions about keeping their children in private schools. To prevent a crisis, the school first must have an awareness of the problem and then act to avert potential negative consequences. In this respect, the public relations program serves a broad purpose of creating a closer relationship between the school and its external publics.

PARENTAL INVOLVEMENT

Selling a product becomes easier if a potential buyer knows a satisfied consumer. The same principle is very true with regard to success in private education. Parents who praise the school, who talk about the successes of their children, are the best recruiters. And while it is true that satisfied parents are, de facto, good ambassadors for the school—that is, they relate positive attitudes to friends, neighbors, and relatives—they can be even more beneficial if they are brought into the general public relations program. In any event, valid parental involvement requires that they receive an ongoing flow of information so that they know the critical issues facing the school (Warner, 1994).

One method of parental involvement is the creation of a public relations advisory committee. Those serving on the committee can suggest creative ideas about how satisfied parents can become a part of marketing, recruitment, and fund raising. Perhaps more importantly, committee members can provide school administrators with their perceptions of the school's strengths and weaknesses. Other possible ways to involve parents include:

- ◆ Staff development projects, especially when the content touches on areas such as discipline and homework
- ◆ Workshops specifically designed to enhance parental roles in education
- ◆ Periodic visitation days that permit parents to shadow their children through the school day
- ◆ Social events that are family-oriented

Parental involvement on a public relations committee or on other task forces also serves a more general purpose. The parents' visibility in school activities conveys a message that the school attempts to engage families—a factor that is often interpreted positively by parents who place a great deal of importance on education. This is the very reason why parent-teacher associations in public schools have been a potent force for developing school image over the years. Most parents react positively to messages that tell them that they are welcome in the school—more, that their direct involvement is welcome and appreciated.

Many parochial schools are quite dependent on parent volunteers (in some instances this includes grandparents). Some schools have even developed volunteer "gift option" books. These booklets outline opportunities for committee work, for assisting in special functions, for aiding teachers, and for other potential volunteer activities. Further, they provide specifications for time and talent so that parents can select an activity that fits their schedule and interest/abilities.

Unfortunately, some schools still resist parental involvement. Most often this myopic stance is predicated on a fear that parents in the school will cause trouble. That is to say, their presence will generate conflict. While this is certainly possible, conflict can often lead to positive changes. For example, a parent working as a volunteer in the cafeteria may point out that the current method of purchasing products is costly. At first, this suggestion may cause friction between the parent and the person doing the purchasing, but ultimately it may lead to improved practices. Isolating parents from the school nullifies one of the real strengths of many private schools—a strong relationship between the school and its publics in which parents, students, and faculty see themselves as a learning community.

FUTURE ISSUES AND PROBLEMS

Because their future is not assured, private schools are dependent on effective long-range planning. For many of these institutions, competition not only occurs with public schools, but with other private schools as well. The political context conveys a great deal of uncertainty about public policy that can affect private schooling. Growing interest in school choice, charter schools, vouchers, and tuition tax credits are examples. While many private school administrators are quick to recognize the potential benefits of these initiatives, few have pondered the possible negative by-products. For example, will vouchers require private schools to adjust their admissions policies? Will choice result in a more heterogeneous student population, and if it does, will this attenuate the asset of strong cultures? Will the indirect funneling of public revenues to private schools result in more government restrictions in areas such as curriculum mandates, accreditation, and teacher licensing?

In large measure the future of private schools depends on how they define themselves. In so doing, the following general issues deserve considerable thought:

◆ Although many small schools may be forced to close or consolidate, new private schools are opening. These new schools often target markets where there is evidence of parental dissatisfaction with public schools. Some of these are entrepreneurial schools that have solid financial backing and attractive programs. While their primary targets are children in public schools, they also may siphon students from existing private schools.

◆ Because private schools are heavily dependent on tuition, changes in the economy have a dramatic effect. Faced with dwindling resources, all consumers must make difficult choices. The option of private education may be dropped quickly if parents are not totally convinced that they are receiving a good return for their investment.

◆ Many private schools have not placed public relations programs in proper perspective. These programs are not frills to cut at the first sign of fiscal difficulty; rather, they are an essential way of reinforcing a major strength of private schools—the linkage of students, parents, and alumni into a school family.

◆ Reform efforts in public education are bringing about certain improvements. Private schools must continuously examine the extent to which they offer parents and students a truly unique option.

◆ In part, the restructuring of public elementary and secondary education in America stems from the transition to a global economy and an information-based society. Private schools also must adapt if they are to remain competitive. This means an investment in technology and staff development, a rethinking of the curriculum, and a planning process that permits constant redefinition of vision.

SUMMARY

From a process perspective, principles of public relations are as applicable to private schools as they are to public schools. Both institutions need to exchange information with their wider environments. But in private schools, the elements of marketing, fund raising, and recruitment take on added importance. They are often dominant features of the public relations program.

While some may be encouraged by the fact that new private schools are opening across the country or by the fact that policy issues such as school choice and vouchers are receiving increased attention, the future of private education at the elementary and secondary level remains uncertain. Parochial schools, for instance, are likely to face added competition from entrepreneurial schools; all private schools may face added competition from restructured and improved public schools. In this context of uncertainty, public relations programs ought not be considered luxuries.

Often private school administrators face the dilemma of knowing that public relations is an absolutely essential activity and yet not having the resources or expertise to implement such programs properly. Successful schools have addressed this problem by building on their primary asset, a strong culture that creates a school family. A common set of values and beliefs brings parental commitment and alumni loyalty that permit the schools to accomplish much with limited resources.

CASE STUDY

Selling A School

Located in an established area of a northeastern city, Metropolitan Hebrew High School has a tradition that dates back to 1951. Many of the alumni are now prominent citizens in the community and regular contributors to the school. Until recently, the school's principal has not had to worry about enrollments, because a new generation of alumni children always filled the available spaces and the enrollment remained stable at about 300 students. In the past three years, however, the incoming freshman classes have declined about 5 percent each year.

Urged by the school's board of directors, the principal has conducted a study to try to determine why the school is suddenly losing enrollment. He has discovered that two factors are most likely responsible. First, there has been a gradual exodus of established families who traditionally enrolled their children in the school. Although most have remained in the general metropolitan area, they have moved to suburbs far enough away to discourage them from enrolling their children in the school. Second, the public school system has just opened a new mathematics and science magnet school in the area. Housed in a new building and equipped with modern computers and science laboratories, the school offers an attractive alternative.

Metropolitan Hebrew High School has defined itself as an academic school. In this context, the faculty are seen as the primary asset. Because of limited resources, only modest investments have been made in technology and materials in the past decade. The following information serves to describe other aspects of the school:

- ◆ The facility in which the programs are offered is now over forty years old. Although there have been periodic improvements, the classrooms remain much as they were when the school was first built.
- ◆ The principal puts out a newsletter twice a year. One issue is designed specifically to solicit contributions.
- ◆ Annual contributions for the last three years have averaged about $54,000, or about $200 per pupil. About 85 percent of that amount has come from a handful of successful businesses.
- ◆ The school has never had an active recruitment program; students of other faiths or students from other parts of the city have not been recruited.
- ◆ The school's last capital campaign occurred about twenty-two years ago. It raised $1.5 million, which was used to make improvements to the buildings.
- ◆ The principal is the only administrator in the school. The school does not have a public relations or marketing plan.
- ◆ Parents often volunteer services for special functions, but there are no task forces or special committees besides the board of directors, which is composed of seven parents and alumni.
- ◆ The school has received periodic support from two local synagogues. This support has been designated for the school's five scholarships.
- ◆ The tuition is currently $4,900 per year, an increase of 6 percent over the previous year.

After reading the principal's report, the board of directors has decided to embark on a five-year program to reverse enrollment trends. They have instructed the principal to outline a plan of action, advising him that a failure to reverse enrollment trends will likely mean the demise of the school. There are mounting fears that continued tuition increases will further erode enrollments. Additionally, several faculty have recently resigned because they received only a 2 percent increase in salary over the past three years.

QUESTIONS AND SUGGESTED ACTIVITIES

Case Study

1. Assume you are the principal of this school. How would you react to the charge given you by the board of directors?
2. What possible strategies could be pursued to save this school?
3. Do you think the school has done a good job of engaging in public relations? Why or why not?
4. Do you think this school has sufficiently defined itself? Why or why not?
5. Is raising money the answer to this school's problem?
6. Given the new magnet school in the area, should Metropolitan Hebrew consider redefining itself?
7. How can school officials determine if the current enrollment pattern will be sustained over the next ten years?
8. Why do you believe most parents elect to send their children to this school? Are those reasons congruent with the definition of the school?
9. Develop a list of activities that could increase parental involvement in this school's activities.
10. Discuss the advantages and disadvantages of attempting to gain additional resources from the two synagogues in the area.
11. How can the principal make the board of directors an integral part of his five-year plan?
12. Is it common for private high schools to have a recruitment plan? A marketing plan?

Chapter

13. How can a principal use the general attractiveness of private schools in his or her action plan?
14. Defining the school for various publics may enhance a principal's action plan. How can the defining process be accomplished?

SUGGESTED READINGS

Coleman, J. S., & Hoffer, T. (1987). *Public and private high schools: The impact of communities.* New York: Basic Books.

Convey, J. J. (1991). Catholic schools in a changing society: Past accomplishments and future challenges. In *The Catholic school and society.* Washington, DC: National Catholic Educational Association.

Convey, J. J. (1992). *Catholic schools make a difference: Twenty-five years of research.* Washington, DC: National Catholic Educational Association.

Cooper, B. (1984). The changing demography of private schools. *Education and Urban Society, 16* (4), 429–442.

Gestwicki, C. (1992). *Home, school, and community relations: A guide to working with parents* (2nd ed.). Albany, NY: Delmar Publishers.

Greeley, A. M. (1982). *Catholic high schools and minority students.* New Brunswick, NJ : Transaction Books.

Greeley, A. M., & McManus, W. (1987). *Catholic contributions: Sociology and policy.* Chicago: Thomas More Press.

Henry, M. E. (1993). *School cultures: Universes of meaning in private schools.* Norwood, NJ: Ablex.

Hogan, S. D., & Knight, H. (1988). *Successful planning for private schools: The administrator's guide.* Arlington, VA: Thornsbury Bailey & Brown.

Holcomb, J. H. (1993). *Educational marketing: A business approach to school-community relations.* Lanham, MD: University Press of America.

Kelly, B. E., & Bredeson , P. V. (1991). Measures of meaning in a public and in a parochial school: Principals as symbol managers. *Journal of Educational Administration, 29*(3), 6–22.

Ries, A., & Trout, J. (1986). *Positioning: The battle for your mind.* New York: McGraw-Hill.

Sergiovanni, T. J. (1994). *Building community in schools.* San Francisco: Jossey-Bass.

REFERENCES

Convey, J.J. (1991). Catholic schools in a changing society: Past accomplishments and future challenges. In *The Catholic School and Society.* Washington, D.C.: National Catholic Educational Association.

Cooper, B. (1984). The changing demography of private schools. *Education and Urban Society, 16*(4), 429–442.

Erickson, D. A. (1983). *Private schools in contemporary perspective.* (ERIC Document Reproduction Service No. ED 231 015)

Greeley, A. M., & McManus, W. (1987). *Catholic contributions: Sociology and policy.* Chicago: Thomas More Press.

Hanson, E. M. (1992). Educational marketing and the public schools: Policies, practices, and problems. *Educational Policy, 6*(1), 19–34.

Kowalski, T. J., & Reitzug, U. C. (1993). *Contemporary school administration: An introduction.* New York: Longman.

Lieberman, M. (1986). *Beyond public education.* New York: Praeger.

Meade, J. (1991). Keeping the faith. *Teacher Magazine, 3*(1), 34-36, 41–45.

Rist, M. C. (1991). Parochial schools set out to win their share of the market. *Executive Educator, 13*(9), 24.

Schlechty, P. C. (1990). *Schools for the 21st century: Leadership imperatives for educational reform.* San Francisco: Jossey-Bass.

Warner, C. (1994). *Promoting your school: Going beyond PR.* Thousand Oaks, CA: Corwin Press.

Name Index

Subject Index